Perl

fast&easy® web development

Perl

fast&easy® web development

Les Bate

Premier Press

Publisher: Stacy L. Hiquet
Marketing Manager: Heather Hurley
Acquisitions Editor: Kevin Harreld
Project Editor: Estelle Manticas
Technical Reviewer: Michelle Jones
Copy Editor: Kate Givens
Interior Layout: Jill Flores
Cover Design: Mike Tanamachi
Indexer: Kelly Talbot
Proofreader: Kim Benbow

ISBN: 1-931841-17-9
Library of Congress Catalog Card Number: 20011096997
Printed in the United States of America

03 04 05 06 07 BH 10 9 8 7 6 5 4 3 2 1

Premier Press, a division of Course Technology
2645 Erie Avenue, Suite 41
Cincinnati, Ohio 45208

To my lovely wife Pauline, and my beautiful daughter Victoria
with all my love…

and to my cats Cassie and Biggles for walking across my keyboard!

Acknowledgments

There are many people that I should like to thank and I am bound to forget someone, I am sorry if one of them is you!

First I should like to thank Julie C. Meloni, who told me my first sample text was good enough. Also thanks to Lynette Quinn for her encouragement in the early stages. Likewise thank you to Estelle Manticas, for encouraging me with her good humor and helpful remarks, and for turning my gibberish into this book. Thanks to Kevin Harreld, who kept me on the rails throughout.

Thank you to my wife Pauline and my daughter Victoria for putting up with my absences.

I would also like to thank my past UWE lecturers, especially Simon Langley, Nigel Baker and Jane Berry, who fired up my enthusiasm for computing, and in the case of Simon, fired up my sense of humor too!

Thank you to Mum and Dad for being my Mum and Dad!

Finally, a special thank you to my good friend Clarisse Craen, who gave me the initial shove to start this project: thank you, my mate!

Les

About the Author

Les Bate is a Senior Analyst Programmer working for CSC at the British Aerospace (Airbus) site in Filton, Bristol, in the UK. He started out as a TV engineer for Visionhire in the West Midlands, England, spending many years at college learning about analogue and digital electronics before becoming a self-employed electronics engineer.

Les later switched careers and moved into systems analysis and programming at British Aerospace. Originally working on mainframe batch and CICS programming, Les finally made the move into Lotus Notes development and from there to Web development.

In 1998 he gained a BSc (Hons) in Computing from the University of the West of England, which he says opened totally new horizons for him in terms of technology and its application in computing.

Les has used many of the currently available technologies, including C, C++, Perl, PHP, Java, JavaScript, VBScript, ASP, and HTML, and he enjoys exploring the possibilities that new technologies offer.

In his spare time he messes around with electronics, plays the guitar (he says very badly!), and enjoys listening to music, traveling, and reading. He attributes his love for reading solely to the works of J.R.R. Tolkien.

Contents at a Glance

Contents

Introduction

Perl was born in October, 1987. Written by Larry Wall as a Ph.D. project, it first appeared on the comp.sources News Group as Perl version 1.0. Perl now offers a standard set of supplied libraries, object-oriented programming facilities, and expanded regular expressions. Perl used to be written as PERL (and sometimes still is), reminding us that it stands for Practical Extraction and Reporting Language. That is what it did, back when it was first written. Now it does much more.

Perl is an interpreted language. That means it isn't as fast as languages like C, but it also means you don't have to keep cycling through the laborious process of editing, compiling testing, then re-editing, recompiling, and so on. With Perl, you just edit and run! It's a fast language to develop in and a great one to prototype with! Perl can also be very concise. It is possible to achieve a lot with very little code. In current parlance, then, Perl is a results-oriented language.

Perl has become the "glue" that allows many other tools to be linked together. It has been "ported" to many platforms and has become an essential tool for OS administrators and Web Programmers. It has been used to build complete systems, and it is also used for creating throw-away code snippets to do one-off jobs. Perl is used world-wide on numerous platforms and with many different Web servers. In many cases it is the default Web language. If an ISP offers any CGI-type programming facilities, it is likely that they will include Perl. If it offers only one language, that language is probably Perl. Perl is powerful, Perl is fast (for an interpreted language!), and Perl is useful! There is virtually no job that cannot be done with Perl, and often jobs can be done with far less code than would be possible using most other languages.

In this book you will explore many of Perl's features before looking at how you can use it to build dynamic Web sites. You will not trawl through huge conceptual discussions on the whys and wherefores of Perl. Rather, you'll take the language and select the methods and mechanisms that can help you most in your quest to write active Web sites. In other words, you'll be exploring ways of solving problems. After all, that's what programming languages are designed to do! My aim in this book is to get you to your destination in the shortest possible time, at the same time seeking to help you understand how Perl works in this field.

How is This Book Organized?

This is very much a "get you started" book. I have deliberately avoided some of the more difficult aspects of learning a language such as Perl, for that way lies the seeds of exasperation, disillusionment, and the probable abandonment of the language.

You will find that first chapters of the book are concerned with the creation of the Web development environment—installing Perl and a Web server. From there to a little over half-way through the book, you'll find bite-sized pieces of Perl code, each designed to demonstrate one particular aspect of the Perl language. The step-by-step code examples are accompanied by screenshots showing the code and its resulting execution.

From there onwards, you will work to wards building real Perl applications—examining CGI and forms, as well as files and e-mail. The book ends with a full Perl database Web application.

Who Should Read this Book?

This book assumes as little as it is possible to assume. It is aimed at someone who has little knowledge of Web development, or someone who has used WYSIWYG point-and-click-type Web authoring tools and now wants to move into creating Web applications in as short a time as possible.

Software/Hardware Requirements

To use this book and the examples supplied, you will need a Web server. If you're using Windows 95 then you can obtain Personal Web Server. This is often to be found on freebie magazine-mounted CDs lurking in a free product called NT Server 4 Option Pack. The Option Pack also contains Peer Web Services for Windows NT 4, which does the same job. Users of Windows 98 / ME should find that they have a copy of Personal Web Server already on their machine. If not, check your Windows installation CD. Windows 2000 professional / XP Professional users should find they have a copy of Internet Information Server (IIS) on their machine, which is even better. UNIX users can make use of the brilliant Apache Web server available from www.apache.org (a Windows version is also available).

Of course, you will need Perl itself; where to obtain it and how to install it are covered in the book.

You will need an editor to code with. You can use a simple editor, such as Notepad in Windows or Vi or Emacs on the UNIX platform. For Windows, a personal favorite of mine is HTMLPad 2000 (http://www.blumentals.net/). There is also OptiPerl (http://www.xarka.com/optiperl/) which offers a full Integrated Development Environment (IDE) for Perl.

You do not need an incredibly powerful machine to develop in Perl; almost anything will do, as long as it has plenty of memory (128Mb+) and few hundred megabytes of space free for you to develop in.

And of course you will need a Web Browser; most of you will have Microsoft's Internet Explorer already on your machine, but you may also want to try Opera (www.opera.com), an excellent browser that comes with a decent mail client built in.

1

Getting Started

This first chapter will cover setting up Perl on your machine. The emphasis here is for Windows users, but there is no shortage of advice for setup on other platforms. See the useful URLs in Appendix B of this book, where you will find Web addresses for the Perl organization and for huge Perl resources supplying detailed advice, examples, and updates. When you are surfing the Internet, take a look at these sites—they really are awesome sources for all things Perl!

Specifically, this chapter will cover:

- Where to obtain Perl
- How to Install Perl
- Configuring Personal Web Server

Where Can I Get Perl?

Perl is available from a number of sources. The best known are http://www.activestate.com and http://www.perl.com.

I advise you not to download a "development version" of Perl, as doing so may cause some confusion if you get any errors. Development versions of software are, as their name suggests, not final, fully debugged versions and may include bugs that could lead you to think that you had made a mistake in your code. For this reason, development versions of Perl are often referred to as "unstable." When you are more experienced in the use of Perl you may want to try development versions, in order to make use of new facilities provided, but until then it is best to stick to the latest "stable" version.

In addition to downloading Perl, you might want might want to look around at some of the resources available for Perl developers. Some useful Internet sites are given here, and there are more in Appendix B.

- http://www.activestate.com/
- http://www.perl.com/
- http://www.perl.org/

These sites will keep you up-to-date with what is happening in the world of Perl and will provide you with invaluable resources for techniques, coding ideas, and loads of news about the Perl language and those who use it. Perl is a natural language for the Internet, so it is equally natural that you will find lots of ongoing support for this powerful and much respected language on the World Wide Web and in News Groups, email lists, and bulletin boards.

How Do I Install Perl?

Before you can use Perl, you need to install it and set up the Web server with which you are going to use it. You will learn how to set up the Web server shortly, but for now, here is the information you need to get started with Perl. Perl can be used at the "command prompt" the way you may have run DOS programs in the old days! Perl began life as a system administration and reporting tool, so it works equally well in this way.

Windows Installation

1. Download Perl from www.activestate.com or www.perl.com.

2. When the download is complete, double-click the file to begin installation.

3. Follow the on-screen prompts to install Perl on your machine. If the installation fails, you may need to obtain the latest copy of the Microsoft Installer. If you are using the Activestate site, you will find a link to the latest MS installer there under the Downloads link.

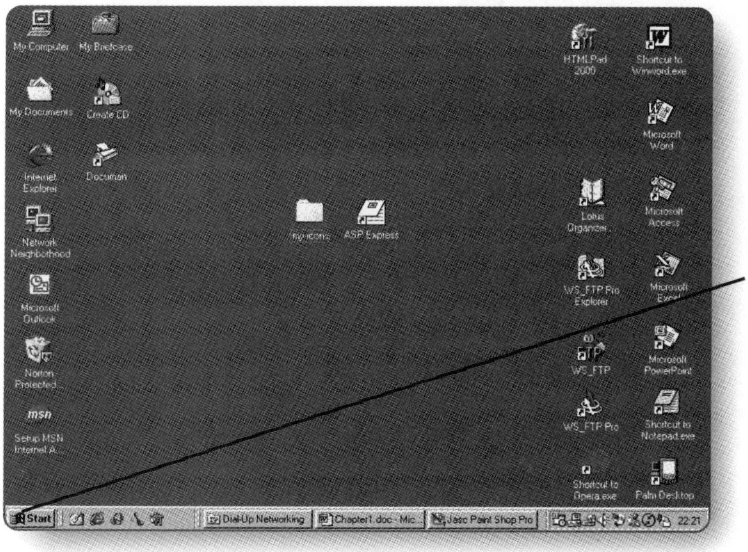

The installation process should update the windows path so that the Perl executable can be found. Open an MS-DOS "prompt" command window to run Perl and verify its version.

4. Click the Start button on the Taskbar.

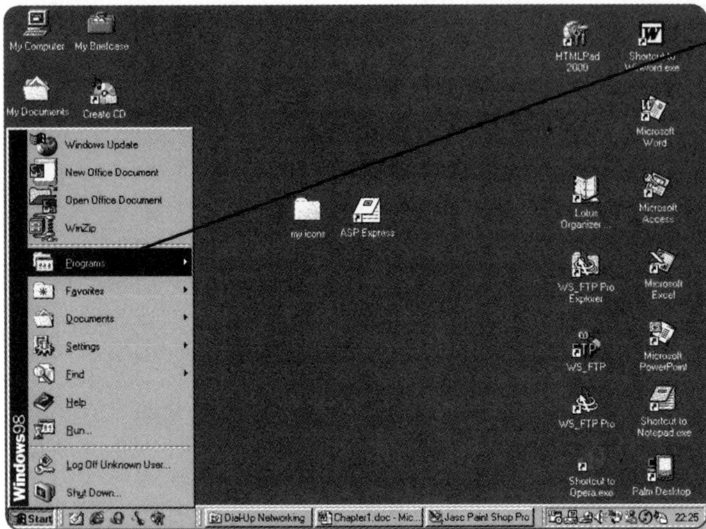

5. Click Programs.

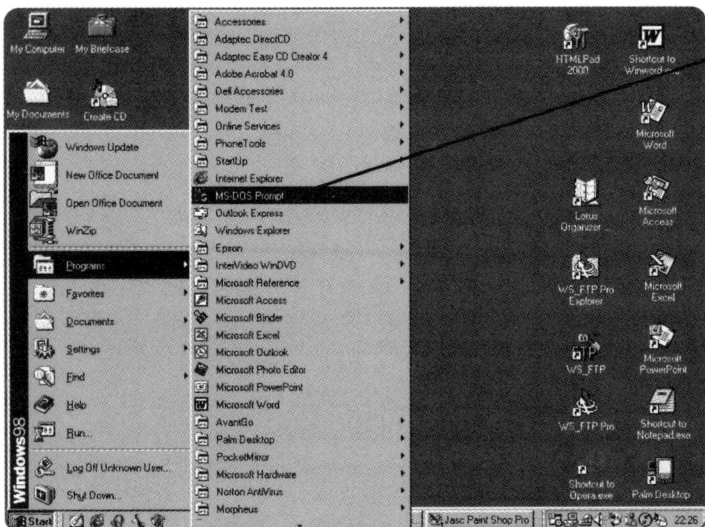

6. Click MS-DOS Prompt. A command window will open.

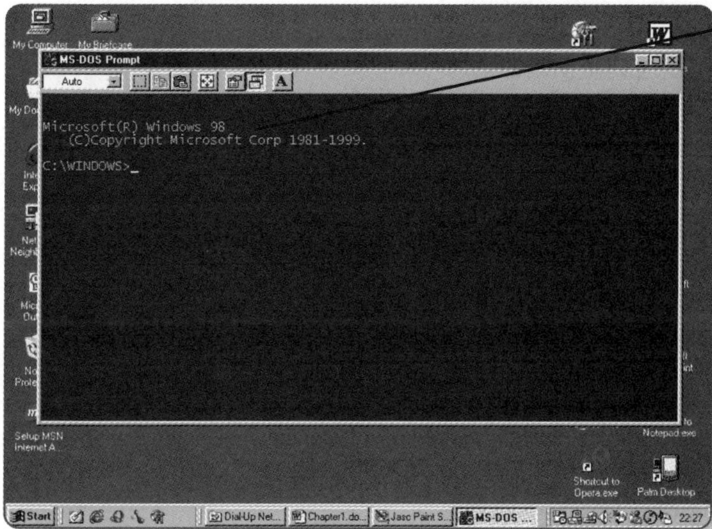

7. Click the left mouse button with the mouse pointer inside the window.

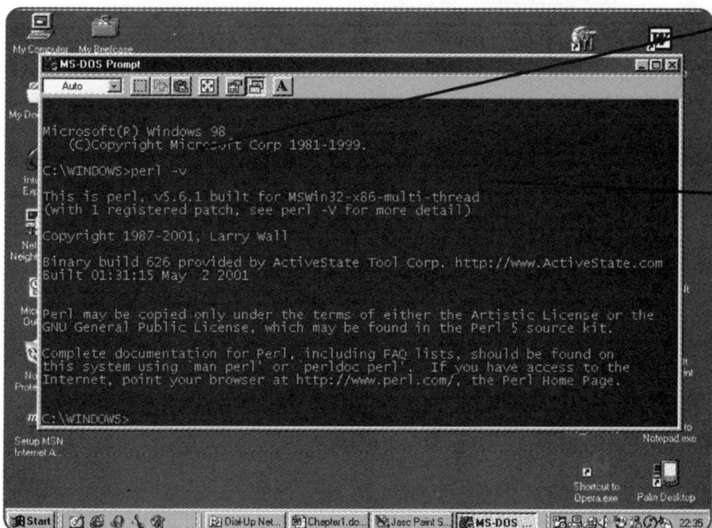

8. At the C: DOS prompt, type:

```
Perl -v
```

9. You should get a report of the version of Perl that has been installed. If you get the "Bad Command or File name" message, then this would suggest that the PATH has not been updated.

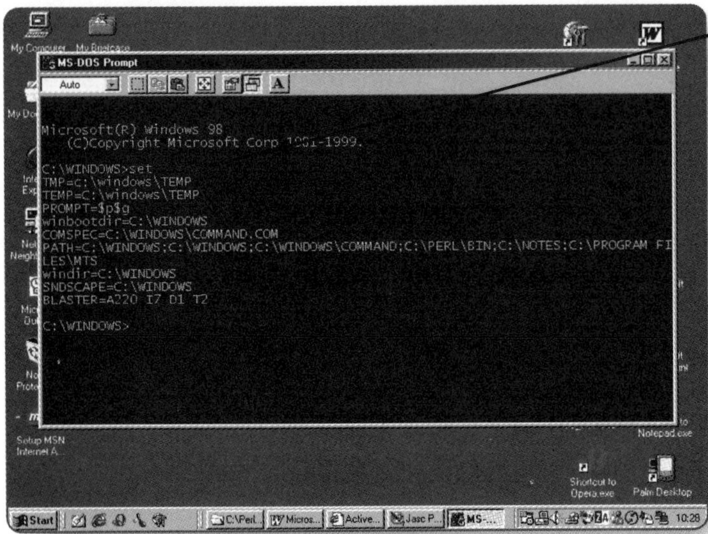

10a. Check this by typing

```
SET
```

at the DOS prompt, which will report the values of the currently set environment variables.

OR

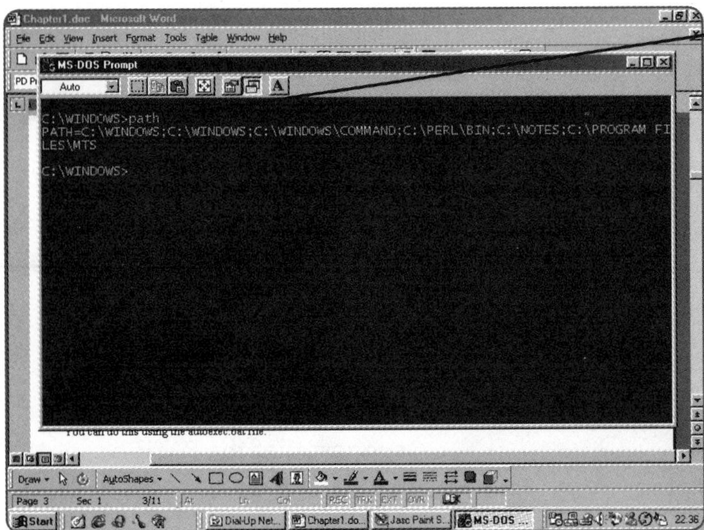

10b. Check it by typing:

```
PATH
```

If the PATH has not been updated, then you need to add the Perl\bin directories to the PATH. You can do this by using the autoexec.bat file.

Windows 95 / 98 allows you to update the PATH variable via the autoxec.bat file. If you are using Windows 98 and you want to use the Windows 98 facilities to update the autoexec.bat, then follow the next set of steps.

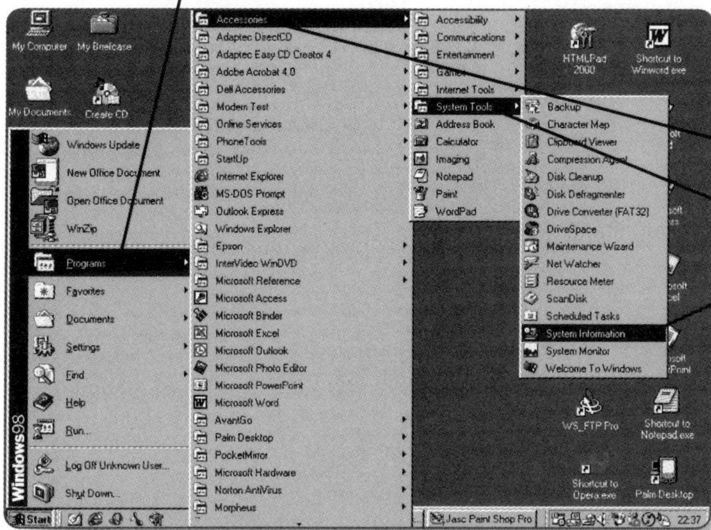

1. Go to the Start menu, at the bottom left of your screen.
2. Click Programs.
3. Click Accessories.
4. Click System Tools.
5. Click System Information. The Microsoft System Information page will appear.

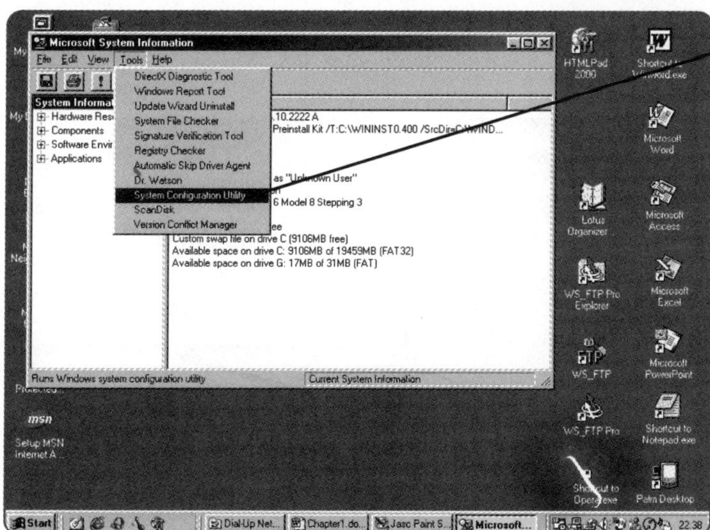

6. From the Tools menu, choose System Configuration Utility.

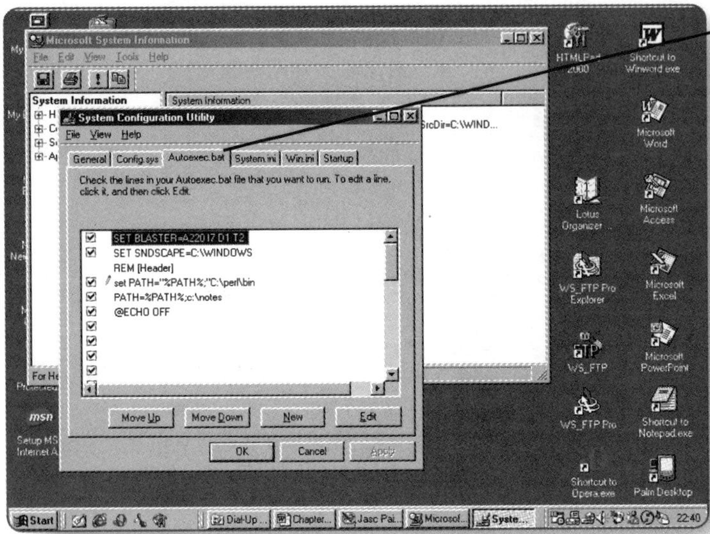

7. Choose the Autoexec.bat tab.

8. Click New and add the following entry:

```
PATH="%PATH%"; C:\perl\bin
```

Note the quotes around %PATH%.

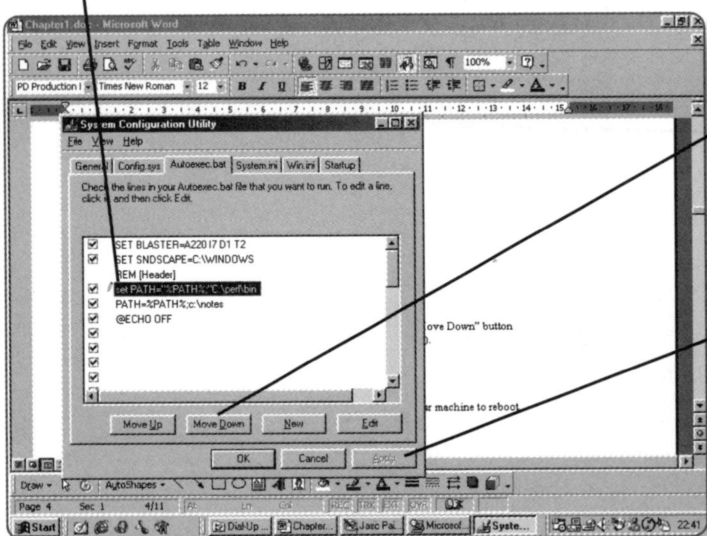

TIP

Use the Move Down button and then click Edit if you want to insert it before other statements.

9. Click Apply.

10. You will now be asked to restart your machine. Do so and wait for your machine to reboot.

Your machine should now have Perl installed and ready to go.

Now run a simple test to make sure that Perl is working and that your operating system knows where to find it.

1. Click on Start.

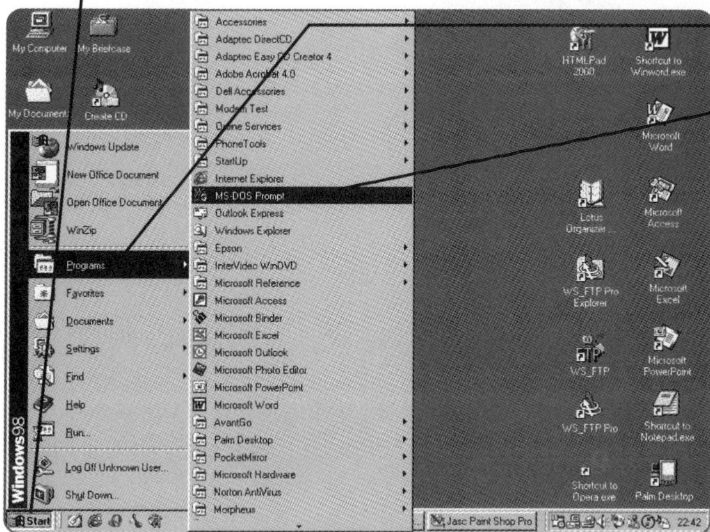

2. Select Programs.

3. Select MS-DOS Prompt. A MS-DOS Command window will open.

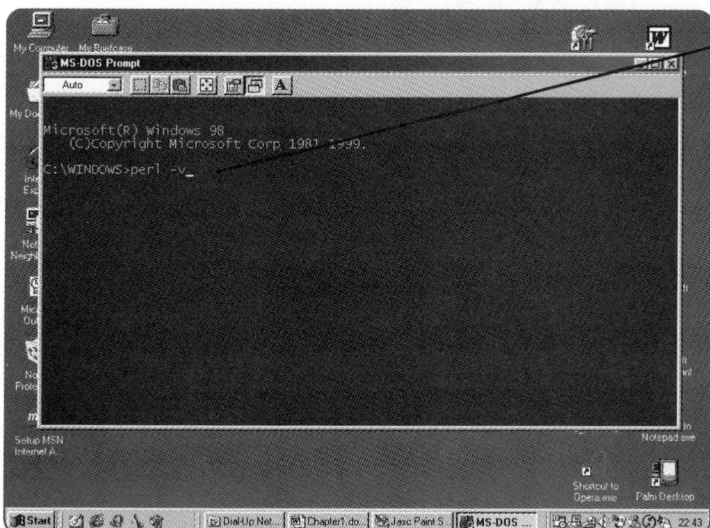

4. At the DOS prompt type

```
Perl -v
```

and press Enter.

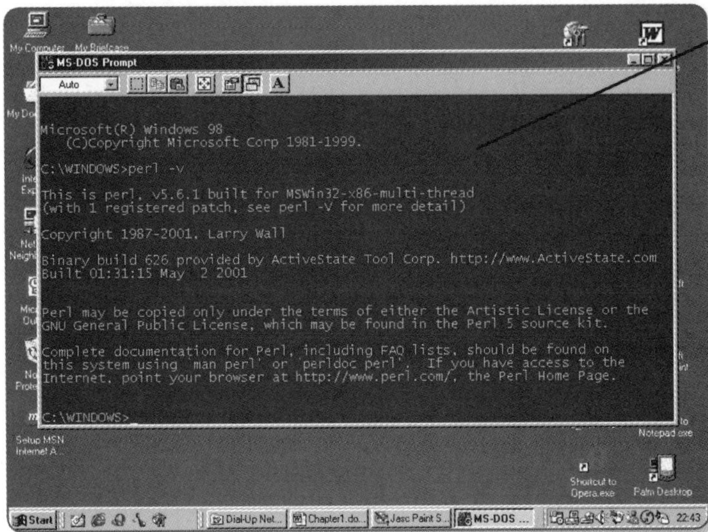

5. You should get a version report back. If you do, then everything has worked correctly. If not, go back and check the installation and verify the path information.

Assuming all is okay, you are now ready to make a start with Perl!

Installing Perl on a UNIX Machine

Installing Perl on a UNIX machine is very different from doing so on a Windows machine. To install Perl on a UNIX machine you must first obtain a copy of the Perl Bundle, as it is known, from either http://www.perl.com or from http://www.activestate.com. Note that there is a Production version and a version that is often marked as "Development." I recommend that you go for the Production version (sometimes referred to as the "Stable" version).

> **TIP**
>
> You will also find a number of other useful tools on these sites, as well as lots of helpful articles, tutorials, helpful hints, and so on.

Having obtained your UNIX Perl Bundle, you must now build your Perl system. For this you will need an ANSI C Compiler. There are a number to choose from, and you may well already have one on your UNIX "box."

In fact, you may already have a copy of Perl on your machine, as many machines are now shipped with Perl as part of the operating system.

As with the Windows test, try typing:

```
Perl -v
```

If you have Perl you will get a version report; if not, you will get a "UNIX command not found" message.

It is worth checking around on the activestate.com or perl.com Web sites to see what packages are available. Things are improving all the time, and it is likely that you will find an easy-to-install version for your platform. Just download it, follow the instructions to the letter, and all should be fine.

> **NOTE**
>
> Of course there is also a version of Perl for the Mac. Known as MacPerl, it is available from http://www.perl.com. You should be able to find a downloadable version there and unpack it using the well-known StuffIt expander program. If you don't have a copy of that, go to http://www.aladdinsys.com/expander/ and download a copy. (Incidentally, StuffIt is available for other platforms, too!)

Personal Web Server (PWS)

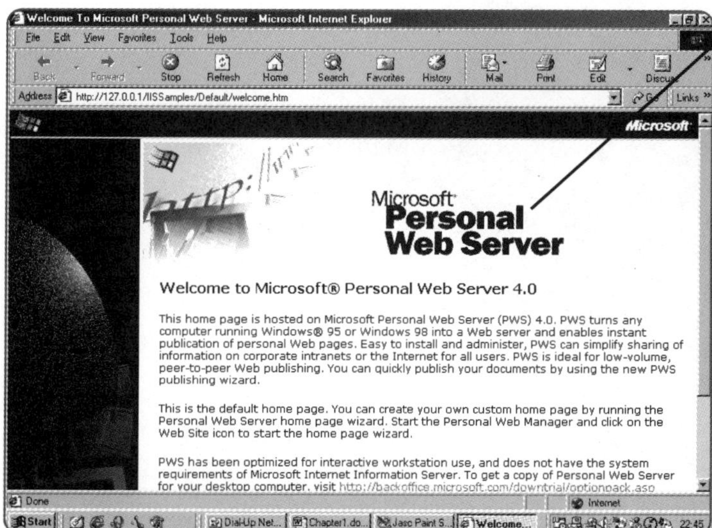

Before you can use Perl in a Web environment, you need a Web server. For Microsoft platforms, you can use Personal Web Server (Peer Web Services on Windows NT) or a Web server such as Apache.

> **NOTE**
>
> Apache can be downloaded from http://www.apache.org, and Personal Web Server can be downloaded as part of a download Option Pack from Microsoft. The easiest way to install Personal Web Server (for Windows NT or for Windows 95) is to use the NT Server 4 Option Pack, which is free when downloaded, or is occasionally available from magazine "freebie disks."
>
> Note that to view pages through your Personal Web Server, you must use a "special" IP address: http://127.0.0.1, or you can use http://localhost/.

If you have Windows 98, you should find Personal Web Server easily; it is already available in your program list:

1. Click Start.
2. Select Programs.

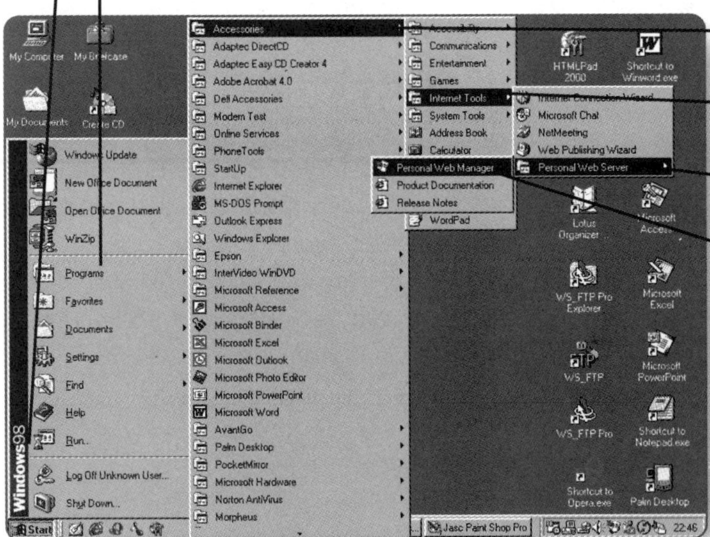

3. Select Accessories.
4. Select Internet Tools.
5. Select Personal Web Server.
6. Select Personal Web Manager.

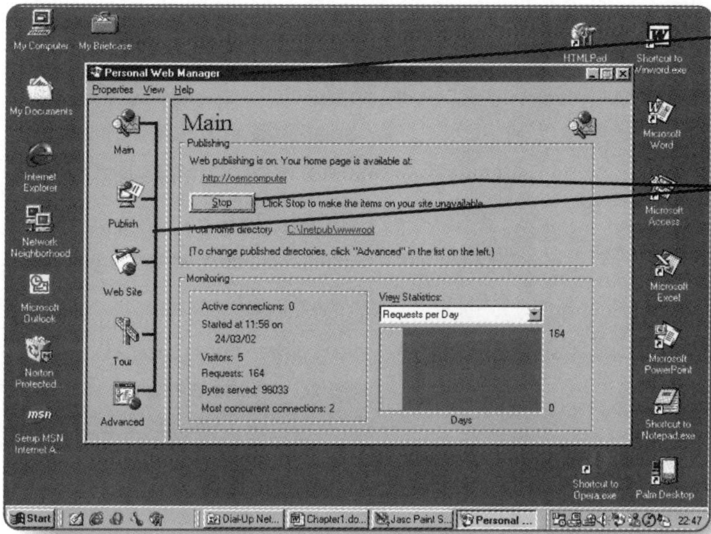

7. Open Personal Web Manager; you will see an interface like this.

Notice that the Personal Web Manager interface has a row of five icons down the left side and the main panel has a button used to start and stop the server.

> **NOTE**
>
> It is not a good idea to have the Web server running when you are connected to the Internet, as it provides a nice gateway for hackers! Make sure that PWS is not in your Startup list, and if it is loaded (you will see an icon in the Taskbar tray), make sure that the server is stopped by using the Stop/Start toggle button when you are on the Internet.

When your Web server is running, you will see that the Stop button is showing—that is, the server is started. Conversely, when the Web server is stopped, the Start button is visible where the Stop button was. (It sounds confusing, I know, but you will see what I mean as you use it!)

The five buttons down the left side are:

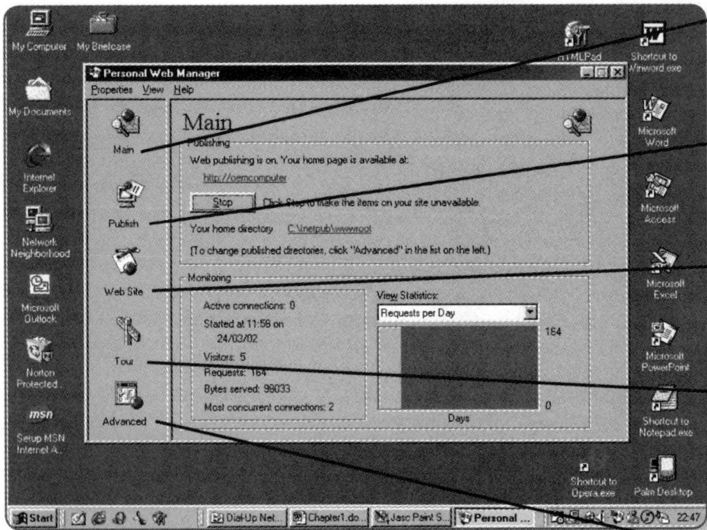

- **Main.** This gives you the main panel that you see at startup with the Stop/Start button.
- **Publish.** This allows you to publish documents to your Web server.
- **Web Site.** Web Site allows you to create a Home Page through the use of a wizard.
- **Tour.** The Tour option takes you through the features of Personal Web Server in true Microsoft Style!
- **Advanced.** This is the most useful option. From here you can configure your Web server, add new folders, change the permissions, and so on.

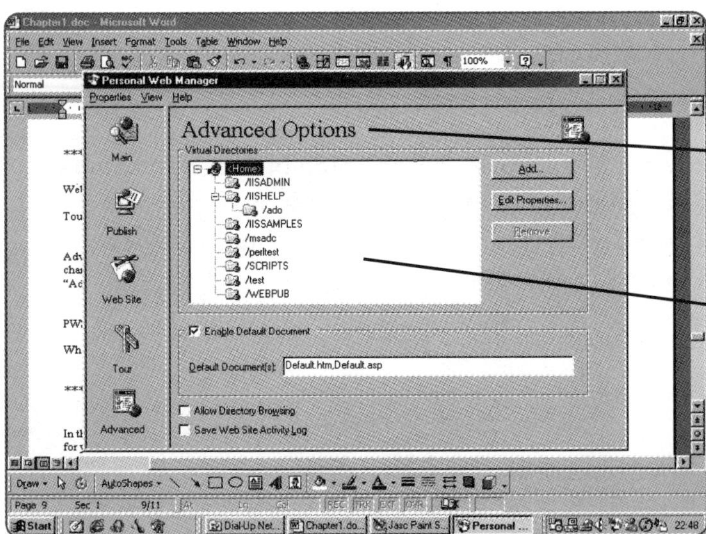

PWS Advanced Options

When you select the Advanced option, you will see a screen like this.

In the main window, you will see a default folder structure; these are the folders that Microsoft has set up for you. The top-level folder is called <Home>. This is often called "wwwroot," and is the top level of any Web server folder hierarchy. All content should be below this level, except for sensitive files and databases.

PWS (and all other servers) allows you to store files other than HTML files in locations outside of the Web server root structure, but allows you to connect the Web server to them by using the Web server alias feature (sometimes referred to as a virtual directory or folder).

Notice also that you get, as a default, a SCRIPTS folder; this is similar to the usual CGI-BIN folder found on most normal Web servers. You will almost certainly find one on your ISP upload (FTP) directory list.

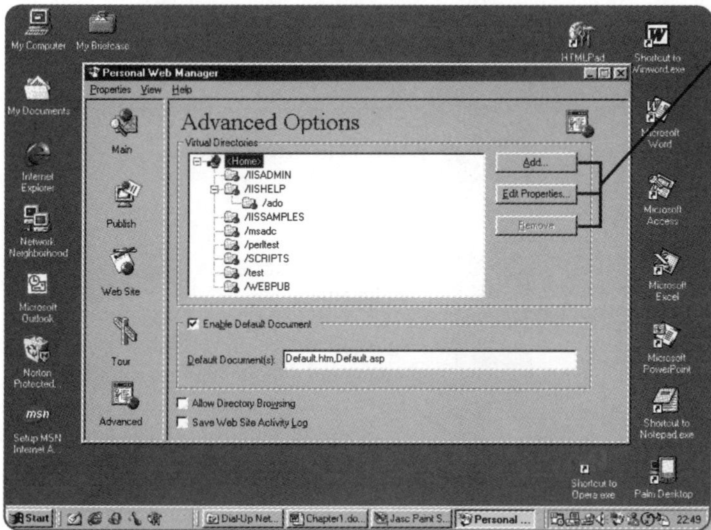

On the right side of the Virtual Directories window you will see three buttons: Add, Edit Properties, and Remove.

The Add button leads you though a wizard to set up a new folder. Let's assume you want to add a new site to your Web server—a site we can refer to as a collection of Web files (HTML and so on) that has a home page at its root and probably a set of other supporting pages, images, and so on.

To illustrate the point, you will now set up a new folder called Test on your Web server.

1. Create a folder called Test under the C:\inetpub\wwwroot folder.

> **NOTE**
>
> You can also create a new folder through the My Computer interface using File, New Options, or through the Windows Explorer interface.

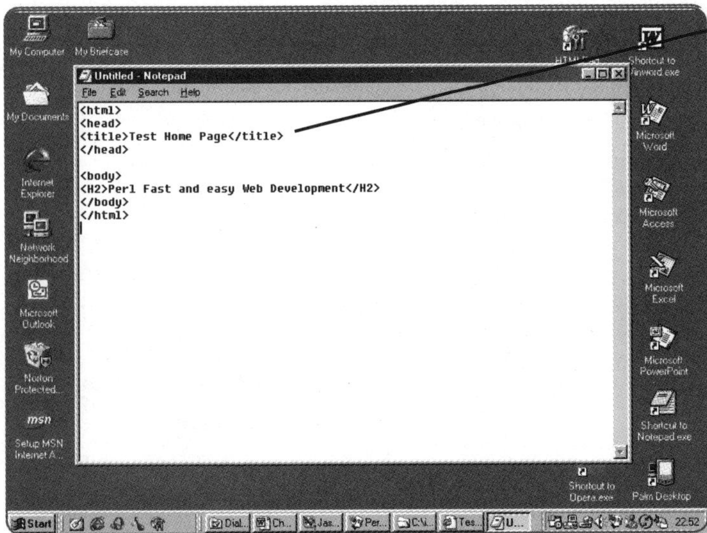

2. Using an editor (Notepad, if you are using Windows, will do), create a simple file containing the following text:

```
<html>
<head>
<title>Test Home Page</title>
</head>

<body>
<H2>Perl Fast and easy Web
Development</H2>
</body>
</html>
```

3. Save the file as default.htm in your new test folder.

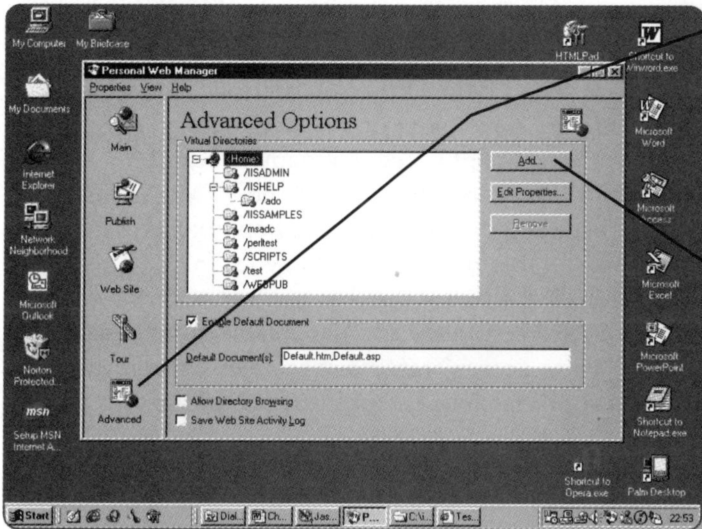

4. Open the Web server dialog and click the Advanced button. You will see the Virtual Directory dialog.

5. Click the Add button. The Add Directory dialog box will open.

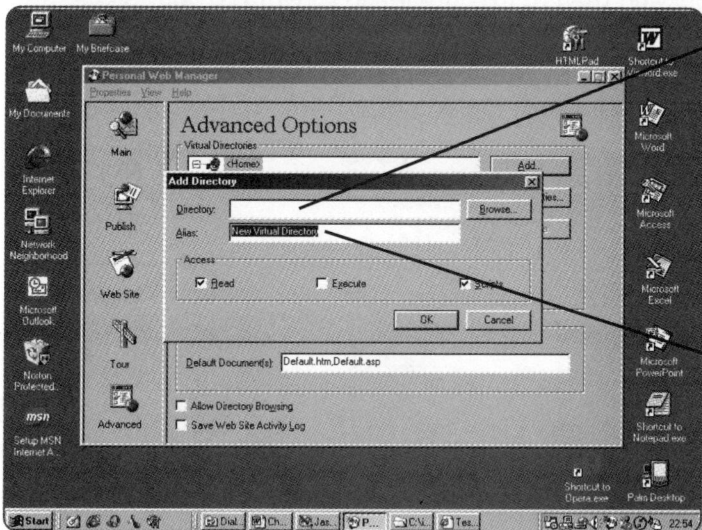

6. In the Directory field, enter the full path of the folder you want to add. Or click the Browse button and search for the folder you want to add.

7. In the Alias field, enter a name by which you want to call the folder. Often this will be the same name as the physical folder name—but it doesn't have to be! The alias is the name you will place after the main part of the URL, but this may point at a folder anywhere on the machine!

CAUTION

Note the Access check boxes below the main window. These set the access options for your new folder or virtual directory. You will probably find Read and Scripts access already checked. These are the "safe" options that allow scripts and HTML pages to be run and read, respectively. The middle option, Execute, is to allow you to run executable programs within your folder. This is potentially dangerous if the folder also has "write" access set up in the Operating System permissions. Also, many commercial Web servers have a "write access" feature in the web server, and UNIX allows you to set permissions through the use of the CHMOD command.

Whichever platform you have, always bear in mind that it is dangerous to have a folder that has both execute and write access. This allows a hacker to potentially install his own program into your folder and then to execute it and to write to your disk – with possibly disastrous results!

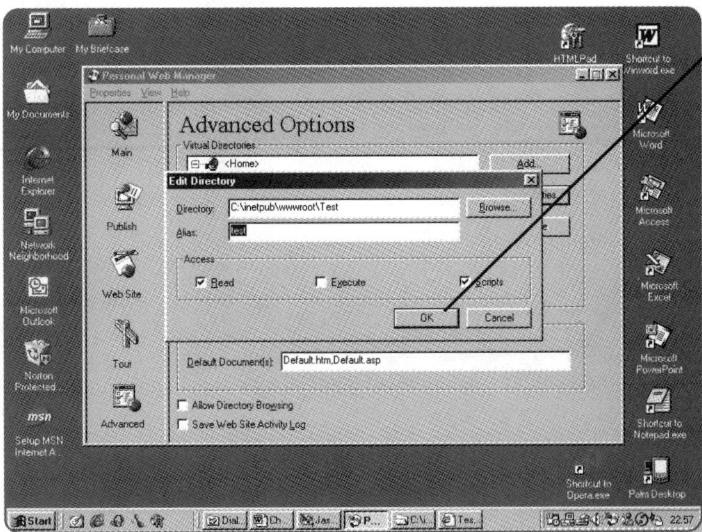

8. Finally, click OK ("un-checking" script access if you do not intend to run any scripts from within this folder). Your Web server now has visibility of your new folder.

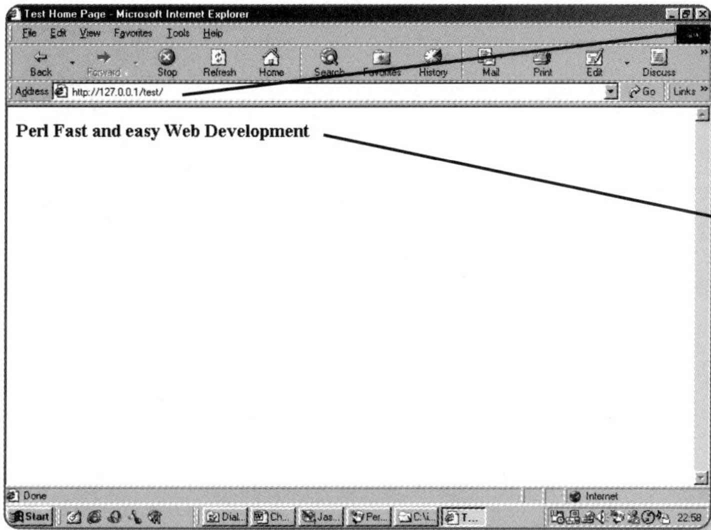

9. Open your browser and enter the following URL:

http://127.0.0.1/test/

You should see this text.

If you are using a different Web server, follow the vendor's instructions to get to a similar point with your chosen server.

You should now have a working Web server and a working copy of Perl, and we can now start to discuss the basics of Perl.

2

Taking Your First Steps with Perl

This fairly short chapter is meant to get you started by writing a simple Perl program and running it, and, hopefully, understanding what's going on in the process.

As Perl is an interpreted language, (a language in which each line of code is converted into machine code and immediately executed) it is fairly easy to test. You can keep your editor open and run your code in another window. If there is a problem, you can nip back into your editor, make changes, and run it again, repeating the process until you get it right. Since most of the problems you encounter will be typos, this is a very convenient way to work.

Though Perl is actually quite fast for an interpreted language, you will eventually be using it in online applications, where speed is not normally a huge issue (compared, for example, to high-volume batch processing).

In this chapter you will learn:

- The basics of coding in Perl
- Basic Perl syntax
- How get input for a Perl program

Before You Start

It will be useful at this stage to decide which text editor you'd like to use to write and edit your programs. There are many available, from Notepad (on Windows) and Vi (on UNIX) to more sophisticated editors with specific language-support functions, buttons, and help. A good starter's editor is HTMLPad 2000. It is great for HTML, Perl, and quite a few other languages, and although it doesn't offer real language support, it does "color code" your source code, making it easier to read. HTMLPad 2000 is a nice, easy-to-use editor to learn with; later, you can choose an editor that includes the language support you want and works in a way that suits you.

For this chapter, and for the next few chapters, create a new folder anywhere on your hard drive. You could create a new folder called "test" (or whatever you prefer to call it) inside the top-level c:\Perl folder, or create a folder called "myPerl" on your hard drive. It doesn't matter where you put it, really, as long as you can find it easily!

The Basics of Coding in Perl

In this chapter, you will begin looking at the structure of Perl, what elements make up a Perl program, and how to use them. So you can learn the basic concepts, the examples at this stage will be kept as simple as possible. As you proceed into later sections, you will be introduced to other useful Perl concepts and gradually increase your knowledge. Finally, a full CGI Perl sample program will bring together all you have learned, and add new practical elements and concepts as you try the example.

Now it's time to learn how to put Perl programs together and how to represent and manipulate data. You'll also have a chance to examine some simple processing mechanisms.

Perl Syntax

You don't need to learn all parts of Perl syntax in this chapter, but there are a few general points you need to understand before you can begin to put together a Perl program.

Statement Formatting

Following are a few definitions to help you with statement formatting:

- A *statement* is the smallest complete unit of code that actually does something. It is the computing equivalent of a sentence in English.
- An *expression* is a value, or an arithmetic, algebraic, or string value.
- A *comment* is a line (or more than one line) that performs no function in the program. It is descriptive text used to help a human reader to understand what is going on in the code. Each line of a comment in Perl starts with a # sign.

Perl is a *free format* language. That is, there can be as much white space (spaces, tabs, line breaks, and so on) as you wish. This means that you can write your code in a manner that makes it a lot more readable than some other languages.

It also means that Perl needs some way of showing when it has reached the end of a statement. This is achieved by the use of the semicolon (;). So a Perl statement may look like this:

```
print "I think Perl is great \n";
```

This is a common method of terminating a statement. C, C++, Java, PHP, and Pascal, among others, all use the semicolon to terminate statements; so if you are coming from one of those languages, you will be familiar with this already.

Okay, assuming you have selected which editor you would like to work with, you can now plunge into some Perl and see how it hangs together!

Beginning Perl

All Perl programs should begin with what is affectionately known as the "shebang" statement. The shebang statement should occur in the beginning at the first column on the first line of the program, and it should contain the file path to the Perl interpreter, perl.exe. Why it should be called the "shebang" statement is open to debate, but it is typical of the type of names that are used in computing for some special characters (the exclamation mark is often referred to as the "shriek" or the "splat").

The shebang statement starts with a # sign, indicating that it is a comment line. However, it is actually the one exception to this! On UNIX systems, this line tells the operating system where to find Perl so that the program can be executed.

NOTE

Remember: A Perl program should always begin with

```
"#!pathname_to_Perl,
```

in column 1, line 1.

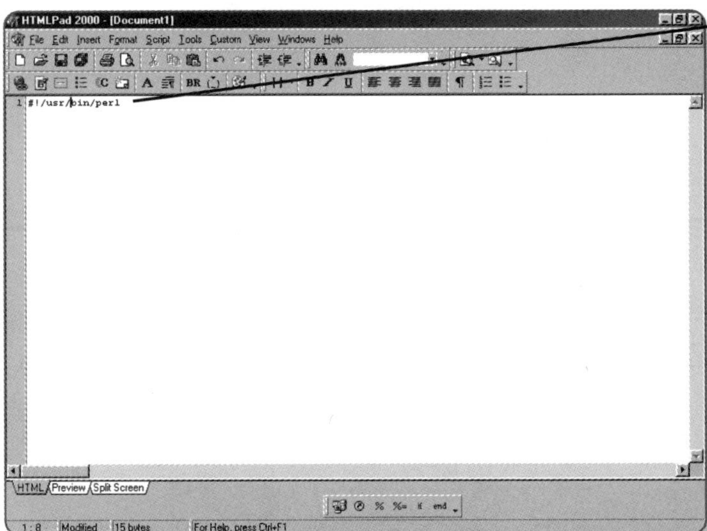

For UNIX, this will look like this:

```
#!/usr/bin/perl
```

Optionally, this may be followed by a flag, which, for example, invokes the Perl syntax checker:

```
#!/usr/bin/perl -w
```

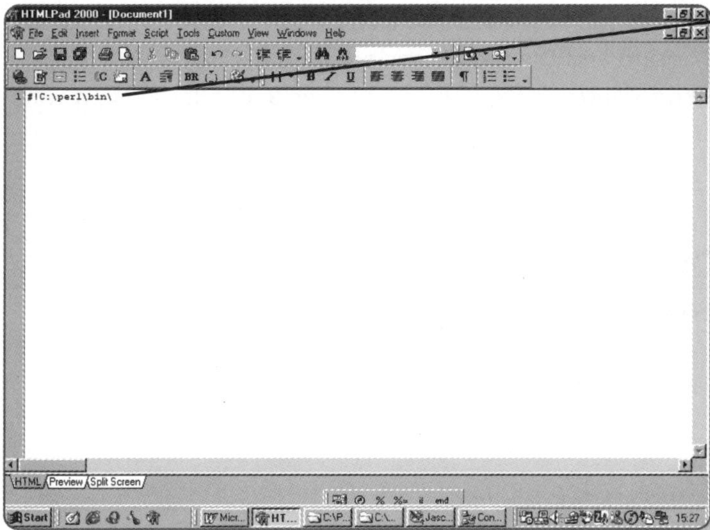

And for Windows, the shebang will look like this:

```
#!C:perl/bin/
```

Note, though, that for Windows, this is purely a comment!

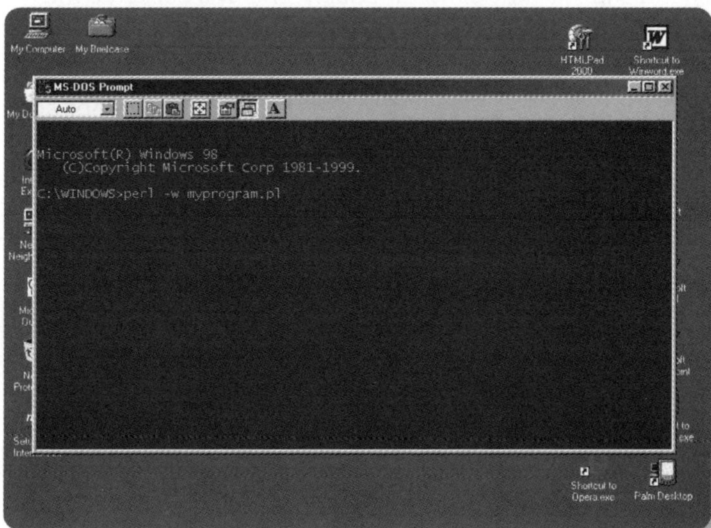

CAUTION

Here is an important difference between the UNIX and NT platforms. Any statement starting with a # is regarded by Perl as a comment and is therefore ignored by the interpreter. An exception to this is the first line of a Perl program, as described earlier. This first statement tells the UNIX operating system where to find the Perl interpreter. As long as the program file is made an executable file (by setting chmod to 755), then just typing its name will cause it to run.

You can of course still use the `-w` flag on the command line in NT.

On the NT platform, this first line will be treated as a comment. However, NT uses "association" between a program and the file extension of its file name. In other words, when Windows NT (and Windows 9x, and so on) sees a .pl extension, it will automatically invoke the Perl interpreter.

Getting Things In and Out of Perl Programs

We have already seen that we can display things on the screen by using the Perl print command:

1. Open your text editor and start a new file.

Many editors like HTMLPad 2000 try to be helpful and add some starting code for you. For now, you will not need what it offers you. To clear the text in the editor window, press the CTRL key and the "A" key simultaneously; this will cause all the text to turn blue. Now press the Delete key, and the editor window will be emptied.

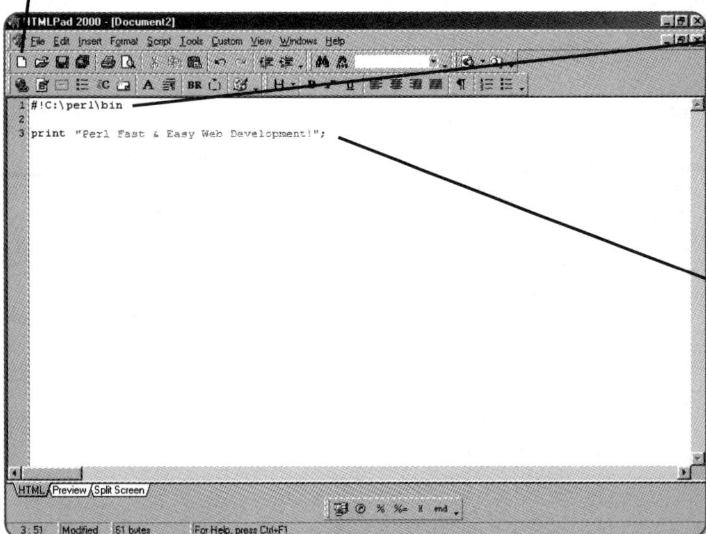

2. On the first line (do not add any spaces in front; that is, start in column 1 line 1), type:

```
#!c:\perl\bin
```

(or `#!/usr/bin/perl` if you are using a UNIX type platform).

3. On the next line (or the one after, to improve readability), type:

```
print "Perl Fast & Easy Web
Development!";
```

(Note the semicolon at the end of the statement.)

4. Save this little program as 02-01.pl in your "Test" folder.

5. Open an MS-DOS command prompt, go to the place where you saved your program, and type:

```
perl 02-01.pl
```

Your program should display the simple message:

```
Perl Fast & Easy Web Development!
```

Print Formatting

Before you can achieve anything very exciting with your Perl print statements, you must take a small diversion. You will revisit the subject again later, in Chapter 3, but it's worthwhile to learn a little about print (screen display) formatting so that you can use it in the early sample program code snippets without getting too confused.

Output to the screen can be formatted using the built-in "escape sequences." Table 2.1 lists some common escape codes.

TABLE 2.1 Common Escape Codes

Escape code	Meaning or effect
\n	Inserts a newline character
\t	Inserts a tab character
\r	Go back to the beginning of the current line (that is, carriage return but no newline)
\\	This is how you add a backslash to the output string (otherwise, it would "escape" the next character.
\"	As above but for double quotes
\'	As above but for single quotes
\$	This is needed to stop Perl interpreting a $ for the beginning of a variable.

So try the following:

1. Open your editor and start a new file.

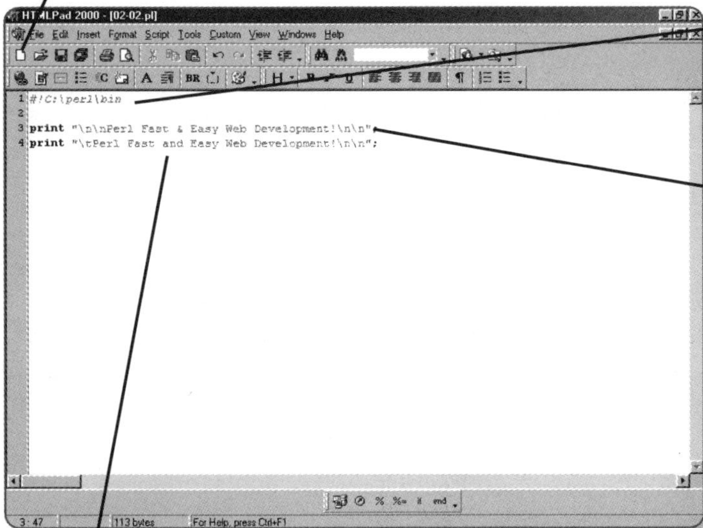

2. Enter the shebang statement:

```
#!C:\perl\bin
```

3. Add a print statement:

```
print "\n\nPerl Fast and Easy
Web Development!\n\n";
```

4. Note the "newline" escape codes, \n\n.

> **NOTE**
>
> A *newline* is an empty line created by forcing carriage returns.

5. Now add another similar print statement with a tab escape code at the front:

```
print "\tPerl Fast and Easy Web Development!\n\n";
```

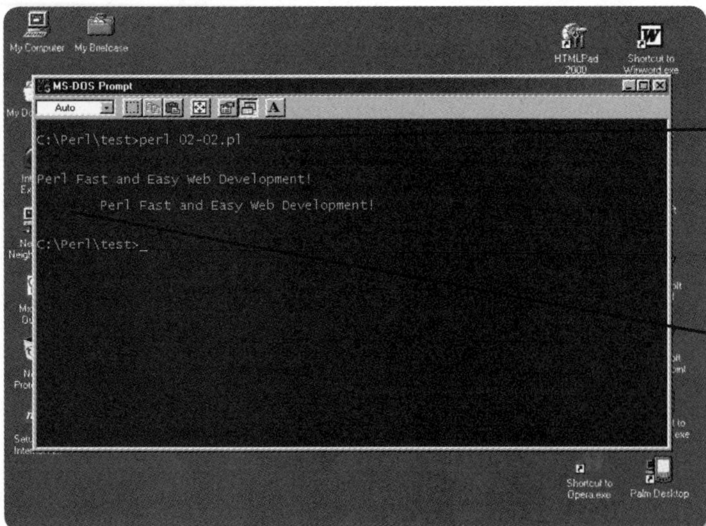

6. Save the program as 02-02.pl in your Test folder.

7. Run your program by opening a command window and typing:

```
Perl 02-02.pl
```

8. The \t at the beginning of the last line of the program causes a tab character to be inserted, which forces the output text to be moved along one tabspace.

Getting Input for a Perl Program

One of the most useful functions provided by any language is to allow the user to provide input for your program, to make your program interactive. Perl can operate as a command line programming language and it can accept input from the user at the command line.

Try the following:

1. Open your text editor.

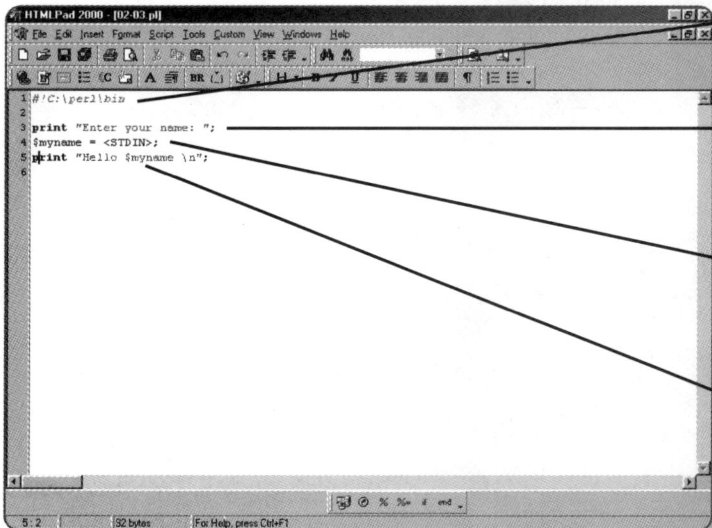

2. Type the shebang statement at line 1, column 1.

3. Leave a blank line then type:

```
print "Enter your name: ";
```

4. On the next line type:

```
$myname = <STDIN>;
```

5. Now type the following on the next line:

```
print "Hello $myname \n";
```

6. Save the program as, say, 02-03.pl.

7. Open an MS-DOS Command box.

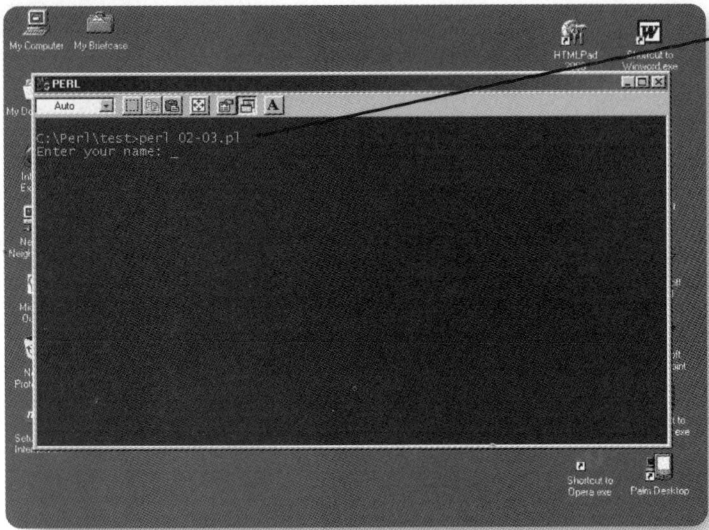

8. Type perl **02-03.pl**. This will run the program, and you should see that the program has displayed the message "Enter your name" and appears to be waiting.

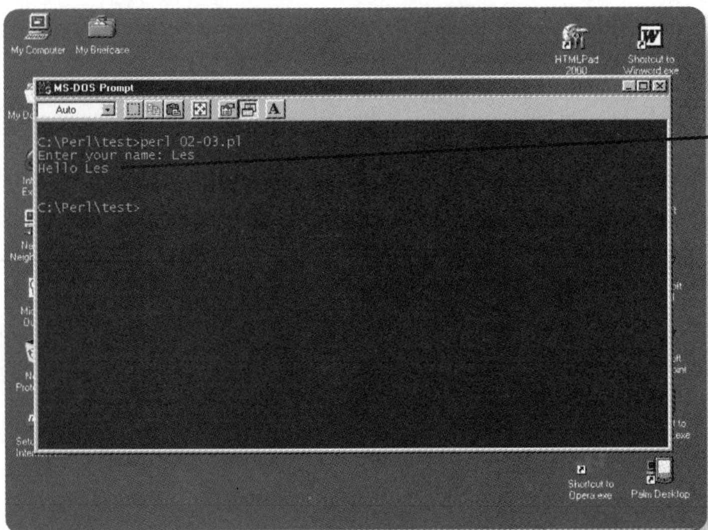

9. Type in your name and press the Enter key.

10. The program will display the message "Hello" followed by whatever name you entered. The program will then end, and the command prompt will be displayed.

So how does this program work?

Here is the program again with line numbers:

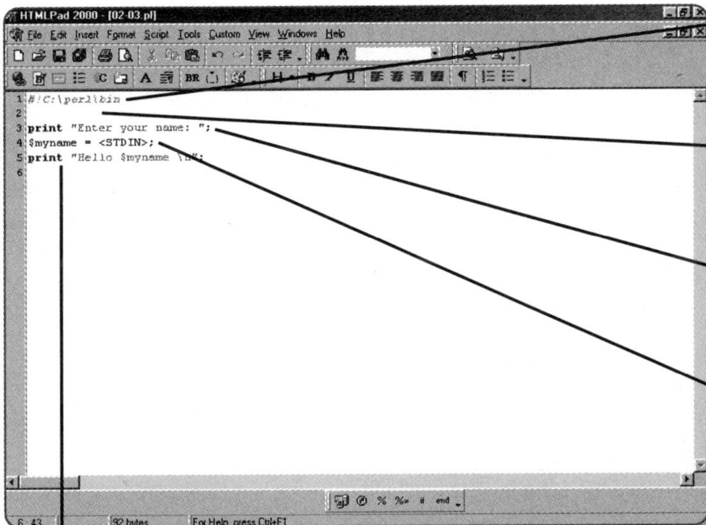

- Line 1 is the shebang statement we described earlier.
- Line 2 is deliberately left blank and just serves to make the program easier to read.
- Line 3 prints a statement to the screen inviting you to enter your name.
- Line 4 takes your typed input from <STDIN> (the Standard Input Stream or Device—the keyboard!) and stores it in a variable called `$myname`; the $ sign tells Perl that this is a Scalar Variable (more on this later).
- Line 5 prints the string "Hello" followed by the value contained within the variable `$myname` followed by a newline character.

Note that the variable remains inside the printed string. Perl substitutes the variable with the value contained within the variable.

You've made a start. You can write a small program to obtain user input and to display a message. But most computing problems are about data. To be able to manipulate data, you need to be able to store it in your programs. So, next you will start to learn about variables.

3

Perl Data Types: Scalars

Perl has four built-in data types. They are scalars, arrays, hashes (also known as associative arrays) and references (used for file handles and so on). *Scalars* are basically single items of data. *Arrays* are lists of data accessed by means of a numeric subscript, and *hashes* are lists of data accessed via another scalar variable or literal; arrays and hashes will be covered in later chapters. A *reference* is a "pointer" to something else. For example, references are used as "file handles" in order to point to a file (you will examine files in Chapter 12, "Using Files in Perl").

This chapter concerns the scalar data type in Perl. Specifically, you will learn about:

- Scalar variables
- Strings
- The $_ variable
- Escape sequences for formatting

Scalar Variables

All scalar variable names are preceded by the dollar sign ($). So, for instance, the variable to hold the age of a person may be written as

```
$age
```

If you are not used to languages that use this kind of variable notation, you could easily forget the $ and find some strange errors creeping into your code.

> **NOTE**
>
> Perl variable names are case sensitive. Case-sensitivity is common in modern languages, but do keep it in mind, as it can be the source of some frustration when debugging Perl programs.

Scalar variables are variables that hold a single value. They can be integer, string, floating-point numbers (real numbers), or references. A reference scalar variable is a variable that simply holds the address of another variable; that is, it is a pointer to that variable.

An integer scalar is simply a variable that holds a whole number:

```
$age = 20;
```

Of course, you can do all the things that you can normally do with a numeric variable. To demonstrate this and to show how you use simple arithmetic in Perl, try the following:

1. Open your text editor.

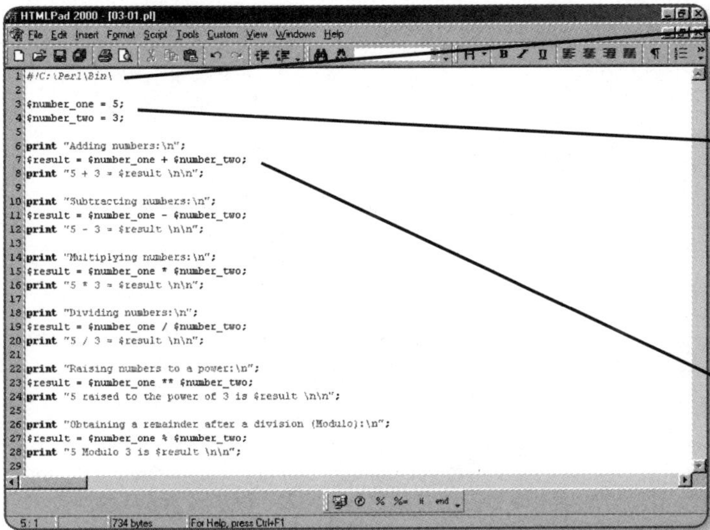

2. Enter the shebang statement.

3. Leave a blank line and then add the following lines to define and initialize two variables.

```
$number_one = 5;
$number_two = 3;
```

4. Add the following three lines:

```
print "Adding numbers:\n";
$result = $number_one +
   $number_two;
print "5 + 3 = $result \n\n";
```

> **NOTE**
>
> Blank lines are optional, but they do help to make the program easier to read. Code that follows on line after line looks a bit crowded. Leaving blank lines between blocks of code that logically belong as a group is easier on the eye and the brain!

The first of the three lines is a print statement to display what you are about to do. The second creates a variable called `$result` and assigns a value to it equal to the result of `$number_one + $number_two`. The third statement is another print statement to demonstrate the result.

5. Enter the next three statements to do the same thing as the last three, using the subtract operator instead.

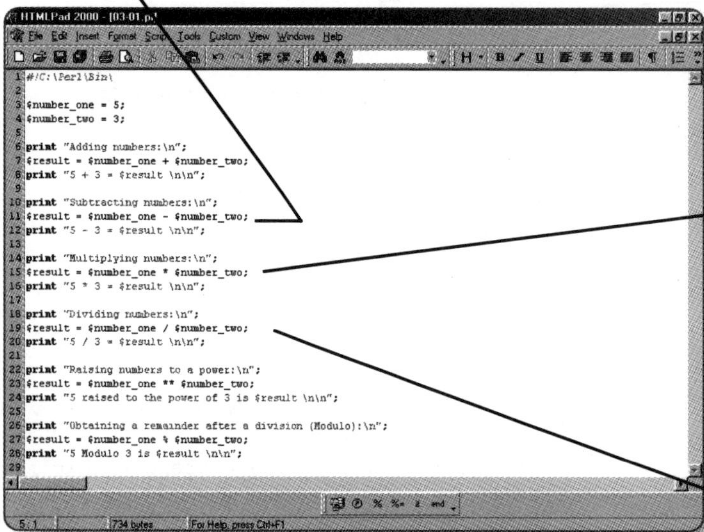


```
print "Subtracting
   numbers:\n";
$result = $number_one -
   $number_two;
print "5 - 3 = $result \n\n";
```

6. Do the same thing for the multiply (*) operator.

```
print "Multiplying
   numbers:\n";
$result = $number_one *
   $number_two;
print "5 * 3 = $result \n\n";
```

7. Enter this code in the same way for the division (/) operator.

```
print "Dividing numbers:\n";
$result = $number_one /
   $number_two;
print "5 / 3 = $result \n\n";
```

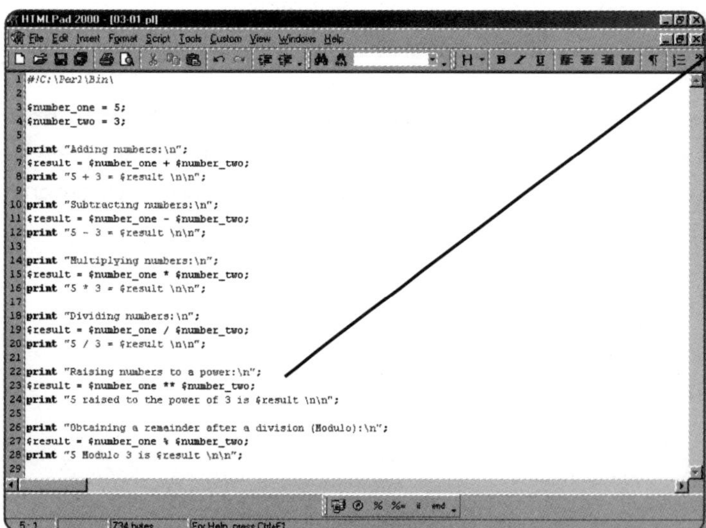

8. Enter the code for the exponentiation (**) operator.

```
print "Raising numbers to a
   power:\n";
$result = $number_one **
   $number_two;
print "5 raised to the power
   of 3 is $result \n\n";
```

The second line of these three causes the `$result` variable to contain the value of `$number_one` raised to the power of `$number_two`.

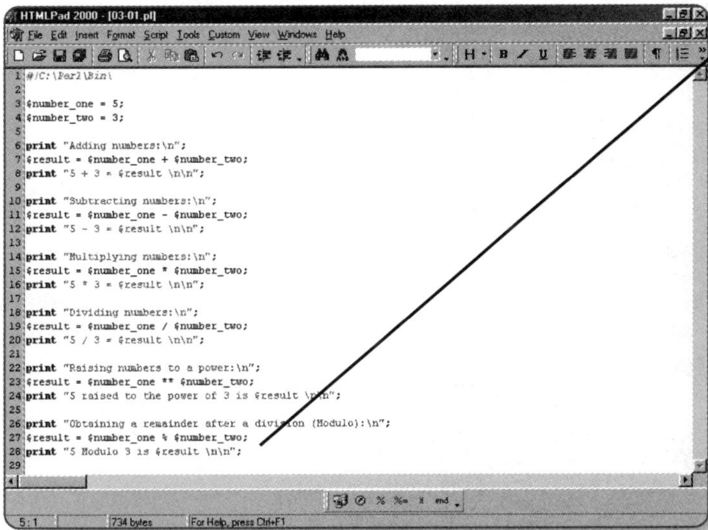

9. Add the last three lines of code to demonstrate the use of the modulo operator.

```
print "Obtaining a remainder
   after a division
   (Modulo):\n";
$result = $number_one %
   $number_two;
print "5 Modulo 3 is $result
\n\n";
```

Here the `$result` variable is assigned the remainder value after the division of `$number_one` by `$number_two`.

10. Save the code in your test folder as 03-01.pl.

11. Open a DOS command prompt.

12. Navigate to your program test folder.

13. Run your code using the perl 03-01.pl command.

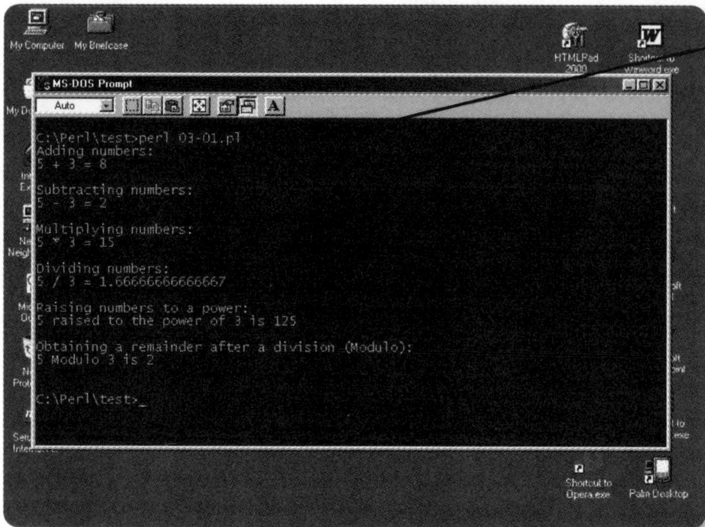

14. You should get output like this.

If your output does not look correct, return to Step 2 and look for any typos.

This exercise demonstrates the simple arithmetic operations you might want to perform using the normal arithmetic operators.

Other Operators

There are a few more simple operators that might look a bit strange. These are the increment, decrement, and the assignment operators. Let's have a quick look at those.

1. Open your text editor.

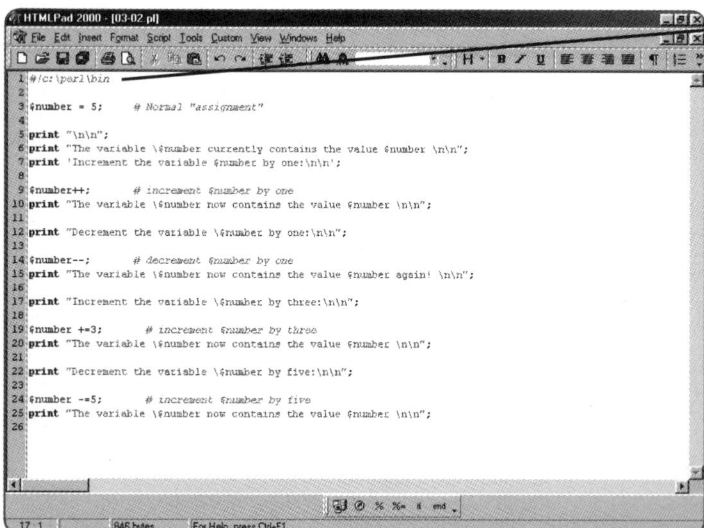

2. Enter the shebang statement.

```
#!c:\perl\bin
```

3. After a blank line, create a variable called `$number` and assign the value 5.

```
$number = 5;     # Normal
"assignment"
```

Note the comment preceded by the hash symbol.

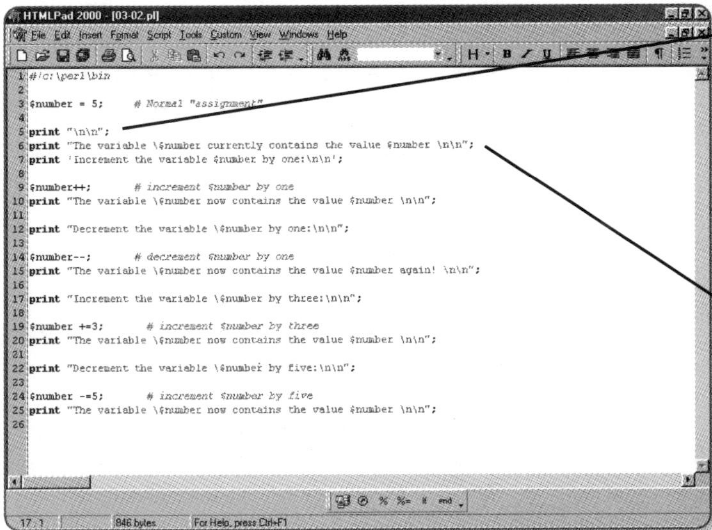

4. Use the following line of code to cause two *newlines* to be printed in the output from the program:

```
print "\n\n";
```

5. Enter this line of code to print the name of the variable and the value it contains:

```
print "The variable \$number
currently contains the value
$number \n\n";
```

NOTE

Note that the variable name, `$number`, is preceded by a backslash (\) so that the variable is not *interpolated* (that is, its name is printed rather than its value). At the end of the line the variable is printed, and this time there is no backslash, so the variable is replaced by its value. There are two further newline characters at the end of the line, so there will be two more carriage returns in the displayed output.

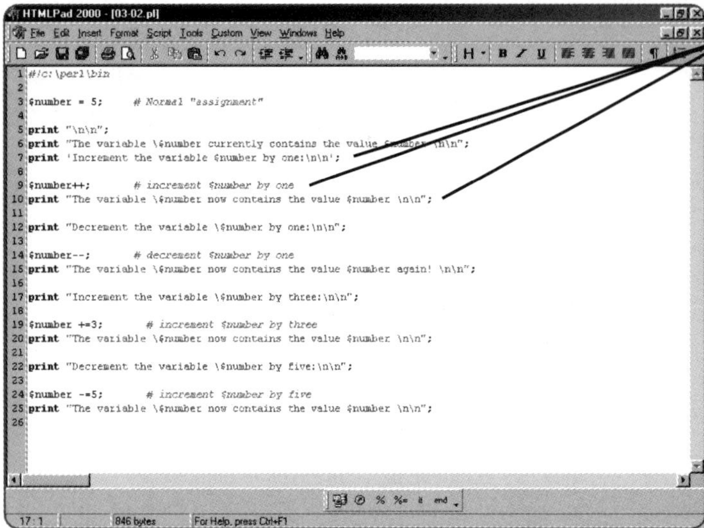

6. Type the next few lines—the first is a simple print statement to announce that `$number` is to be incremented. In the next line, `$number++` causes the variable to be incremented. The last of the three lines displays the new value of the variable `$number`.

```
print 'Increment the variable
$number by one:\n\n';

$number++;  # increment
     $number by one
print "The variable \$number
   now contains the value
   $number \n\n";
```

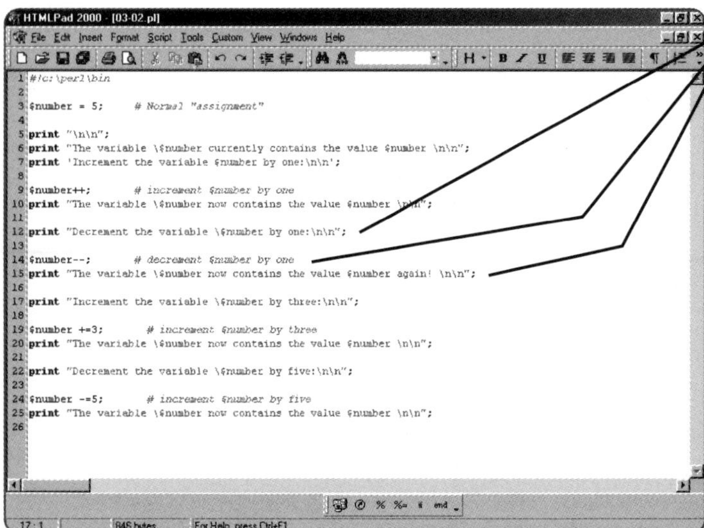

7. Now enter the following lines to do a similar thing, this time using the decrement operator.

```
print "Decrement the variable
\$number by one:\n\n";

$number--;        # decrement
     $number by one
print "The variable \$number
     now contains the value
     $number again! \n\n";
```

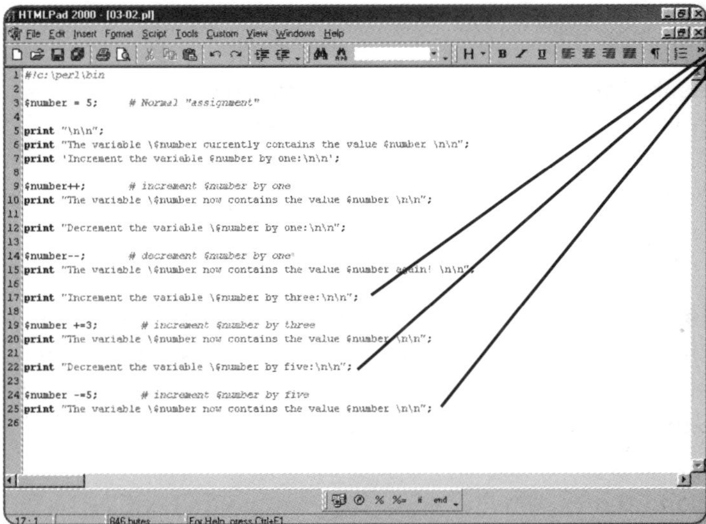

8. Add these lines to demonstrate how variables can be incremented or decremented by values other than 1.

```
print "Increment the variable
   \$number by three:\n\n";

$number +=3;   # increment
   $number by three
print "The variable \$number
   now contains the value
   $number \n\n";

print "Decrement the variable
   \$number by five:\n\n";

$number -=5;   # increment $number by five
print "The variable \$number now contains the value $number \n\n";
```

9. Save the code in a test folder as 03-02.pl.

10. Open a DOS command prompt.

11. Navigate to your program test folder.

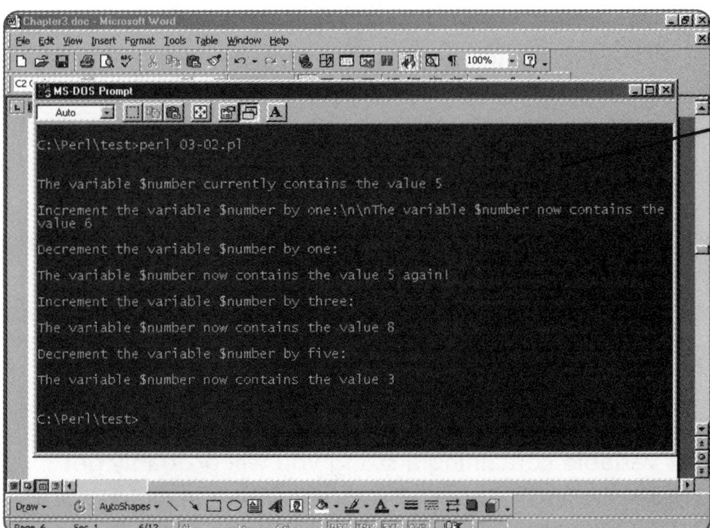

12. Run your code using the perl 03-02.pl command.

13. You should get something like this as output.

NOTE

Note the way that comments appear automatically in italics. This is a function of the editor I have chosen to use here. If you are using another editor your comments may not appear in italics, though it is common in most modern editors.

Looking back at your program, note the backslash (\) before the variable name in lines 6, 10, 15, and so on. This is used so that Perl will print `$number` as a literal and not try to treat it as a variable. Where the `$` is not preceded by a backslash you will notice that the value is substituted for the variable name.

There is a slight complication to the increment and decrement assignment operators. This is that they can occur either before or after the variable. The effect of the operator is the same except that when the operator is before the variable, the value of the variable is updated before the variable is used. If the operator is after the variable, the value of the variable is updated after the variable is used. If you are at all familiar with C, C++, Java, PHP, and so on, you will be familiar with this; otherwise it might sound confusing. Don't worry too much about it for now—uses for these techniques will suggest themselves as you get deeper into Perl.

Strings

Strings are also held in scalar variables, for instance, a person's surname might be held in a scalar, like so:

```
$surname
```

But remember, a scalar is a scalar. For example, I can also use the `$surname` variable to hold a number. However, it is not all chaotic. Perl will recognize that you are using a scalar as a number by the action you are carrying out upon it. For example, if you carry out an arithmetic operation upon a numeric scalar you will get a sensible result.

If you do the same on a scalar variable containing a string you will probably get zero. In other words, Perl recognizes a variable type by the *context* in which it is used; you will often hear the word *context* used in conjunction with Perl data types. If you are used to a "strongly typed" language this will seem a little strange, but you'll soon get used to it.

The $_ Variable

If you use some functions in Perl that require a parameter or argument but do not supply one, Perl will use its special "default" variable. This variable is `$_`, and it can have many uses as well as being occasionally the source of confusion.

For example, you would normally expect the print statement to have a parameter passed to it—the thing you want printed. If you do not pass a parameter to print, print does not fail, it merely prints the contents of `$_`.

Try this:

1. Open your editor.

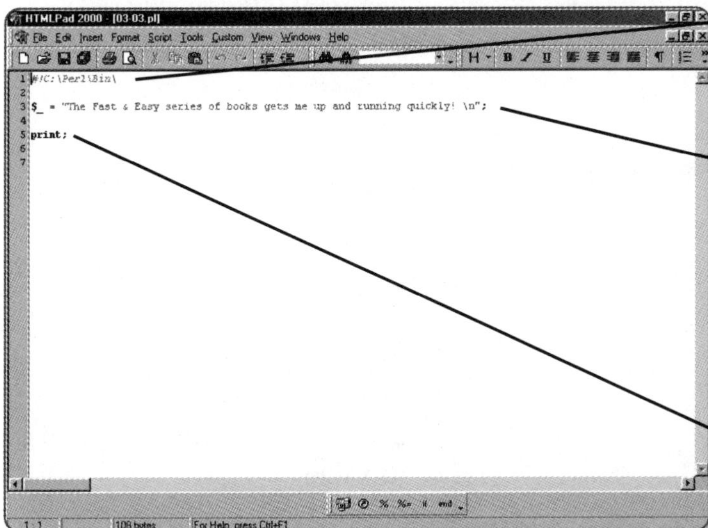

2. Enter the usual shebang statement, then leave a blank line.

3. Enter the following statement to load the `$_` variable with a string as shown:

```
$_ = "The Fast & Easy series
   of books gets me up and
   running quickly! \n";
```

4. Next type

```
print;
```

5. Save your program as 03-03.pl.pl.

6. Run the program by using the usual command prompt and typing perl 03-03.pl

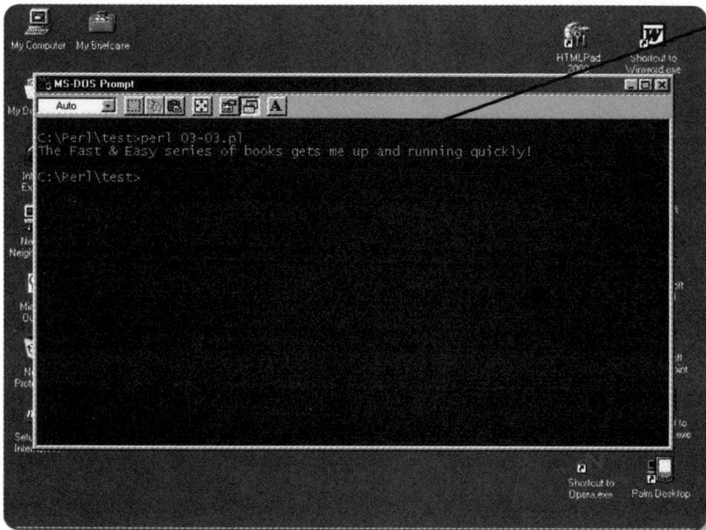

Here is the result.

Now, just to prove all of the previous points, try the following program and run it from the command prompt.

1. Open your editor.

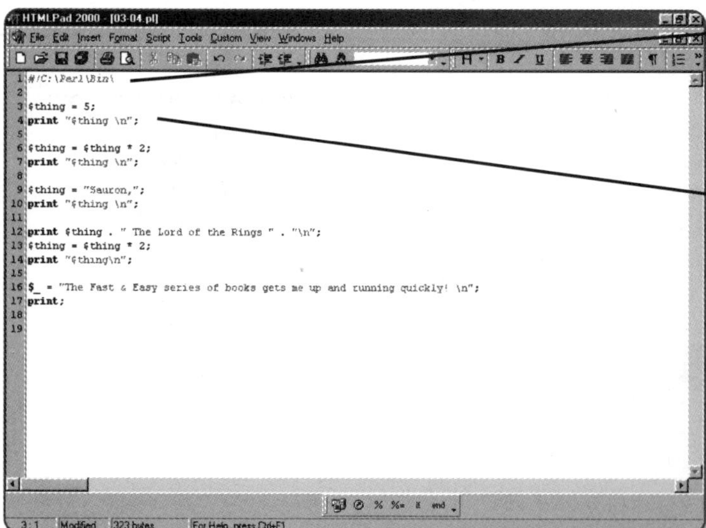

2. Enter the usual shebang statement.

```
#!C:\Perl\Bin\
```

3. Create a variable called `$thing`, initialize its value to 5, and tell your program to display its value.

```
$thing = 5;
print "$thing \n";
```

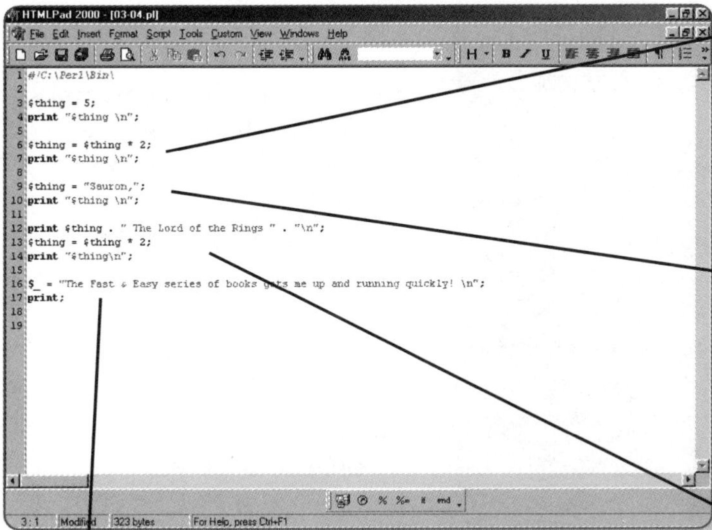

4. Now add these two lines to multiply `$thing` by two and display the result.

```
$thing = $thing * 2;
print "$thing \n";
```

5. Now assign the value "`Sauron`" and display the value of `$thing` again.

```
$thing = "Sauron,";
print "$thing \n";
```

6. Add the following lines to concatenate `$thing` with the string literals "`The Lord of the Rings`" and "`\n`". Then try to multiply the result by 2 and display the result.

```
print $thing . " The Lord of the Rings " . "\n";
$thing = $thing * 2;
print "$thing\n";
```

7. Finally, set the `$_` variable to "`The Fast & Easy series of books gets me up and running quickly! \n`" and display the result.

```
$_ = "The Fast & Easy series of books gets me up and running quickly! \n";
print;
```

8. Save your program as 03-04.pl.

9. Run the program (perl 03-04.pl from the command prompt).

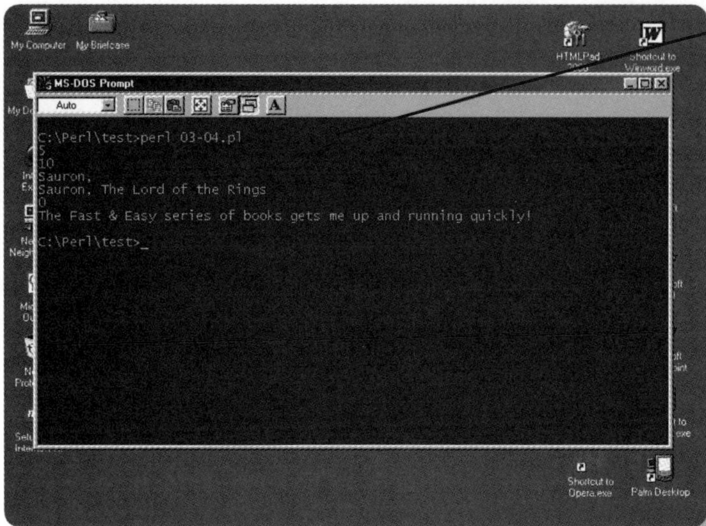

Here is the result.

This example shows how scalars can be used for numeric or string values and also what happens when you try to perform arithmetic on a string scalar value.

The last two lines demonstrate the use of the `$_` variable. You will use this again as you continue through your exploration of Perl.

Once again, note that the variables in the print statement are enclosed in quotes. Double quotes allow you to interpolate a variable within a string. It is important that you fully understand this mechanism.

```
$thing = "Fred";

print "the value of the string is $thing \n";
```

will give you

```
the value of the string is Fred
```

Single quotes work in a similar way for literals, but they *do not* cause interpolation to occur, and so variables are *not* evaluated within a string.

In other words, the following code:

```
$thing = "Fred";
print 'the value of the string is $thing';
```

will give you

```
the value of the string is $thing \n
```

Try it and you'll see what I mean.

Finally, note the \n characters at the end of the print statements. Those familiar with C, C++, Java, PHP, and so on will recognize that this is the newline character. This causes any subsequent text output to move to the next line on the screen. Note that this, too, will not be interpolated as a newline character if singles quotes are used in the print statement.

Single quotes cause escape sequences to be ignored. If you put one of the print statements in the previous program in singles quotes, the \n sequences will be displayed and there will be no newlines.

Note that a scalar variable can contain nothing. For example, if you do the following:

```
print $string1;
```

`$string1` now exists but has no value. However, you can check for the existence of a scalar using the following:

```
if (defined $string1)
  {
     print "That variable has been defined! \n";
  }
```

You can even "uninitialize" a scalar variable like this:

```
undef($string1);
```

or

```
$string1 = undef;
```

You will be examining more things that you can do with strings in Perl as you come to use strings for real.

Escape Sequences For Formatting

You have already used the print function in Perl. And you recently learned about the use of an escape character \n to give a newline character—that is, to force a line break and move the text cursor to the next line, and \t to give a tab character.

In Chapter 2 you saw a short table of escape sequences. There are a number of other escape sequences that provide text formatting. See Table 3.1 for a more complete list of these common escape sequences.

TABLE 3.1 Escape Sequences

Escape codes	Meaning
\b	Backspace
\n	Newline
\r	Carriage return (go to the beginning of the line)
\t	Tab
\b	Backspace
\u	Convert the next character to uppercase
\U	Convert the following characters to uppercase
\l	Convert the next character to lowercase
\L	Convert the following characters to lowercase
\\	Display a backslash
\'	Display a single quote
\"	Display a double quote
\E	End an U or L effect

Note that the backslash can also be used for purposes other than text formatting. For example, what if you want to display a string such as \n or even just a \ ?

You'd place another backslash in front of what you want to print (or to place the string in single quotes). So, if you want to display \n, use

```
print \\n;
```

If you want to display a backslash, use

```
print "\\";
```

Also, if you want to display quotes, you can do this:

```
print "One of the words here has \"quotes\" around it \n";
```

Now you know how to set up a string value and how to display it. Next you will learn about something that you cannot do much programming without—operators.

4

Operators

You have used some operators already, such as the addition (+) and subtraction (-) operators. In this chapter you will learn a little more about them, and about a few new ones.

In this chapter you'll have a chance to examine:

- The Assignment operator
- String operators
- Comparison operators
- Logical operators

The Assignment Operator

The first operator to mention is the assignment operator. This is the equals sign (=), and you have already used it. The assignment operator is common to almost every programming language and doesn't need a lot of explanation.

Very simply, the value on the right of the equal sign is copied—not moved—to the variable on the left.

```
$surname = "Smith";
$age = 30;
```

Try the following little program:

1. Open your editor.

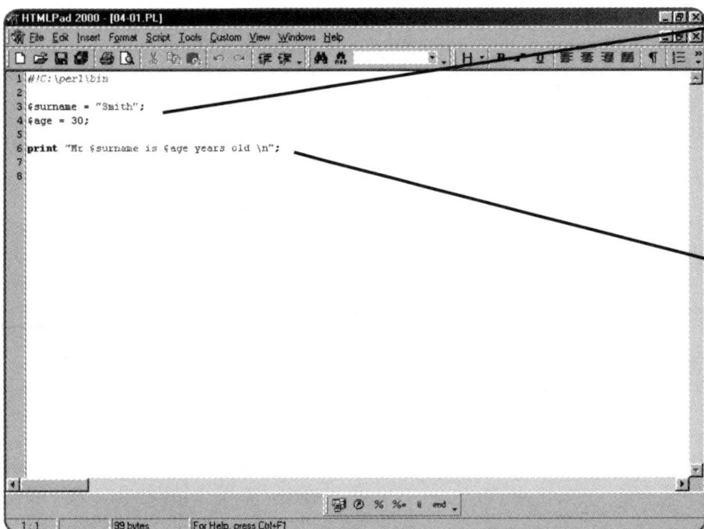

2. After the usual shebang statement, create a couple of variables like this:

```
$surname = "Smith";
$age = 30;
```

3. Now, using *interpolation* (wrapping the variables inside a double quoted string), embed the values of the variables in the string like this:

```
print "Mr $Surname is $age
   years old \n";
```

4. Save the program as 04-01.pl or the name of your choice.

5. Open a command window and run the program (perl 04-01.pl).

The result should look like this.

Again, like most other languages, you can *daisy chain* assignments together, so that all variables have the same value and that value is the last one in the chain. (This is often done to set lots of variables at the beginning of a program.)

Try this program.

1. You start, of course, with the shebang.

```
#!C:\perl\bin
```

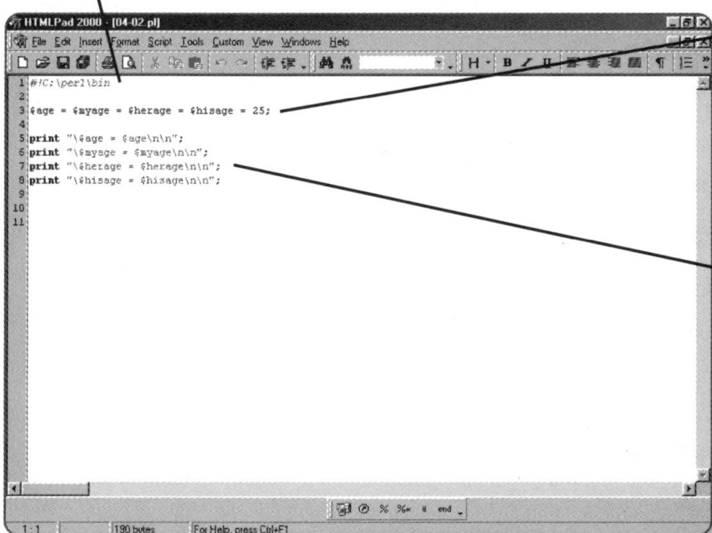

2. Define a set of variables and assign them to each other and finally assign a value, like this:

```
$age = $myage = $herage =
    $hisage = 25;
```

3. Now display them one at a time to prove that it worked.

```
print "\$age = $age\n\n";
print "\$myage = $myage\n\n";
print "\$herage =
   $herage\n\n";
print "\$hisage =
   $hisage\n\n";
```

Your program should look like the one shown here.

4. Save your program (I've used the name 04-02.pl, you can use any name that suits you).

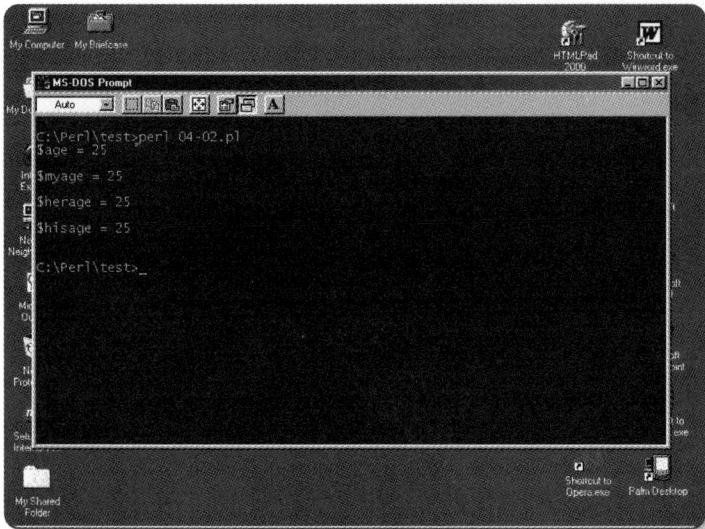

5. Run your program. You should see that all the variables have been set to the same value.

Arithmetic Operators

Perl has a familiar (to programmers) list of arithmetic operators.

(+) The addition operator

(-) The subtraction operator

(*) The multiplication operator

(/) The division operator

(%) The modulus operator

(**) The exponentiation operator

We have mentioned most of them before, but here's a description of the last two:

- The modulus operator (%) gives the value of the remainder following a division operation. For example:

  `33 % 7 gives the value 5  (33 / 7 remainder 5).`

- The exponentiation operator (**) gives the value of a number after being raised to a power. A simple demonstration would be

  `5 ** 3 would give 125`

  That is, 5 raised to the power of 3 (5^3) gives 125.

Just so that you know what they look like when coded, here are a few examples of arithmetic operations as used in Perl.

1. Open your editor.

2. Enter the shebang (I'll not mention the shebang again...I'm sure you've got the message by now).

```
#!C:\perl\bin
```

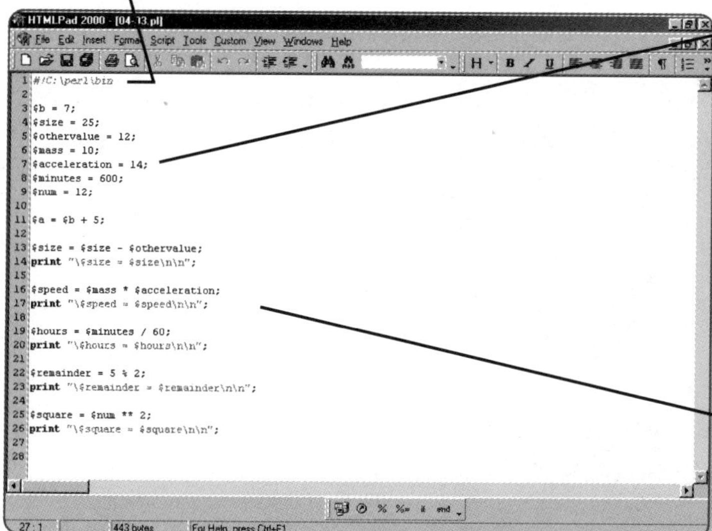

3. Enter the following code to set up a number of variables.

```
$b = 7;
$size = 25;
$othervalue = 12;
$mass = 10;
$acceleration = 14;
$minutes = 600;
$num = 12;
```

4. Enter the code (listed on the next page) to perform arithmetic operations on your variables and to display the results.

```
$a = $b + 5;

$size = $size - $othervalue;
print "\$size = $size\n\n";

$speed = $mass * $acceleration;
print "\$speed = $speed\n\n";

$hours = $minutes / 60;
print "\$hours = $hours\n\n";

$remainder = 5 % 2;
print "\$remainder = $remainder\n\n";

$square = $num ** 2;
print "\$square = $square\n\n";
```

5. Save your program as 04-03.pl.

6. Open an MS-DOS command prompt window.

7. Run your program (perl 04-03.pl).

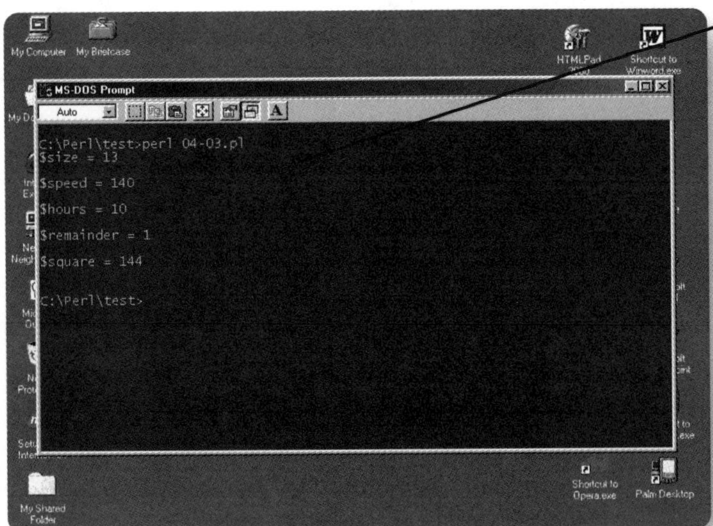

You should get this output.

Play with some examples in a simple Perl program of your own and use the `print` statement to display the effect.

Other Operators

Perl also supports the increment and decrement operators, as you discovered earlier; now you can take a look at them in a little more detail. These operators are a shorthand way of updating the value of a numeric variable.

```
$counter++;          # This is the same as:      $counter = $counter + 1;
$counter–;           # This is the same as:      $counter = $counter - 1;
```

If you want to add more than one to a numeric variable, you can do the following.

```
$counter+=5;         # This is the same as:      $counter = $counter + 5;
```

Similarly:

```
$counter-=5;         # This is the same as:      $counter = $counter - 5;
```

This shorthand method of updating variables also works with other operators, as shown here:

```
$counter %=5;        # This is the same as       $counter = $counter % 5;
```

(That is, divide `$counter` by 5, and then place the remainder into `$counter`.)

```
$counter*=5;         # This is the same as       $counter = $counter * 5;
```

By way of a reminder, here is a little program to demonstrate these operators.

1. Open your editor.

2. Use this simple code to assign a number to a variable.

```
$number = 5;     # Normal "assignment"
```

3. Enter the following code to print a couple of blank lines and then display the variable.

```
print "\n\n";
print "The variable \$number currently contains the value $number \n\n";
```

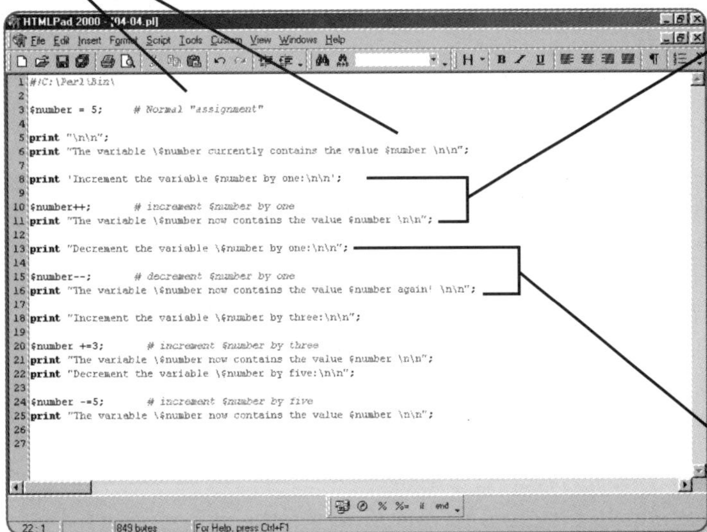

4. Now display a message and then increment the variable like this:

```
print 'Increment the variable
   $number by one:\n\n';

$number++;    # increment
   $number by one
print "The variable \$number
   now contains the value
   $number \n\n";
```

5. Now use this code to display a message and then decrement the variable.

```
print "Decrement the variable \$number by one:\n\n";

$number–;        # decrement $number by one
print "The variable \$number now contains the value $number again! \n\n";
```

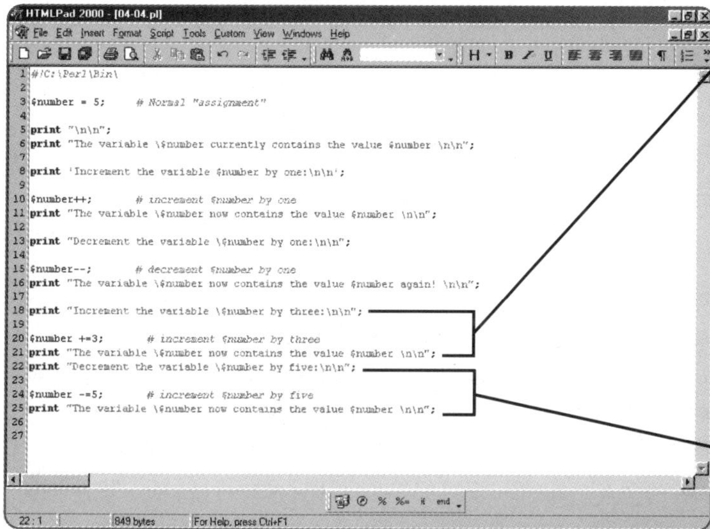

6. Then type the following to increment the variable by 3 and display the result.

```
print "Increment the variable
   \$number by three:\n\n";

$number +=3;        # increment
   $number by three
print "The variable \$number
   now contains the value
   $number \n\n";
```

7. Finally, enter the code to decrement the variable by 5.

```
print "Decrement the variable \$number by five:\n\n";

$number -=5;       # increment $number by five
print "The variable \$number now contains the value $number \n\n";
```

8. Save it as 04-04.pl.

9. Open an MS-DOS command prompt window.

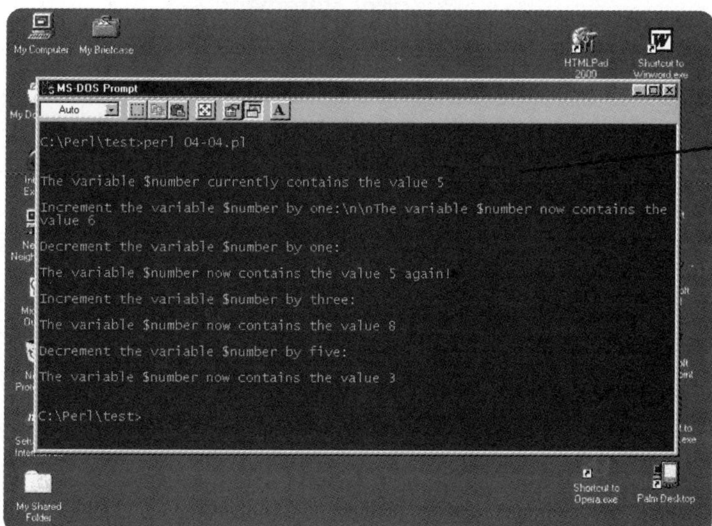

10. Run the program (perl 04-04.pl).

You should get the results shown.

There is one more thing that is probably worth mentioning before you move on. The increment and decrement operators can occur before the variable name, like this:

```
++$count;
```

Initially, it might not appear to be any different than the following:

```
$count++;
```

And there isn't a lot of difference. After all, the value still ends up incremented by 1. The only difference is that, in situations where the variable is used in a loop, the value contained in the variable `$count` is incremented *before* its value is used in the first case, and *after* it is used in the second case. It might not appear to matter much at first sight, but remember it; I guarantee you will find a reason to use one rather than the other.

Try this simple example to demonstrate the subtle difference.

1. Open your editor.

2. Start a new file.

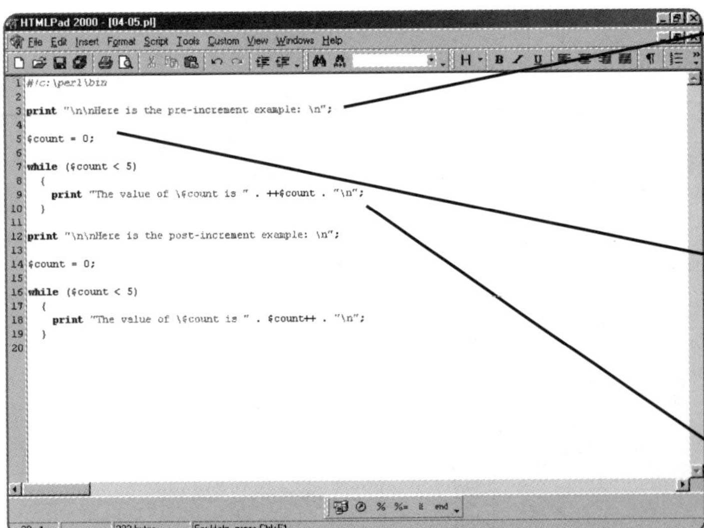

3. After the usual shebang statement, enter the following print statement:

```
print "\n\nHere is the pre-
   increment example: \n";
```

4. Now create a variable to act as a counter and set its value to zero.

```
$count = 0;
```

5. Use a simple `while` loop, setting the limit of the loop iterations to 5. In this case, use the pre-increment operator (`++$count`).

```
while ($count < 5)
  {
   print "The value of \$count is " . ++$count . "\n";
                                                       }
```

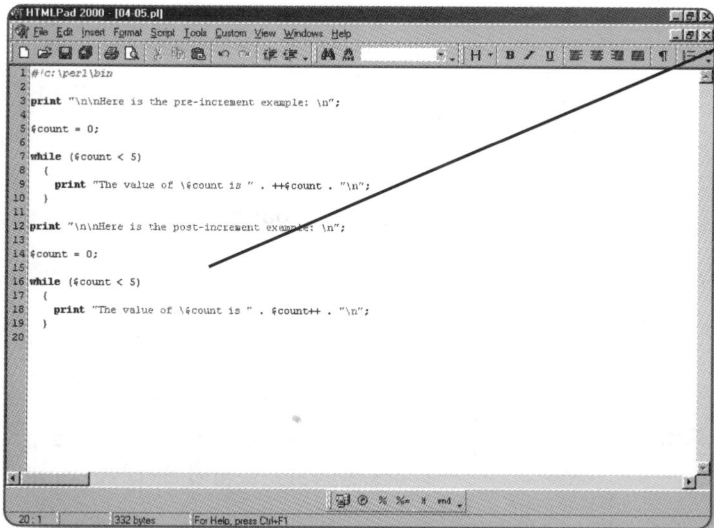

6. Now repeat the above code, but this time using the post-increment operator.

```
print "\n\nHere is the
   post-increment example: \n";
$count = 0;
while ($count < 5)
  {
  print "The value of \$count
     is " . $count++ . "\n";
  }
```

7. Save the program as 04-05.pl.

8. Open a command window.

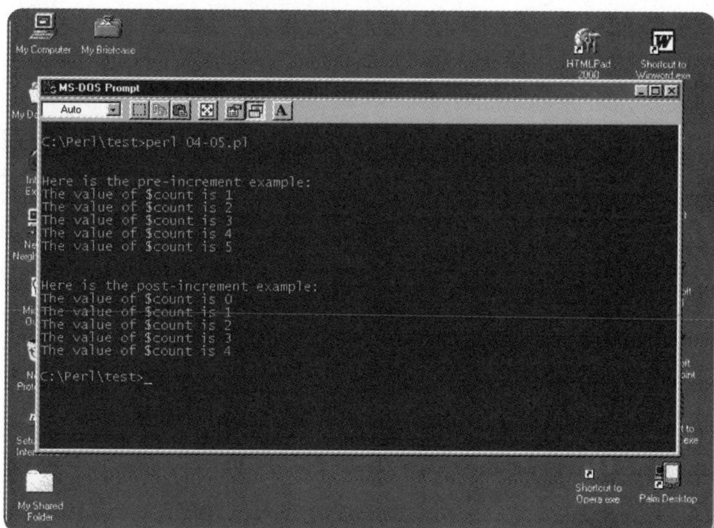

9. Run the program and observe the results. Can you see the subtle difference?

That is probably enough about numeric operators to give you an idea of how they work. Next you will learn about string operators.

String Operators

String operators provide you with some useful methods of manipulating strings; with these operators you can join strings together (known as *concatenation*) or extract "substrings" from other strings. You will learn about some different string operators in the next sections.

The Concatenation Operator

You can join strings together in Perl using the "dot" (concatenation) operator. Try this example.

1. Open your editor.

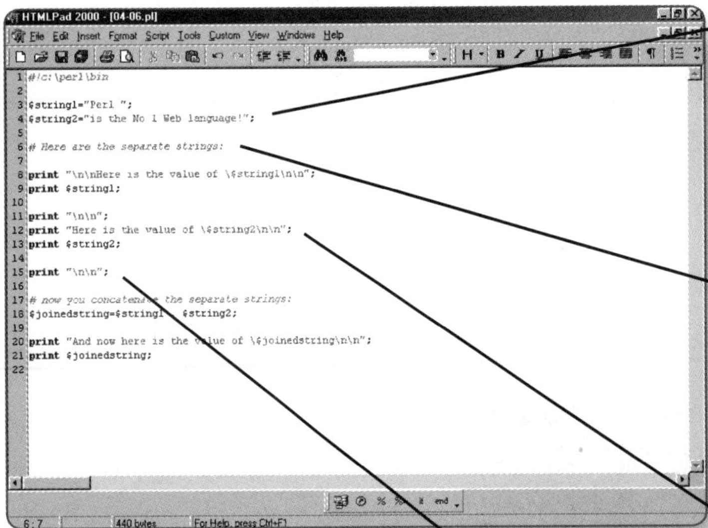

2. Enter the Perl code to set up a couple of string variables, assign values, and display them.

```
$string1="Perl ";
$string2="is the No 1 Web
   language!";
```

3. Enter a comment to remind you of what you are doing.

```
# These are the separate
   strings:
```

4. Display the value of `$string1`.

```
print "\n\nHere is the value
   of \$string1\n\n";
print $string1;
```

5. Print a couple of empty lines to keep it tidy.

```
print "\n\n";
```

> **NOTE**
>
> It is good practice to do this throughout your programs—you'll be glad you did when you come back later to fix them!

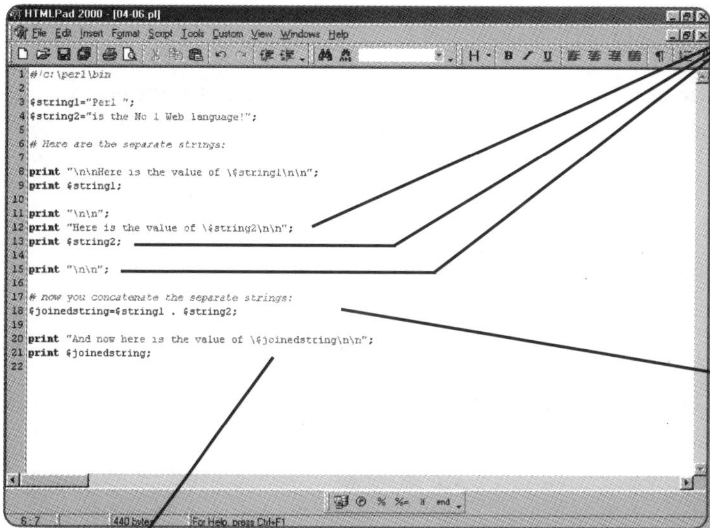

6. Enter the following to display the value of the second string variable, `$string2`.

```
print "Here is the value of
   \$string2\n\n";
print $string2;

print "\n\n";
```

7. Add another comment and then join the strings together.

```
# now you concatenate the
   separate strings:
$joinedstring=$string1 .
   $string2;
```

8. Display the result.

```
print "And now here is the value of \$joinedstring\n\n";
print $joinedstring;
```

9. Save it as 04-06.pl.

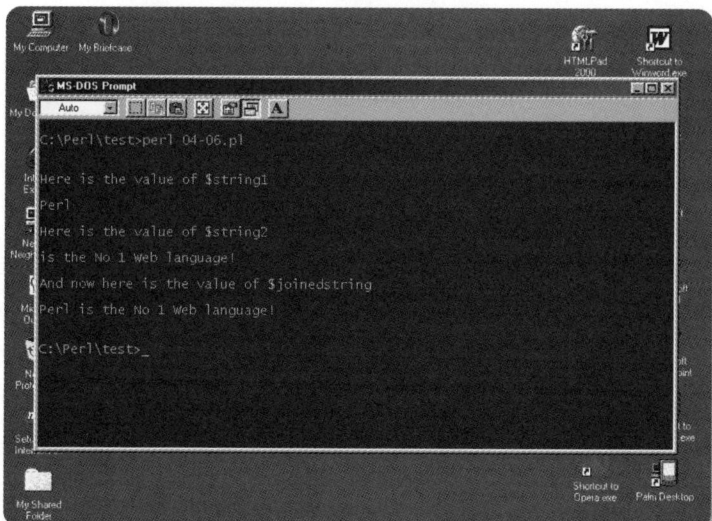

10. Open a command window.

11. Type **perl 04-06.pl** to run your program and observe how the strings have been joined together or concatenated.

As you can see, concatenating strings and string variables is easy in Perl, once you know how!

Variable Interpolation Revisited

You have learned already about interpolation, wherein if a variable is contained within a string enclosed in double quotes, the variable will be replaced by the value of that variable.

```
$language = "Perl";
print "The best Web Programming language is $language \n";
```

will give you

```
"The best Web Programming language is Perl"
```

There are occasions when you want a variable value when interpolated to join up to an adjacent word. Consider the following example:

```
$something = "comfort";
print "This chair is very $somethingable\n";
```

This is trying to join `$something` to the literal part `able` of the main string. Unfortunately, it will not work, as Perl will try to expand a variable called `$somethingable`. If you add a space to try to fix it, obviously you'll get a space in the result.

Try this example and prove it to yourself.

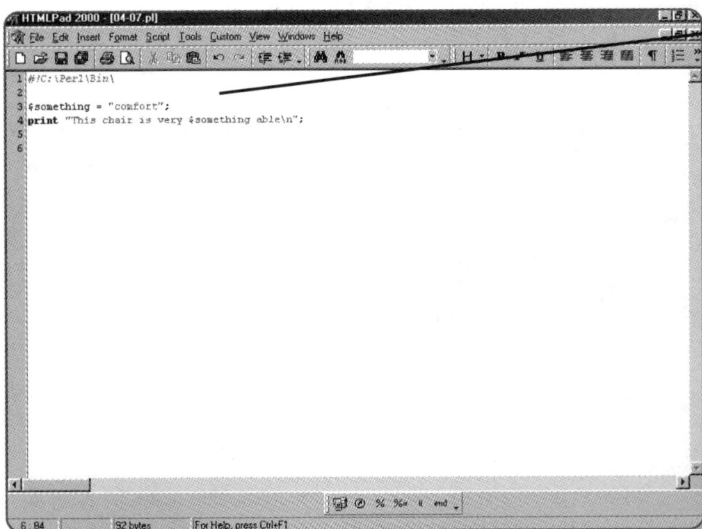

1. You are becoming familiar with the editor now and using the command window, so, using your editor, enter this code into a new file:

```
$something = "comfort";
print "This chair is very
   $something able\n";
```

2. Save the code as 04-07.pl.

3. Open a command window.

4. Run your program.

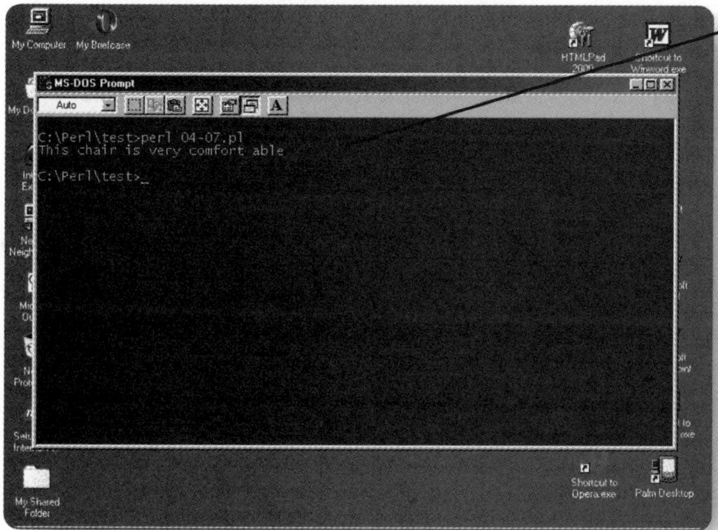

The output should look like this.

Note that you have a space between `comfort` and `able`—that's not what you want!

But Perl has a fix for this. You can wrap your variable name in braces.

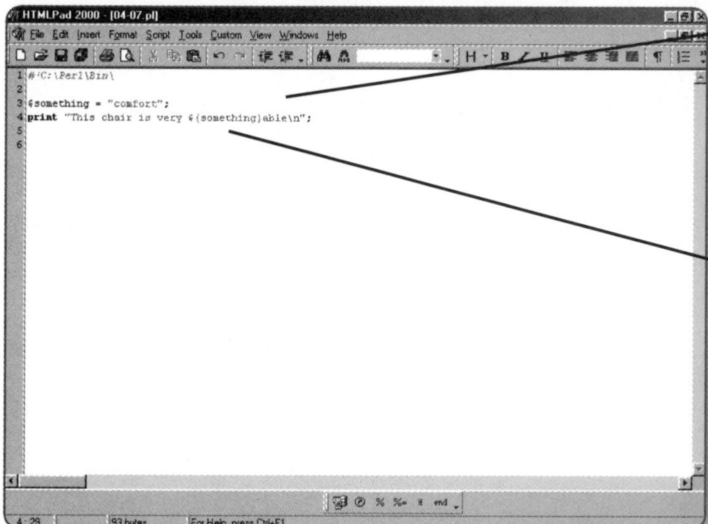

1. Change the program so the two lines look like this:

```
$something = "comfort";
print "This chair is very
   ${something}able\n";
```

2. Note there are no spaces between `${something}` and `able\n`.

3. Re-save your program.

4. Open a command window.

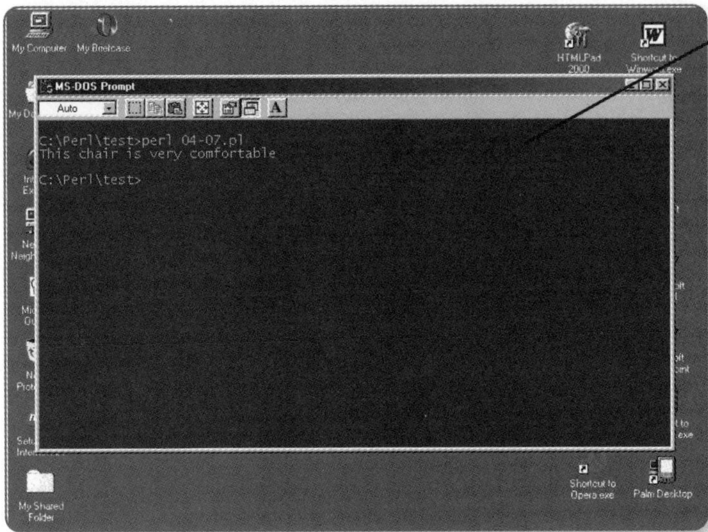

You should now see this.

That's better! Again, this is another example of something very simple, but very useful, fixing a potentially frustrating problem.

Substrings

Perl enables you to extract a part of a string and print it or place it in another variable. However, the Perl function that performs the substring action is more sophisticated. The syntax of the function is

```
substr(stringb, startpos, length)
```

This means you should obtain the value to be found in `stringb;` that value being taken from the character at `startpos` for `length` number of characters.

If that's confusing, try this small program.

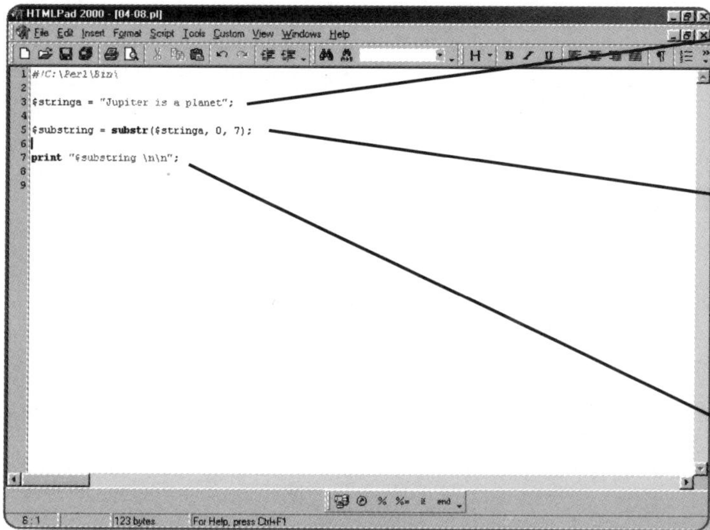

1. Set up a string.

```
$stringa = "Jupiter is a
   planet";
```

2. Use the `substr()` function to extract the first 7 characters.

```
$substring = substr($stringa,
   0, 7);
```

3. Display the result.

```
print "$substring \n\n";
```

4. Save the program as 04-08.pl.

5. Open a command prompt window and run the program (perl 04-08.pl).

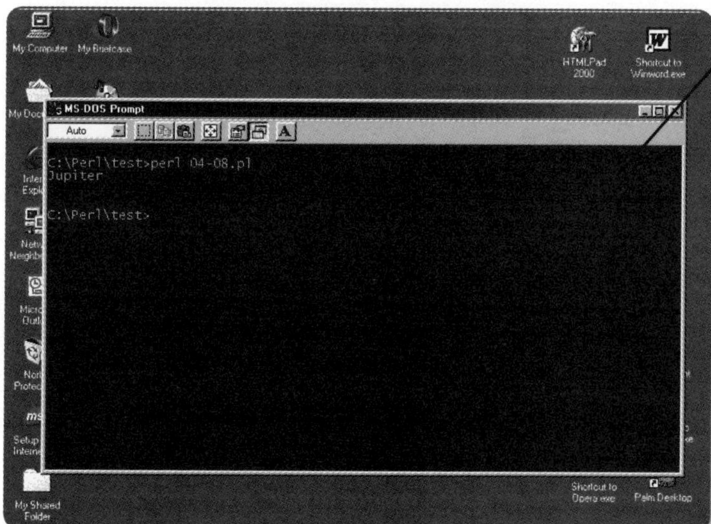

You should see something like this.

> **NOTE**
>
> The `length` parameter of the `substr()` function is optional. If you omit it, then `substr()` will assume that the length value is to the end of the string.

Changing Case

You may want to change the "case" of a string, for example, prior to doing a comparison of values. Perl has several strings that perform this function.

Very simply, these Perl functions perform the following operations:

- **uc.** Converts a string to all uppercase.
- **lc.** Converts a string to all lowercase.
- **ucfirst.** Converts just the first character of a string to uppercase.
- **lcfirst.** Converts just the first character of a string to lowercase.

Try this sample program.

1. Set up a couple of string variables like this:

```
$stringlower = "perl fast & easy";
$stringupper = "PERL FAST & EASY";
```

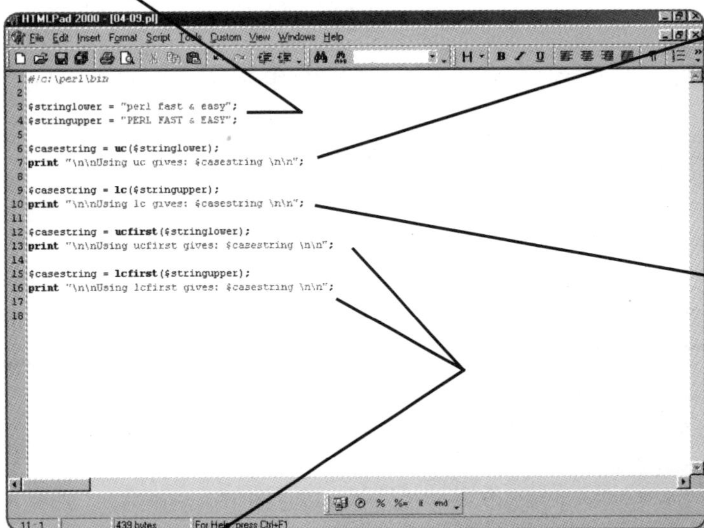

2. Show the effect of the uppercase function, `uc`.

```
$casestring =
   uc($stringlower);
print "\n\nUsing uc gives:
   $casestring \n\n";
```

3. Show the effect of the lowercase function, `lc`.

```
$casestring =
   lc($stringupper);
print "\n\nUsing lc gives:
   $casestring \n\n";
```

4. Similarly, show the effect of the `ucfirst` and `lcfirst` functions.

```
$casestring = ucfirst($stringlower);
print "\n\nUsing ucfirst gives: $casestring \n\n";

$casestring = lcfirst($stringupper);
print "\n\nUsing lcfirst gives: $casestring \n\n";
```

5. Save your program as 04-09.pl.

6. Open a command prompt and run your program.

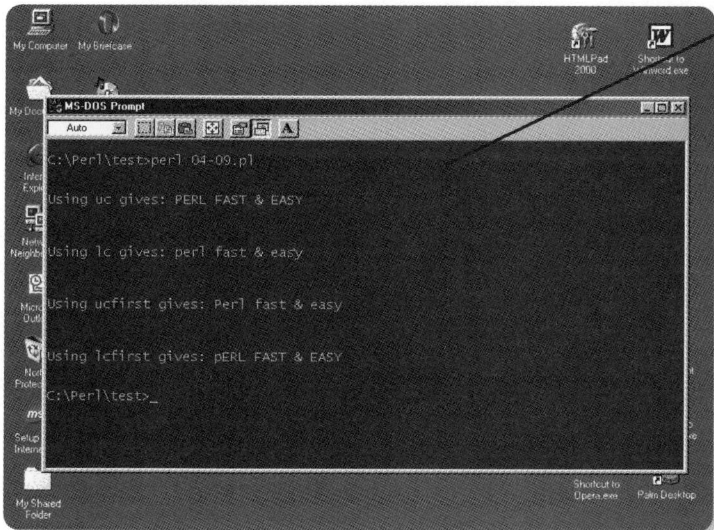

This should give these results.

As you can see, Perl is a very powerful language with some very useful string functions. In fact, Perl is extremely rich in functions for all kinds of purposes. You are learning a lot of the most useful ones, and there is a wealth of others just waiting for you to discover them. And all the time, the army of Perl authors and programmers are creating more functions, helping to keep Perl as one of the most powerful languages around.

Mixing Strings and Numbers

As you learned earlier, Perl decides what to do with a scalar variable based on context in which it is being used. This can lead to some confusion unless you're ready for the results!

Try the following code example and read the comments against each line in order to understand what is happening; then, if you wish, enter the code into your editor and try the program out.

1. Set up some numeric variables, assign values, and display them.

```
$num1=25;
print "\n\n\$num1 = $num1\n";

$num2=10;
print "\n\n\$num2 = $num2\n";
```

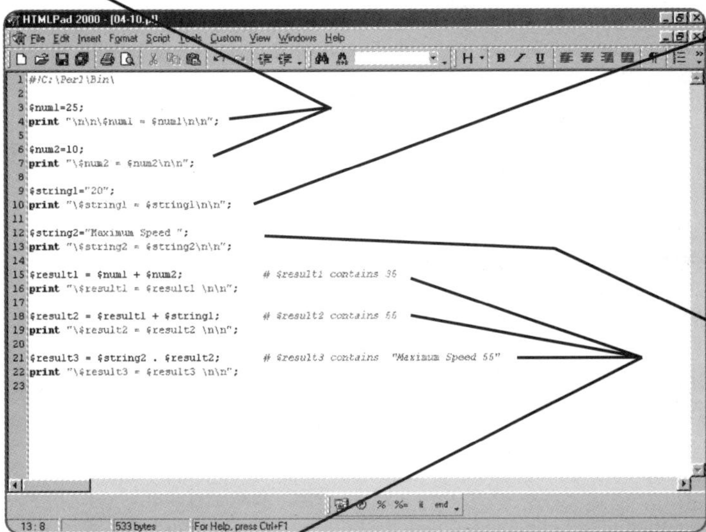

2. Now set up a string variable, give it the string `"20"` (rather than `20`), and display it to prove it is okay.

```
$string1="20";
print "\n\n\$string1 =
   $string1\n";
```

3. Set up another string variable and display the value assigned.

```
$string2="Maximum Speed ";
print "\n\n\$string2 =
   $string2\n";
```

4. Now perform a few operations on the variables—read carefully!

```
$result1 = $num1 + $num2;          # $result1 contains 35
print "\$result1 = $result1 \n\n";

$result2 = $result1 + $string1;    # $result2 contains 55
print "\$result2 = $result2 \n\n";

$result3 = $string2 . $result2;    # $result3 contains  "Maximum Speed 55"
print "\$result3 = $result3 \n\n";
```

5. Save the program as 04-10.pl.

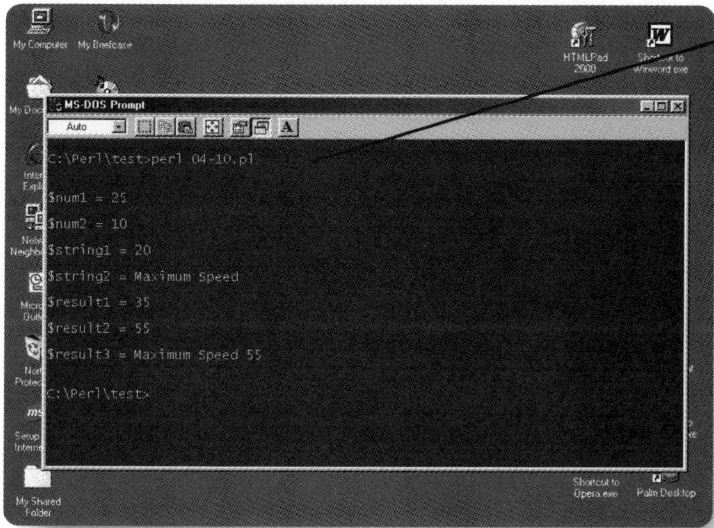

6. Run the program; you should get these results.

Can you follow through what's happening? The rule is that Perl will treat a scalar variable as the type it appears to be. If it looks like a number, Perl will most likely treat it like one. Copy the above snippet of code into a new Perl program file in your editor, save it, and try running it. Play with the code and test what works and what does not.

Comparison Operators

When you write `if` statements, you use comparison operators to test the value of strings, numbers, and so on.

Numeric Comparison Operators

If you are testing numeric scalar values you would use the following comparison operators.

- (`>`) Greater than
- (`= =`) Equal to
- (`<`) Less than
- (`>=`) Greater than or equal to
- (`<=`) Less than or equal to
- (`!=`) Not equal to

Try the next program to see the use of numeric operators.

1. Open your editor.

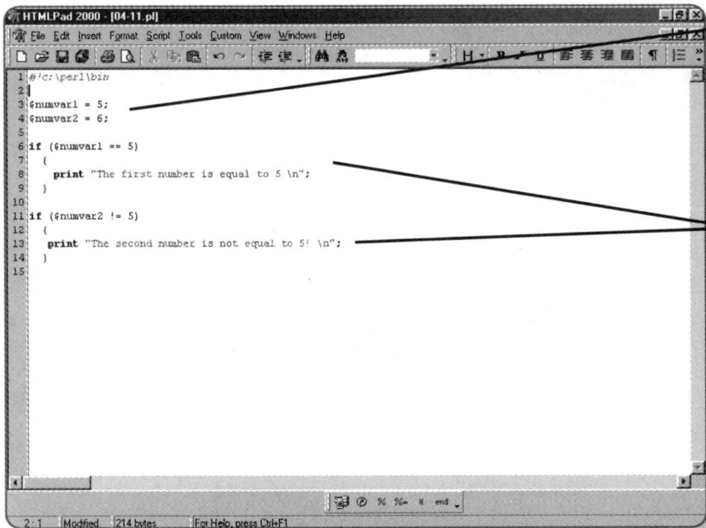

2. Define a couple of variables and assign values like this:

```
$numvar1 = 5;
$numvar2 = 6;
```

3. Using an `if` statement (we haven't covered that yet, but it is simple enough here), test the values of the variables and print a message if the value passes a test using the == and the != comparison operators.

```
   if ($numvar1 == 5)
{
print "The first number is equal to 5 \n";
}

if ($numvar2 != 5)
{
print "The second number is not equal to 5! \n";
}
```

NOTE

The `if` statement is described in Chapter 7, "Program Flow," but I hope you have been able to follow the simple `if` statements used here. If not, return here after reading Chapter 7 and reexamine this code.

4. Save your program as 04-11.pl.

5. Open a command window.

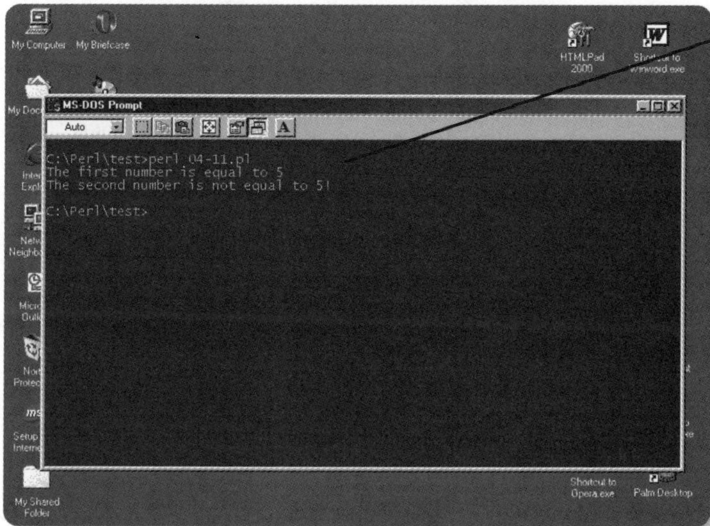

6. Run your program.

> **NOTE**
>
> It cannot be emphasized enough about the use of the equality comparison operator == when checking for equality of values. Remember that the = sign is an *assignment* operator. This is the source of many bugs.

Other similar operators are used in exactly the same way as the previous example.

```
if ($numvar > 5)
   {
      print "You chose a number greater than 5 \n";
   }


if ($numvar >= 5)
   {
      print "You chose a number greater than 4 \n";
   }
```

And so on.

You will be using numeric operators again later. Their use is pretty obvious, as later examples in real Web application code will show.

String Comparison Operators

The above operators (==, <, >, and so on) should only be used for testing numeric values. Why? Try the following program, which will demonstrate the difference between numeric comparisons and string comparisons.

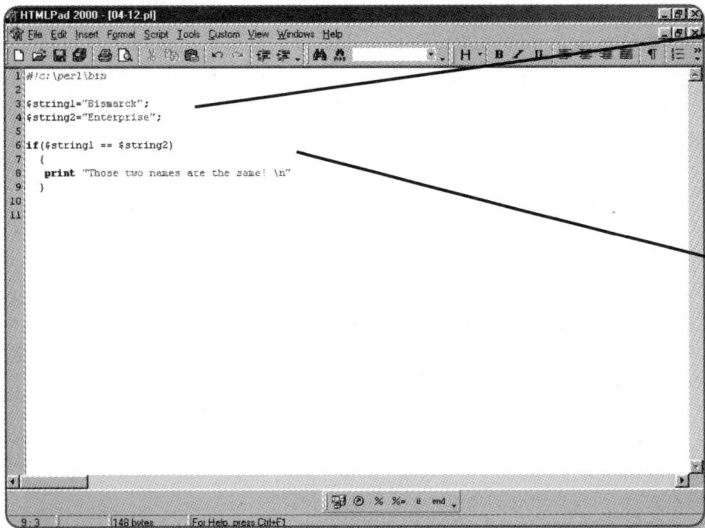

1. Set up a couple of string variables and assign values to them.

```
$string1="Bismarck";
$string2="Enterprise";
```

2. Perform a similar test to the previous program and print the result if they are equal (which obviously they are not!).

```
if($string1 == $string2)
{
print "Those two names are the
   same! \n"
}
```

3. Save your program as stringcomp1.pl.

4. Open a command prompt window and run your program.

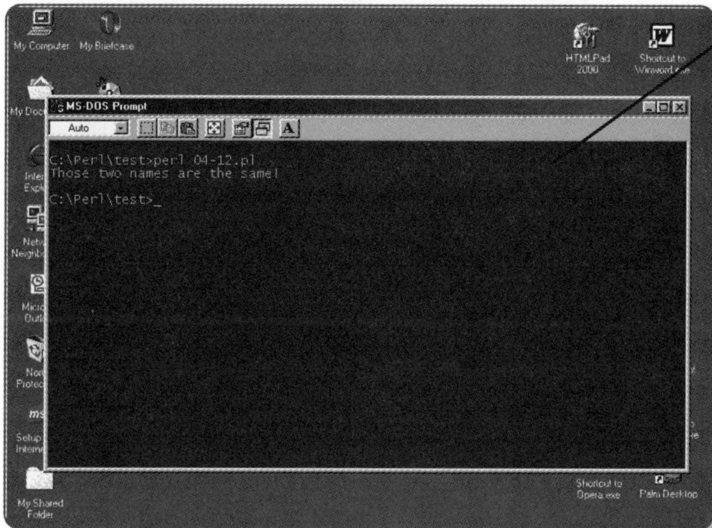

The comparison decided that the two strings were the same.

The reason for this is that = = is a numeric comparison operator, and so Perl will interpret `$string1` and `$string2` as numeric variables. Because Perl will be unable to evaluate them as numbers, they will be set to zero. Therefore, both variables are numerically equal and so the test is passed and the string `"Those two names are the same!"` is printed.

For this reason, Perl has a different set of comparison operators for strings.

- **eq.** Equal to
- **ne.** Not equal to
- **it.** Less than
- **gt.** Greater than
- **le.** Less than or equal to
- **ge.** Greater than or equal to

These operators are used in a similar manner to the numeric ones, but obviously only with string variables.

Here is an identical program, except you will be using the string `eq` comparison operator, and there is an `else` option to catch the result; otherwise you would see no output.

1. Open a new file or copy the previous one.

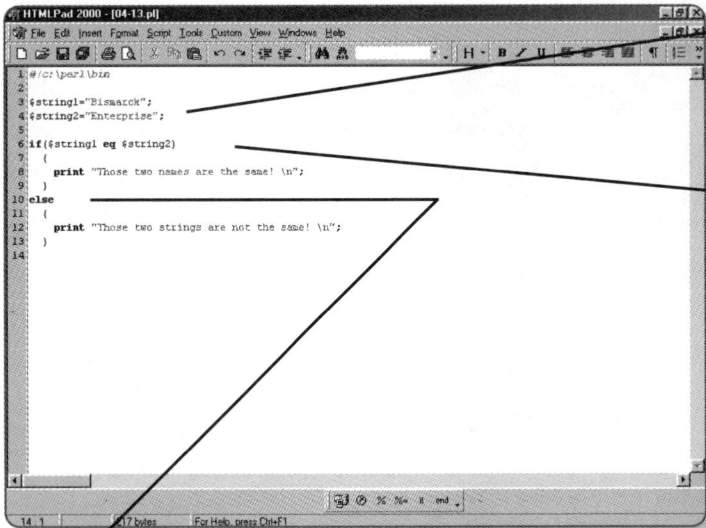

2. Use the same variables.

```
$string1="Bismarck";
$string2="Enterprise";
```

3. Again use the same `if` statement, but this time using the eq operator rather than the == operator.

```
if($string1 eq $string2)
  {
    print "Those two names are
       the same! \n";
  }
```

4. Now add an `else` statement, and if the above works as we hope, then as it stands nothing would be printed.

```
else
  {
    print "Those two strings are not the same! \n";
  }
```

5. Save your program as 04-13.pl.

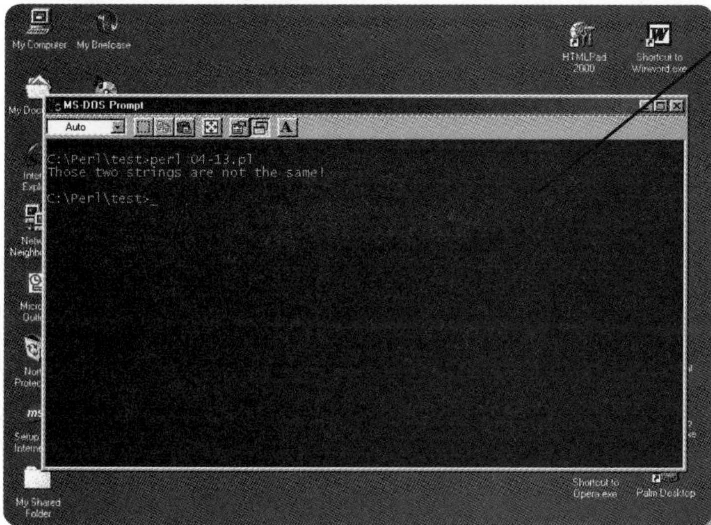

6. Run this version of the program. This time you should find that you get the desired result.

Before we leave operators for now, you will learn a little about logical operators.

Logical Operators

Finally, in your brief examination of operators, comes the logical operator. A *logical operator* is used to evaluate whether or not a condition being tested is true or false. You will often see True and False capitalized, as here, to emphasize that this is a logical, or Boolean, value.

The term *Boolean* comes from the name of a mathematician, George Boole, who pioneered the rules of a logical form of algebra. Computers rely on the logic to work, and so you will often come across the terms *True* (often represented by the value 1, but can be represented by any non-zero value) and *False* (often represented by the value zero).

A numeric True value is any non-zero value and, therefore, numeric zero equates to False. So 1, 5, 7, 232, -175, and so on are all True. Only numeric zero is False. We can apply True/False checks to strings, too. The word Olympic is True, a string containing "0" is True, and a single empty space is True. Only the absence of any alphanumeric characters at all is False.

There are basically three logical operators: and, or, and not.

This means that you can check whether two variables have a value simply by doing this:

```
if ($num1 and $num2)
  {
     print "Both of those variables have a non-zero value.\n";
   }
```

Or you can say:

```
if (not $num1)
  {
     print "That variable is empty.\n";
   }
```

And you can say:

```
if ($num1 OR $num2)
  {
     print "One of those variables has a non-zero value.\n";
   }
```

You can combine conditions such as:

```
if ($num1 and $num2 or $num3)
  {
     print "Both of the first variables have a non-zero value or that last one
       does!.\n";
   }
```

The logical operators all work in exactly the same way. As you have discovered, the empty string equates to False, and all other values equate to True.

Finally, there are symbols that can be used instead of `and`, `or`, and `not`.

`||` is the same as the `or` logical operator

`&&` is the same as the `and` operator

`!` is the same as the `not` operator

The only difference between using these instead of the word operators `and`, `or`, and `not` is that the symbol version has a greater precedence. That is, a `||` will be dealt with before an `or`. Don't worry about that too much. If you want something evaluated before something else, just enclose the one want you want done first in parentheses.

Logical operators seem simple, but misuse can lead to very confusing errors. You will use logical operators quite a lot later. Try using the previous examples and playing with the code, or just read on and wait for some real examples.

5

Arrays

Arrays are simply collections of scalars. The array has a name much like the simple scalar does, but it also has a number of elements. Each element has the same name and is pointed at by a numeric subscript.

In this chapter you will learn about:

- Declaring arrays
- Loading arrays
- Joining arrays
- Array function and manipulation

Conceptually, an array can be thought of as a number of "pigeon-holes," each of which can contain separate items of data. As mentioned, each element shares a common name with all of the others, and uses a *subscript* (a sort of address) to determine which element in the array is being referenced.

You will remember that the scalar variable was preceded by the dollar sign ($). The array uses a prefix to make it instantly recognizable just as the scalar variables do. Scalar variables use the $ sign as a prefix, whereas arrays use the @ sign instead, so that you can instantly recognize that it is an array in a program source code listing.

> **NOTE**
>
> As in most programming languages, the first item in an array is element zero. I will mention this again as time goes on, and I'll make no apology for doing so, as it cannot be emphasized enough. This concept can be the source of some confusing programming errors if you are not used to it.

Declaring Arrays

You can declare an array prior to use, or you can load the array at the same time that you declare it.

An example will illustrate the point.

1. Open your editor and start a new program.

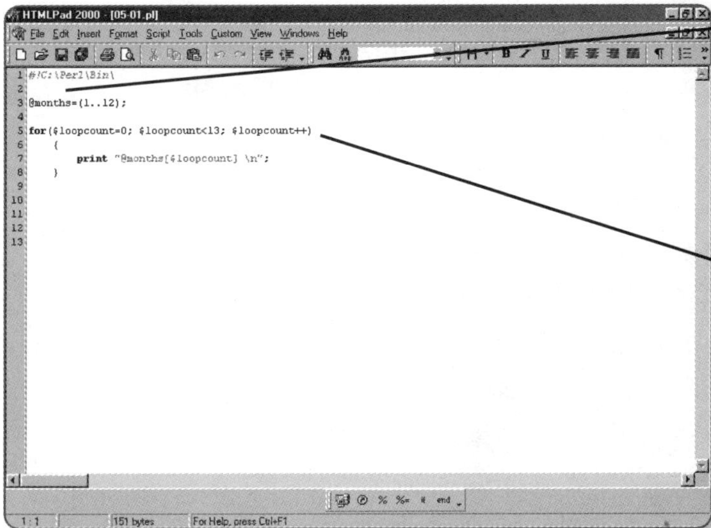

2. Type an array definition like this: This will create an array and load it with the values 1 through 12.

```
@months =(1..12);
```

3. Now add a simple loop construct to display the values contained within the array. Use a `For` loop.

```
For ($loopcount = 0;
$loopcount < 13; $loopcount++)
{
  print "@months($loopcount)
     \n";
}
```

4. Save your program as 05-01.pl.

5. Now open a command window.

6. Run the program (perl 05-01.pl)

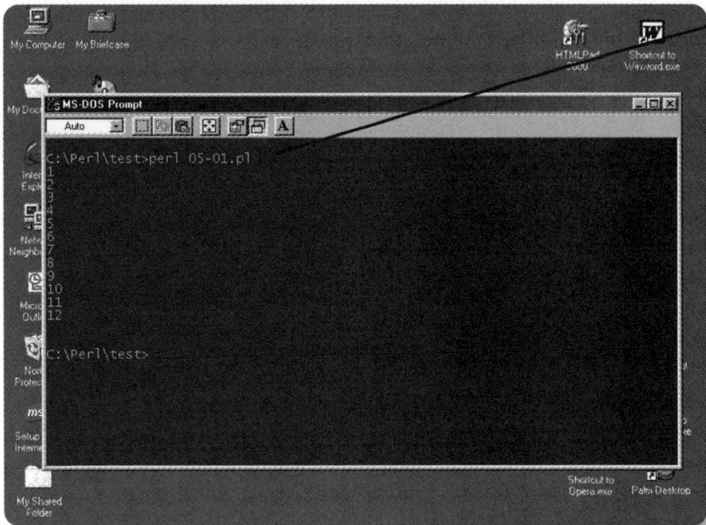

You should get a list of numbers (the contents of each element of the array), like this.

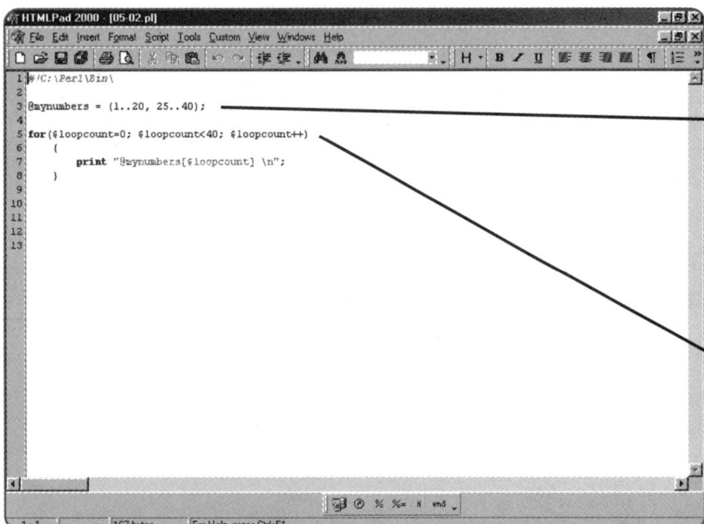

You can have a break in a range when defining an array, like this:

1. Repeat the above example with this array. Note there is a break in the numbers from 21 to 24 inclusive.

```
@mynumbers = (1..20, 25..40);
```

2. Add the loop as before.

```
for($loopcount=0;
   $loopcount<40;
   $loopcount++)
    {
       print "@mynumbers
           [$loopcount] \n";
    }
```

3. Save your program as 05-02.pl.

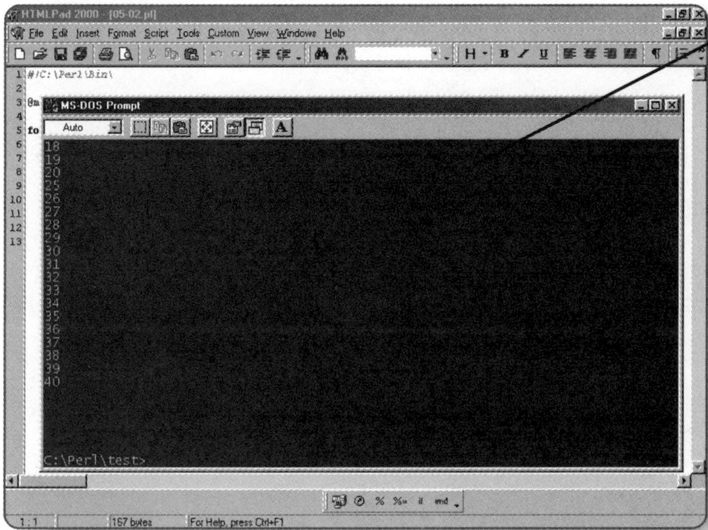

4. Run the program—you should see this. Note the gap in the numbers as set up in the array definition.

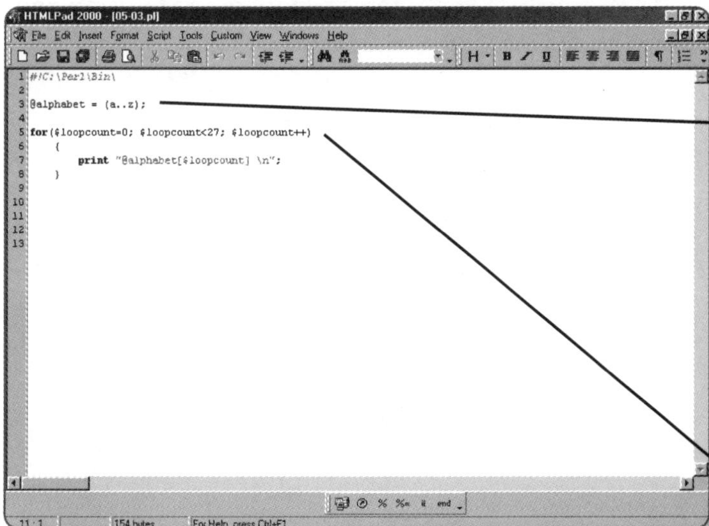

You can do the same thing with characters, like this:

1. Once again, modify the program using the following array:

```
@alphabet = (a..z);
```

This will create an array of 26 scalars, each containing a letter from the alphabet.

2. You will need to change the loop counter to cover the number of letters in the alphabet.

```
for($loopcount=0; $loopcount<27; $loopcount++)
    {
        print "@alphabet[$loopcount] \n";
    }
```

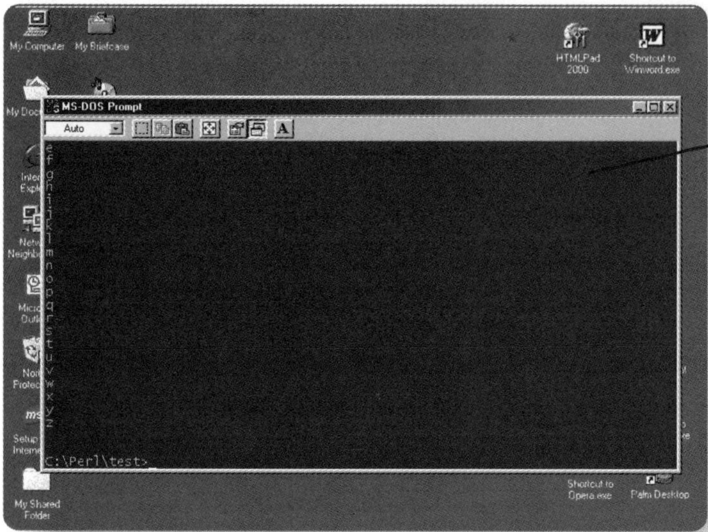

3. Save your program as 05-03.pl.

4. Run your program and you should see this.

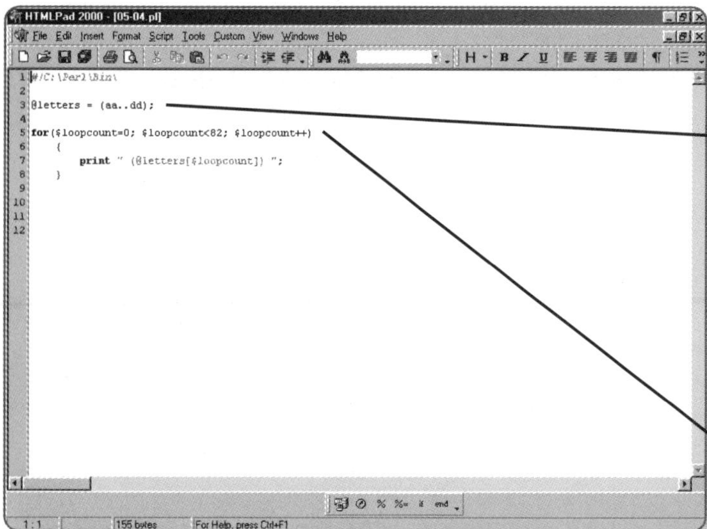

You are not limited to using one character, either.

1. Change the array to look like this.

```
@letters = (aa..dd);
```

You will create an array containing 82 values; aa, ab, ac, ad, and so on, through dd.

2. Again, change the loop code to process the new array.

```
for($loopcount=0;
  $loopcount<82; $loopcount++)
   {
   print "
    (@letters[$loopcount]) ";
   }
```

This time brackets (parentheses) have been used rather than the simple carriage return so that you can see all of the values and validate the output from this program.

3. Save the program as 05-04.pl.

4. Open a command prompt and run your program. As you can imagine, you need to watch how far you take this.

And finally, you can mix the element types, like this:

```
@things = ("Fred", 16,
   57.23456, $title);
```

Here, there is a literal string, an integer, a floating point number, and a scalar variable containing whatever it does.

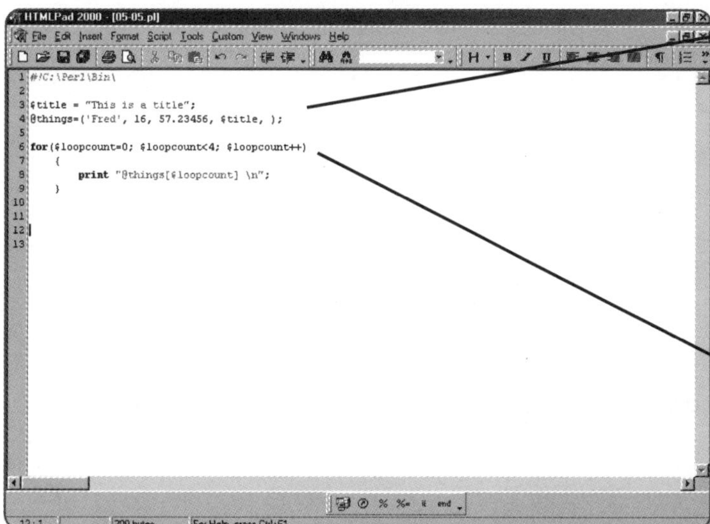

1. Once again, modify the program to include a string variable (`$title` and set to `"This is a title"`) and to accommodate the previous array.

```
$title = "This is a title";
@things=('Fred', 16,
   '57.23456', $title, );
```

2. Modify the loop so that you are using the new array `@things`.

```
for($loopcount=0;
  $loopcount<4; $loopcount++)
    {
       print " @things
          [$loopcount] \n ";
    }
```

3. Save it as 05-05.pl.

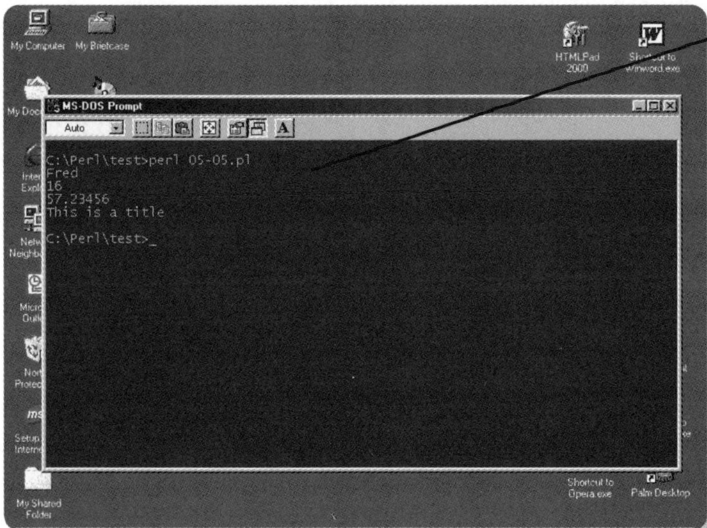

4. Open a command window.

5. Run the program. You should see this.

Loading Arrays

There is a lot that you can do with arrays, and many functions are available to manipulate them. Here are a few examples.

Say you have an array called `ships`. You can load it like this:

```
@ships=('Bismarck', 'Titanic', 'Hood', );
```

And you can refer to the individual elements of the array by the use of a numeric subscript like this:

```
$shipname = @ships[1];
```

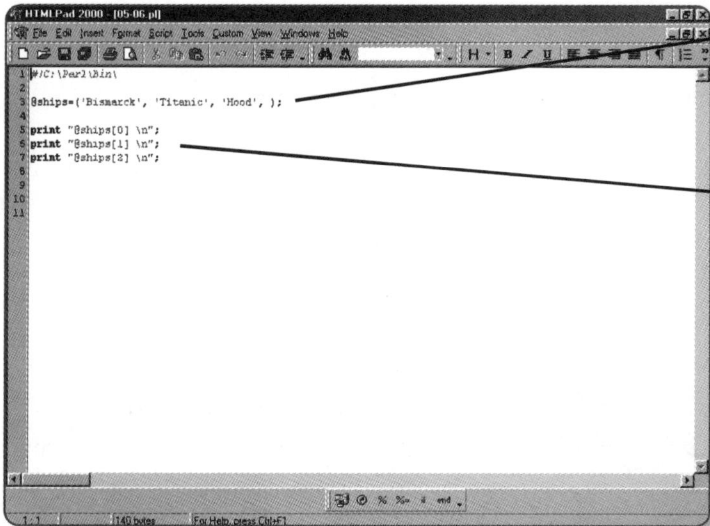

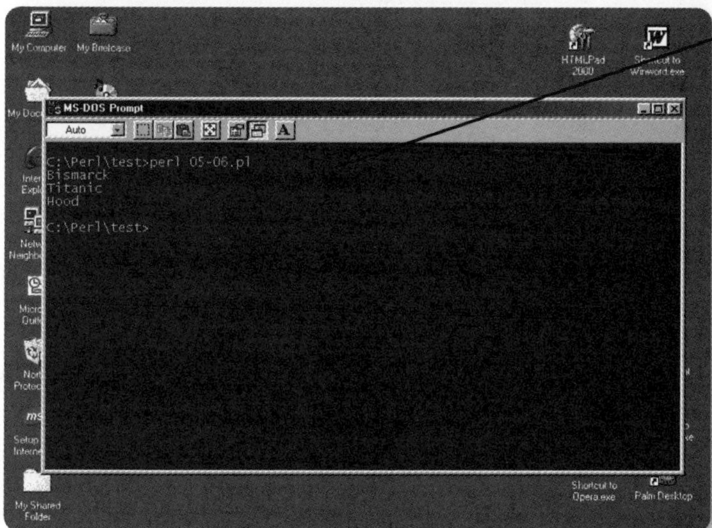

1. Start a new program in your editor.

2. Set up the array like this.

```
@ships=('Bismarck', 'Titanic',
   'Hood', );
```

3. Now print out the value of each element.

```
print "@ships[0] \n";
print "@ships[1] \n";
print "@ships[2] \n";
```

4. Open a command window.

5. Run your program. You should get this result.

Note that as arrays start with element 0 (zero), the subscript 1 points at the *second* element in the array. So the following statement:

```
Print @ships[1];
```

will print

```
Titanic
```

Joining Arrays

You can also join arrays together. If you take two arrays like this:

```
@warships = ('Hood', 'Bismarck', 'Washington');
@passengerships = ('Titanic', 'Olympic', 'Britannic');
```

You can join them together like this:

```
@ships = (@warships, @passengerships);
```

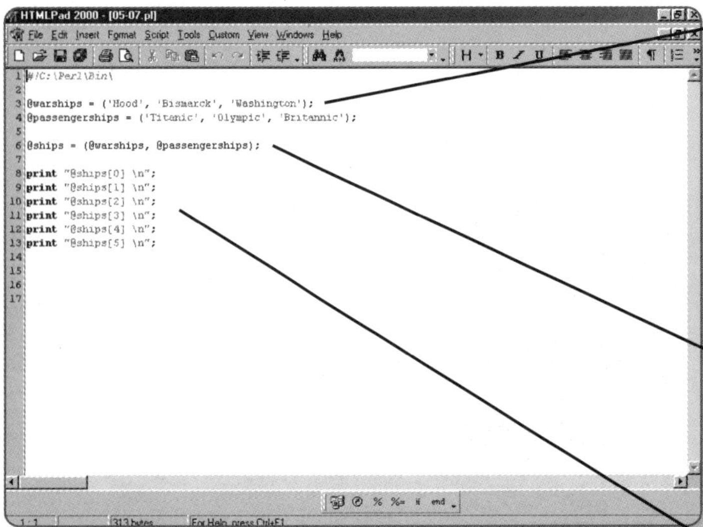

1. Open a new program in your editor, and in a similar way to the last single array example, set up two arrays.

```
@warships = ('Hood',
   'Bismarck', 'Washington');
@passengerships = ('Titanic',
   'Olympic', 'Britannic');
```

2. Now join the two arrays in the following manner:

```
@ships = (@warships,
   @passengerships);
```

3. Print out the values of each element of the `@ships` array

```
print "@ships[0] \n";
print "@ships[1] \n";
print "@ships[2] \n";
print "@ships[3] \n";
print "@ships[4] \n";
print "@ships[5] \n";
```

NOTE

You could use a loop, as you did in some previous examples, to display the contents of the array.

4. Save your program as 05-07.pl.

5. Open a command window.

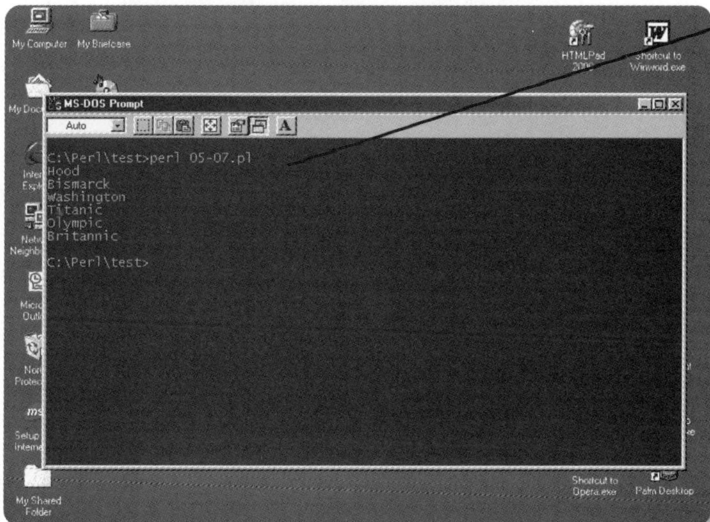

6. Run your program. You should get this output.

Array Functions and Array Manipulation

Perl arrays are pretty flexible, and really, you have only just scratched the surface of what they can do. There are also lots of built-in functions that are designed to help you manipulate arrays, as you will learn.

Would you like to know how many elements there are in an array? Try this:

```
print $#ships;
```

Now try the modified program.

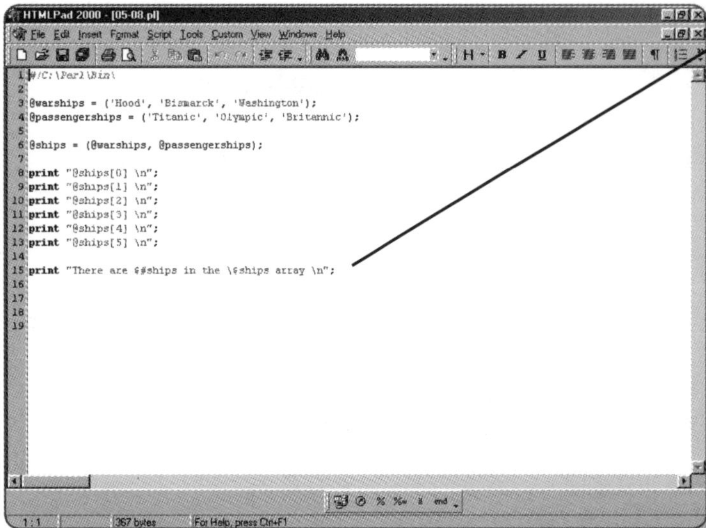

1. Take the previous program and add the following line at the end:

```
print "There are $#ships in
   the \$ships array \n";
```

2. Save your program as 05-08.pl.

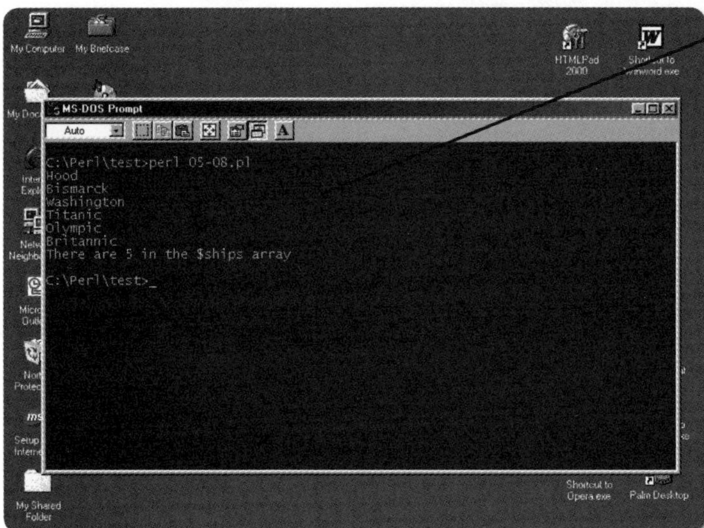

3. Open a command window and re-run your program. This is the result.

> **NOTE**
>
> If you used the array example you tried a minute ago, you will get a result of 5. (Don't forget that Perl arrays start at element 0, so if there are 6 elements, that will give you a result of 5).

Want to fill an array with 250 zeros? This will do the trick:

```
@zeros = (0) x 250;
```

It looks a little confusing doesn't it? But it just means to take a zero and load it into a new array element 250 times and then call the array "zeros"!

Try it and see for yourself.

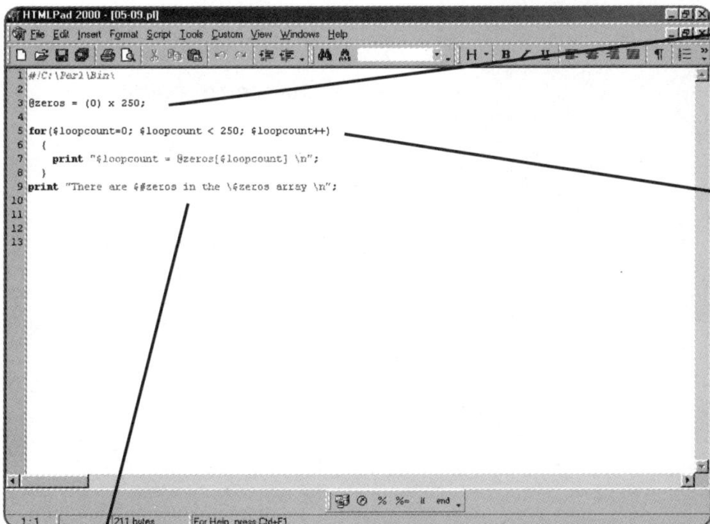

1. Open your editor and set up a new array.

```
@zeros = (0) x 250;
```

2. Because there are lots of elements in the array, you will have to use a `for` loop to display them all, but doing so is fairly simple:

```
for($loopcount=0; $loopcount <
250; $loopcount++)
  {
    print "$loopcount =
@zeros[$loopcount] \n";
  }
```

3. Now you can display the total number of elements in the array.

```
print "There are $#zeros in the \$zeros array \n";
```

4. Save the program as 05-09.pl.

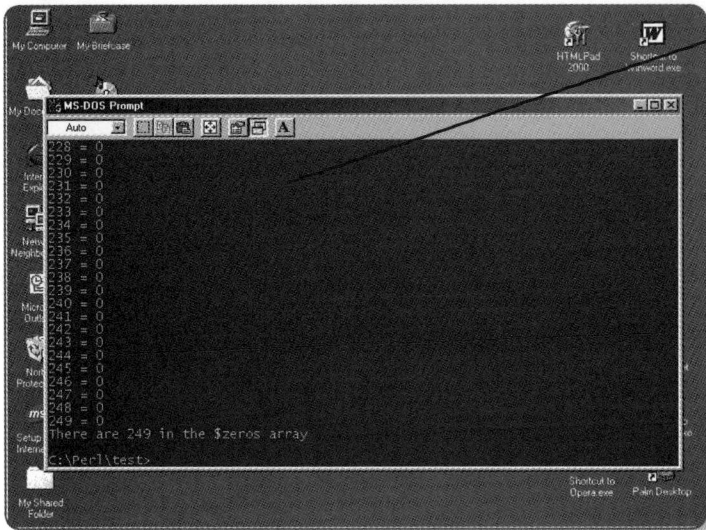

5. Open a command window and run the program to see the result. You should see this.

Perl, unlike most other languages, supports only single-dimensional arrays, and so two-dimensional arrays must be simulated using arrays of references, or pointers. You'll have a chance to examine references soon.

6 Hashes

Hashes are sometimes regarded as a difficult subject in Perl. This perception is largely due to the so-called "misleading and inconsistent" syntax. For this reason, the beginning of this short chapter includes a discussion of what hashes are and how you refer to them in Perl. Hopefully, you will see that hashes are not only useful, but also perfectly logical! You will then learn and practice how to use this powerful data structure. So, read on and bear with me; the short ride will be worth it.

In this chapter you will learn what a hash is and how to use hash prefixes, as well as how to:

- Initialize a hash
- Create a hash
- Load and search hashes
- Remove keys from hashes

What are Hashes?

Hashes (sometimes referred to as *associative arrays*) are similar to "normal" arrays in as much as they are a list of scalar values. However, the way in which they are accessed is different—the mechanism utilizes "keys" rather than the simple numeric subscript. The important thing to remember about hashes is simply the order in which you quote or specify them, that is, the key and then the value. In most other respects, hashes might be considered a bucket into which you can pour data.

Hashes have a prefix just like scalars and arrays do. For hashes, the prefix is the % symbol. This denotes, when used, that you are referring to the whole hash; if you want to access a single element of a hash you use the $ prefix as you do with arrays. This might seem confusing until you consider that you are only referencing a single scalar within the hash; therefore, you use the scalar notation. Only when you are accessing the whole hash do you use the hash % prefix symbol.

Hashes provide you with a useful lookup mechanism that is a bit like some database tables. A unique key is used to locate a given value. Hashes are uniformly fast; that is, hashes can grow very large with very little degradation in speed, and, as long as your machine has the resources to cope with them, you can make them as large as you like!

Hashes have many uses, not least in Web applications, where they are useful for handling input from HTML forms, CGI environment variables, and other elements, as you will see.

Hash Prefixes

You have just learned that you refer to a hash using the % sign. You will also see the prefixes $ and @ used. Confusing? Well, actually it is quite simple. Always try to think what it is that you are doing with Perl, and all will become clear.

For example, if you are trying to return a single item from a hash, you will see

```
$item = $hashname{'keyvalue'}
```

Notice that the hash is using the $ prefix. That makes sense doesn't it? It does, because you are returning a single item, that is, a scalar. Similarly, when you want to return a number of values you use this:

```
@arrayofvalues = @hashname{'keyvalue1', 'keyvalue2'}
```

This means: return an array of item values from the given hash that correspond to (in this case) the two key values supplied. You are returning more than one item, so you use the @ prefix. Why? You are returning more than one item into an array.

Just to make it more fun, you can even do this:

```
@arrayofvalues = @hashname{@arrayofkeys}
```

Instead of supplying the keys in a list in the braces (yes, those are braces, not parentheses), you supply an array of keys. Still, you are returning a number of values just like in the previous example, so you use the hash name prefixed by @.

Like a lot of things in Perl, at first sight things might seem contradictory or illogical, but when you look at them and think about it, it all makes perfect sense. Perl does force you to think, but you soon realize that if it is logical, it will work in Perl. As you become more proficient in Perl, you will grow ideas of your own and you will be amazed to discover that your logical idea works just fine.

You are now going to try creating and manipulating hashes. It's easier than it seems at first, I promise.

Initializing a Hash

To initialize a hash, simply do this:

```
%animals = ();
```

You now have a hash called `animals`, with no keys or values.

You will try this out in a moment, but let's cover a few more simple hash operations first. You will begin by adding keys and values to a hash.

Creating a Hash

You can add key-value pairs to a hash individually or many at a time. To add elements to a hash you can do something like this:

```
$animals{'Horse'} = 'Red Rum';
```

This adds one key-value pair to the hash `animals`. (Note the $ prefix. As you saw previously, you use the $ prefix because you are accessing a single element of the hash).

If you want to add several at once, you can do so in the following manner:

```
%animals = ('Red Rum', 'Horse', 'Jaws', 'Shark', 'King Kong', Gorilla);
```

Now, this is okay, but have you noticed what starts to happen as you read along the list? As you grow the list, imagine what happens when you try to jump into the middle of the list. With the subjects and names you're using here it is fairly obvious which is a key and which is a value. However, in some cases this will not be quite so obvious, and so Perl has another notation that helps you to determine which is which, no matter how long the list. The notation is known as the *comma-arrow operator* and looks it like this:

```
%animals = (Horse => 'Red Rum', Shark => 'Jaws', Gorilla => 'King Kong');
```

Now you can easily see that the => operator is pointing from the key to the data for that pair in the hash. Not only that, but you can now add newline / carriage returns and other whitespace characters and it will still work, so you can make your hash definitions more readable in your programs by using one key-value pair per line, like this:

```
%animals = (Horse => 'Red Rum',
            Shark => 'Jaws',
            Gorilla => 'King Kong'
);
```

This notation is probably called the comma-arrow operator because the => replaces a comma in the previous example. Whatever the reason, the comma-arrow operator makes the pairs easier to identify.

Let's load your first hash.

Loading and Searching Hashes

Now you'll learn how to load hashes and how to find data within them. As you are beginning to see, hashes are not much more difficult to use than arrays, and they are very powerful.

1. Open your editor.

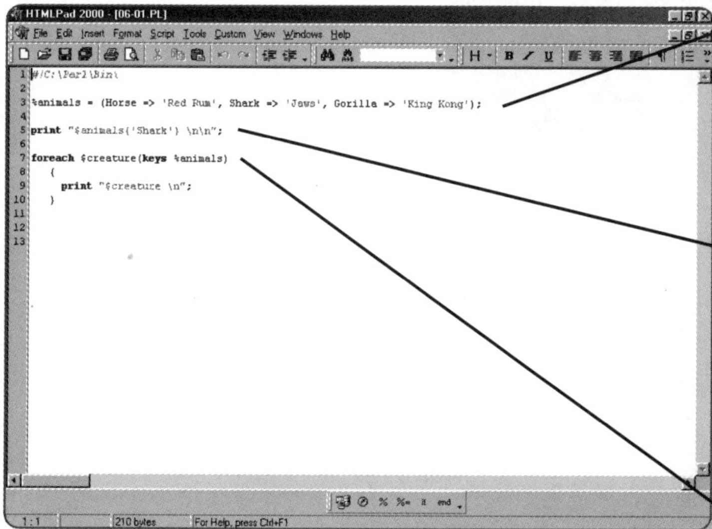

2. Create a hash using the following code:

```
%animals = (Horse => 'Red
   Rum', Shark => 'Jaws',
   Gorilla => 'King Kong');
```

3. You are going to display the animal in the hash that corresponds with the name "Shark."

```
print "$animals{'Shark'}
   \n\n";
```

4. Now you will list out the keys of the whole hash by using a `foreach` loop.

```
foreach $creature(keys %animals)
   {
     print "$creature \n";
   }
```

5. Save the program as 06-01.pl.

6. Open a command window.

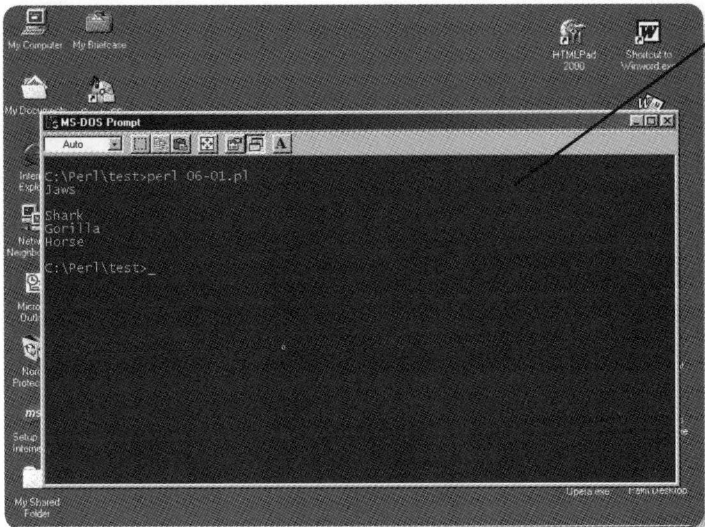

7. Run the program—you should see this.

Here is a brief examination of the last program:

Line 3 shows a method of loading a hash.

Line 5 shows how to get a single value back from a hash, given a key.

Lines 7 through 10 show how you can list all of the keys of a hash.

Finally, note that you can print the whole of a hash very simply by using a statement such as

```
print %animals;
```

But the results are printed one joined onto the other, which isn't very useful at all!

Removing Keys from a Hash

To remove a single key from a hash, simply use the `delete` function.

```
delete($animals{Shark});
```

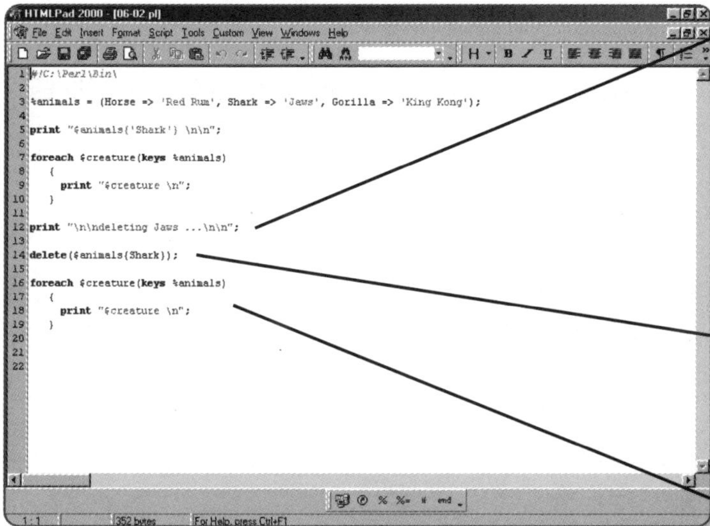

1. Using the last program as a starting point, add the following line after the last line (This just announces what you are about to do):

```
print "\n\ndeleting Jaws
   ...\n\n";
```

2. To delete the hash entry, enter this line.

```
delete($animals{Shark});
```

3. Now just repeat the `foreach` loop to prove that it has gone.

```
foreach $creature(keys %animals)
   {
     print "$creature \n";
   }
```

4. Save the program as 06-02.pl.

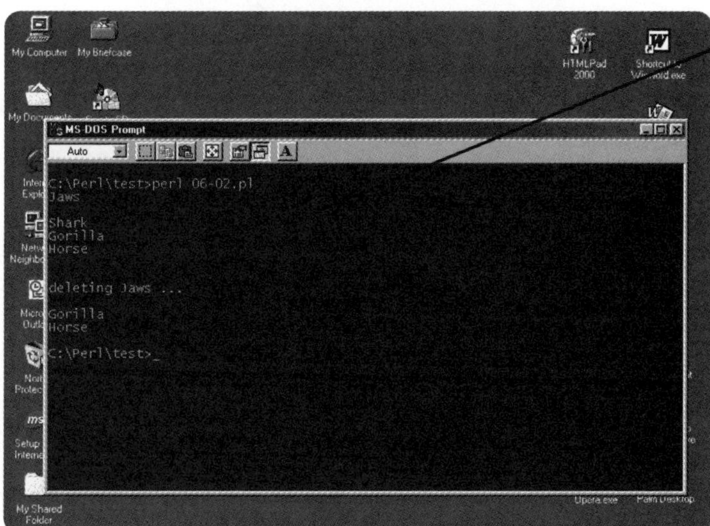

5. Open a command window and run the program. You should see this.

You can also remove all the keys (and values) from a hash, like this:

```
%animals=();
```

Notice that you have not really deleted anything. You have just *re-initialized* the hash, or started it afresh. But the effect is the same.

Once again, modify the previous program and try it.

1. Again taking the previous program as a starting point, add the following lines at the end of the program:

```
print "\n\n'emptying' the hash …\n\n";
%animals=();
```

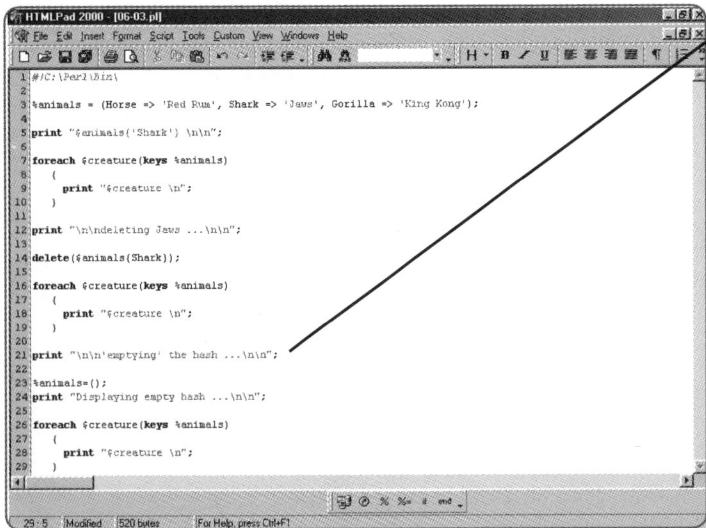

2. Then use the `foreach` loop to display the values in the hash again.

```
print "Displaying empty
   hash…\n\n";

foreach $creature(keys
   %animals)
{
    print "$creature \n";
}
```

3. Save the program as 06-03.pl.

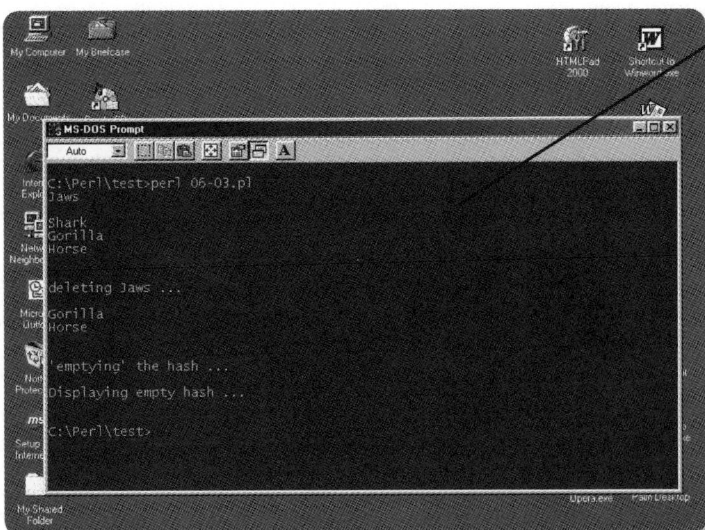

4. Open a command window and run the program. It should look like this.

As a last demonstration of hashes (for now), you can test whether a particular key exists in a hash.

1. Open your editor.

2. Take a copy of 06-01.pl.

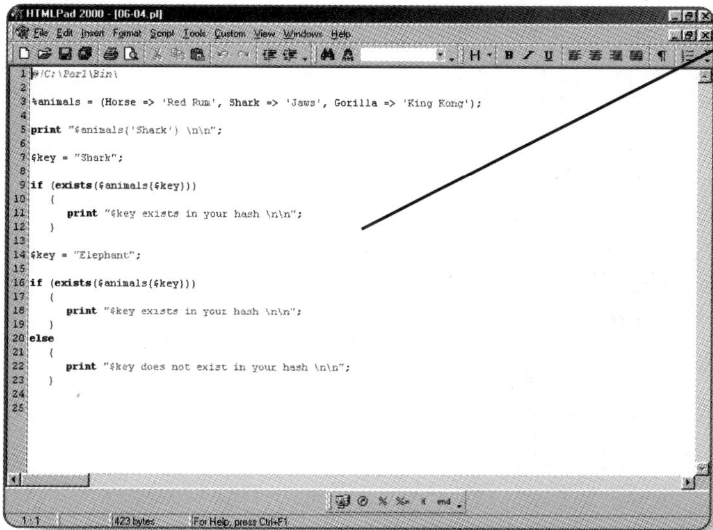

3. Replace the `foreach` loop displaying the values with the following code:

```
$key = "Shark";

if (exists($animals{$key}))
   {
      print "$key exists in
        your hash \n\n";
   }

$key = "Elephant";

if (exists($animals{$key}))
   {
      print "$key exists in your hash \n\n";
   }
else
   {
      print "$key does not exist in your hash \n\n";
   }
```

4. Save the program as 06-04.pl.

5. Open a command window.

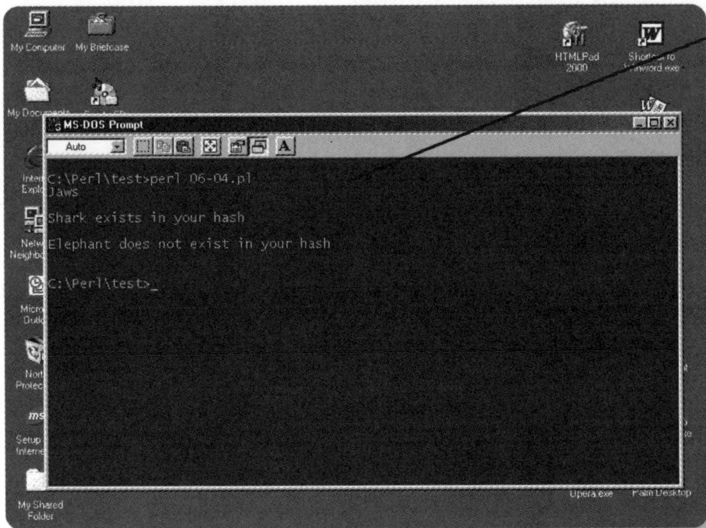

6. Run the program; the results should look like this.

As you have discovered, hashes are very powerful and probably easier to use than you first thought. When you get into Web CGI programming, you will use them extensively and you will be thankful that they exist.

This has been enough information to serve as a gentle introduction to hashes. Following this and the previous chapters, you should now have a feel for some of the ways of handling data in Perl.

Next, you will learn a little more about how to control the flow of a program in Perl—how you make decisions and control loops for performing repetitive actions. You have seen some of this already, but the next chapter is entirely dedicated to this subject.

7

Program Flow

This chapter will begin with a basic discussion on what program flow is (regardless of the language being used, there is always some kind of flow control in a program). You will then learn how to use flow control to produce the result you want from your Perl programs.

If you are already familiar with basic programming techniques, you may want to skip this short introduction. If you're a Web author branching out into Web development, or someone fairly new to programming who wishes to become a Web developer, you may find this section to be of interest.

In this chapter you will learn:

- What program flow is
- How program flow works in Perl
- How to use the `if` statement
- How to use loops in Perl

What Is Program Flow?

Program flow is the property of a program that gives that program the capability to make decisions or to do repetitive work. In programming logic, there are basically three program structures: sequence, selection, and iteration.

Sequence

Sequence is a mode of programming in which a sequence of instructions is executed in the order in which the instructions are written until the program reaches the end. Most of the old assembly language programs were of this type (with a few "go to" statements or something similar thrown in).

Selection

Selection is concerned with the route through a program dependent upon values presented to it or values calculated or derived within a program. In other words, when a program is executed, the statements that are executed are decided upon based on certain data. Some of that data might come from outside the program under consideration; other data might be the result of calculations occurring within the program.

The main tools used in selection are variants of the IF and CASE statements.

Iteration

Iteration is a fancy name for looping. *Looping*, when it is unintentional, can be a programmer's nightmare. But it can also be very useful if used correctly; for example, a loop construct can be used to process records in a file or database.

There are a number of loop constructs; the most common in most languages are the `for` loop, the `while` loop, and the `repeat` loop.

Program Flow in Perl

First of all, let us discuss the program block. This is a group of statements that are always executed one after the other. They are wrapped in braces, like this:

```
{
     statement one;
     statement two;
     statement three;
     statement four;
}
```

You can nest a block of statements inside another block. Note that although it makes no difference to the way a program works, blocks of code are usually indented from the rest of the code before and after them. This helps to make code more readable and to simplify future maintenance. Blocks are usually found in loop constructs and IF statements, and these too will be indented, again, just to make the program easier to read.

The If Statement

The `if` statement is one of Perl's selection statements. It enables Perl to make decisions based on the values contained in variables.

The `if` statement in Perl is similar to that in C, C++, and other languages.

```
If (condition)
  {
      statement …;
      statement …;
  }
elsif
  {
     statement …;
     statement …;
  }
else
    {
```

```
        statement …;
        statement …;
    }
```

Note that often you will find the first curly brace on the same line as the `if (condition)` part of the statement, like this:

```
If (condition)    {
      statement ...;
    }
```

Once again, this is just convention and it is up to you whether or not to adopt it. If you are not working to any set rules within an organization, just be consistent. Otherwise you might confuse people who attempt to maintain or learn from your program.

The `elsif/else` part of the `if` construct is optional. You might not need one; in fact, often you will not. Also note that spelling of `elsif`.

You can also have `if` statements within `if` statements or within `else` clauses, and you will come across many differing examples. You have leaned the basic syntax of the `if` statement, so now it is time to try one out. You have actually seen this example before, but it won't hurt to cover it again.

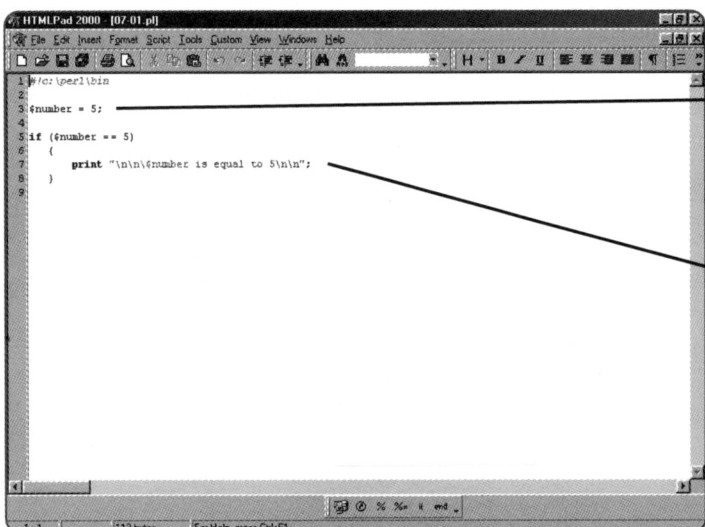

1. Open your editor.

2. Set up a variable called `$number` and initialize it to 5.

```
$number = 5;
```

3. Using the simple `if` statement you used earlier, check that the value is equal to 5. (Note the double equal signs, ==.)

```
if ($number == 5)
   {
      print "\n\n\$number is equal to 5\n\n";
   }
```

4. Save the code as 07-01.pl.

5. Open a command window and run the program.

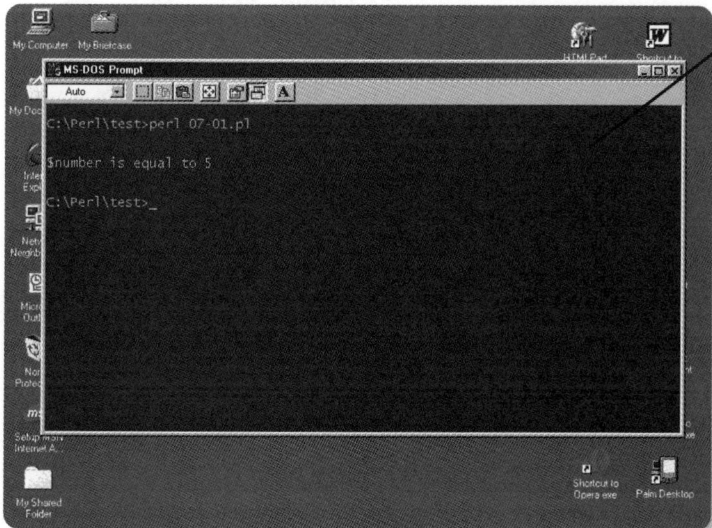

You should see these results.

That was a simple `if` statement. Here is an `if` statement using the full `if` statement syntax.

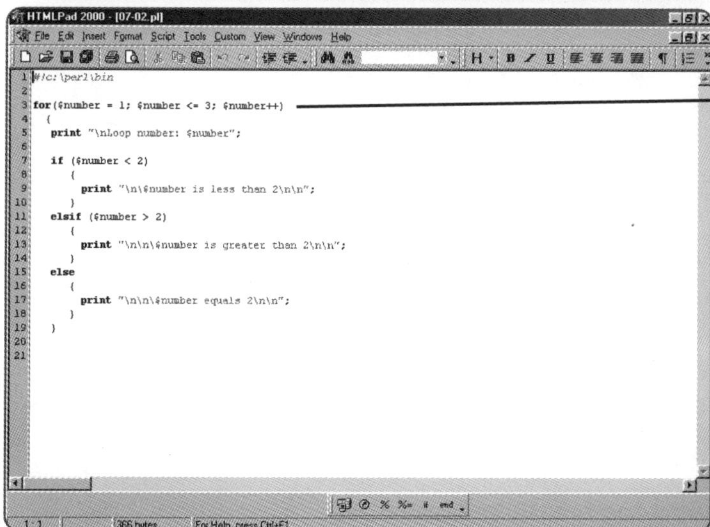

1. Open your editor.

2. This time you are going to use a `for` loop to test values. Begin with this:

```
for($number = 1; $number <= 3;
   $number++)
  {
```

> **NOTE**
>
> This sets the value of `$number` to 1; then, do whatever is in the loop (between the following curly braces) as long as `$number` <= 3. `$number++` increments the value of `$number` on each execution of the loop.

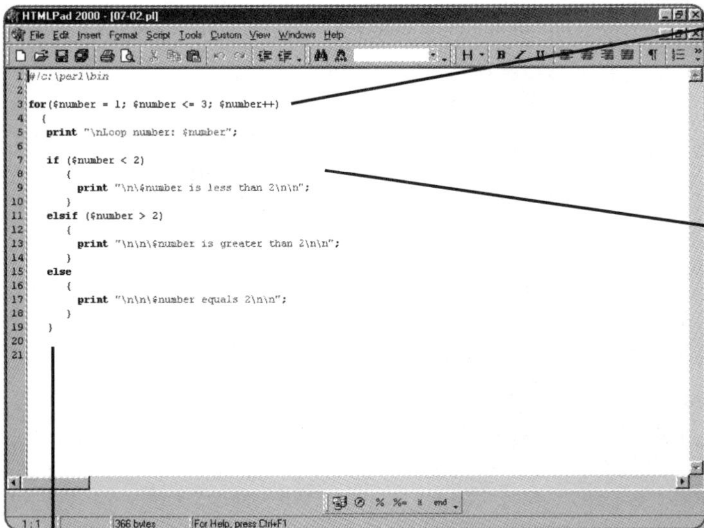

3. Display the value of the loop variable.

```
print "\nLoop number:
   $number";
```

4. Now the `if/elsif` bit will check the value of `$number` and display the appropriate message.

```
if ($number < 2)
       {
         print "\n\$number is
           less than 2\n\n";
       }
elsif ($number > 2)
   {
     print "\n\n\$number is greater than 2\n\n";
   }
else
   {
     print "\n\n\$number equals 2\n\n";
   }
```

5. Finally, don't forget the closing brace for the `for` loop.

```
}
```

6. Save the code as 07-02.pl.

7. Open a command window and run the program.

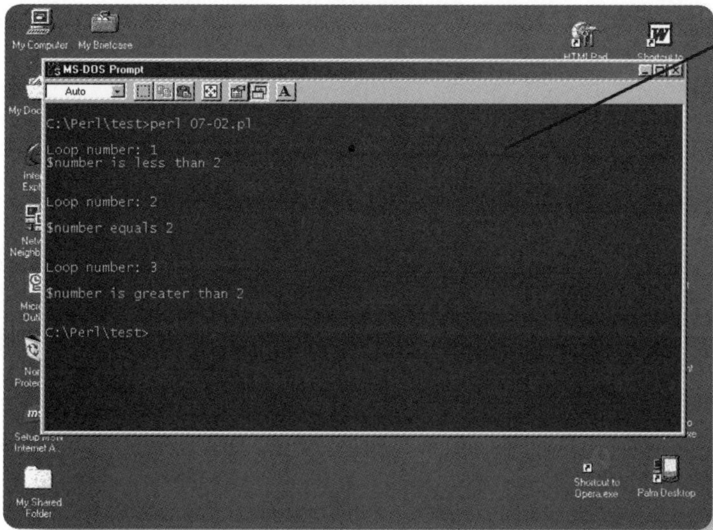

8. You should see this output from your program.

Loops in Perl

Perl is fairly rich in its loop facilities. Perl can loop while a condition is True. It can loop until a condition is True. Perl can do a loop while or until a condition is True or False, performing the loop at least once. Finally, Perl can loop a predetermined number of times using the `for` loop. Next you will learn how to use each of these loop structures.

The while and until Loops

The `while` loop runs a loop as long as a given condition is True. If the condition specified is not True to begin with, the code within the `while` loop is never executed. The `while` loop looks like this:

```
While (condition)
  {
     statement …;
     statement …;

  }
```

> **NOTE**
>
> Note that again you will often see the opening brace on the same line as the `while(condition)`—it is just another convention.

The `until` loop is very similar to the `while` loop. As the names of these loops suggest, the `while` loop continues to loop *while* a given condition is satisfied, whereas the `until` loop continues to loop *until* a condition arises.

Here is an example with both types of loops.

1. Start a new program in your editor.

2. Announce what you are going to do (this is optional, of course).

```
print "The While Loop:\n";
```

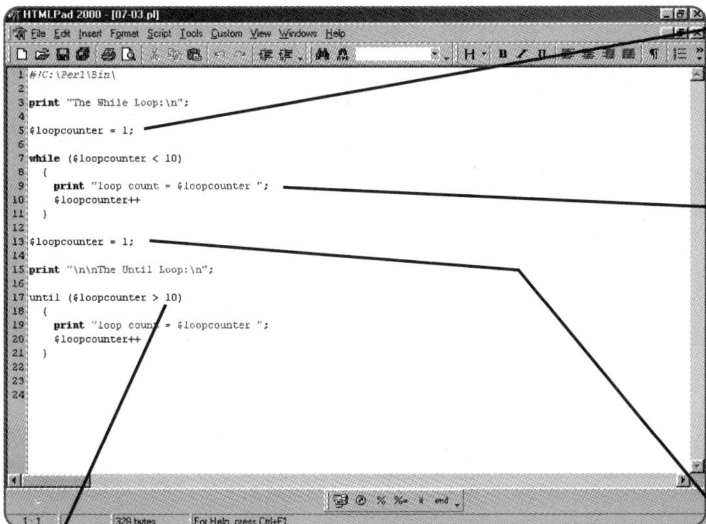

3. Initialize a variable (`$loopcounter`) to 1.

```
$loopcounter = 1;
```

4. Use the `while` loop code to demonstrate its operation.

```
while ($loopcounter < 10)
  {
    print "loop count =
       $loopcounter ";
    $loopcounter++
  }
```

5. Reset the counter variable, `$loopcounter`, to 1.

```
$loopcounter = 1;
```

6. Again, announce what you are going to do (optional).

```
print "\n\nThe Until Loop:\n";
```

7. Use the `until` loop code on the next page to demonstrate its operation.

```
until ($loopcounter > 10)
  {
    print "loop count = $loopcounter ";
    $loopcounter++
  }
```

8. Save your program as 07-03.pl.

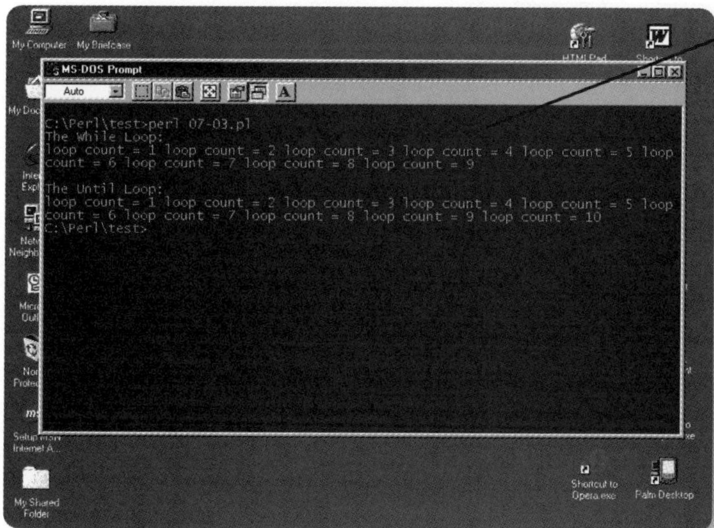

9. Open a command window and run it. You should get something like this.

> **NOTE**
>
> I have not inserted line breaks in the print statements of the program so that the output is captured on a single screen.

This example uses the shorthand increment operator:

```
$loopcounter++;
```

You could of course use

```
$loopcounter = $loopcounter + 1;
```

The Do Loop

The `do` loop is a variation on the `while` and `until` loops; the important difference is that the condition is tested at the end of the loop (either "while a condition is True" or "until a condition is True") thus ensuring that the loop executes at least once.

Here is an example of both the `do-while` and the `do-until` loop.

1. Open your editor, starting a new program file.

2. Add a print statement to announce the `do-while` example.

```
print "The do - while Loop:\n";
```

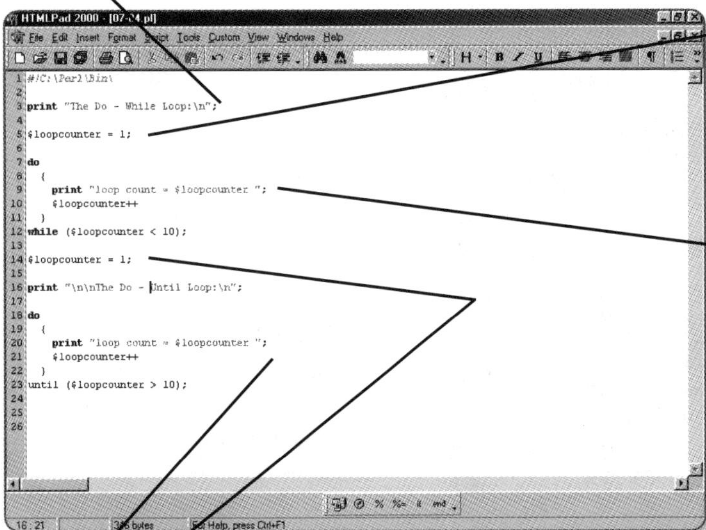

3. Set a scalar variable to be used as a counter and initialize its value to 1.

```
$loopcounter = 1;
```

4. Now code the main `do-while` loop.

```
do
  {
    print "loop count =
       $loopcounter ";
    $loopcounter++;
  }
while ($loopcounter < 10);
```

5. Reset the counter scalar variable.

```
$loopcounter = 1;
```

6. Add a similar loop but this time using the `do-until` loop.

```
print "\n\nThe Do - Until Loop:\n";

do
  {
    print "loop count = $loopcounter ";
    $loopcounter++;
  }
until ($loopcounter > 10);
```

7. Save the program as 07-04.pl.

8. Open an MS-DOS command window and execute the program.

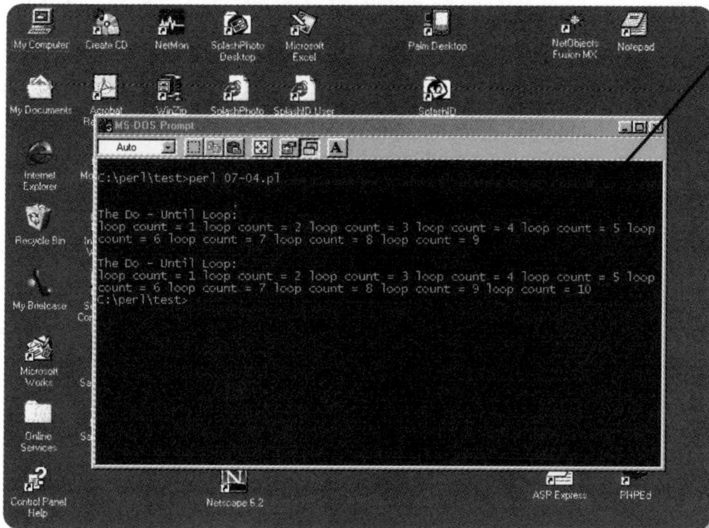

9. The results should look like this.

Both of the loops in this example are similar to the preceding `while` and `until` loops, but as has already been stated, the main difference is that the loop in the `do` versions is executed at least once.

The For Loop

This is similar to the C/C++ `for` loop. The format of the `for` loop is

```
for(loop_variable = initial_value; loop_termination_condition;
   loop_variable_update)
```

The syntax begins with the keyword `for`, followed by an open bracket, and then the initial condition of the `for` statement, followed by the test that determines whether the loop should finish or not, followed by the update to the variable being tested. Often this is an increment, but it can also be a decrement value. Finally, there is the closing bracket. Then there is the block of code to be executed while the test condition allows.

Following is an example of the Perl `for` loop.

1. Open a new program in your editor.

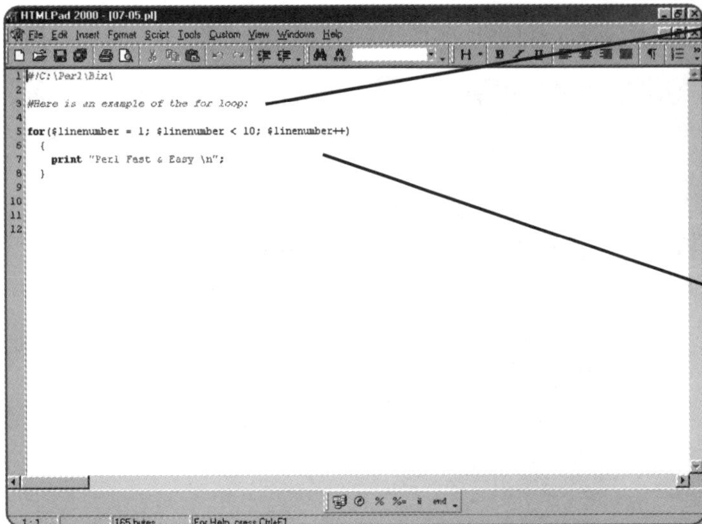

2. Enter a comment to remind you what you are doing. (Your programs should be, of course, full of comments.)

```
#Here is an example of the for
   loop:
```

3. Here is a simple `for` loop. It is similar to what you have seen in other previous examples when we weren't talking about loops but it was convenient to use them.

```
for($linenumber = 1; $linenumber < 10; $linenumber++)
  {
    print "Perl Fast & Easy \n";
  }
```

4. Save the program as 07-05.pl.

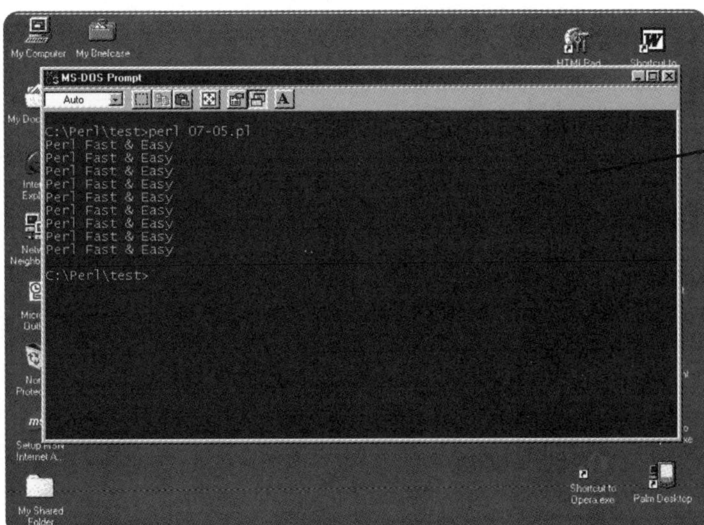

5. Open a command window and run the program.

Your program should repeatedly print "Perl Fast & Easy" until `$linenumber` is no longer less than 10.

The increment can also be a decrement, so you might see this instead:

```
for($linenumber = 1;
   $linenumber < 10;
   $linenumber–)
```

You will sometimes see odd implementations of `for` loops. Try this one:

```
for(;;)
  {
   print "Perl Fast & easy \n";
  }
```

This loop has no initialized variable, no test, and no update of any test variable, so it will loop forever. Often, this means that you don't always know under what conditions the loop should terminate, and so this technique is sometimes used to allow you a different method of deciding when you should break out of the loop. An unusual use of this type of loop, but it serves to illustrate the flexibility of the Perl `for` loop.

We have discussed the data types used in Perl and given a few examples of how they can be used. You have also learned the syntax of some program flow processing elements of the Perl language. There is more to learn in these respects, and you will be extending your knowledge of the language as you need to. The rest of this book will provide much of that knowledge; your own experience and looking at the work of others (who were once where you are now) will fill in the gaps and extend your experience.

8

Perl Functions

Perl is a very function-rich language. In this chapter you will explore many of the functions that Perl provides, especially those that help you with your Web applications. Some functions are found in many languages, others are unique to Perl; after you've learned to use them, you'll wish that all languages provided the same facilities.

In this chapter you will learn how to use:

- String functions
- Array functions
- Hash functions
- Subroutines

What is a Function?

A *function* is normally considered to be a section of code that performs a limited set of related actions. It might act upon a value (or a number of values passed to it, called *arguments* or *parameters*), and it often returns a *result*. A function that does not return a result is often called a *subroutine*.

To begin with, take a look at some of the functions you can use in Perl, a few of which you have seen before in earlier chapters.

String Functions

There are many string functions provided by Perl. In this chapter you will learn about the following:

- `chop()`
- `chomp()`
- `length()`
- `substr()`
- `lc()`
- `uc()`
- `lcfirst()`
- `ucfirst()`

Chopping a String: chop()

The `chop` function removes a character from the end of a scalar variable (in other words, it will work with numeric values as well as strings).

The basic syntax for the `chop` function is

```
$scalar_variable = chop($other_scalar_variable);
```

For example:

1. Open a new program in your editor.

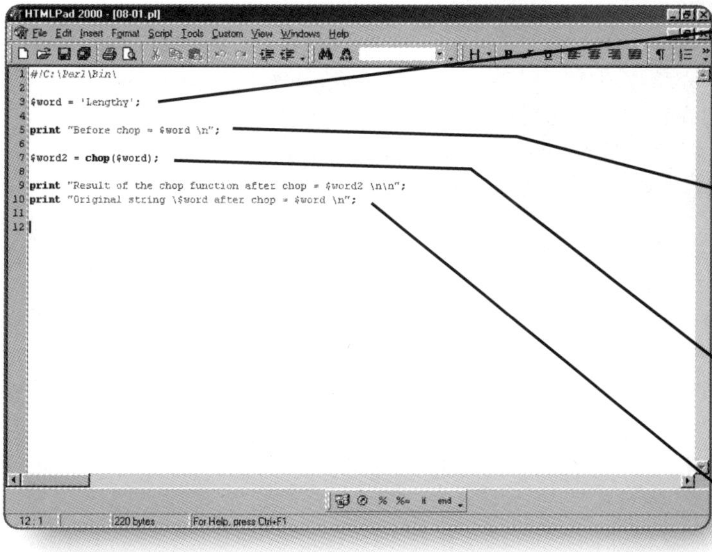

2. Set up a variable and initialize it like this:

```
$word = 'Lengthy';
```

3. Display the string before the `chop` function.

```
print "Before chop = $word \n";
```

4. Now do the chop function.

```
$word2 = chop($word);
```

5. Display the results using code like this:

```
print "Result of the chop function after chop = $word2 \n\n";
print "Original string \$word after chop = $word \n";
```

6. Save the program as 08-01.pl.

7. Open a command window.

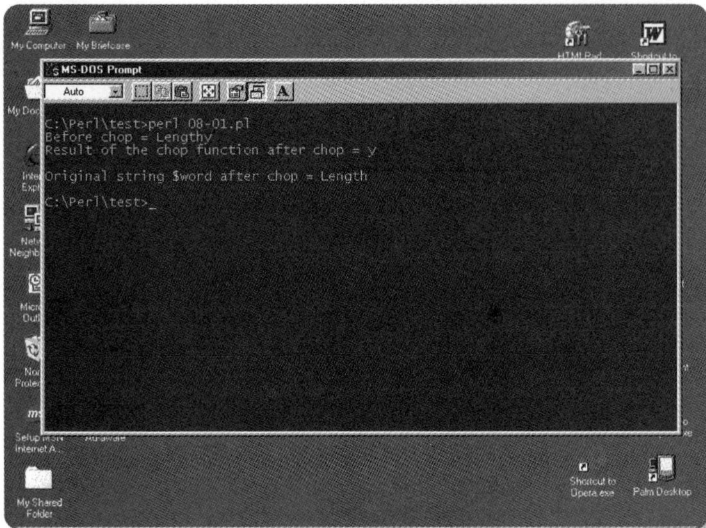

8. Check out the result.

9. After executing the previous code, `$word2` will contain the string "y". (The character "chopped" and `$word` contains the original string minus the "y".)

So, the `chop()` function is doubly useful, simultaneously giving you the chopped word and the character it chopped.

As you have already learned, this will also work with numbers; try this example to prove it.

1. Open your editor.

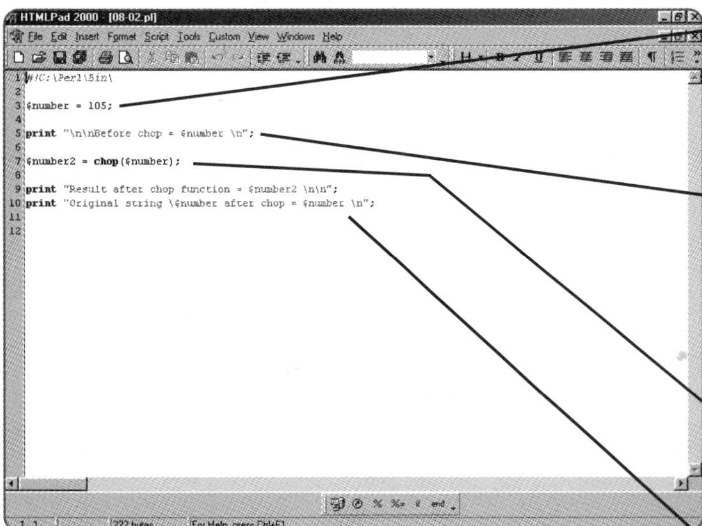

2. Set up a scalar variable with a numeric value.

```
$number = 105;
```

3. Again, print the value of the variable before applying the `chop`.

```
print "\n\nBefore chop =
   $number \n";
```

4. Now do the `chop`.

```
$number2 = chop($number);
```

5. Display the results.

```
print "Result after chop function = $number2 \n\n";
print "Original string \$number after chop = $number \n";
```

6. Save the program as 08-02.pl.

7. Open a command window.

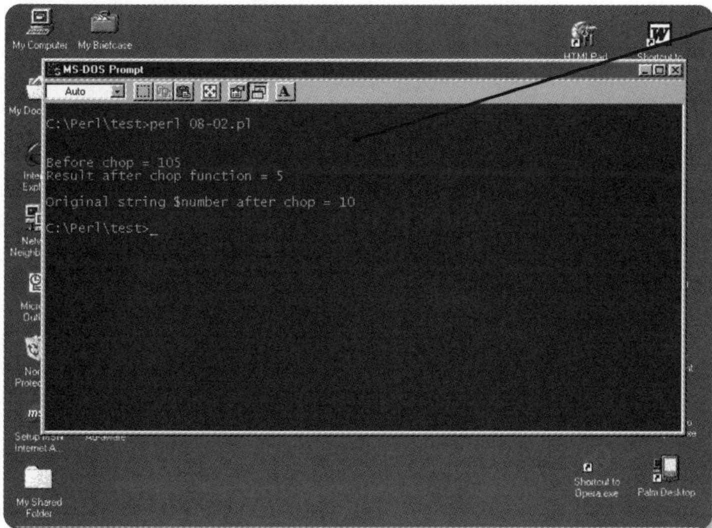

8. Run the program to check the results.

`chop()` has behaved in exactly the same way as it did for the string variable. This is not altogether surprising; as you will remember, a scalar can be string or numeric, in fact any single value of any data type. `Chop()` receives a scalar variable as its argument (or parameter) and so regardless of what it contains, `chop()` deals with it in the same way.

The `chop` function is very useful when it comes to things like removing the carriage return character at the end of a line in a file, for example. But you will find other uses for it as you go along.

A Smart Chop: chomp()

`chomp` is similar to `chop`, except that you have some control over what it chops...err, chomps. It too takes characters from the end of a line (string), but this time only the characters you tell it to. It does this through the use of a special variable known as the input record separator. The *input record separator* is represented like this:

```
$/
```

$/ will contain the character you want removed from the end of a string, which means if the string you give it doesn't have the character(s) you wanted removed, the original string is returned. Check out the example on the next page.

```
$/ = "\n";
$stringvalue = "This is a string \n";
print ($stringvalue);
```

This will return

```
This is a string
```

If you do the following:

```
$/ = "\n";
$stringvalue = "This is a string";   # note no \n in this string
print ($stringvalue);
```

Then this will still return

```
This is a string
```

To illustrate this, try the following program.

1. Open your editor.

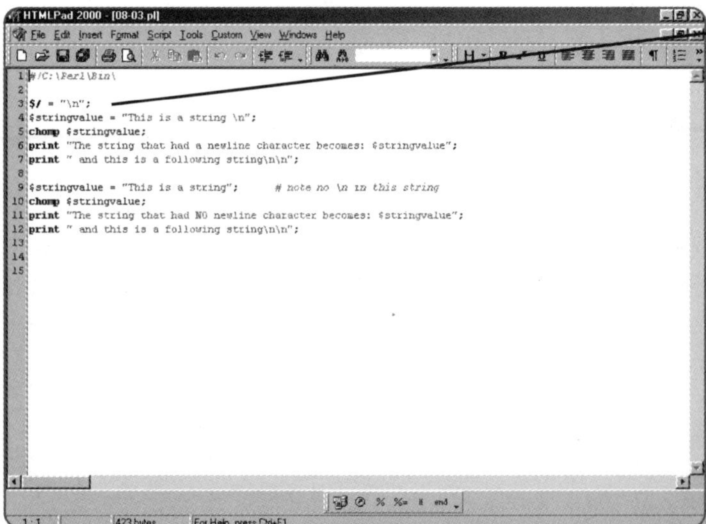

2. Start your program by storing a newline character in the input record separator variable.

```
$/ = "\n";
```

> **NOTE**
>
> Note though, that \n is the default value for $/, so you do not really need to do this unless $/ previously contained something else.

3. Set up another variable and initialize it like this.

```
$stringvalue = "This is a string \n";
```

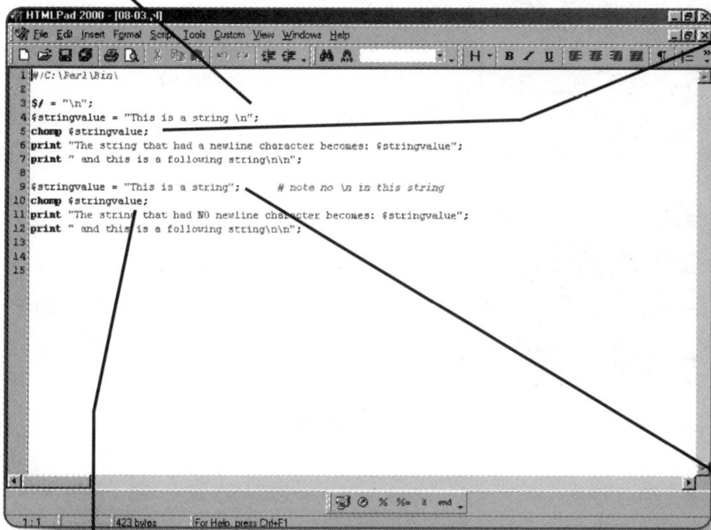

4. Use the chomp function to remove the newline character from the end of the string.

```
chomp $stringvalue;
```

5. Display the result.

```
print "The string that had a
   newline character becomes:
   $stringvalue";
print " and this is a
   following string\n\n";
```

6. Now, restore the string scalar variable. (Note though, that after the previous coding this variable will already have this value.)

```
$stringvalue = "This is a string";   # note no \n in this string
```

7. Do the chomp again.

```
chomp $stringvalue;
```

8. Display the result.

```
print "The string that had NO newline character becomes: $stringvalue";
print " and this is a following string\n\n";
```

9. Save the program as 08-03.pl.

10. Open a command window.

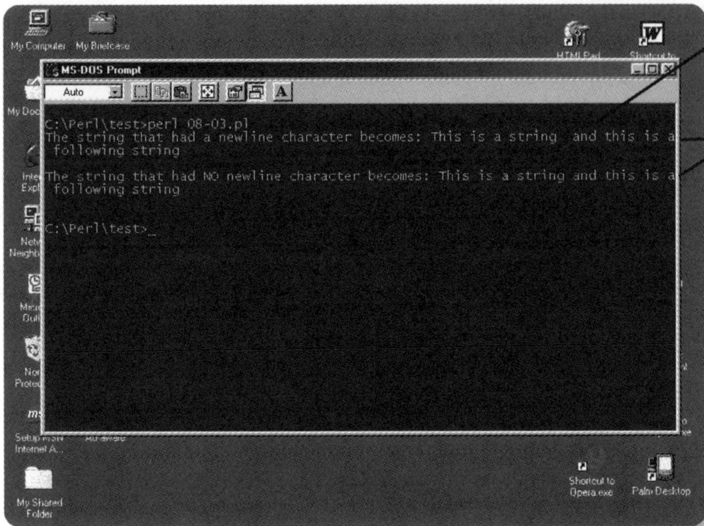

11. Run the program and look at what happened.

12. Note that in the first case the"\n is removed and in the second case there was no \n, and so it appears that the two cases are the same.

As you can see, `chomp()` is a bit more flexible than `chop()`, and it saves you having to check if the unwanted character is at the end of the string before chopping it.

Let's look at a few more Perl functions.

Measuring String Length: length( )

This is a simple function that enables you to measure the length of a string.

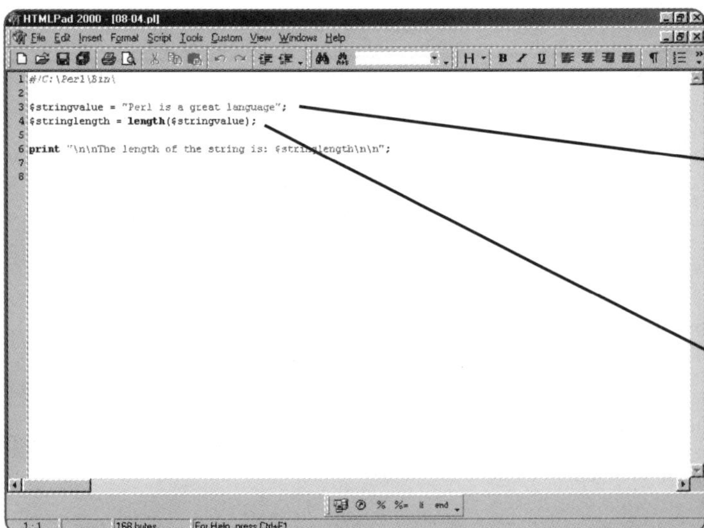

Try this easy example.

1. Open your editor.

2. Initialize a scalar variable with a string like this:

```
$stringvalue = "Perl
   is a great language";
```

3. Now use the `length` function to measure the length of the string.

```
$stringlength =
   length($stringvalue);
```

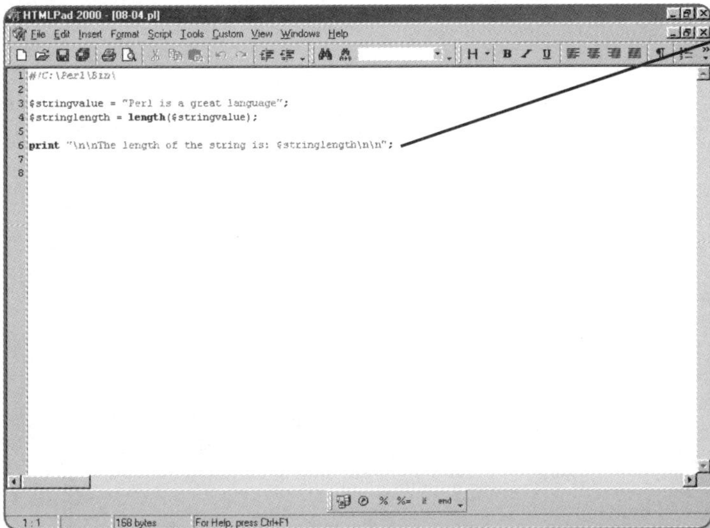

4. And display the result.

```
print "\n\nThe length of the
   string is:
   $stringlength\n\n";
```

5. Save the program as 08-04.pl.

6. Open a command window.

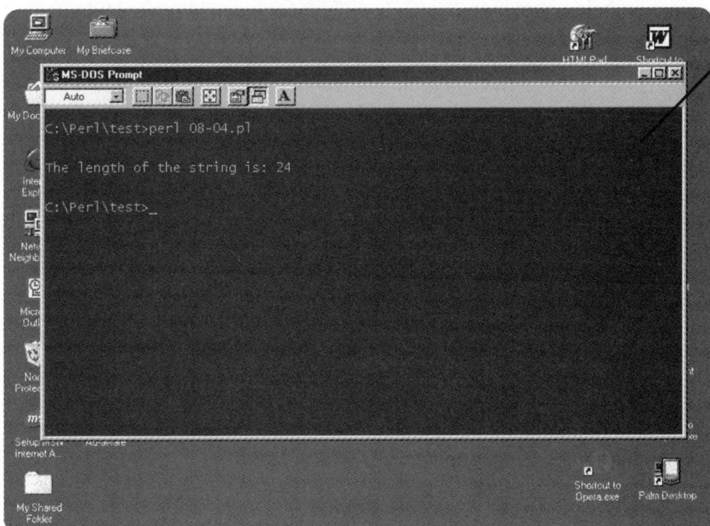

7. Run the program and view the result.

The `length()` function is a very simple but a very useful Perl string function, with many uses in many different applications. You'll be surprised how often you use it.

Getting Substrings: substr( )

The `substr` function enables you to extract a part of a string. Perl needs this function as, unlike C, a Perl string scalar is not an array of `chars`, and therefore you cannot address characters individually using things like the example on the next page.

```
$stringvalue = "Perl is a great language";
$char = $stringvalue[5];              # This will NOT work!!
```

The `substr` function allows you to extract one or more characters from a string scalar like this:

1. Open your editor.

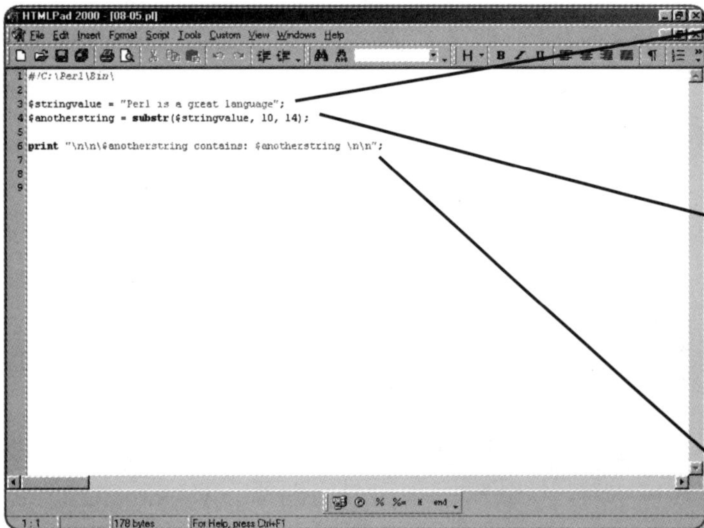

2. Set up a scalar variable to contain a string.

```
$stringvalue = "Perl is a
   great language";
```

3. Get the characters from position 10 for a length of 14 characters.

```
$anotherstring =
   substr($stringvalue,
   10, 14);
```

4. Display the result that was stored in the variable `$anotherstring`.

```
print "\n\n\$anotherstring contains: $anotherstring \n\n";
```

5. Save the program as 08-05.pl.

6. Open a command window.

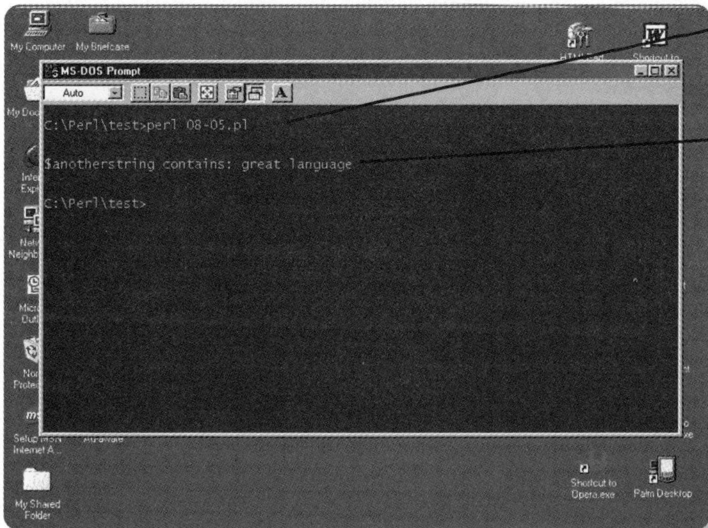

7. Run the program and observe the output.

8. `$anotherstring` contains

```
"great language"
```

The `substr` function therefore accepts three parameters; the string being worked upon, the starting character position for the substring you want to extract, and the length (number of characters) to extract.

> **NOTE**
>
> The starting position for a string is ZERO, that is, in the above example,
>
> ```
> $anotherstring = substr($stringvalue, 1, 3);
> ```
>
> would return
>
> ```
> erl
> ```

`Substr` is a very useful function and you will no doubt be using it a lot. There will be many times that you will want to extract a domain from an e-mail address or a page name from a URL.

Changing Case: lc ( ), uc ( ), lcfirst ( ), ucfirst ( )

You first learned about these functions in Chapter 4, but you'll examine them in more detail here.

The `lc( )` function simply changes any uppercase characters in a string to lowercase. In this example, `string2` will contain "smith".

```
$string1 = "SMITH";
$string2 =  lc($string1);
```

As you would expect, `uc( )` has the opposite effect. In this example, `string2` will contain "SMITH".

```
$string1 = "smith";
$string2 =  uc($string1);
```

`lcfirst( )` does what you might expect it to do. I assume that this function has been added for completeness, as there are few occasions when you'd really need to use it. In this example, `string2` will contain "sMITH".

```
$string1 = "SMITH";
$string2 =  lcfirst($string1);
```

Finally, a slightly more useful function is `ucfirst( )`. This takes a string and capitalizes the first letter, as you might want to do for a name. In this example, `string2` will contain "Smith".

```
$string1 = "smith";
$string2 =  ucfirst($string1);
```

The short example here will illustrate all of these functions.

1. Open your editor.

2. Set up two variables, one with a lowercase string and one with an uppercase string.

```
$stringlower = "perl fast & easy";
$stringupper = "PERL FAST & EASY";
```

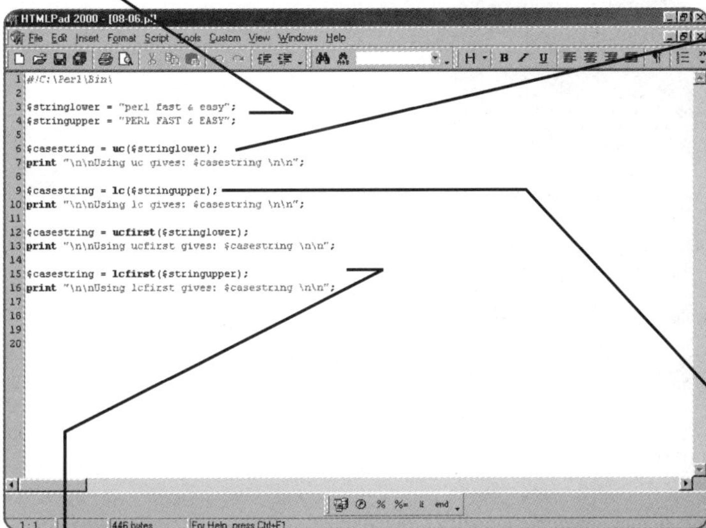

3. Try using the `uc()` function to convert the lowercase string to uppercase.

```
$casestring =
   uc($stringlower);
```

4. Display the result.

```
print "\n\nUsing uc gives:
   $casestring \n\n";
```

5. Now use the `lc()` function to convert the uppercase string to lowercase.

```
$casestring = lc($stringupper);
```

6. Again, display the result.

```
print "\n\nUsing lc gives: $casestring \n\n";
```

7. Finally, use the `ucfirst()` and `lcfirst()` to convert the case of the first character to upper- and lowercase, respectively, and display the results.

```
$casestring = ucfirst($stringlower);
print "\n\nUsing ucfirst gives: $casestring \n\n";

$casestring = lcfirst($stringupper);
print "\n\nUsing lcfirst gives: $casestring \n\n";
```

8. Save it as 08-06.pl.

9. Open a command window.

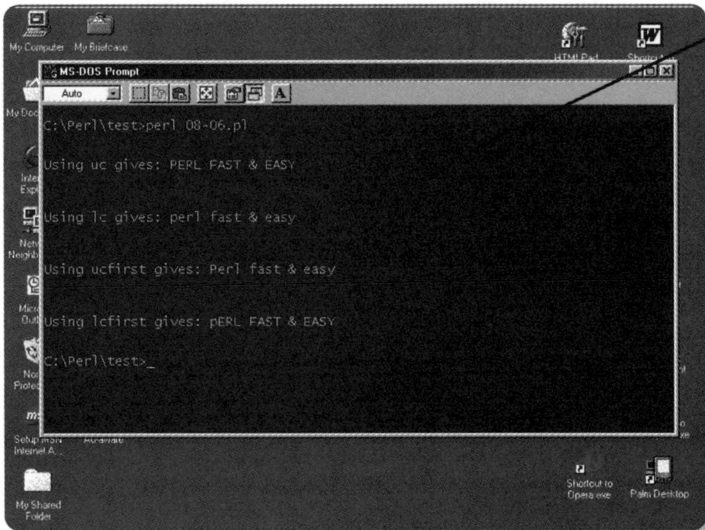

10. Run the program to demonstrate the case functions.

Array Functions

In this section you will learn about some of the functions provided by Perl for manipulating arrays.

Printing Arrays: print

Earlier, you learned a little about a concept called "context." This concept also affects functions, and what functions do can depend upon what is sent to them.

The `print` function will easily print an array. Try this simple array example.

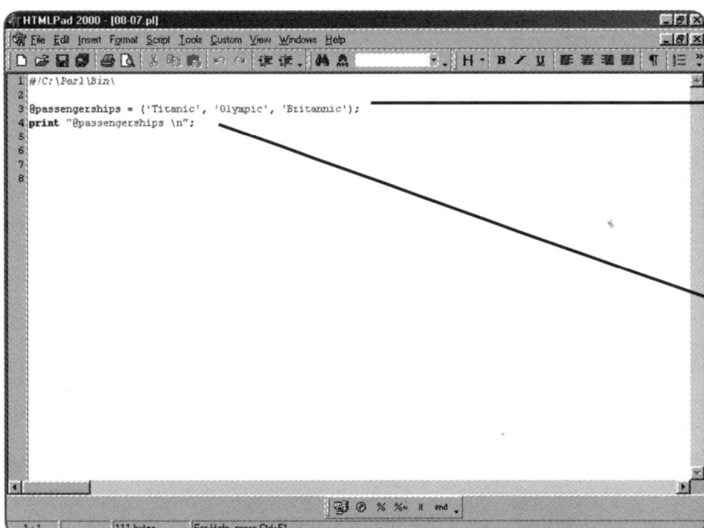

1. Open your editor.

2. Create an array with three elements like this:

```
@passengerships = ('Titanic',
   'Olympic', 'Britannic');
```

3. Then simply print the array.

```
print "@passengerships \n";
```

4. Save the program as 08-07.pl.

5. Open a command window.

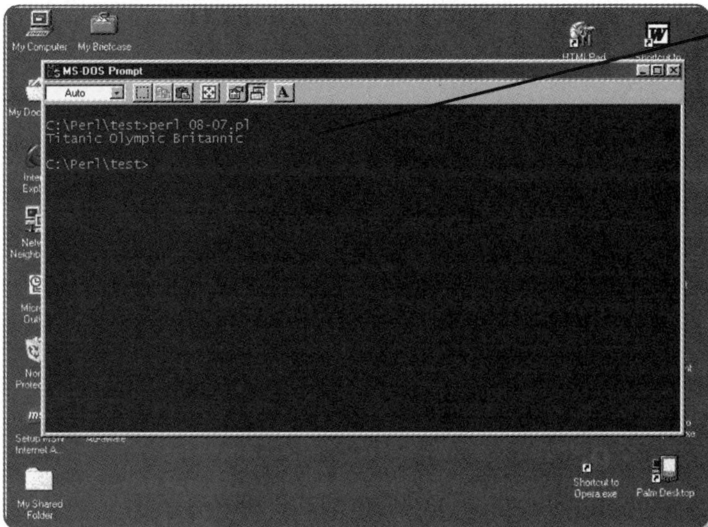

6. Running the program causes the array to print out.

You might not often want to print an array like that, but Perl can do it easily if ever you do.

Finding the Size of an Array: scalar

In Chapter 5, you saw how to print the size of an array. The function `scalar( )` returns the size of an array so that it can be stored in a variable to be used for some other purpose or again to allow the size of the array to be printed. Beginning with that method, here are a few examples describing the measurement of the size of an array.

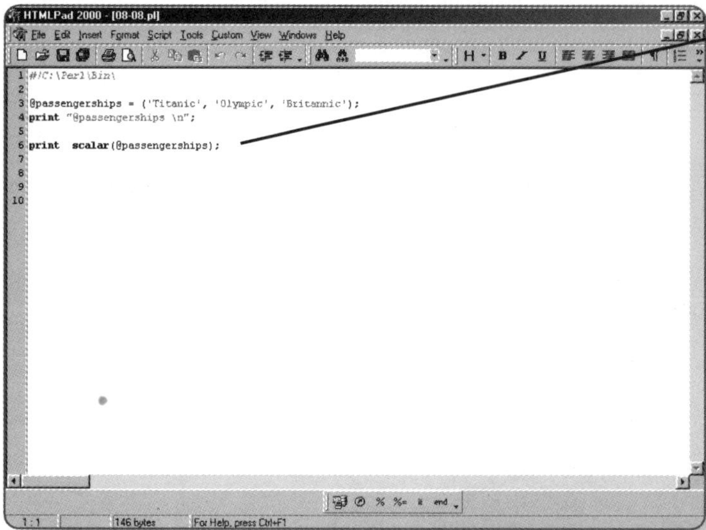

1. Using the same array as in the previous example, add the following line to the end of your program:

```
print
   scalar(@passengerships);
```

2. Save your program as 08-08.pl.

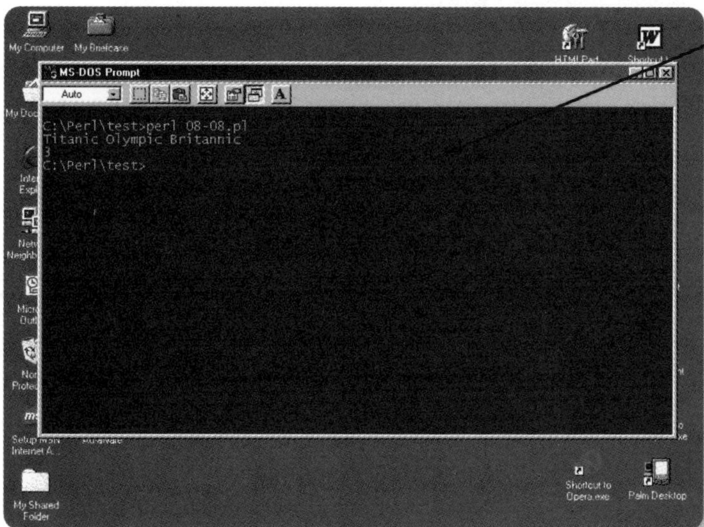

3. Running your program should give this result.

That gives you the number of elements in your array. Here is another way of determining the size of an array.

To print the size of an array, as you learned about in Chapter 5, you can do this:

```
print $#passengerships;
```

This prints 2 as the array size, because the value returned is a count of elements starting at 0.

Finally, you can use

```
$arraysize = @passengerships;

print $arraysize;
```

which will return a value of 3.

To show these techniques in action, once again modify the previous program.

1. Display a couple of newlines just to space the output from the previous part of the program.

```
print "\n\n";
```

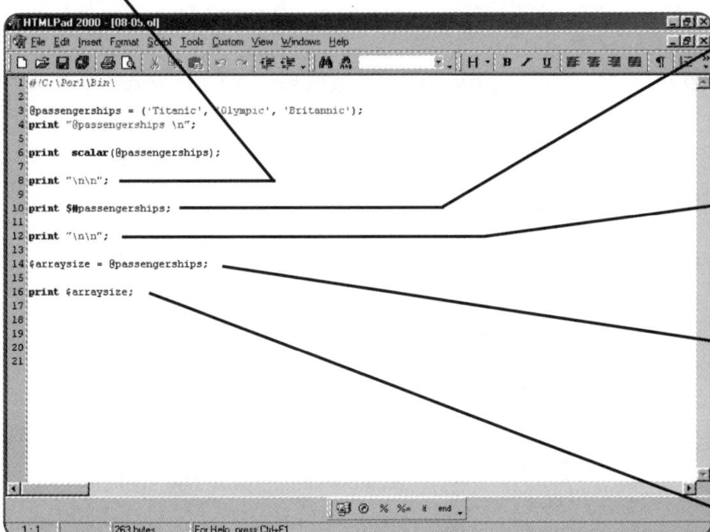

2. Display the size of the array like this:

```
print $#passengerships;
```

3. Display two more newlines.

```
print "\n\n";
```

4. Store the size of the array in a variable.

```
$arraysize = @passengerships;
```

5. Print the result.

```
print $arraysize;
```

6. Save it as 08-09.pl.

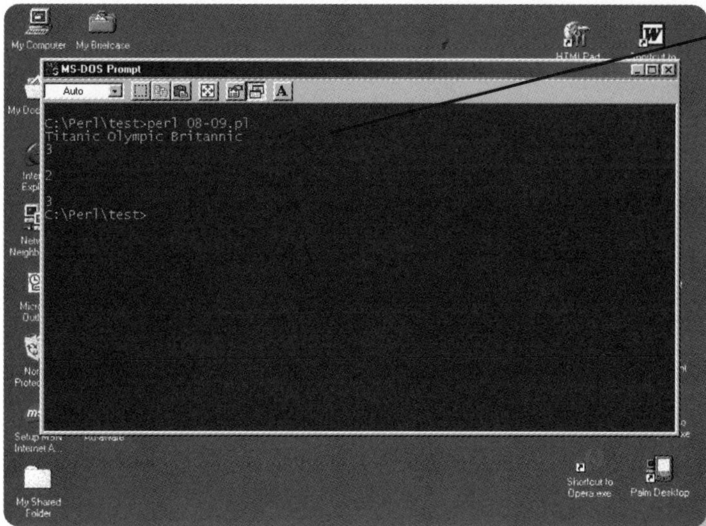

7. Run the program and observe the results.

As you will see, measuring the size of an array will prove to be very useful, and Perl enables you to easily obtain the information you need.

Adding to the End of an Array: push( )

You can add elements to the end of an array by using the `push( )` function.

Sticking with the array in the previous example, you can add another element to the end of the array like this:

```
push(@passengerships, "QE2");
```

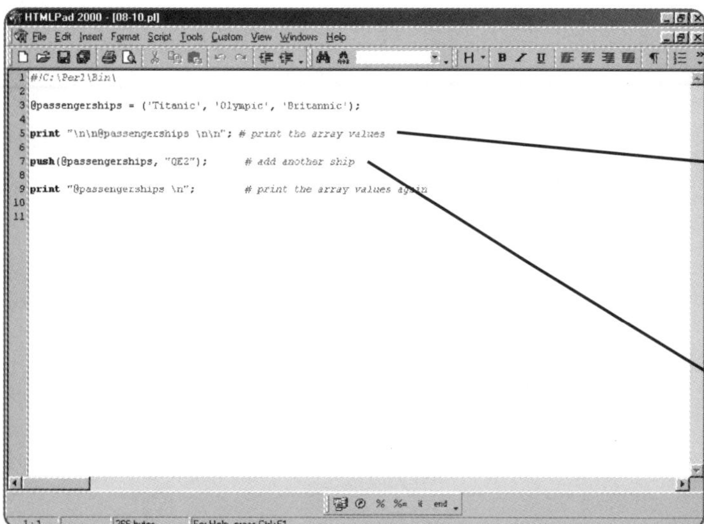

Try this example.

1. Open your editor.

2. After the array definition, print the array as you did before.

```
print "\n\n@passengerships
   \n\n"; # print the array
   values
```

3. Use the `push` function to add another element to the array like this:

```
push(@passengerships, "QE2");
   # add another ship
```

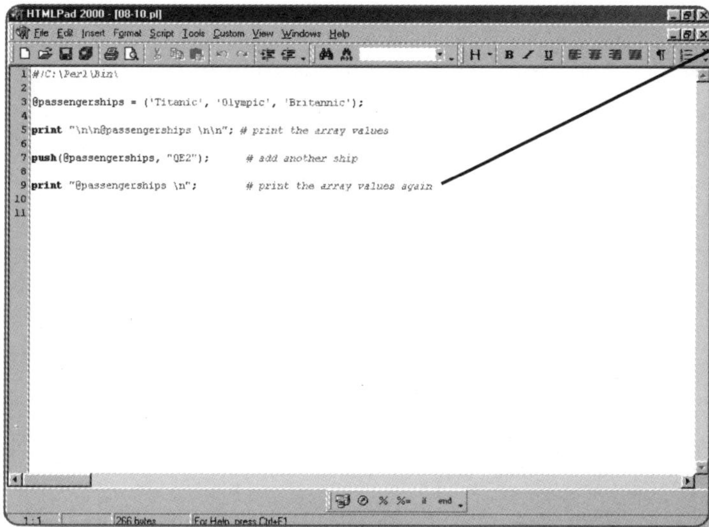

4. Display the array again to prove that it worked.

```
print "@passengerships \n";
   # print the array values
   again
```

5. Save the program as 08-10.pl.

6. Open a command window.

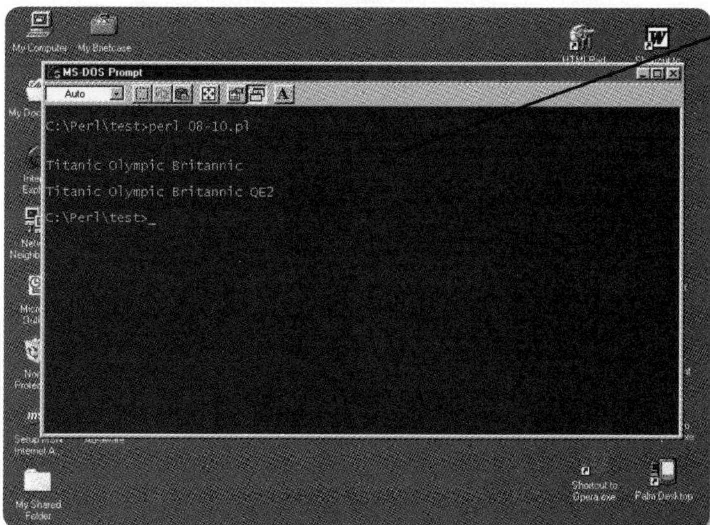

7. Run the program and verify that the new ship, QE2, has appeared in your array.

Perl arrays are not sized at definition time or fixed in size at any point, so you can keep adding elements. And of course, in the previous example, you could have added more elements at the same time by just adding more values separated by commas.

Removing an Element from an Array: pop( )

You can remove the elements from the end of an array using the `pop( )` function.

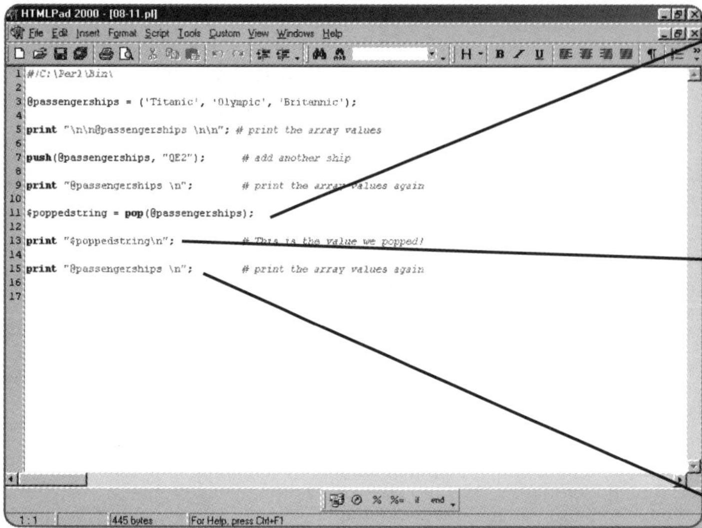

1. Remove an element from the array using the `pop()` function.

```
$poppedstring =
   pop(@passengerships);
```

2. Display what is now in the `$poppedstring` variable, which is where `pop()` should have put its result.

```
print "$poppedstring\n";
```

3. Display the array to prove that the element has been removed.

```
print "@passengerships \n";
```

4. Save the modified program as 08-11.pl.

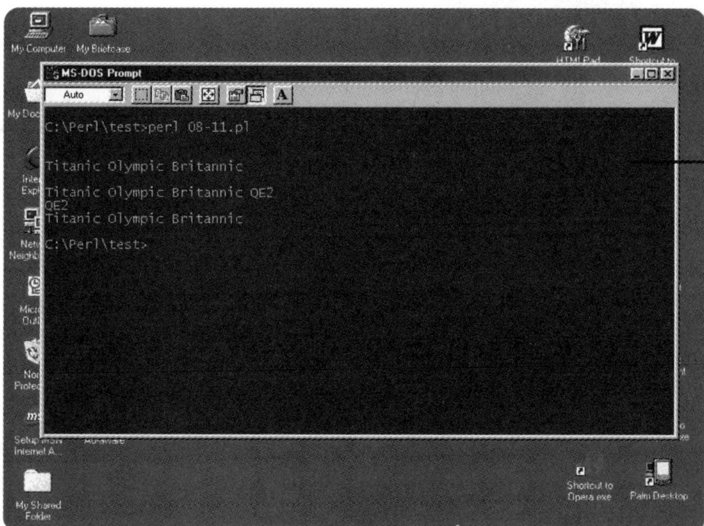

After the "pop" function call, `$poppedstring` will contain "QE2".

5. Run your program and view the effect of the `pop()` function in the output.

Now you have a few useful array functions to get you started with working on arrays.

Hash Functions

Perl provides a number of hash functions. Take a brief look at a much-used one. The `each` function enables you to run through the key value pairs of a hash so that you can do what ever you want with the values. A simple example would be to print all the values of a hash.

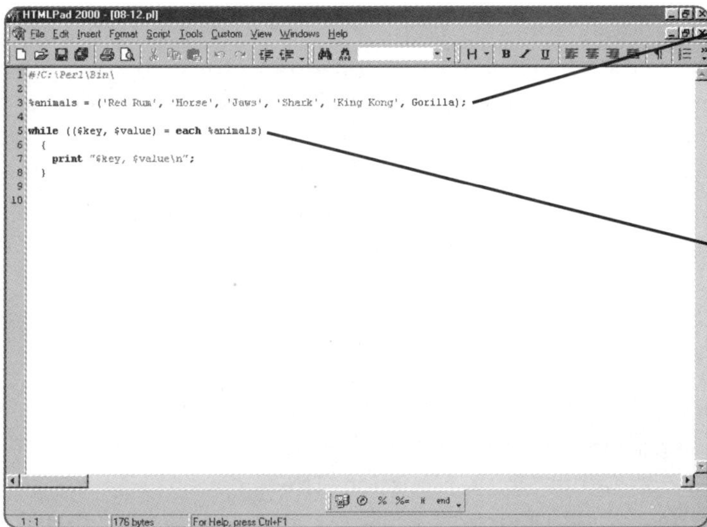

1. To do this, create a hash like this:

```
%animals = ('Red Rum',
   'Horse', 'Jaws', 'Shark',
   'King Kong', Gorilla);
```

2. Use a `while` loop to display the contents of the hash.

```
while (($key, $value) = each
%animals)
  {
    print "$key, $value\n";
  }
```

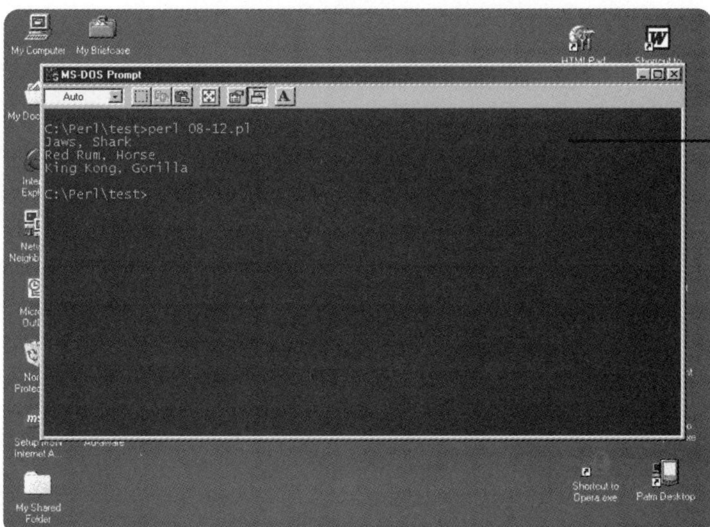

3. Save the program as 08-12.pl.

4. Run the code and you should see this output.

> **NOTE**
>
> Note that the `each` function should not be confused with the `foreach` loop. `foreach` is a loop construct with many purposes and not a specific function for processing hashes.

I have kept the examples of Perl functions very simple in order to help you to understand the material in this chapter. You have just started to scratch the surface of some of the built-in functions available in Perl, though. There are many more, as you will see.

For now though, take a look at another type of function—the *subroutine*.

Subroutines

Subroutines are very similar to functions, except they are *user-defined functions*. You can go and write your own subroutines and when they are written, your program can call them like it does a built-in Perl function. These days, the term subroutine is used interchangeably with *function*. However, so that it is clear that you are looking at sub-routines that you have written yourself, the distinction will be maintained in this text.

Subroutines are created using the following syntax:

```
Sub subroutine_name
  {
     statement1 …;
     statement2 …;
     statement3 …;
     statement4 …;
      . . . . . .
   }
```

The subroutine is called in a similar way to a function.

```
Subroutine_name( );
```

To get a subroutine to return a value as a Perl built-in function does, you use the `return` statement. Usually this will be a matter of returning a value of a variable.

```
Sub subroutine_name
  {
     statement1 …;
     statement2 …;
     return($variable);
   }
```

If you are expecting a value to be returned, you can capture that value like this:

```
$result = subroutine_name();
```

You can also pass parameters as you do with many built-in functions.

```
$result = subroutine_name($);
```

If this looks odd, try this simple example to help you fully understand what is going on.

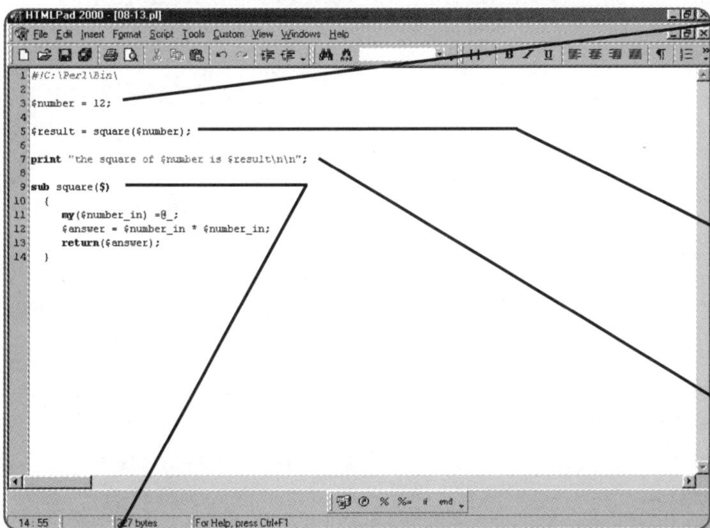

1. Start a new file and set up a variable containing the number 12.

```
$number = 12;
```

2. Now call a subroutine with your variable as a parameter.

```
$result = square($number);
```

3. Add this line to display the result:

```
print "the square of $number
   is $result\n\n";
```

4. Now code the subroutine that is called in Step 2.

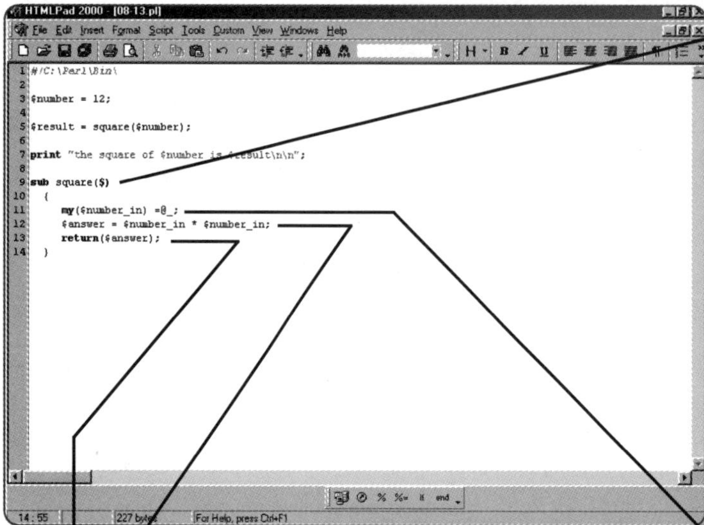

5. To do this, use the Perl keyword `sub` followed by the name of the subroutine. Also, use a $ sign as a placeholder for your parameter.

```
sub square($)
```

6. Now open a set of braces to contain the block of code that is the body of the subroutine.

```
{
```

7. The next line is simply to transfer the contents of the parameter placeholder into the variable `$number_in`, from a special variable @_, which contains the list of parameters sent to the subroutine. The Perl keyword `my` simply states that the variable is private to this subroutine and therefore cannot be seen (accessed) from outside of this subroutine.

```
my($number_in) = @_;
```

8. Now you can take the value passed into `$number_in` and multiply it by itself to achieve the square operation.

```
$answer = $number_in * $number_in;
```

9. As mentioned previously, you now need to "pass" the answer from the square operation (using the return statement) back to the statement that called the subroutine, so that ultimately, the value produced by the square operation is loaded into the `$result` variable.

```
return($answer);
```

10. Finally, you must close the braces to end your subroutine.

```
}
```

11. Save the program as 08-13.pl.

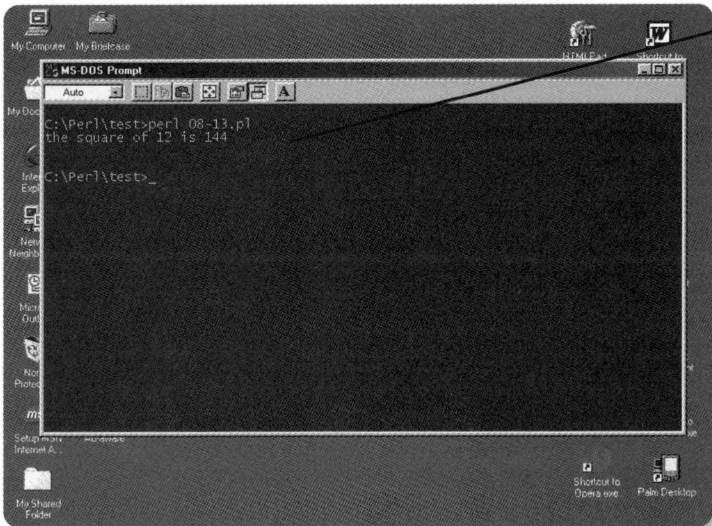

12. Now run the program and observe the result; you should get 144, as shown here.

You have seen just one way of writing a subroutine. You will see different approaches and techniques used; read through these examples carefully and see if you can work out what is going on. In Perl, there are many ways to achieve the same result.

When writing your own subroutines, there are many aspects to consider, such as scope and global versus local variables (or Perl's answer to them—the `my` keyword, for example). It is best to introduce yourself to those subjects slowly, when they can be best shown with practical usage.

You have just begun to scratch the surface of Perl. That is not to say you have not learned much, because you have! But Perl is a huge language, and there are many experienced programmers and Web developers out there who still do not know all there is to know about Perl. Right now, you need to begin covering some groundwork for Web applications. So far, you have looked at Perl from the point of view of using it as a "console" or "command line" programming language. However, in order to use Perl for the Web, you have to use it in a slightly different way. Before you can do that, you have to know all about the main language of the Web: HTML.

9 A Diversion: HTML

In order to use Perl for the Web, you have to know the main language of the Web, HTML. This chapter is bit of a diversion into HTML for those who don't have any experience with it (or for those who use WYSIWYG editors). Even if you do prefer to use point and click editors, an understanding of HTML is useful if you want to know what is really going on in an application.

If you're already familiar with HTML, you can skip this chapter. If you have never seen any HTML, then read on. If you are unsure, treat it as a refresher course—we all need those from time to time!

In this chapter you will learn how to:

- Write an HTML document
- Add headers and color
- Add images and hyperlinks
- Add frames

Saving HTML Files and Testing HTML Pages

HTML is merely text, and so can be written using any text editor (like Notepad, WordPad, Word, HTMLPad 2000 and so on). There are many HTML editors on the market but they differ from ordinary text editors only in so far as they have specialized tools that enable you to write HTML more quickly and with (hopefully) fewer errors.

When you save an HTML file, you will normally save it so that it has an .htm extension.

```
Home.htm
```

> **NOTE**
>
> You can also use the .html extension, which is usually the standard on UNIX-based systems. The three-character .htm extension probably came about because of the 8.3 filename limitation in DOS and Windows 3.1

Be careful when using editors such as Notepad or Word because they might (unless you explicitly ask them to do otherwise) add a .txt or a .doc extension to your HTML filename.

You can test your HTML pages simply by opening a file directly in the Web browser. In Windows, you would do this simply by double-clicking the file, which causes the browser to open, displaying the contents of the HTML file. Of course, a better way to test the files is to save them into a folder under wwwroot or htdocs (depending upon your platform, Web server, and so on). You can then use the http://127.0.0.1/*foldername* type of address in your browser location window.

> **NOTE**
>
> When you actually write Perl Web (CGI) programs, you *must* save them in a scripts folder (or another folder with execute permissions) under your Web server or they will not work.

From this point on, it's up to you to decide which method to use for testing your HTML files.

The Structure of an HTML Document

HTML tags tell the Web browser all about your page and how to format it. In most cases, HTML tags have a *start tag* and an *end tag* so that the browser knows when to start the formatting and when to end it. Often, you can get away without the end tag, but it is poor practice and might cause problems with some browsers.

There are many optional elements in an HTML document, but basically, an HTML document consists of the <HEAD> tag and the <BODY> tag. In turn, the <HEAD> tag and the <BODY> tag may consist of a number of other tags.

The <HEAD> tag can contain:

- The <TITLE> tag. This is the title that appears on the title bar right at the top of the browser window.
- The <SCRIPT> tag. Optionally, scripts can be added inside the HTML header, for example, for Form field validation—more on that later.
- Other tags such as <META ...> tags, which contain information about the Web page and are used by search engines to find and catalogue your page.

The <BODY> tag contains the actual content of the page—often referred to as the *document*—which consists of a wide range of possible HTML tags.

Writing an HTML Document

In this chapter, you'll learn the basics of HTML to get you up and running with Web applications as quickly as possible, but you should know that there are formal, recognized standards for HTML as there are most other things in computing. As you become more proficient in writing Web applications, you will want to know more about these standards. There are many sites on the Web, as well as some excellent books, that will help you to extend your knowledge.

HTML is simple, but like most things in life, it does have rules. Follow the text and try the examples; by the time you get to the end of this chapter, you should be able to write a Web page from scratch, using little more than a simple text editor and your Web browser.

Start by telling the browser that this is an HTML document. To do this, you use the <HTML> tag. You end the HTML document with the </HTML> tag. All end tags are the same as the start tags, except they have the forward slash at the start of the tag name.

So, the header tag is <HEAD> and ends with </HEAD>. And the body tag is <BODY> and ends with </BODY>. Get the idea?

Open your editor and start coding some HTML.

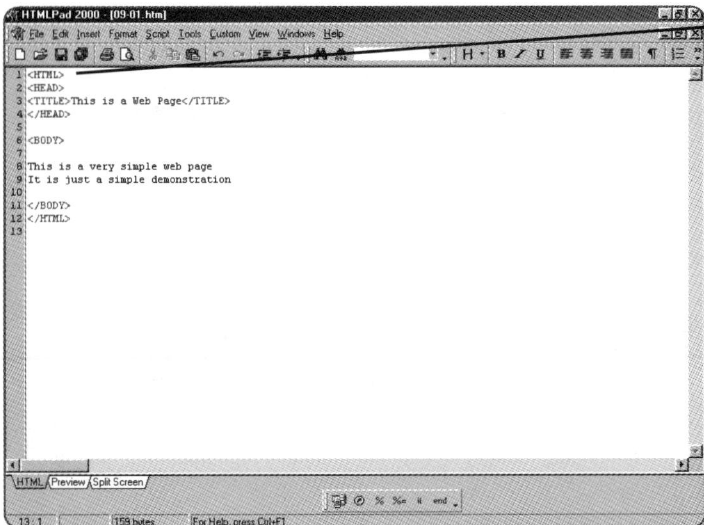

1. Start the HTML page like this.

```
<HTML>
```

The title for an HTML page (the one that appears on the blue title bar at the top of your Web browser, not in the Web page itself!) is coded as

```
<HEAD>
<TITLE>This is a Web
   Page</TITLE>
```

NOTE

The <HEAD> tag opens the HTML page header. The <HEAD> is used to contain the title and other things such as script code, for example, JavaScript, VBScript, and so on. You will see a little of this when you come to code forms.

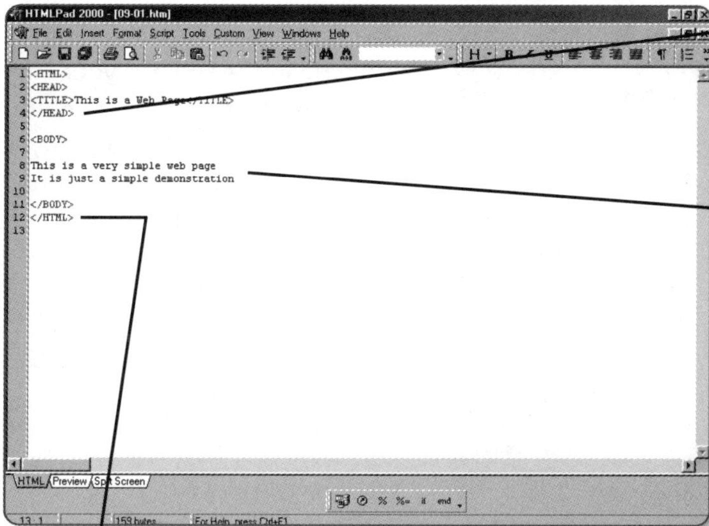

2. The <HEAD> is closed with the </HEAD> tag.

```
</HEAD>
```

The main part of an HTML page is contained within the <BODY> and </BODY> tags. In this case, just use a couple of lines of text like this:

```
<BODY>

This is a very simple web page
It is just a simple
demonstration

</BODY>
```

3. Finally, an HTML page is closed with the </HTML> tag.

```
</HTML>
```

> **NOTE**
>
> Notice that the HTML tags are all in uppercase letters. This is purely by convention. You can use uppercase or lowercase, whichever you prefer.

4. Save it as 09-01.htm on your hard drive.

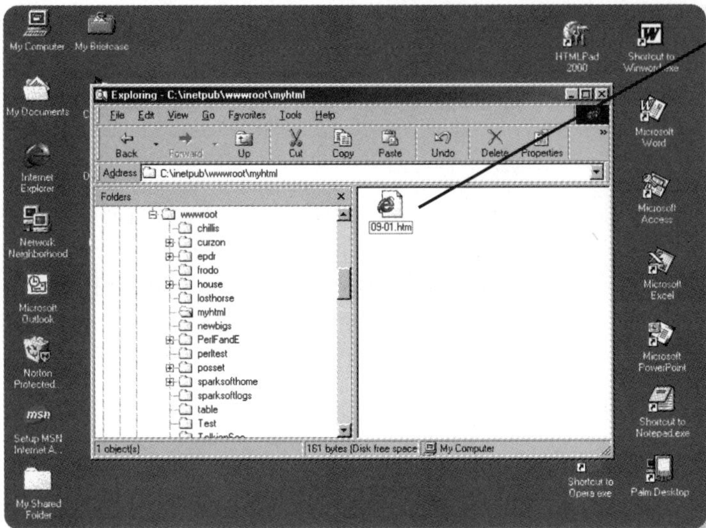

5. Go to your Web browser and type in the URL for your HTML file, then press the Enter key, or find the file through My Computer on Windows Explorer. You should see an Internet Explorer icon.

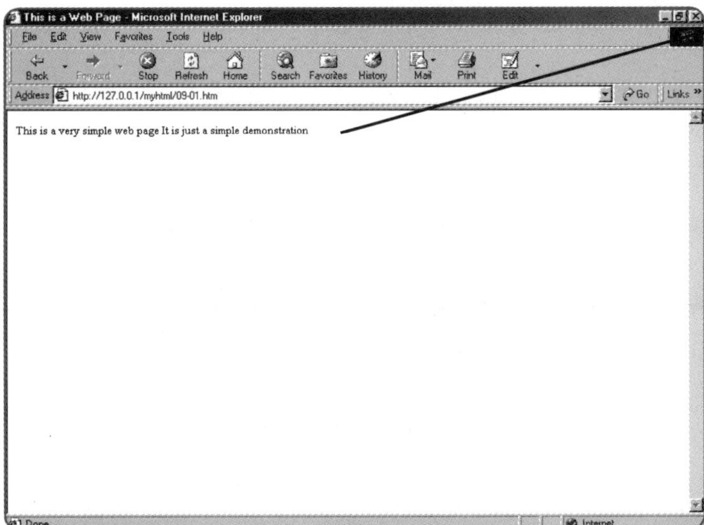

6. If you are using the file method of viewing your Web page, double-click on your new 09-01.htm file and you should find that Internet Explorer automatically starts and loads your file. Did you notice anything?

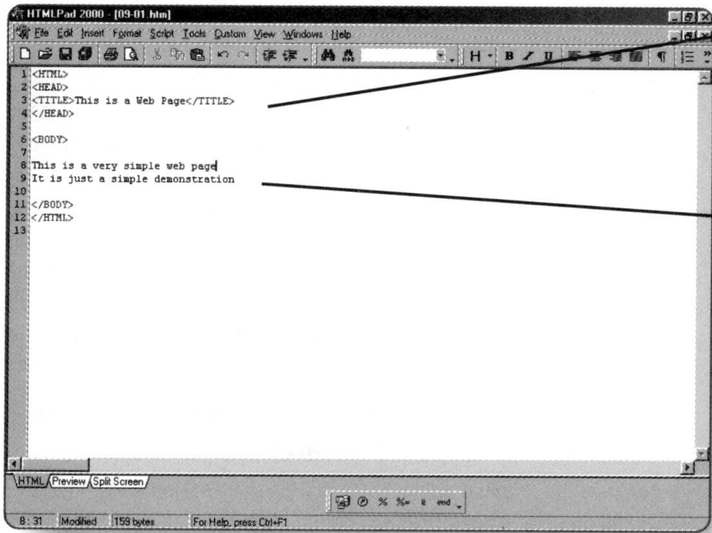

7. Look at the page as displayed by the browser and then look again at the listing for 09-01.htm.

8. Despite the fact that you pressed return after

```
"This is a very simple web
   page"
```

You got

```
"This is a very simple web
   page it is just a simple
   demonstration"
```

The browser joined the two lines of text together. In an HTML document, carriage returns are ignored.This is done so that the document flow can be flexible so that if you change the size of the browser window, the text moves around to occupy the available space. If you put ordinary carriage returns in the document this resizing would not work very well.

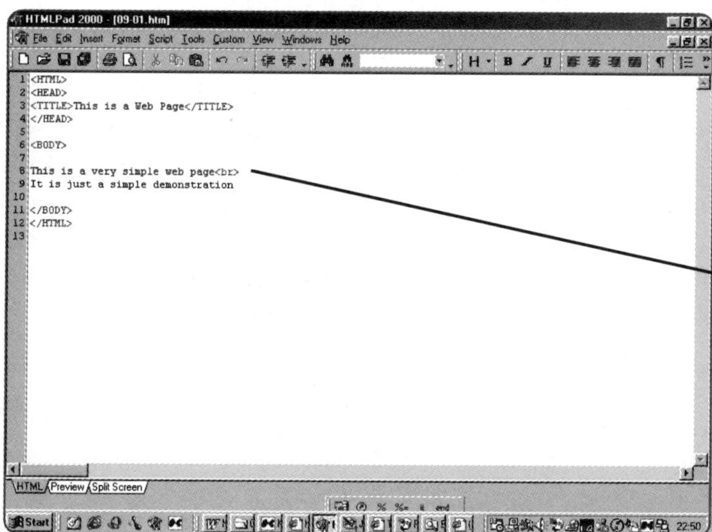

If you want to force a carriage return you must use the HTML tag <BR>. This stands for break (line break).

To demonstrate this

1. Edit your 09-01.htm and add a <BR> to the end of the first line of text in the body.

```
This is a very simple web
   page<BR>
```

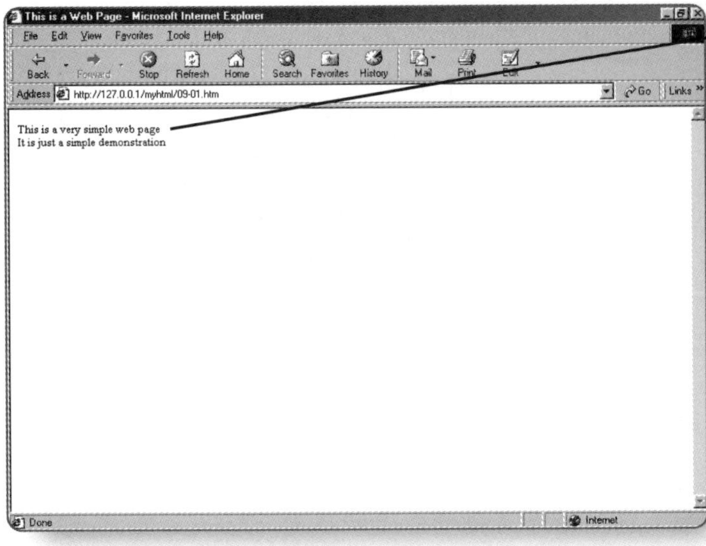

2. Re-save your file and double-click it again, or run it through the http address in your browser. Now you can see two separate lines of text.

 is one of the many simple HTML text-formatting commands. There are many others and you will see more of them as you continue through this chapter.

Spaces

The Web browser only notices the first space character it encounters. If you place three spaces between words, one space will be displayed but any subsequent spaces will be ignored. To overcome this problem you must enter an HTML *non-breaking space*. This is not an HTML tag, but an escape code:

```
 
```

It is called an *escape code* (or *escape sequence*) because it causes the system to escape from the current process, carry out the code, and then return to the system. The & character starts the escape and the semicolon signifies the end of the code.

You can group a number of ` ` codes together to move a piece of text further along a line, giving another form of simple text formatting. There are much better ways, but this method does have its uses.

Once again, modify your HTML code to add some ` ` escape codes.

1. Open the previous HTML page in your editor.

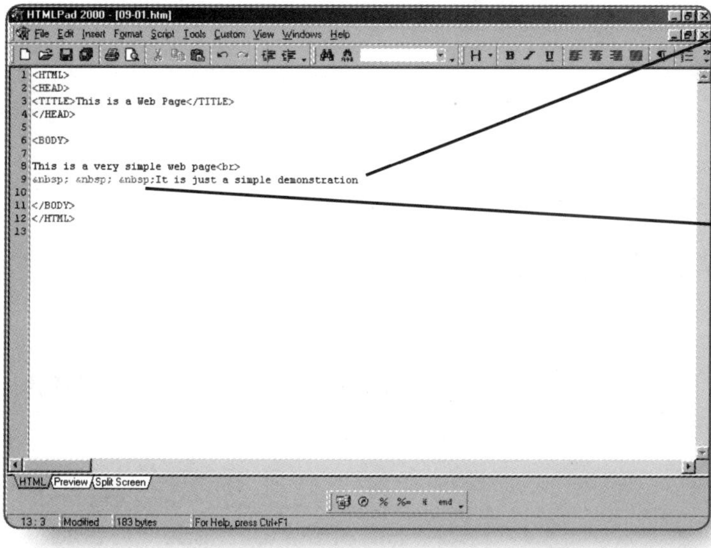

2. Locate the line that says this:

```
It is just a simple
   demonstration
```

3. Add three non-breaking spaces at the front of the line so that it looks like this:

```
     It is just
   a simple demonstration
```

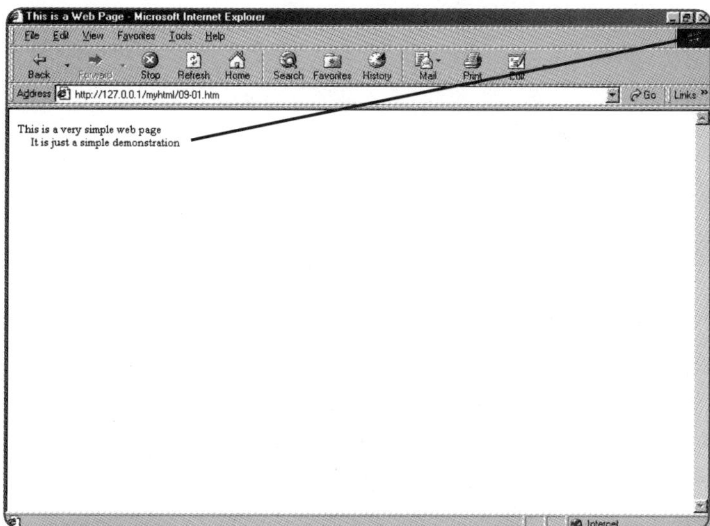

4. Save it again and observe the effect.

Three   codes have been added and each one gives a single space, so the second line of text is moved along by three spaces.

More Text Formatting

Okay, so now you can create a new document, give it a title, display text, force line breaks, and put larger gaps comprised of spaces into your HTML document.

Here are some more simple text formats you can use:

- **Bold** is achieved using the <B> tag and ends with the </B> tag.
- *Italics* are achieved using the <I> tag and ends with the </I> tag.
- Underline is achieved using the <U> tag and ends with the </U> tag.

You can combine any or all of these tags to combine the effect. So now you can make your test1.htm document look a bit more interesting.

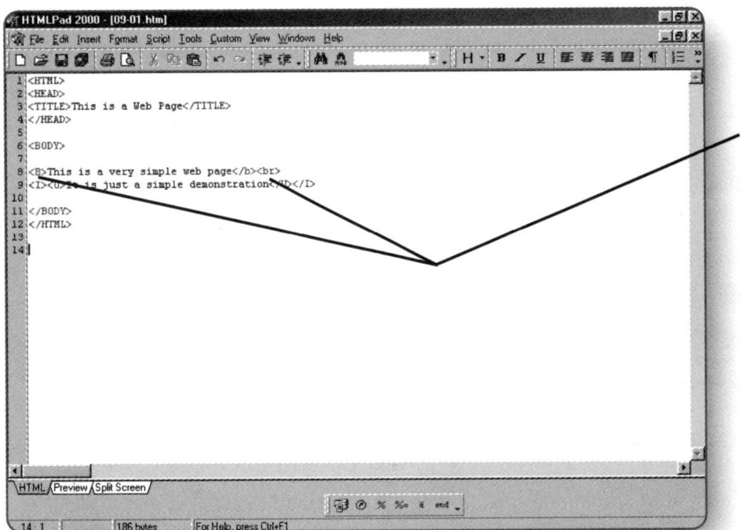

1. Modify the previous HTML file.

2. Add tags to make the first line of the text appear in bold text; do this by wrapping the line in <B> and </B> tags, like this:

```
<B>This is a very simple web
   page</B><BR>
```

NOTE

You still have the <BR> tag at the end of the line to give a line break. On the second line of text, add italic and underline effects by using the <I>...</I> and <U>...</U> tags respectively:

```
<I><U>It is just a simple demonstration</U></I>
```

There are no ` ` codes this time. This is just for clarity so that you can focus on the subject at hand. If you want to include them to see the effect, please do.

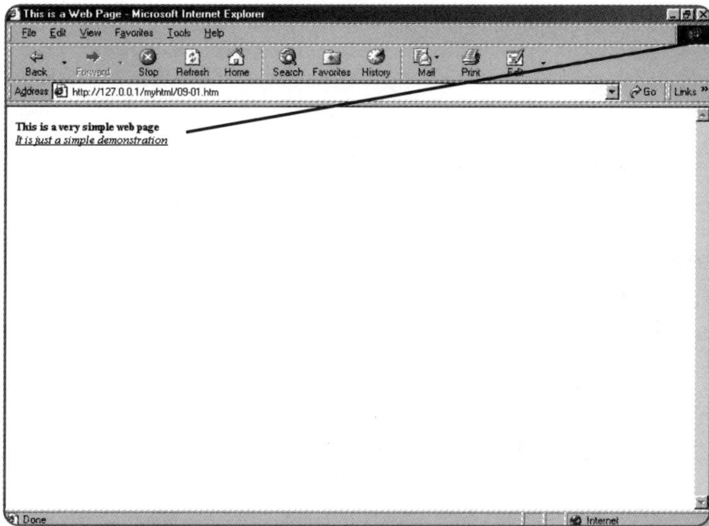

3. Save the modified file and view the effects.

It is normal to end tags in the reverse order to the way you started them. If you open the italic tag first, you close it last (as you have done above). But it is not mandatory to do this, and the browser will forgive you if you get the order wrong. However, it is good practice to get the order right, as it makes modifying or debugging the page much easier.

Adding Structure and Color

Web Pages were originally about text and then, later, images. Now however, Web pages are much more complex, and a wide variety of tags and associated attributes can be used to give your pages structure and color. Next, you will learn more about some of the most useful tags that add richness to your Web pages.

HTML Headings

What you have so far is all very well, but you still need to be able to add things like titles and, if you are to use the main advantage of the Web, you also need to be able to use hyperlinks.

Titles, or in HTML-speak *headings* or *headers*, are easily implemented using the <Hx> tags (where x = a number between one and six). <H1> is a start tag for the largest header. As usual, an end tag </H1> is placed after the heading text. Once again, an example will show the effect.

In your editor, open a new file and write a new HTML page.

1. Start the HTML page as you did before, with the header.

```
<HTML>
<HEAD>
<TITLE>This is the Title Example Page</TITLE>
</HEAD>
```

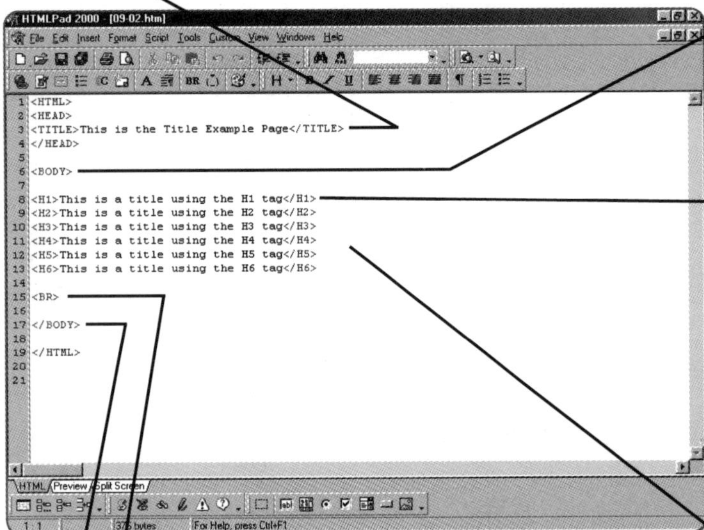

2. Now open the main <BODY> of the HTML page.

```
<BODY>
```

3. For this demonstration, you'll use header tags to create titles on the displayed page. <H1>...</H1> encloses a title when you want a large title:

```
<H1>This is a title using the
   H1 tag</H1>
```

4. As you go up through the numbers, the titles get smaller, with <H6> being the smallest. So now, code some more titles using all of the header tags through to <H6>.

```
<H2>This is a title using the H2 tag </H2>
<H3>This is a title using the H3 tag </H3>
<H4>This is a title using the H4 tag </H4>
<H5>This is a title using the H5 tag </H5>
<H6>This is a title using the H6 tag </H6>
```

5. Now use a <BR> tag to leave an empty line.

```
<BR>
```

6. Close the <BODY> tag using the </BODY> end tag.

```
</BODY>
```

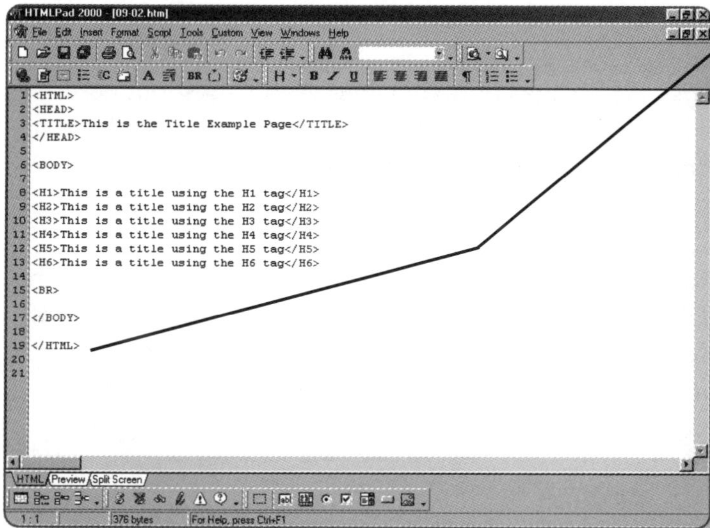

7. Close the HTML file using the </HTML> end tag.

```
</HTML>
```

8. Save it as 09-02.htm, or any other name you are happy with.

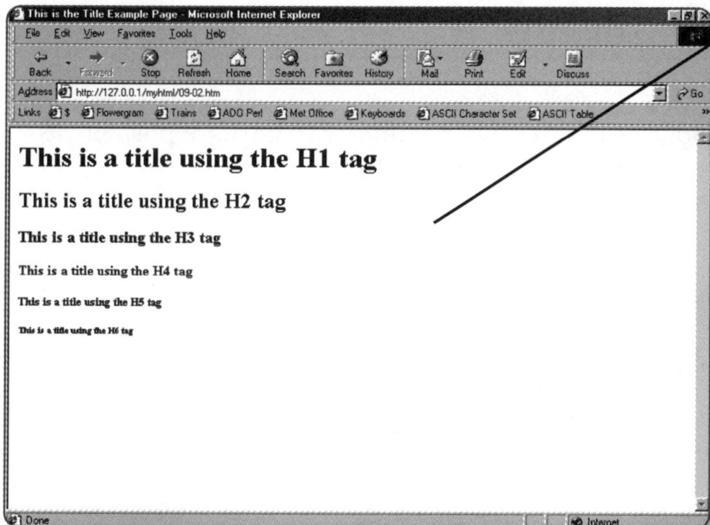

9. Now find your new file as you did with the last one, or double-click it; you should see something like this.

> **NOTE**
>
> <H1> tags can also be combined with most other text formatting tags to produce desired effects, such as the <B>, <I>, and <U> tags (just don't forget the end tags—</B>, </I> and <U>).

There are other tags that might also be combined, and more of these will be covered later.

Text Positioning

Now you can create headings for passages of text in your Web pages, but note that in the previous example, the titles are all left-justified, that is, they are lined up with the left hand edge of the page. Sometimes, you might want to have a title or heading that is centered on the page.

There are two ways of doing this—by using the <CENTER></CENTER> tags or the <DIV ALIGN=CENTER></DIV> tags. (The <DIV> tag can be used for a number of purposes but here is used for centering text). The <CENTER> tag is a deprecated tag, and it is therefore preferable to use the <DIV> tag.

> **NOTE**
>
> A *deprecated tag* is a tag that is now considered obsolete but is still supported by current versions of HTML and browsers but may be dropped from future versions.

Notice that here, the DIV tag uses the ALIGN= parameter to perform positioning. This can also be used to position text (or images) to the left or to the right. As you would expect, the tags then read as <DIV ALIGN=LEFT></DIV> or <DIV ALIGN=RIGHT>.

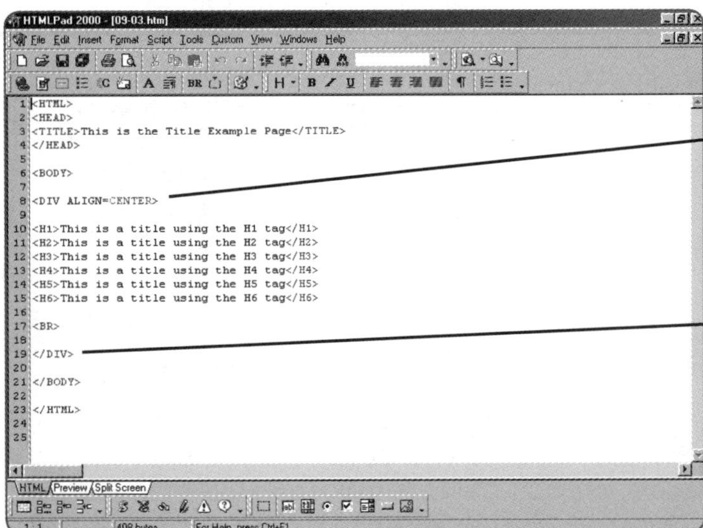

1. Re-open the previous HTML page.
2. Insert a <DIV ALIGN=CENTER> tag at the beginning of the <BODY> of the page.
3. Add an end </DIV> tag before the end of the <BODY>.

NOTE

The <DIV></DIV> tag can enclose one title or line of text or as many as you want so that you do not have enclose each line you want to be centered with separate <DIV></DIV tags.

4. Now save the page as 09-03.htm.

5. Open 09-03.htm in your browser.

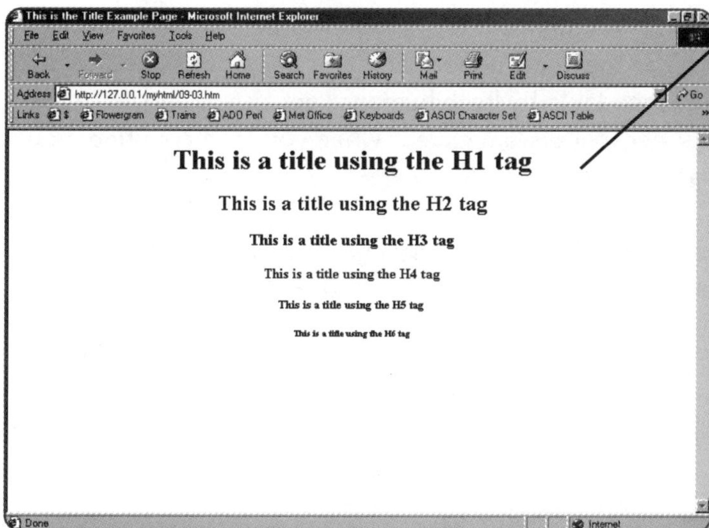

The lines of text are now centered on the page.

Now you are getting quite good at formatting and positioning text, but it still looks a bit bland! Next, you will take a quick look at adding some color to your pages.

Color

Now you can create HTML documents, you can create titles of different sizes and position them across the width of the page, and you can create text for the pages and render it bold, italicized, underlined, and so on. Unfortunately, it looks a bit boring because the text is all black on a white background. This would be even worse on some browsers, especially older ones, as the background will be gray.

But you can liven up your pages with a bit of color. The subject of color can be as simple or as complicated as you want to make it. You will see what I mean in a moment.

The Web, and in particular Web browsers, uses the RGB color system, as does your PC (usually). With this system, using a mixture of red, green, and blue colors in varying strengths makes all of the required colors available. The strength (or saturation) of each color is variable in 255 discrete steps. So, maximum saturation of red = 255, green = 255 , and blue = 255, gives white, and black is given by red = 0, green = 0 and blue = 0—it's rather like mixing paint at school.

A further complication is that computers often use a number representation known as *hexadecimal*. Humans count in multiples of ten, probably because we have ten fingers. Computers use *binary* as they only understand 1 or 0, on or off, and so on. Hexadecimal is a hybrid that is readable by both humans (just about) and computers. It is similar to our decimal system except when you start counting, you don't go into double figures until you reach 16.

To represent the digits greater than 9 you use A through F, so you count like this in Hex (as hexadecimal is abbreviated): 0, 1, 2, 3, 4, 5, 6, 7, 8, 9, A, B, C, D, F… .

Then it continues…10, 11, 12, 13, 14, 15, 16, 17, 18, 19, 1A, 1B, 1C, 1D, 1E, 1F…20, and so on.

Got the idea? (Don't worry if you haven't; you don't need to understand it unless you are interested, as you will see in a moment).

As I have said, white is represented by 255 red, 255 green, and 255 blue. In HTML you convert these numbers to Hex and join them all together. In Hex, 255 is represented as FF, so when you convert all three numbers and join them together, white becomes FFFFFF (3 FFs joined together, in the order red, green, blue).

HTML precedes these numbers with a # sign. This merely signifies that the number is in Hexadecimal. So now white is represented as #FFFFFF. Black is #000000. Bright yellow would be #FFFF00.

Note I said that you do not need to worry about the representation of colors using hexadecimal values. There are two main reasons for this.

- The Web browser is capable of displaying colors from a palette of 216 colors.
- Many HTML editors or other Web authoring tools have some kind of color palette that enables you to point and click to set colors.

Finally, many of the colors have been given names so that you can set colors using English names such as YELLOW and BLUE, and so on that then replace the #FFFF00 and #0000FF, respectively.

Okay, now that you know how to represent colors, let's try using them.

Backgrounds

Setting the background color of a document is achieved through the use of the BGCOLOR attribute of the <BODY> tag. Using what you have learned, you can now set the background color of the page.

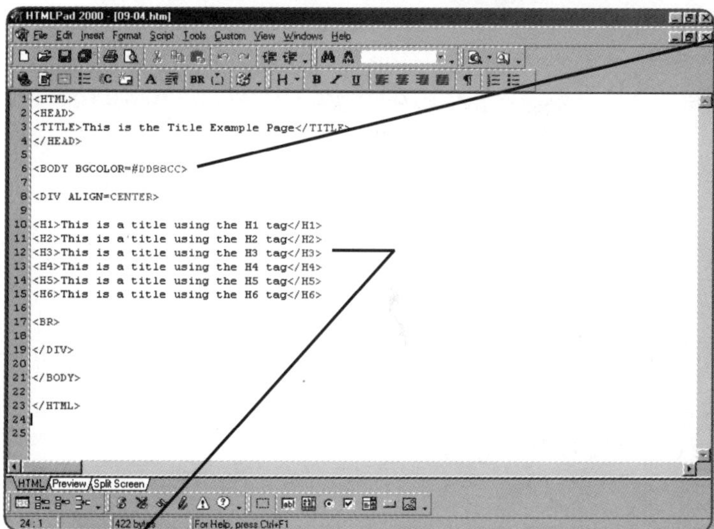

1. Modify the 09-03.htm listing to add the BGCOLOR attribute. This is done by simply inserting the BGCOLOR=xxxxxxx attribute to the <BODY> tag, like this:

```
<BODY BGCOLOR=#DD88CC>
```

NOTE

The hex characters after (#) character describe the color being used as three pairs of hex numbers, or you can use the color name without a hash sign.

2. The HTML for the modified page now looks like this.

NOTE

Notice that BGCOLOR is an attribute of a tag, and not a tag in its own right. Attributes modify the behavior of the tag they belong to and you will come across many more as you continue learning HTML.

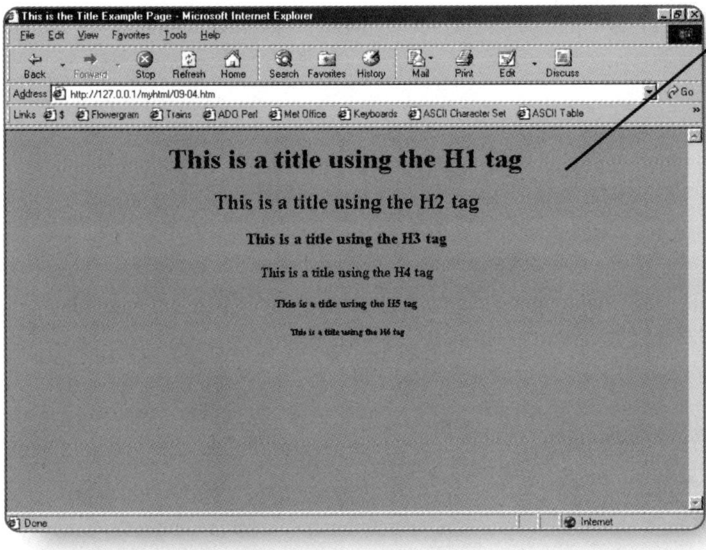

3. Save your modified 09-04.htm file and then find and open it again to observe the difference with your new background color. (Okay, you can't see the color in this book, but you should be able to see it in your browser.)

4. Experiment with changing the #xxxxxx numbers and see the difference. If you increase the first two digits, your background will be more red. If you increase the middle two digits there will be more green and of course, if you increase the last two digits there will be more blue. If you increase them all or decrease them all the color will get brighter or darker, respectively.

Background Images

You can also make the background even more interesting by using the BACKGROUND attribute of the <BODY> tag.

Try modifying the previous example to demonstrate the difference. Use a simple background texture graphic. In the example shown here, the graphic has been called bground.jpg.

The graphic does not have to be the size of the page—a small graphic will tile over the whole page. This enables you to fill the screen with a background graphic using a very small file, which means that it takes very little time to download to the browser. Graphics packages (such as Paint Shop Pro) are available that will enable you to produce seamless graphics so that when they tile on your page background they do not produce a horrible grid of joins.

Where before you put the BGCOLOR=#, put

```
BACKGROUND="bground.jpg"
```

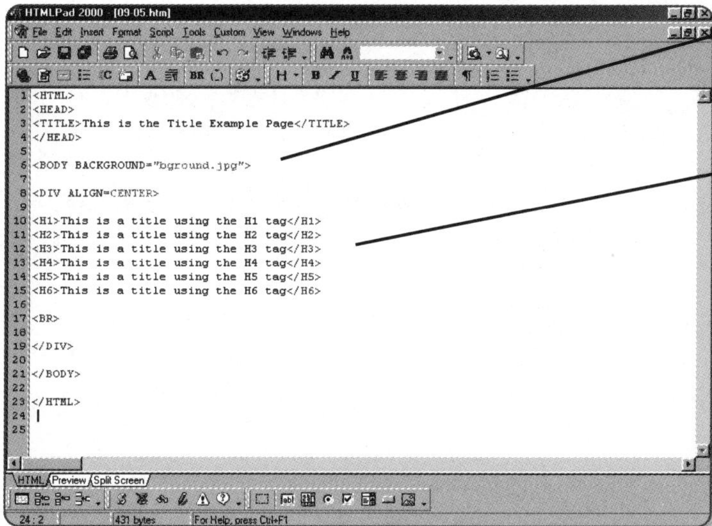

1. Enter the background HTML code into your editor in the <BODY> tag.

2. Your HTML should then look like this.

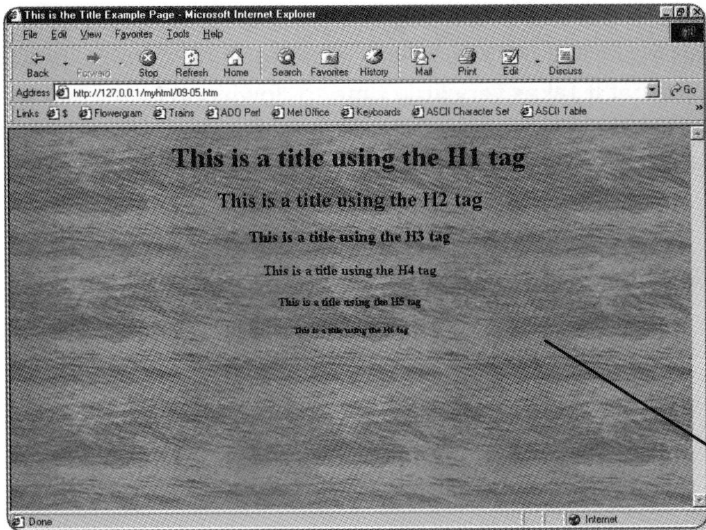

3. Save your HTML file as 09-05.htm and then test it in your browser.

Save whatever image you have decided to use into the same folder as your HTML as bground.jpg so that the BACKGROUND="bground.jpg" attribute of the BODY tag can find the graphic.

4. Your page should now look something like this.

You can also use this principle to produce some interesting effects that you have probably seen during your Web surfing.

For example, replace the graphic used above with one that looks like this (call it bground2.jpg and alter the BACKGROUND= attribute accordingly).

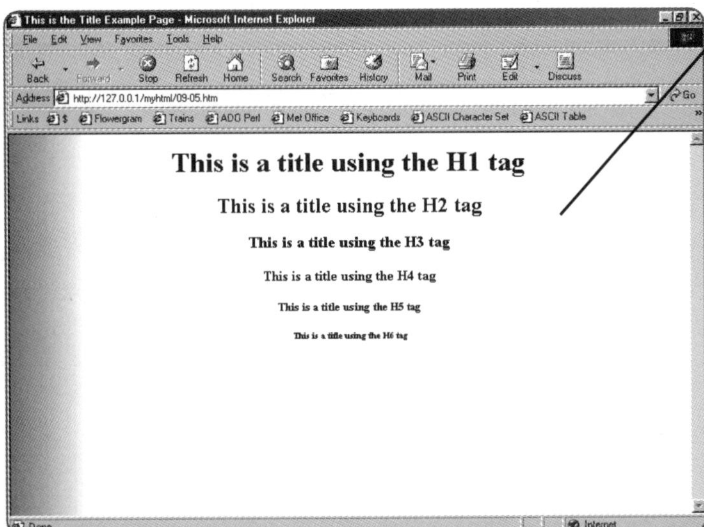

Your page now looks like this.

There are many other effects that might be achieved using similar techniques—experiment with some ideas of your own.

Fonts in HTML

So now you can set background colors and position headings of various sizes where you want them on the page. But what about "normal" text?

You can do a lot with that too, using the <FONT></FONT> tag. With <FONT> you can set the size, typeface, and color, and of course you can again combine the <FONT> tag with any of the other text formatting tags.

A typical font tag looks like this:

```
<FONT FACE=facename SIZE=n COLOR=#xxxxxx>here is some text</FONT>
```

Try modifying the previous HTML page to include some <FONT> settings; you can then combine them with some of the other tags you learned about earlier.

Here are some examples for you to add to your HTML page.

```
<FONT FACE="arial" SIZE="2" COLOR=#804040>This is funny reddish arial
text</FONT><BR>
<FONT FACE="Tahoma" SIZE="5" COLOR=#FF0000>This is red tahoma text</FONT><BR>
<FONT FACE="arial" SIZE="3" COLOR="#0000FF"><B>This is medium sized blue arial
bold text</B></FONT><BR>
<FONT FACE="Times New Roman" SIZE="1" COLOR="GREEN"><I>This is tiny green
Times New Roman italic text</I></FONT><BR>
<FONT FACE="arial" SIZE="7" COLOR=#000000><B><I>This is large black arial bold
italic text</I></B></FONT><BR>
<FONT FACE="Courier" SIZE="6" COLOR="White"><U>This is fairly large white
Courier underlined text</U></FONT><BR>
```

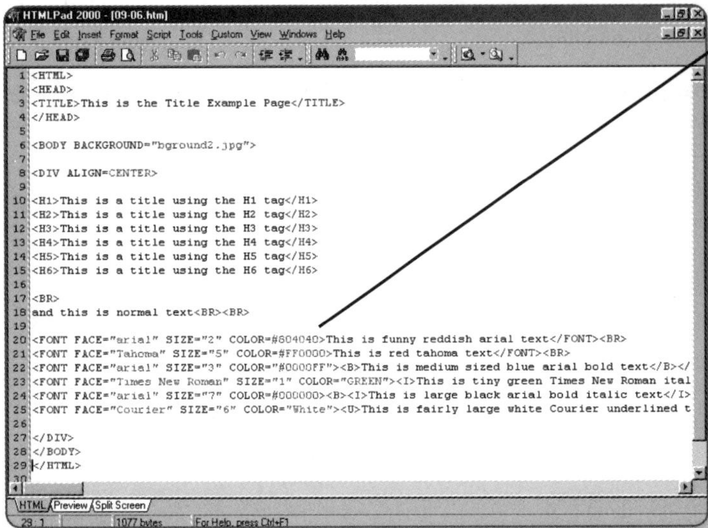

1. Insert the code into your HTML page so that it now looks like this.

2. Save it as 09-10.htm.

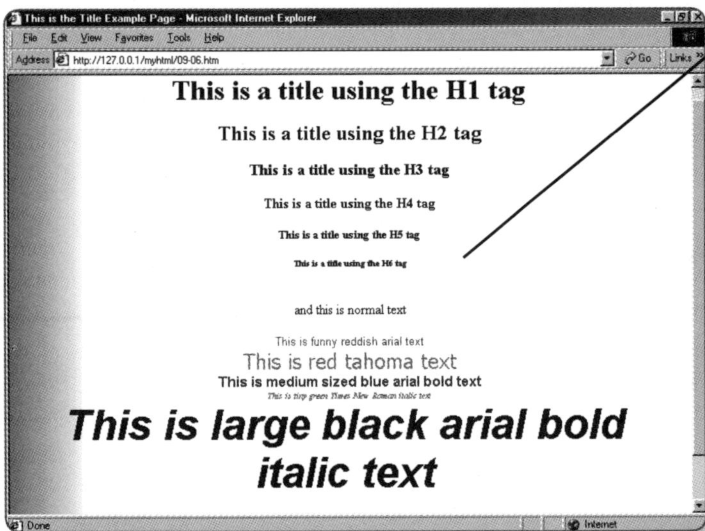

3. Take a look at it in your browser; it should look like this.

NOTE

A single <FONT></FONT> tag can be wrapped around many paragraphs of text. Also note that you lose sight of the white text, as it is on a largely white background.

The Horizontal Rule Tag

One other tag of interest at this point is the <HR> tag. HR stands for *horizontal rule*, and it gives a dividing line across the screen. It is not employed as often as it used to be because authors now favor more graphical methods, but it is useful as a simple page divider. Note that an end tag is not required.

Modify an earlier page to show what HR looks like (it doesn't matter which example you use, or whether you make up your own).

The horizontal rule tag can be a very simple tag, as shown here:

```
<HR>
```

Or you can add other attributes to it such as its width as a percentage, like this:

```
<HR WIDTH=75%>
```

And you can even add a color attribute like this:

```
<HR WIDTH=500 SIZE=5 COLOR="#804040">
```

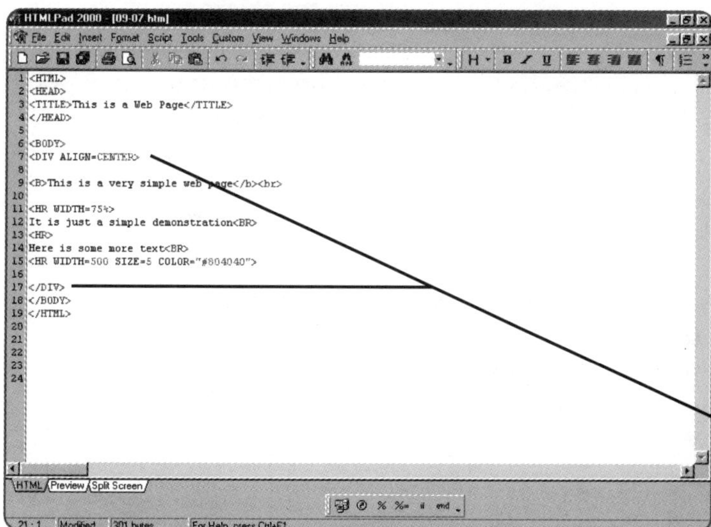

1. Add the following to the second sample Web page (09-02.htm):

```
<HR WIDTH=75%>
It is just a simple
   demonstration<BR>
<HR>
Here is some more text<BR>
<HR WIDTH=500 SIZE=5
   COLOR="#804040">
```

2. Also add <DIV ALIGN=CENTER> before the first line of text and </DIV> before the </BODY> tag.

3. Save this example as 09-07.htm.

NOTE

Notice that there are three examples in the previous listing. The first one states that the horizontal rule should be 75% of the width of the page. This means that the rule will adjust its width to always be 75% of the current width of the page, so that if you change the browser window size the width of the rule will change with it.

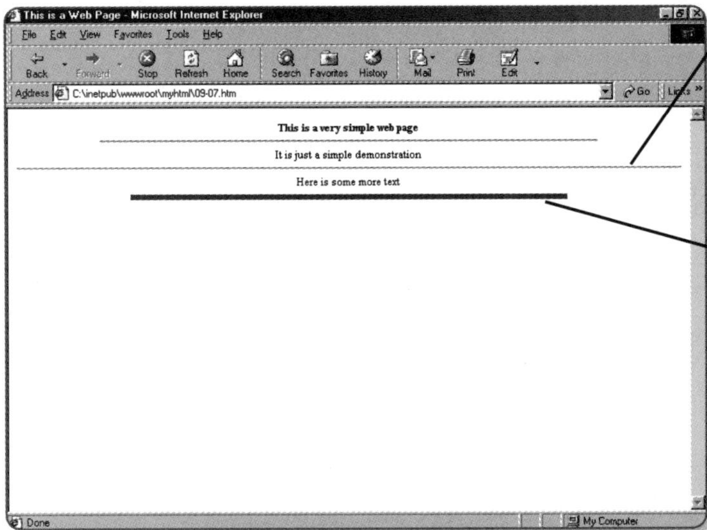

4. The second example in the listing is the simplest use of the <HR> tag. If it is used like this you will see a rule that occupies the full width of the page.

5. The third example also sets the width of the rule, but this time it is not a percentage for a value measured in pixels. The SIZE attribute is also set and affects the thickness of the rule. Finally you can also set the color using the same notation as you used for background color and font colors (#xxxxxx).

TIP

Drag the corner with your mouse and watch what happens to the width of the lines. Note that the 75% rules adjust themselves to maintain their width relative to that of the window.

The Paragraph Tag

The paragraph tag <P> is used to split up sections of text into paragraphs. It is preferable to the <BR> tag, which is used simply for breaking lines. The <P> tag has an end tag </P> and this should be used. Right now you might be able to get away with not using it, but it is meant to be there, and there is no guarantee that future browsers will not insist on it being present. Anyway, it helps keep your HTML tidy, so use it!

Here is a simple example of the paragraph tag.

1. Open a new HTML file in your editor.

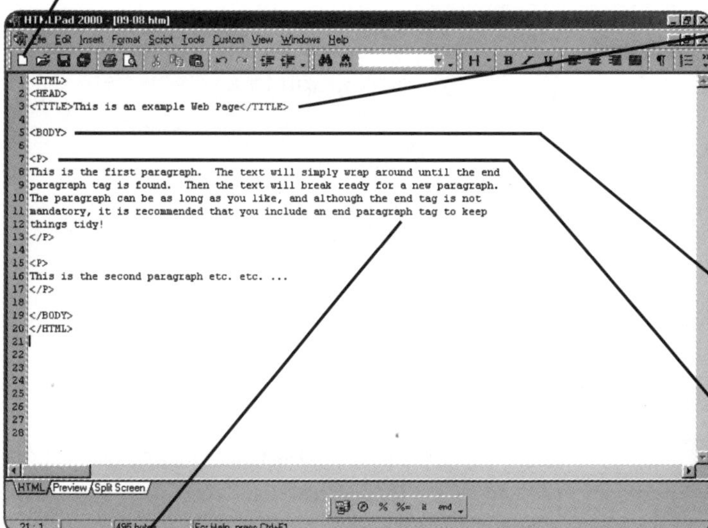

2. Create the usual opening <HTML> and <HEAD> tags.

```
<HTML>
<HEAD>
<TITLE>This is an example Web
   Page</TITLE>
```

3. Open a <BODY> tag.

```
<BODY>
```

4. Open a paragraph tag like this:

```
<P>
```

5. Now enter some text:

```
This is the first paragraph. The text will simply wrap around until the end
paragraph tag is found. Then the text will break ready for a new paragraph.
The paragraph can be as long as you like, and although the end tag is not
mandatory, it is recommended that you include an end paragraph tag to keep
things tidy!
```

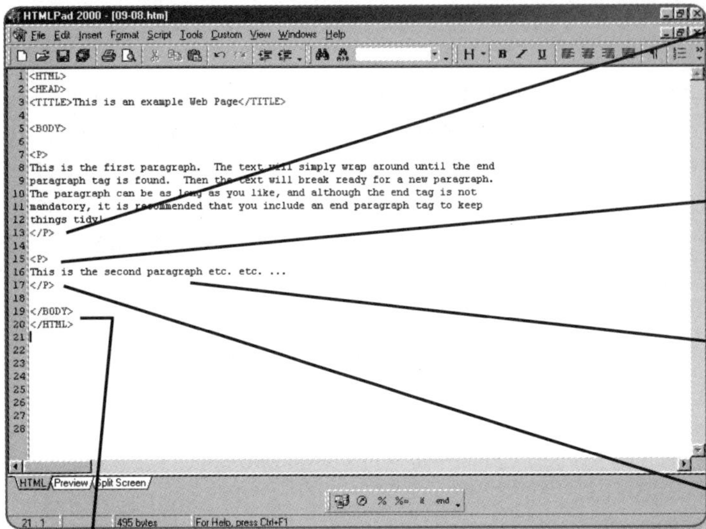

6. Now close the paragraph tag.

```
</P>
```

7. Open a new paragraph tag.

```
<P>
```

8. And add some more text.

```
This is the second paragraph
   etc. etc. ...
```

9. And of course, close the paragraph tag.

```
</P>
```

10. Finally, as usual, close the <BODY> and <HTML> tags.

```
</BODY>
</HTML>
```

11. Save your HTML as 09-08.htm.

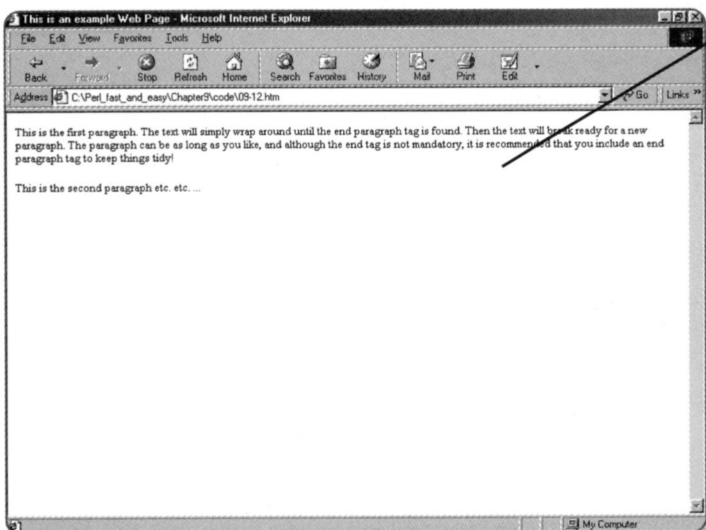

12. The resulting page will look like this.

Images

In addition to text, a Web page can also hold pictures, sound, video, and almost anything you want. Right now, you can find out more about images and using them in your Web pages. Web browsers normally support two image formats, the JPEG and the GIF image.

JPEG Files

JPEG files are very good where there are lots of colors, such as in photographs, as they can achieve a high degree of compression so that the file size is reduced and the time taken to download them is shorter.

GIF Files

The GIF format was developed by the ISP CompuServe and has become a popular image standard. It achieves a degree of compression by limiting the maximum number of colors to 256. GIF images are better where there are fewer colors in an image. It is possible to remove all unused colors to reduce the file size and download time.

There is a new image format (PNG) that seemed likely to rise to prominence in the near future, but so far has failed to catch on. You don't need to worry about that here. In any event, the same principle will apply in so far as Web pages are concerned.

Let's add an image to a Web page. Create a new Web page for this example; keep it nice and simple.

You can use an image like this one. (Create or use one of your own, or borrow one from another Web site, just to try it out.)

1. Create a new HTML page.

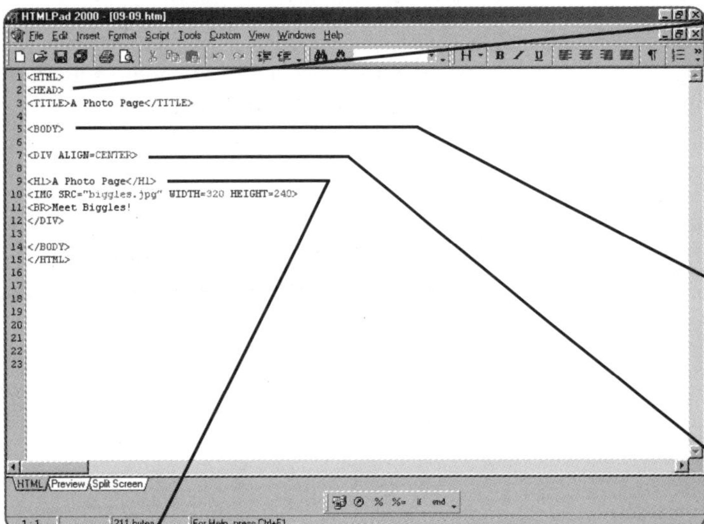

2. Create the <HEAD> section as you did before.

```
<HTML>
<HEAD>
<TITLE>A Photo Page</TITLE>
</HEAD>
```

3. Now create the <BODY> section.

```
<BODY>
```

4. Use the <DIV> HTML tag to (in this case) center anything inside it and the </DIV> tag.

```
<DIV ALIGN=CENTER>
```

5. Create a heading on the page using the <H1> tag.

```
<H1>A Photo Page</H1>
```

6. Now display an image.

```
<IMG SRC="biggles.jpg"  WIDTH=400 HEIGHT=486>
```

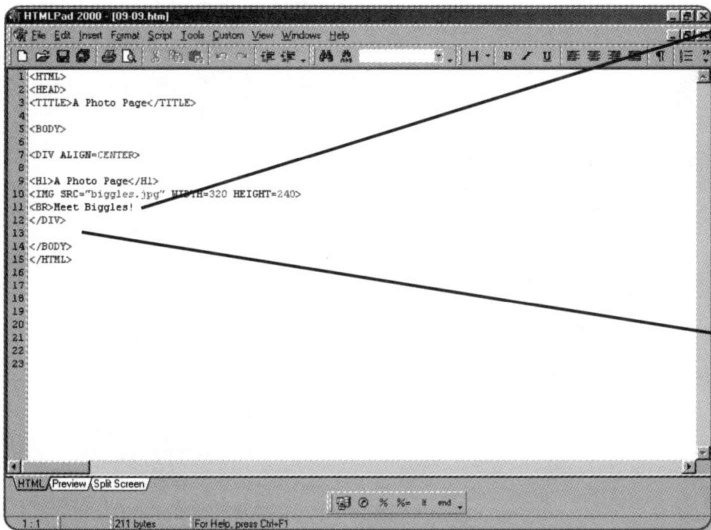

7. Use a break tag <BR> to move down one line.

```
<BR>
```

8. Enter some text.

```
Meet Biggles!
```

9. Then close the <DIV> tag, the <BODY> tag, and the <HTML> tag.

```
</DIV>
</BODY>
</HTML>
```

10. Save your HTML as 09-09.htm.

11. Use a photograph of your own and change the name accordingly in the `SRC=` attribute. (And don't forget to put the image in the same folder as your HTML.)

12. Now load 09-09.htm into your browser.

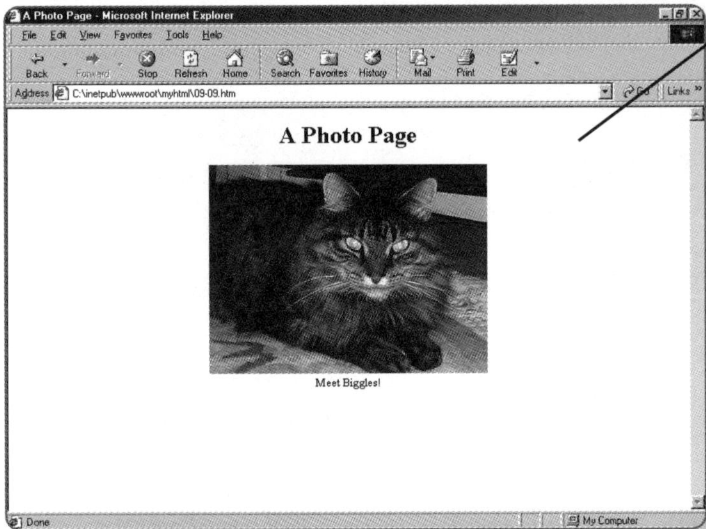

13. You should have something like this.

There are a couple of things to note here. The `SRC=` attribute gives the name of the file and the path to the file if it is not in the same folder as the HTML file. The image file could even be at another location, in which case you could give the full URL. If the image file is in a folder called Images below the current folder (that is, below the folder the HTML file is in), you would specify the `SRC` attribute as:

```
Images/biggles.jpg
```

If your Images folder is stored above the current folder you would denote this as

```
../images/biggles.jpg
```

If the Images folder were right at the top of the site, you would indicate this by

```
/images/biggles.jpg
```

All this might seem a little confusing, but you will come across it again when you learn about hyperlinks, and you will find it gets clearer as you go along.

Hyperlinks

You will shortly be learning about frames. Before you do, you need to understand hyperlinks, because frames are pretty useless without them. Indeed, the whole Internet would cease to exist without hyperlinks (sometimes called *hypertext links*)

Linking pages is very simple; you use *anchor* tags to accomplish it. The anchor tag looks like this:

```
<A HREF="http://www.microsoft.com">Go to the Microsoft Home Page</A>
```

This anchor tag shows the text "Go to the Microsoft Home Page." When displayed on the Web page it is (usually) colored blue and underlined to show that it is a hyperlink. You can set the color of the link text in the <BODY> tag. (HREF stands for hypertext reference).

You can use images instead of the link text shown in the previous example.

```
<A HREF="http://www.microsoft.com"><IMG SRC=image1.jpg WIDTH="30"
HEIGHT="10" BORDER ="0"></A>
```

> **NOTE**
>
> The `BORDER= "0"` attribute is used to prevent a box being displayed around the image.

Linking within a Page

You can link to a location within a page by using the anchor `NAME` attribute.

```
<A HREF=#placename</A>
```

Lower in the page you must put an anchor name tag.

```
<A NAME=placename>
```

You can also jump to a location within another page by combining the URL type HREF and the "place name," or anchor name.

```
<A HREF="http://www.mydomain.com/index.htm#location2">Go to the Microsoft Home
Page</A>
```

This will cause index.htm to be loaded and to be immediately scrolled down the place in the page containing the <A NAME=location1> tag.

Try this simple hypertext link demonstration.

1. Create an HTML page using the usual <HEAD> tags and so on and with an appropriate title.

```
<HTML>
<HEAD>
        <TITLE>Hyperlink Test Page</TITLE>
</HEAD>
```

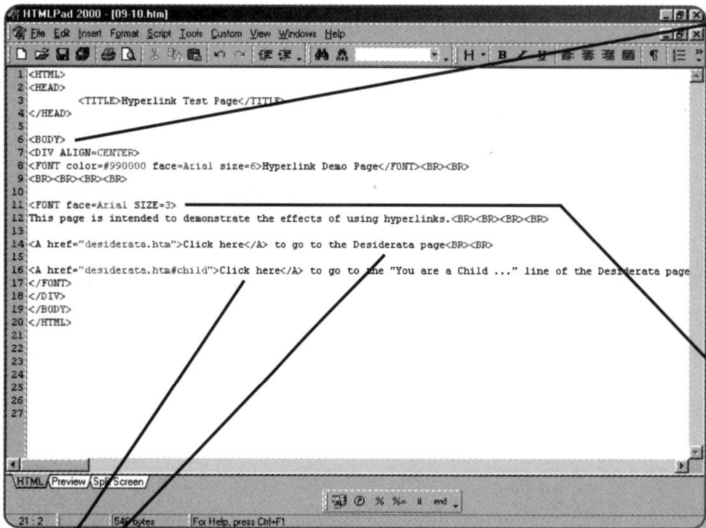

2. Start the <BODY> section of the page, using a suitable header title.

```
<BODY>
<DIV ALIGN=CENTER>
<FONT color=#990000 face=Arial
   size=6>Hyperlink Demo
   age</FONT><BR><BR>
<BR><BR><BR><BR>
```

3. Set the font for any following text:

```
<FONT face=Arial SIZE=3>
This page is intended to
   demonstrate the effects of
   using hyperlinks.<BR><BR>
   <BR><BR>
```

4. Now code an anchor tag pointing to another page called Desiderata.htm.

```
<A href="desiderata.htm">Click here</A> to go to the Desiderata page<BR><BR>
```

5. Code another anchor, this time pointing to a place within the Desiderata.htm page.

```
<A href="desiderata.htm#child">Click here</A> to go to the "You are a Child
..." line of the Desiderata page<BR><BR>
```

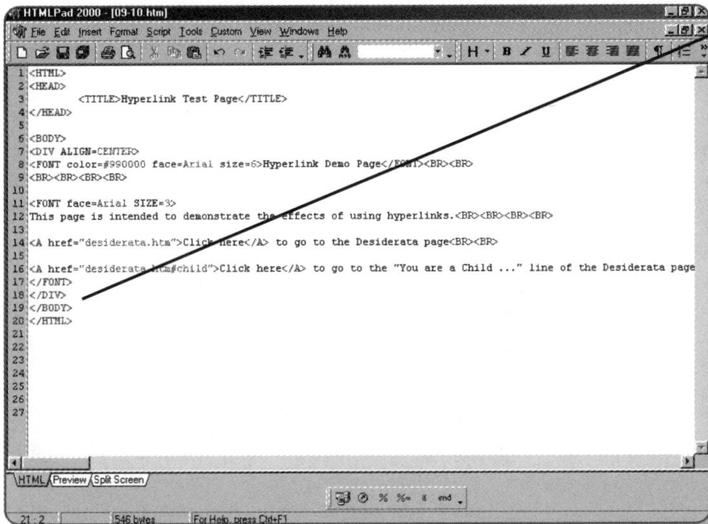

6. Tidy up by closing the <FONT>, <DIV>, <BODY>, and <HTML> tags.

```
</FONT>
</DIV>
</BODY>
</HTML>
```

7. Save the listing as 09-10.htm.

8. Now type the following listing into your editor (It's *The Desiderata*, by Max Ehrmann):

```
<HTML>
<HEAD>
<TITLE>The Desiderata</TITLE>
</HEAD>
<BODY ALINK=FUCHSIA BGCOLOR=#C8FFFF LINK=BLUE VLINK=BLUE>
<H1 ALIGN=CENTER>
<FONT FACE="arial" COLOR=#cc3333>The Desiderata<BR></font>
</H1>
<BR>
<DIV ALIGN=CENTER>
<FONT FACE="arial" SIZE=3>
Go placidly amid the noise and haste, and remember what peace there may be in
silence. <BR><BR>
As far as possible, without surrender, be on good terms with all persons.
<BR><BR>
Speak your truth quietly and clearly; and listen to others,<BR><BR>
even to the dull and ignorant; they too have their story.<BR><BR>
Avoid loud and aggressive persons; they are vexations to the spirit.<BR><BR>
If you compare yourself with others, you may become vain or bitter,<BR><BR>
for always there will be greater and lesser persons than yourself.<BR><BR>
Enjoy your achievements as well as your plans. <BR><BR>
Keep interested in your own career, however humble, <BR><BR>
it's a real possession in the changing fortunes of time.<BR><BR>
Exercise caution in your business affairs, for the world is full of trickery.
<BR><BR>
```

```
But let this not blind you to what virtue there is; <BR><BR>
many persons strive for high ideals, and everywhere life is full of heroism.
<BR><BR>
Be yourself. <BR><BR>
Especially do not feign affection. Neither be cynical about love; <BR><BR>
for in the face of all aridity and disenchantment,<BR><BR>
it is as perennial as the grass.<BR><BR>
Take kindly the counsel of the years, <BR><BR>
gracefully surrendering the things of youth.<BR><BR>
Nurture strength of spirit to shield you in sudden misfortune. <BR><BR>
But do not distress yourself with dark imaginings. <BR><BR>
Many fears are born of fatigue and loneliness. <BR><BR>
Beyond a wholesome discipline, be gentle with yourself. <BR><BR>
<A NAME=child>You are a child</a> of the universe no less than the trees and
the stars; <BR><BR>
you have a right to be here. <BR><BR>
And whether or not it is clear to you, <BR><BR>
no doubt the universe is unfolding as it should. <BR><BR>
Therefore be at peace with God, whatever you conceive him to be. <BR><BR>
And whatever your labours and aspirations, in the noisy confusion of
life,<BR><BR>
keep peace in your soul. <BR><BR>
With all its sham, drudgery and broken dreams, it is still a beautiful world.
<BR><BR>
Be cheerful. Strive to be happy.
<BR><BR>
</FONT>
</DIV>
</BODY>
</HTML>
```

9. Note the <A NAME=child> tag. This is where the second link in the previous HTML page will link to.

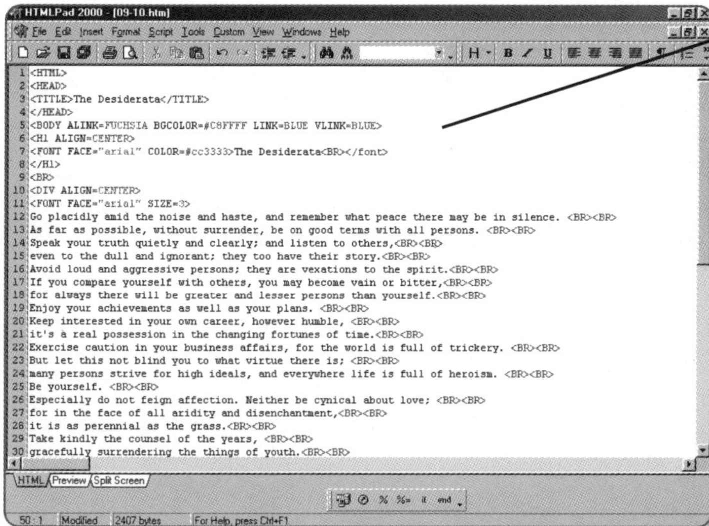

10. The HTML code should look like this in your editor.

11. Save the listing as desiderata.htm.

12. Now open 09-10.htm in your browser and test the links to see the effects.

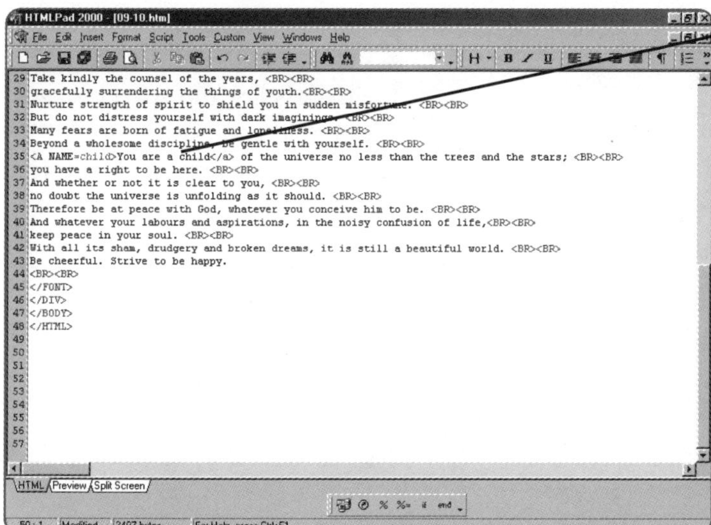

13. Note that the second link should take you straight down to the "You are a child…" line.

14. Try adding a link at the bottom of desiderata.htm to take you back to 09-10.htm.

15. Then try adding a link at the bottom of desiderata.htm back to the top of the page. (You will need a new <A NAME= tag.)

Finally, you can also direct the link to open a new browser window for the new page by using the TARGET attribute.

The TARGET attribute has a number of predefined values that can be used. For the time being, just use the "_new" attribute.

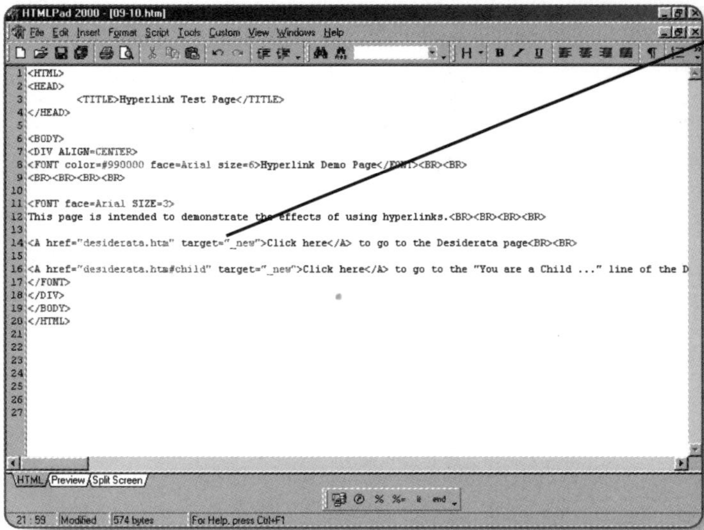

1. Modify 09-10.htm adding

`target="_new"`

in both the <A HREF=... tags so that the listing looks like this.

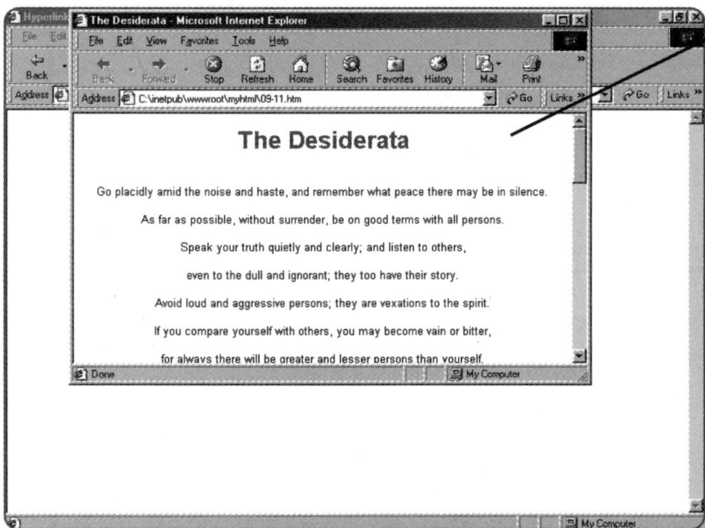

2. Test the 09-10.htm page again and click the third link—you should see desiderata.htm open in a new window like this.

> **NOTE**
>
> You can use the attribute `_blank` instead of `_new`–it has the same effect.

That's all on hyperlinks for the time being, but you will be using them again shortly during our discussion on frames.

Frames

Before you start, a warning: use frames sparingly—they can make your site slower to load and they don't always look the same in all browsers. However they do have their uses. The most common purpose is to aid navigation.

You have seen Web sites where you have a menu of options down the left side and perhaps a banner at the top of the screen. If you find that when you scroll down the main screen the left side menu doesn't move, this site has probably been created using frames.

Frames (or "framesets," as collections of frames are called) are not part of any of the pages that you normally see. Rather, they are a container for the other frames that contain, for example, the menu banner and the main page that displays the site content pages selected from the menu. Such an arrangement then looks like this.

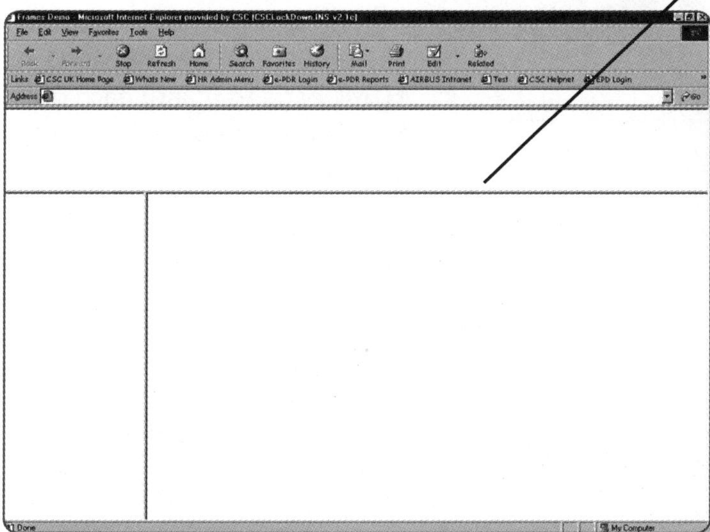

Of course, this is only one option. You can create frame layouts of any type you want to set up, but this is one of the most commonly used.

NOTE

If you created a page that described the above layout and then tried to view it in a browser, you would see nothing. As I have already said, the frame page merely describes the frame layout that will contain the pages that fit into each frame. Those pages are set up separately as conventional HTML pages and are then loaded into the required frame.

In summary, a *frameset* is a collection of frames designed to contain HTML pages, which are then displayed as one page in the browser.

Frame Tags

There can be several frames in a frameset but more than two or three becomes impractical. For each frame, you specify the size of the frame. The frames effectively divide up the page area that you see in the browser. This is achieved by specifying the width or height of each frame.

To get the frames to look like you want them to appear can be difficult at first, but it is logical. Honestly.

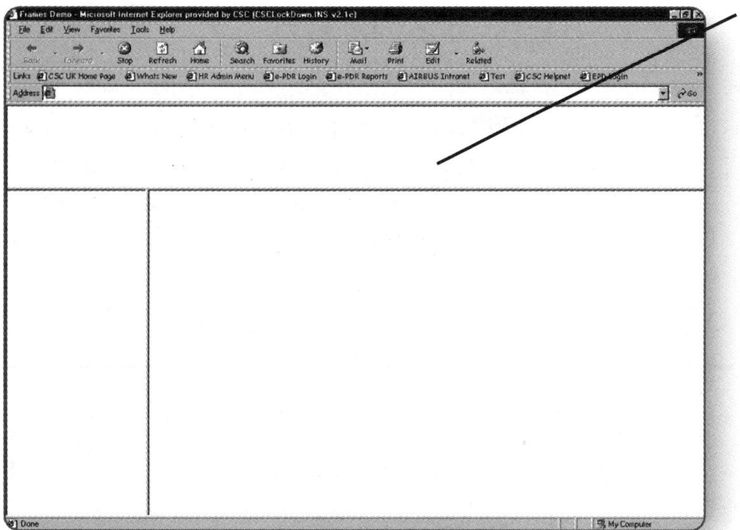

Let's copy the earlier "typical" frame design.

Remember that you will need an HTML page to fit into each of the above frames. To fit in with the scheme, you can call them Banner.htm, Menu.htm, and Page1.htm.

The coding needed to produce the frames page to achieve the layout is as follows:

```
<HTML>
<HEAD>
<TITLE>Frames Demo</TITLE>
</HEAD>
<FRAMESET ROWS="20%,80%" COLS="*" FRAMEBORDER="0">
<FRAME SRC="banner.htm" NAME="banner">
<FRAMESET COLS="20%,80%" ROWS="*">
<FRAME SRC="menu.htm" name="menu">
<FRAME SRC="page1.htm" name="main">
```

```
</FRAMESET>
</FRAMESET>
<NOFRAMES><BODY BGCOLOR="#FFFFFF">
Sorry, Your browser does not support frames.
</BODY></NOFRAMES>
</HTML>
```

1. Copy this into your editor.

2. Save it as framedemo.htm.

3. Open the file in your browser in the usual way.

4. When you open it in your browser you will see the three frames that you expected, but they will all be displaying 404—Not Found messages because the HTML pages to fit into each frame have not yet been written.

This code might need some explanation.

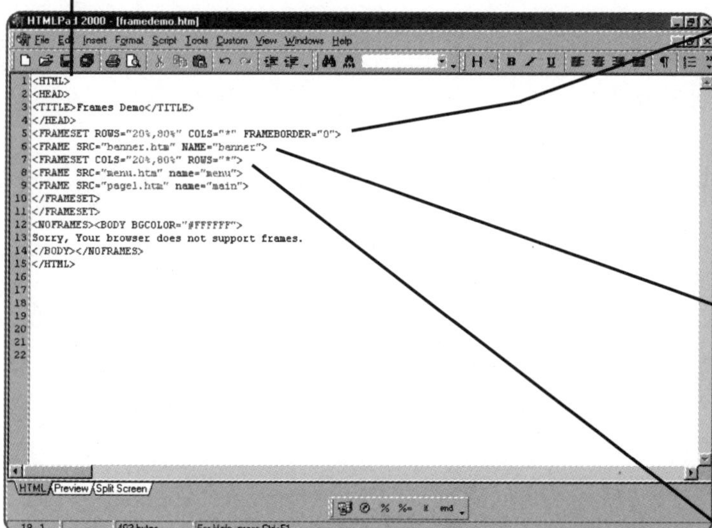

5. The first FRAMESET tag says create two FRAMES as "rows" (that is, split the screen horizontally) and make the first row (the upper one) 20 percent of the page height, and the second (lower) row 80 percent.

6. The next tag is a FRAME tag and it is describing what the first (20 percent) frame should contain—an HTML page called banner.htm.

7. The next tag will describe what goes into the lower (80 percent) frame.

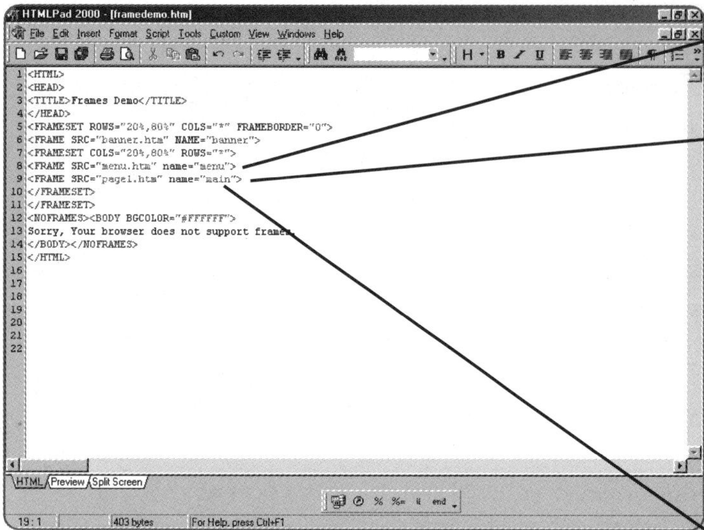

8. In this case it is another FRAMESET tag.

9. This new FRAMESET tag is this time splitting the lower 80 percent of the frame into two further frames. Notice that this time the FRAMESET is a COLS frameset, so you are going to split the lower 80 percent vertically. The left-hand frame is 20 percent wide and the right-hand frame is 80 percent.

10. The left-hand frame is to contain a page called menu.htm, and the right-hand frame will contain a page called main.htm.

11. Notice that the COLS attribute in the first FRAMESET is set to *, which means ALL or in this case the whole width. Similarly, the second FRAMESET has ROWS set to *, the whole height.

Try changing the values of the numbers in the FRAMESET tags to observe the effect.

Try replacing the * values in the ROWS and COLS attributes with numbers and see what you get.

Now add additional numbers separated by commas to the FRAMESET attributes.

```
<FRAMESET ROWS="100,500,100" COLS="100,200">
```

Also, note that although here the values are specified as a numbers of pixels, you can also use percentage values.

```
<FRAMESET ROWS="10%, 90%" COLS="*
>
```

Now let's put something into the frames.

For this demo, you will need to build five pages.

1. You should already have the framedemo page. If not, copy the following into your editor and save it as framedemo.htm.

```
<HTML>
<HEAD>
<TITLE>Frames Demo</TITLE>
</HEAD>
<FRAMESET ROWS="20%,80%" COLS="*" FRAMEBORDER="0">
<FRAME SRC="banner.htm" NAME="banner">
<FRAMESET COLS="20%,80%" ROWS="*">
<FRAME SRC="menu.htm" name="menu">
<FRAME SRC="page1.htm" name="main">
</FRAMESET>
</FRAMESET>
<NOFRAMES><BODY BGCOLOR="#FFFFFF">
Sorry, Your browser does not support frames.
</BODY></NOFRAMES></HTML>
```

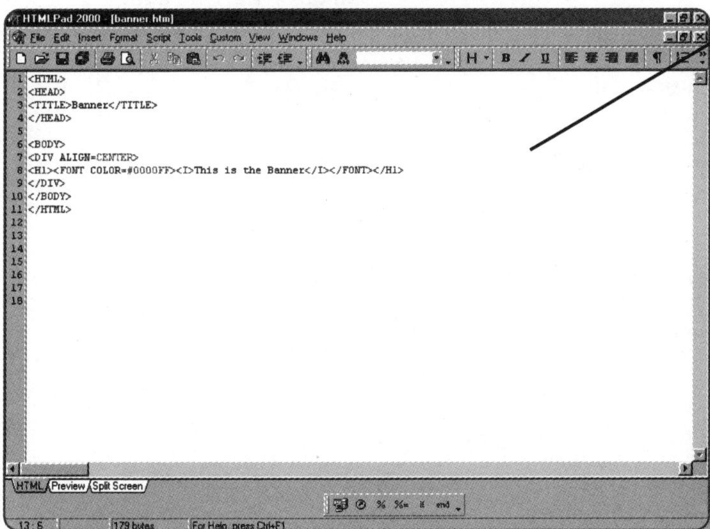

2. For the banner, copy this listing into your editor and save it as banner.htm.

```
<HTML>
<HEAD>
<TITLE>Banner</TITLE>
</HEAD>

<BODY>
<DIV ALIGN=CENTER>
<H1><FONT
COLOR=#0000FF><I>This is the
Banner</I></FONT></H1>
</DIV>
</BODY>
</HTML>
```

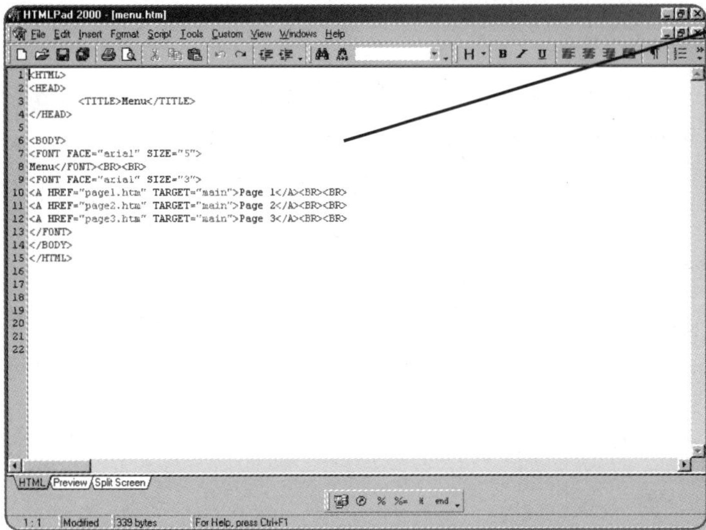

3. For the menu page, copy this listing into your editor and save it as menu.htm.

```
<HTML>
<HEAD>
        <TITLE>Menu</TITLE>
</HEAD>

<BODY>
<FONT FACE="arial" SIZE="5">
Menu</FONT><BR><BR>
<FONT FACE="arial" SIZE="3">
<A HREF="page1.htm"
   TARGET="main">Page
   1</A><BR><BR>
<A HREF="page2.htm"
   TARGET="main">Page
   2</A><BR><BR>
<A HREF="page3.htm"
   TARGET="main">Page
   3</A><BR><BR>
</FONT>
</BODY>
</HTML>
```

NOTE

Notice the TARGET attributes—this means open the page in the frame called "main," the main window. Of course, this name can be anything you want it to be.

And now, three pages to go into the main window.

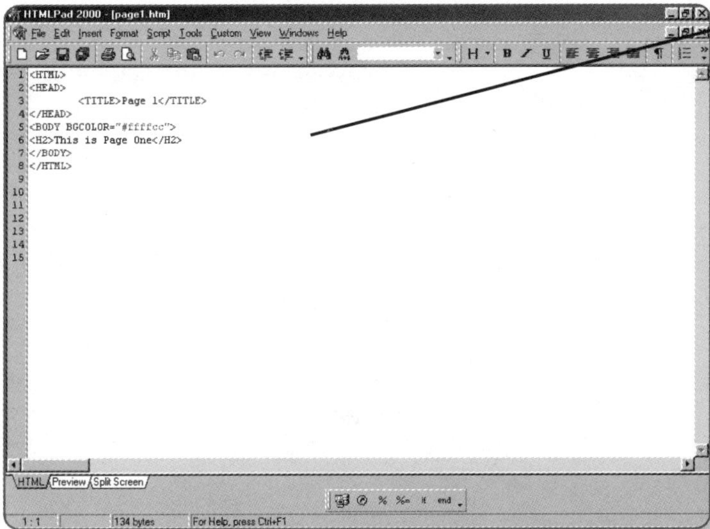

4. For page 1, copy this listing into your editor and save it as page1.htm.

```
<HTML>
<HEAD>
        <TITLE>Page 1</TITLE>
</HEAD>
<BODY BGCOLOR="#ffffcc">
<H2>This is Page One</H2>
</BODY>
</HTML>
```

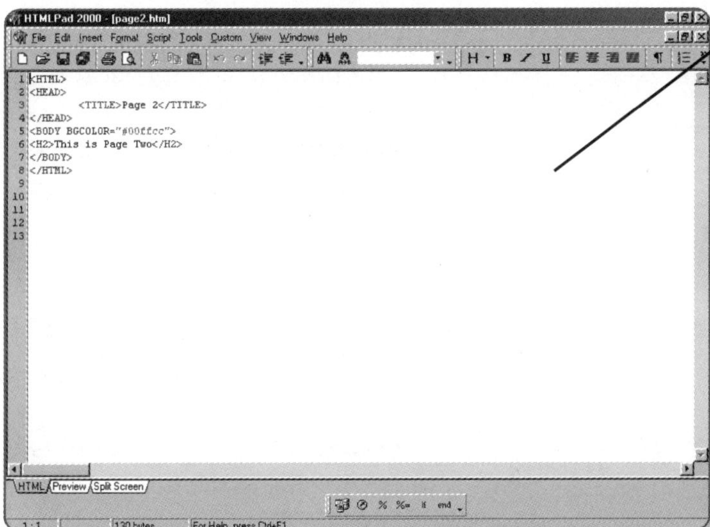

5. For page 2, type this listing into your editor and save it as page2.htm.

```
<HTML>
<HEAD>
    <TITLE>Page 2</TITLE>
</HEAD>
<BODY BGCOLOR="#00ffcc">
<H2>This is Page Two</H2>
</BODY>
</HTML>
```

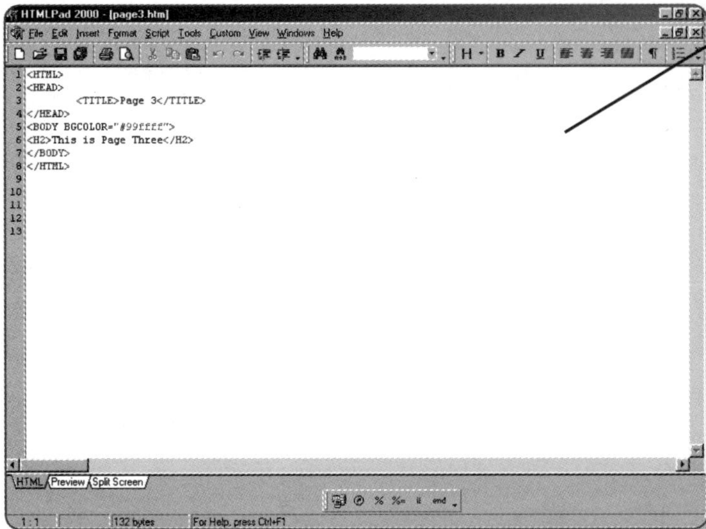

6. For page 3, type this listing into your editor and save it as page3.htm.

```
<HTML>
<HEAD>
    <TITLE>Page 3</TITLE>
</HEAD>
<BODY BGCOLOR="#99ffff">
<H2>This is Page Three</H2>
</BODY>
</HTML>
```

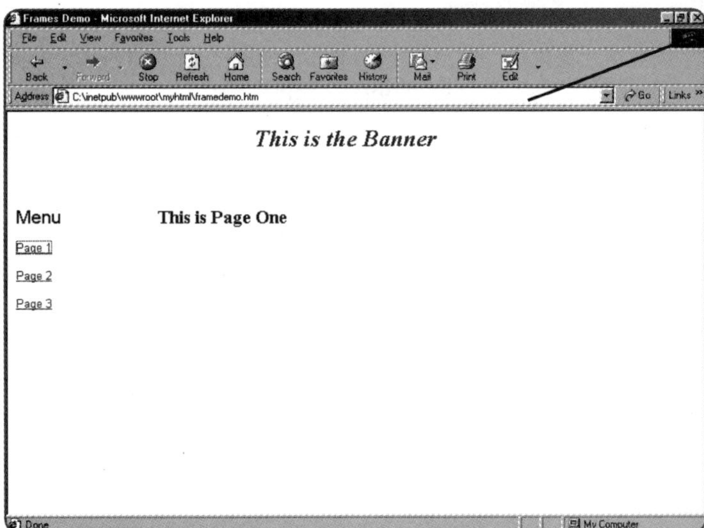

Now, load framedemo.htm into your browser and try out the links on the left—you should see the pages in the main window change as you click the links in the left menu window.

Sometimes you might not want to see the lines that separate the windows or frames—you can remove these using the FRAMEBORDER="0" attribute. Try modifying the first FRAMESET tag in framedemo.htm so that it looks like this:

```
<FRAMESET ROWS="20%,80%" COLS="*" FRAMEBORDER="0">
```

8. Save it and try again.

9. Re-open the page; the lines should have disappeared.

That's enough on frames to get you started.

A couple of major components of HTML, forms and tables, have been omitted. You will learn about these as you learn about writing Web applications.

10

CGI Programming

Remember right back at the beginning, in Chapter 1, when you installed your Web server and tested it? Now it is time to start using it.

In this chapter you will:

- Learn what CGI is and what you can do with it
- Try your first Perl CGI Program
- Use HTML forms

What Is CGI?

Let's have a quick overview of what the Web server does. Normally, the Web server receives a *request*, as it is known, from the user's Web browser. That is, the user requests a page from a Web site. The Web server receives the request, finds the page, and returns it to the browser. The browser renders the page using the HTML tags we talked about earlier to format the page on the user's screen.

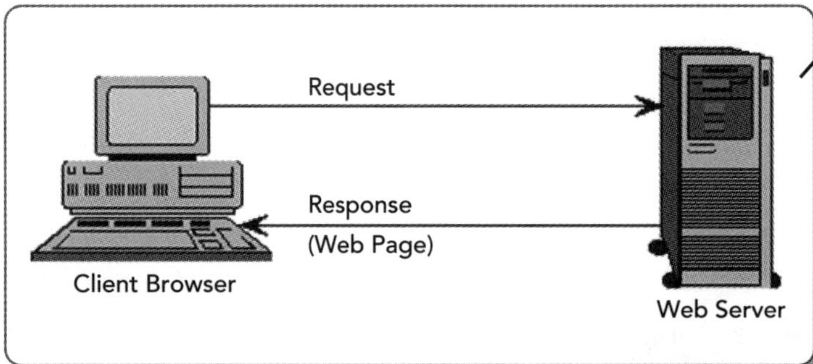

The setup then is a bit like this.

This is fine for HTML pages, but what happens when you want your Web page to use a Perl program to update a database? A Web server cannot handle that by itself. When such a request arrives at the Web server it is passed to other external software. This is achieved through the *Common Gateway Interface*; and this is what CGI programming is all about.

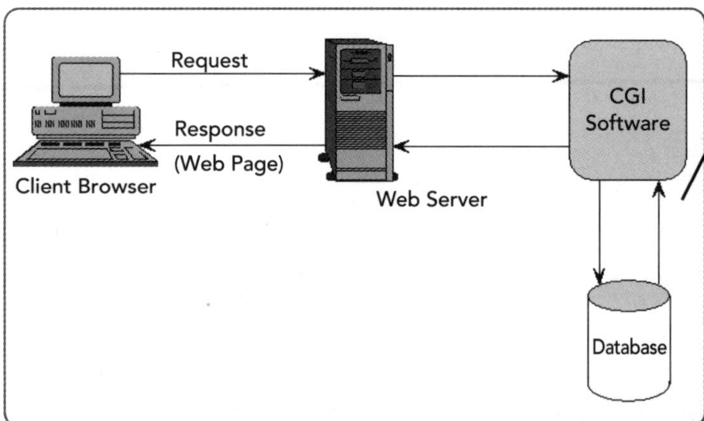

CGI Processing

So now the set up looks like this.

The CGI box shown can consist of many things. For instance, if you intend to use ASP for your Web applications, any requests for an ASP page will be diverted to the program asp.dll. But of most interest right now is Perl; requests for Perl scripts or programs are passed to perl.exe. In Chapter 1 you installed Perl on your machine, so now you should be all ready to go.

What Can I Do with CGI?

CGI programming allows you to do almost any Web-based task you could ever want to do with a Perl CGI program.

There are some rules for using Perl to talk to its Web surroundings that you'll need to learn. There are also some features of CGI itself to learn that you will find useful.

A Simple Perl CGI Program

At last you are going to try a real CGI program. You are going to write a very simple Perl program to display the IP address of your machine on a Web page.

> **NOTE**
>
> An IP *address* is the network address of your PC. Every computer connected to the Internet has an IP address. An IP address looks like this: 121.236.157.53. That is, four sets of numbers separated by dots (periods). The Internet uses names to find Web site addresses, but these names are converted into IP addresses by Domain Name Servers (DNS), computers whose job it is to carry out this conversion so that computers can find each other.

In Chapter 1, you learned about the Web server and how to set up folders for Web sites. You also learned about the cgi-bin, or scripts folder. You will be putting your Perl program in the scripts folder if you are using Microsoft Personal Web Server or into the cgi-bin folder if you are using a UNIX machine and something like Apache Web Server (an excellent choice).

Of course, if your ISP enables you to run your own Perl scripts, find out from them where you should put your scripts and if there are any do's and don'ts for your Web space. You will be using the 127.0.0.1 address to access your Web pages from your Web browser. Remember though, that if you choose to host your programs on your ISP Web space, you will use an address like:

http://*www.mydomain*.com/scripts/

for the Perl code, and something like:

http://*www.mydomain*.com/

for the HTML.

Of course, if your IP address is static (that is, it doesn't change—most of them do) then you can use that instead of your domain name.

To create your first Perl CGI program, follow these steps, paying careful attention to the actual coding to make sure you don't leave out any code or make any typos.

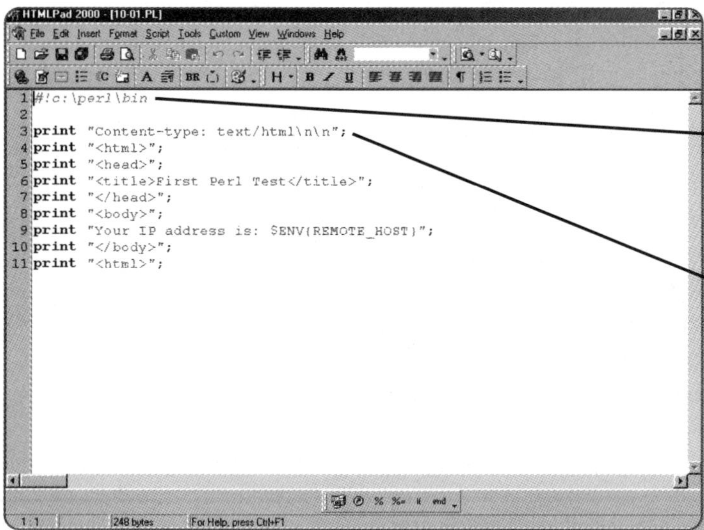

1. Open your editor, creating a new file.

2. Start with the usual shebang statement (you still need it for CGI programs).

3. Now enter the following line:

```
print "Content-type:
   text/html\n\n";
```

This line tells the Web server what kind of data is being sent. In this case, you are telling the server that this is going to be an HTML document, which is a subtype of a text document (hence the text/html part).

Note the two newline characters. These are very important—they are not for cosmetic purposes. The `Content-type: text/html` statement *must* be followed by two newline characters; otherwise, your program will not work and you will get a message telling you that you sent back incomplete headers or something similar.

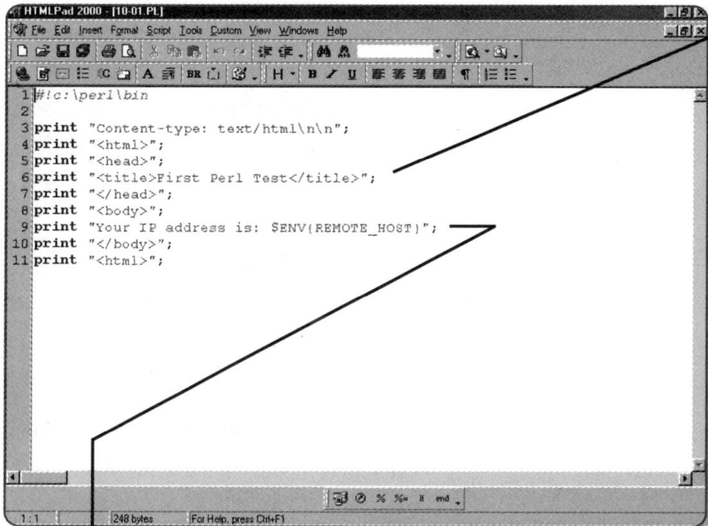

4. You have told the server to expect some HTML, so now you can send it some.

Use print statements as you did for the console programs you wrote earlier when you were learning some simple Perl examples, but now embedding the HTML within them.

```
print "<html>";
print "<head>";
print "<title>First Perl
Test</title>";
print "</head>";
print "<body>";
```

All of this is standard HTML; it's just wrapped in Perl print statements so that Perl will send it to the Web server. The text enclosed in the quotes of the print statements will be received by the Web server as ordinary HTML and so will be returned to your browser in the normal way.

5. Now you are going to do something different. Enter the following line exactly as shown:

```
print "Your IP address is: $ENV{REMOTE_HOST}";
```

The above statement says: Print the following text (the following text is an environment variable).

The environment variable you want to display is one called REMOTE_HOST.

> **NOTE**
>
> Environment variables are variables that contain information about the server and the client (your Web browser). This information can be very useful when it comes to writing Web applications.

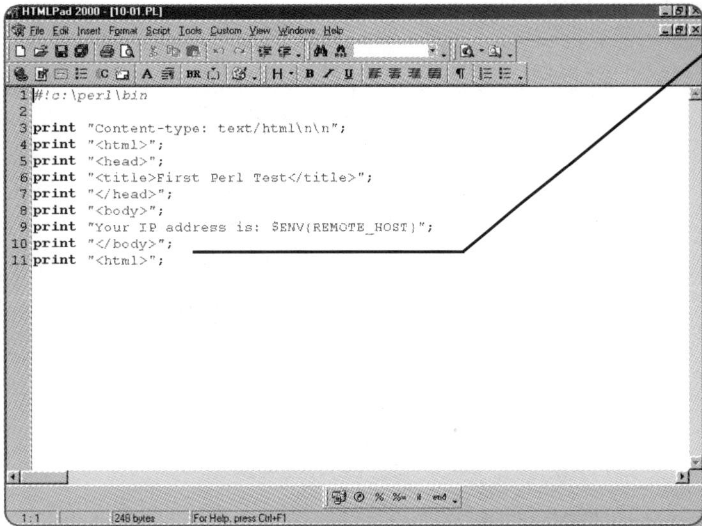

6. Having displayed the string "Your IP address is :" followed by the REMOTE_HOST variable, you then close off the HTML in the normal way, but of course wrapped up in Perl print statements:

```
print "</body>";
print "<html>";
```

And that's it—your first Perl CGI program. Not very exciting perhaps, but it's a good start and you will use it to check that your Perl/Web server setup is working.

7. Save your program in the scripts (or cgi-bin folder) as cgi1.pl, or if you want to follow the chapters in this book, call it 10-01.pl.

Now, open your Web browser, and in the location or address box, type the address of your server followed by the path to your script. Do you remember what the local IP address of you machine is? It's127.0.0.1.

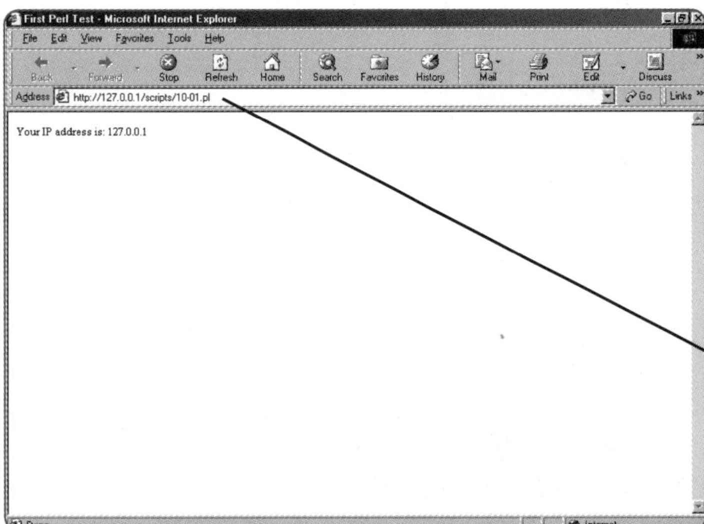

OR

You can also use *localhost* as a name instead of the IP address, like this: http://localhost. So, you'd type in the following address and press the Enter key:

http://localhost/scripts/10-01.pl

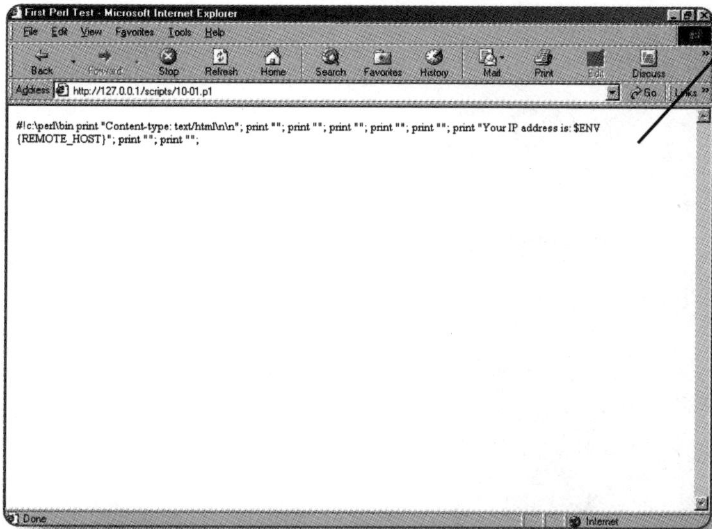

If you see something like this instead, then your Web server is not recognizing that your script is a Perl program. UNIX users shouldn't have this problem because Perl is pre-installed in most cases.

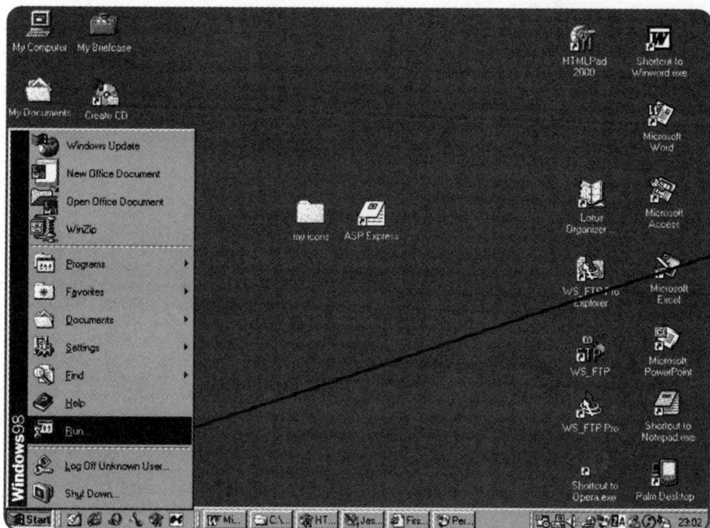

If you are a Windows user and you get this problem, then do this:

1. Open the Start menu.
2. Click Run.

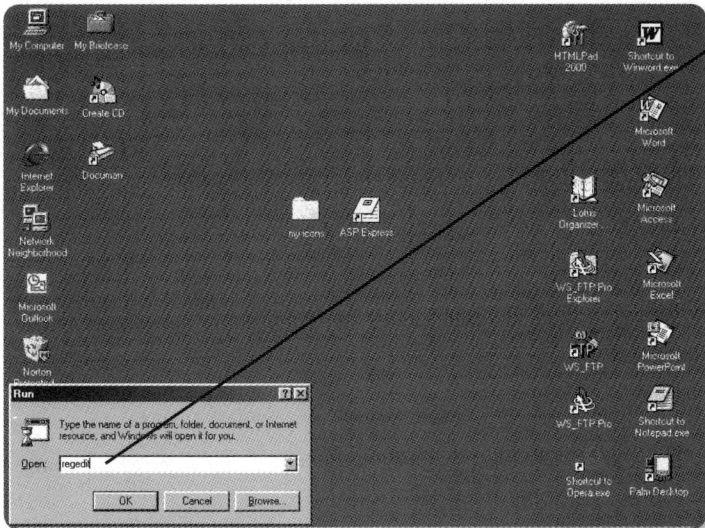

3. In the Run dialog box, type **Regedit** and click OK.

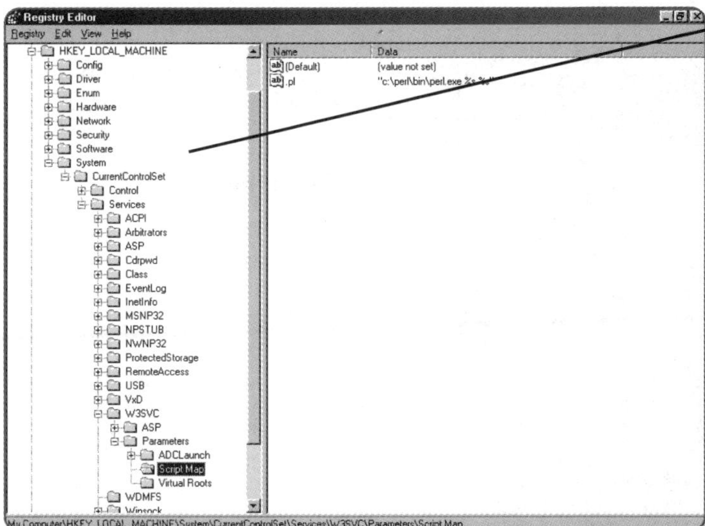

4. Open the following registry key:
HKEY_LOCAL_MACHINE\SYSTEM\CurrentControlSet\Services\W3SVC\Parameters\ScriptMap

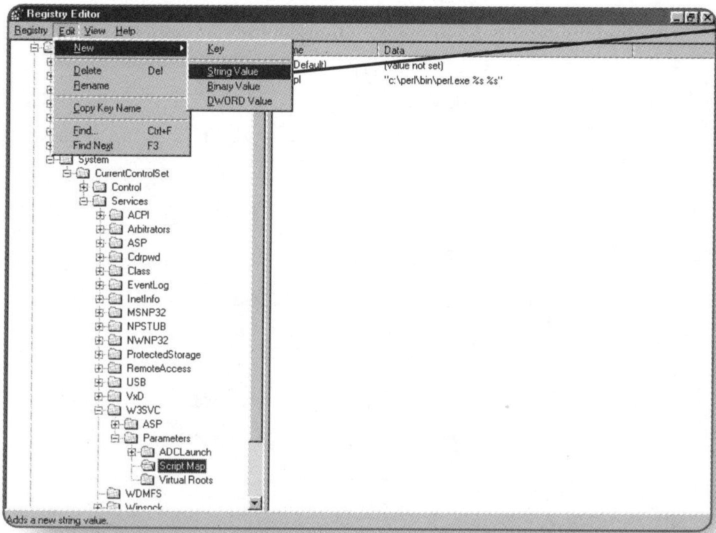

5. From the Edit menu, select New, then click String Value.

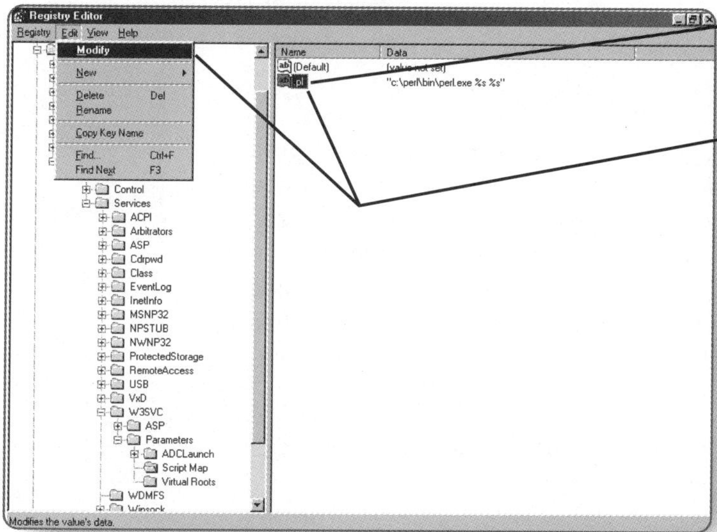

6. Type **.pl** for the value and press Enter.

7. Select .pl, and select Modify from the Edit menu.

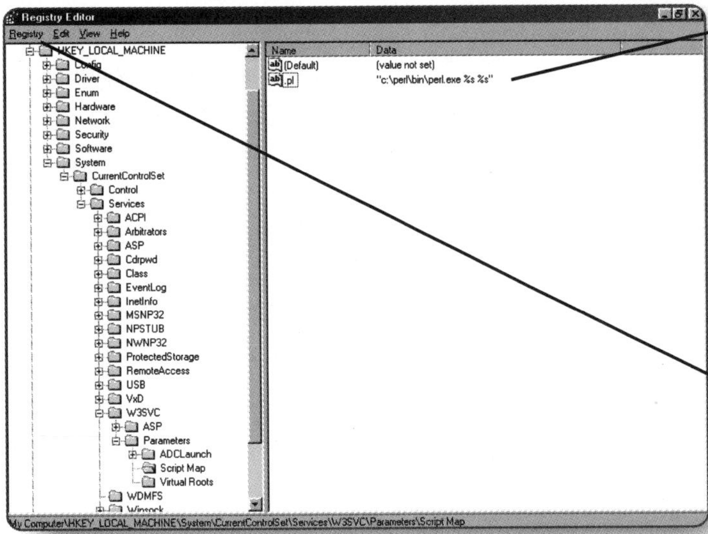

8. In the Data column box, type

```
c:\perl\bin\perl.exe %s %s
```

> **NOTE**
>
> Use lowercase s in the %s %s; %S %S will not work.

9. Close the Registry Editor by selecting Registry from the top menu, and then clicking Exit.

Restart your computer.

> **CAUTION**
>
> If you are at all unsure about modifying values in your computer's registry, then do not attempt to make any modifications. If you make a mistake when making changes to the registry, you can render your computer unusable, perhaps requiring the re-installation of Windows! Always follow your computer vendor's instructions on backing up the registry before making any changes.

You have now proven that your programs should work with your setup. Now you can go a little further.

You just used a Perl program to display your IP address using an environment variable. You can display all of these variables with another simple Perl CGI program.

1. Start your editor.

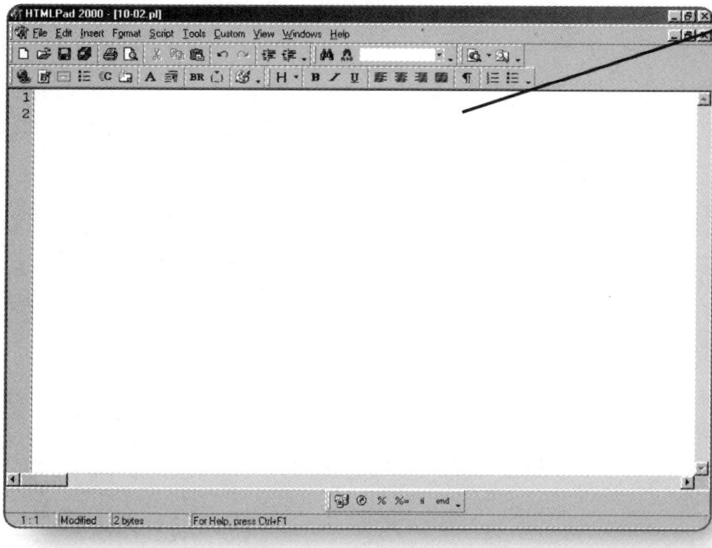

2. Open a new file. If you are using an editor that tries to create a skeleton HTML page, then empty the page.

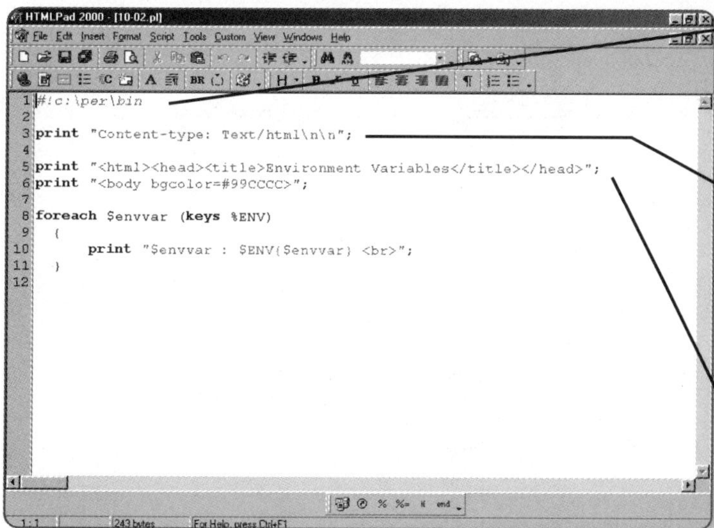

3. Type the usual shebang statement.

```
#!c:\perl\bin
```

4. Type a Perl statement to direct output from the server back to the browser.

```
print "Content-type:
   Text/html\n\n";
```

5. Enter the following to start building a Web page using Perl "print" statements:

```
print "<html><head><title>Environment Variables</title></head>";
print "<body bgcolor=#99CCCC>";
```

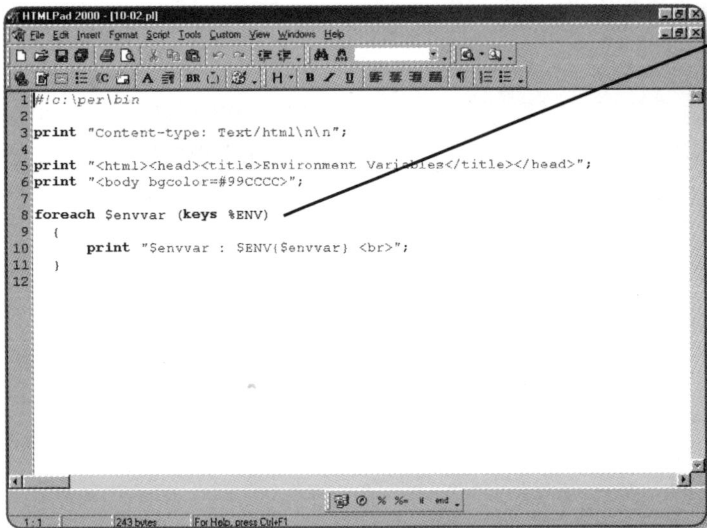

6. Now use a simple `foreach` loop to display the values and keys of the environment variables.

```
foreach $envvar (keys %ENV)

  {

      print "$envvar :
         $ENV{$envvar} <br>";

  }
```

7. Save your program as 10-02.pl.

8. Open your Web browser.

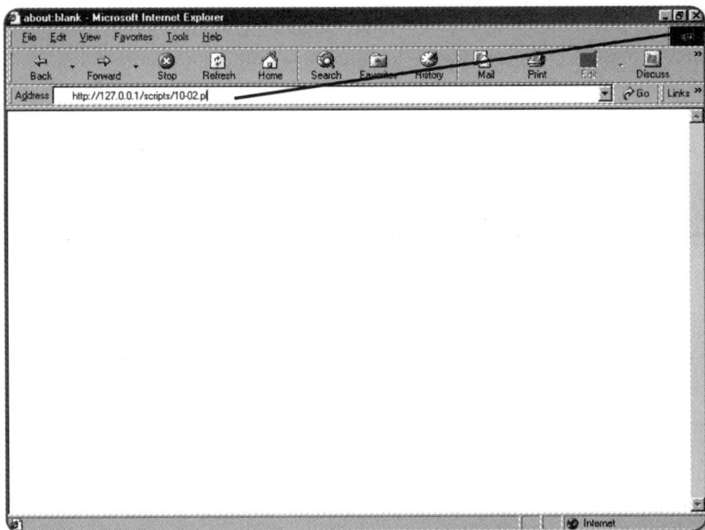

9. Type the URL into the address bar of your browser and press the Enter key.

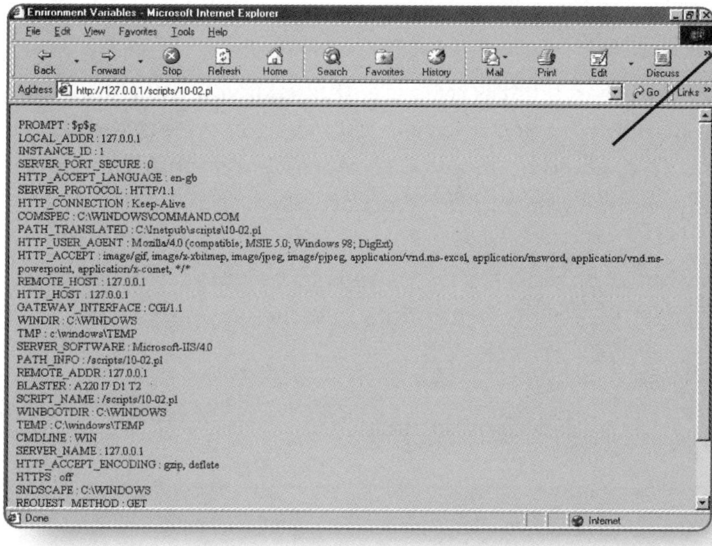

You should see this.

Keep this program handy because it is useful to see what each environment variable does. You will want to use many of them when you start to build your own Web applications.

Your Perl Web applications are beginning to get just a little more interesting. But what can you do with them? You can find out information about the client browser and so on, but there is something missing.

HTML Forms

To make Web applications really useful, you have to be able to "talk" to them—to send them data and to get data back. You can get data back using the print HTML type statements we have used already. But how do you send data? To do this you need a little more HTML than we have covered so far. You need HTML forms.

> **NOTE**
>
> Before you go any further, create a folder called myhtml under the wwwroot folder if you have not done so already. It will be useful for the examples you are about to try.

HTML forms allow users to interact with Web sites by entering data which can then be used to populate a database or file, or perhaps to send an email to the owner of the site. Forms make Web pages useful! Using forms, you can collect information from users of your site and give them the information they want and need.

What Are Forms?

If you are to build anything other than a flat HTML site; that is, if you want the page to do something other than display text and images, you have to connect the page to some storage mechanism. This would enable you to store data so that you can capture data from users and send data to a user's Web browser.

Normally, data is held in databases or files. If your page is to be able to manipulate data of some kind then you must be able to enter data in some way—this entry mechanism is the form.

The form has a number of elements, described in Table 10.1.

TABLE 10.1 Form elements and their purposes

Element	Purpose
Text	Enables entry of short strings.
Textarea	Enables the entry of longer strings occupying a number of lines of text.
Radio Button	A "one of n" choice selection mechanism.
Check Box	A true/false indicator—a box with a tick or an X when selected.
Select Boxes	A pull-down list of options from which one (or more) options can be selected.
Hidden	A text box wherein the box is not visible on the page. It is often used to carry data that the user does not need to see.
Password	Similar to a text box, but represents each character with an asterisk as the user types.
Submit Button	A button that enables the data entered into the form to be transferred to the processing mechanism.
Reset Button	A button that clears all data from the form so that the user can begin again.

The form itself is defined using the <FORM> </FORM> tags and within them are tags to represent all of the data items needed.

Here is a typical FORM tag:

```
<FORM NAME="myform" METHOD="POST" ACTION="/scripts/myscript.pl">
```

The NAME attribute enables elements within the form to be referenced by scripts within the page, such as JavaScript, VBScript, and so on. You'll learn more about JavaScript in Chapter 15.

METHOD usually is set to either "POST" or "GET." This is a method of sending data to a script or other program.

METHOD="GET"

Data sent by the GET method is sent along with the URL to the script all as one string. You might have noticed, when filling in a form on the Internet, something like this in the URL location box of the browser:

```
http://www.somedomain.com/scripts/ascript.exe?dataitem1=value1
```

Note the question mark separating the name of the script from the data that follows it.

The main disadvantages of this method are that the data that is being passed can be easily seen and also the length of the data string is limited.

METHOD="POST"

This method sends the data to the "standard input" of the program to which the data is being sent. Programmers, especially those who have written software in C, C++, and so on, will understand what this means. Suffice it to say that this is a standard method of getting data into a program.

The main advantage of this method is that the amount of data that can be transferred is unlimited.

ACTION

The ACTION is the attribute that describes the location and the name of the script or program to be executed. It will be something like

```
/scripts/myprogram.pl
```

Of course, you can use a program that lives elsewhere, perhaps on another server at another domain, in which case you can use the full syntax for the program like this:

```
http://www.mydomain.net/scripts/myprogram.pl
```

Using the Form

Place the tags you need to represent all of the data to be collected by the form between the <FORM> and </FORM> tags.

You will now look at some typical tags used to describe the data input fields. Almost all fields in an HTML form are of the INPUT tag type.

> **NOTE**
>
> Tag names in the following text will appear both all capitalized (example: SELECT) and all lowercase (example: select). In the early days of HTML it was a convention to always uppercase HTML tags. In recent years, it has become the convention to use lowercase characters through an HTML document, probably because HTML (or the programs that generate the HTML) is now often coded by programmers who are used to using lowercase in languages such as C, C++, Java, and so on. You should get used to seeing tag names written both ways.

Text Fields

The text field is probably the most commonly used. Often, almost all fields on forms are of this type. They give you the usual rectangular input box that takes a single line of text.

The HTML code for the text field looks like this:

```
<INPUT TYPE="TEXT" NAME="surname" SIZE="30" MAXLENGTH="25">
```

The size attribute is optional and determines the size of the box in characters.

The MAXLENGTH attribute is also optional, and is used when you want to limit the amount of text that can be typed into the box. In this case, the limit has been set to 25 characters.

Password Fields

The password field is, in most respects, the same as the text field. The main difference is that text typed into a password field cannot be seen. Each character entered is replaced by an asterisk.

The HTML code for a typical password field would look like this:

```
<INPUT TYPE="Password" NAME="pwrd">
```

Obviously, the password field is useful for login type functions in Web applications.

Hidden Fields

Hidden fields are also very similar to text fields. The main difference is that you cannot see the field on the Web page at all. You might think that pretty useless, but it's very handy for quietly passing data from one page to another page or to a Perl CGI program.

The HTML code for a typical hidden field would look like this:

```
<INPUT TYPE="hidden" NAME="secret" value=3000>
```

Radio Buttons

The radio button gets its name from the old radios with the mechanical selection buttons for waveband. You used to press the button and any previously selected buttons would pop out. These radio buttons behave in a logically similar way. They are round in appearance (on most browsers.); if there are several of them and you select one by clicking it with the mouse, any previously selected buttons will be deselected.

The syntax of the radio button is

```
<INPUT TYPE="RADIO" NAME="choice1">
```

If you want this type of field to be already selected, you add the `SELECTED` attribute.

```
<INPUT TYPE="RADIO" NAME="choice1" SELECTED>
```

The radio button can also have a value like this:

```
<INPUT TYPE="RADIO" NAME="choice1"  value="1" SELECTED>
```

Here is a very simple HTML example just so that you get the idea.

1. Open your editor.

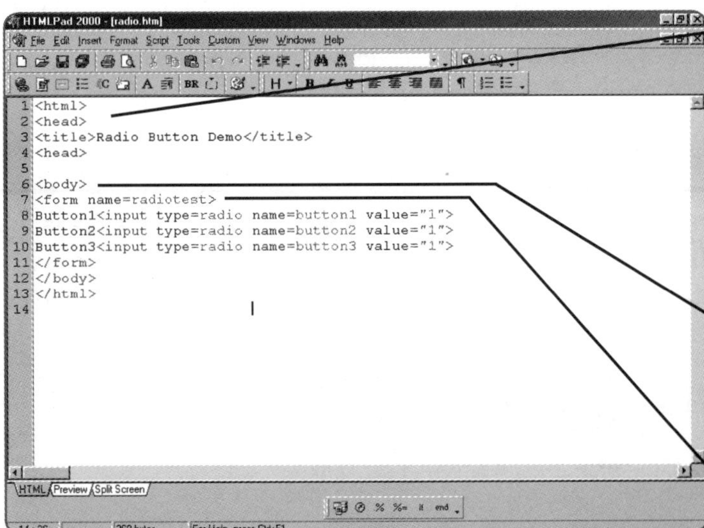

2. Start an HTML page like this:

```
<html>
<head>
<title>Radio Button
   Demo</title>
<head>
```

3. Open the body of the Web page.

```
<body>
```

4. Now start the form. Because you are not going to use this with a CGI program, you do not need an `action` or a `method` attribute.

```
<form name=radiotest>
```

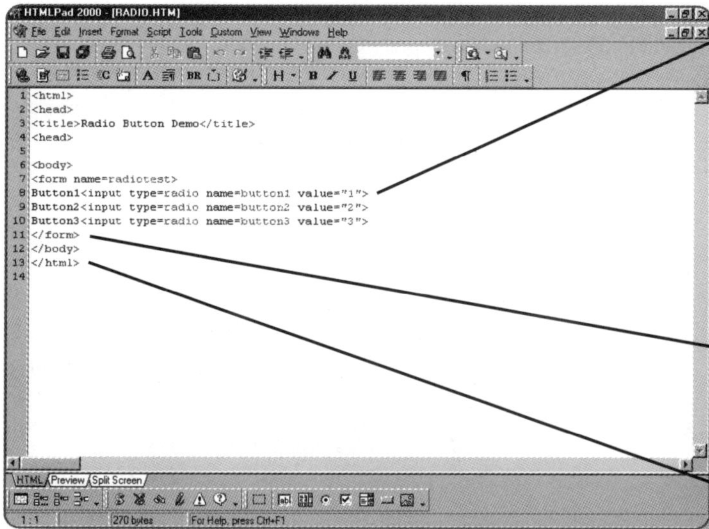

5. Code three radio buttons like this:

```
Button1<input type=radio
   name=button1 value="1">
Button2<input type=radio
   name=button1 value="2">
Button3<input type=radio
   name=button1 value="3">
```

6. Close your form.

```
</form>
```

7. Close the body and the HTML tags of your HTML page.

```
</body>
</html>
```

NOTE

The name attributes of the radio buttons all have the same name. It is this that causes the radio button effect. If you give them all different names, you can select any or all of them at once. Try it and see.

8. Save your HTML in your myhtml folder or wherever you want to save it.

9. Open your Web browser.

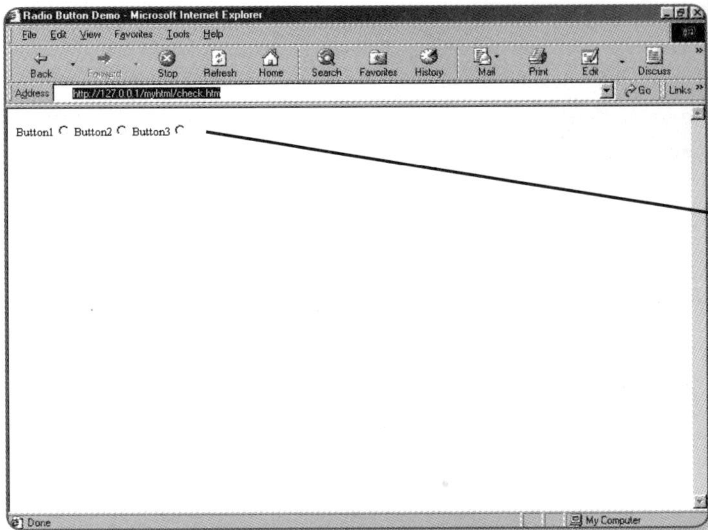

10. Type the address to your new HTML file in the address box of your browser and press the Enter key.

You should see a result like this.

11. Play with the radio buttons and observe the effect.

12. Change the names of the radio button `name` attributes and see how they no longer reset each other when you select them.

Check Boxes

The check box is another useful type of input box. It is similar in principle to the radio button, except that it is designed for multiple choices—you have no doubt seen the online survey forms wherein you are asked to choose from a list all of the items that you like or agree with.

Even giving the check boxes the same name does not change their behavior. It does make them a little more difficult to deal with, so it would make more sense to give them their own individual names. You can have a page full of check boxes and select as few or as many as you want.

Also, note that you deselect check boxes by clicking them again.

```
<INPUT TYPE="CHECKBOX" NAME="selection1">
```

Again, if you want to show this field already checked, then add the `checked` attribute.

```
<INPUT TYPE="checkbox" NAME="choice1" checked>
```

Here is an example similar to the previous one, but for check boxes instead.

1. As in the previous example, open your editor and start a new HTML file.

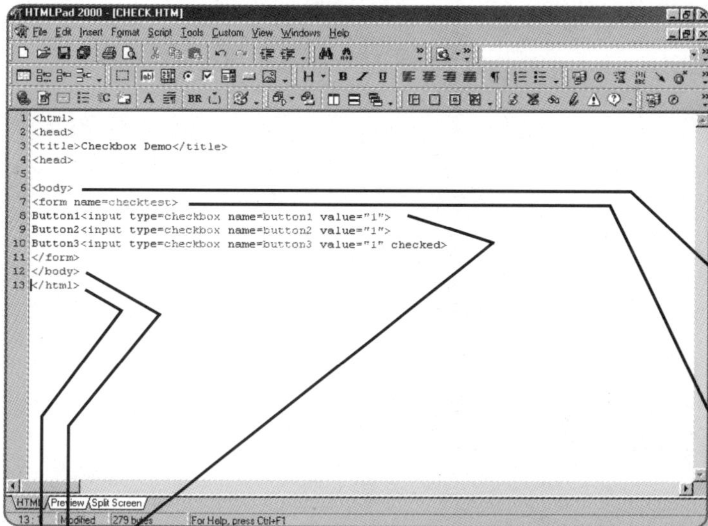

2. Complete the usual HTML header.

```
<html>
<head>
<title>Checkbox Demo</title>
<head>
```

3. Open the body of the HTML page.

```
<body>
```

4. Start a form (again, no method or action is needed).

```
<form name=checktest>
```

5. Now create three buttons in a similar way to the last example.

```
Button1<input type=checkbox name=button1 value="1">
Button2<input type=checkbox name=button2 value="1">
Button3<input type=checkbox name=button3 value="1" checked>
```

The last button has the `checked` attribute. This will cause it to be displayed as though it had already been selected (clicked with the mouse).

6. Close the form.

```
</form>
```

7. And of course, close the body of the page and the HTML.

```
</body>
</html>
```

8. Save your program in your myhtml folder as check.htm.

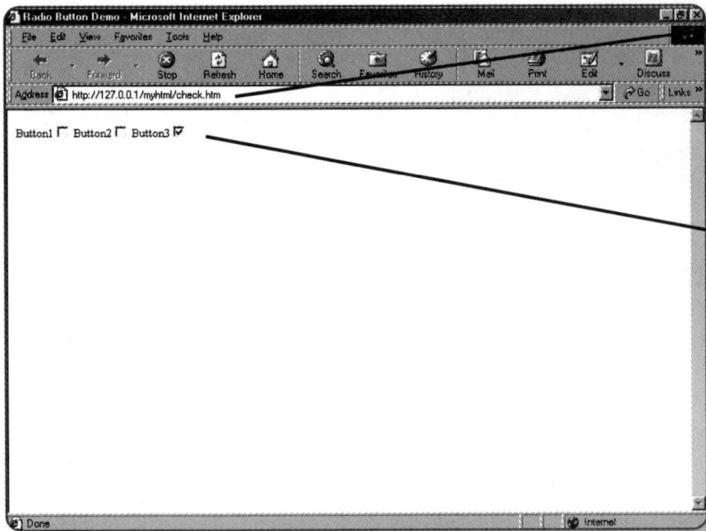

9. Open your browser and go to the following URL:

```
http://127.0.0.1/myhtml/
   check.htm
```

You should see something similar to this.

Drop-Down Boxes

For drop-down boxes you use the <SELECT> tag. The select tag is a little different from the others in that it is not a variation on the <input type= > type tag.

A typical select tag looks like this:

```
<SELECT NAME="country">
       <OPTION value="UK" SELECTED>UK</OPTION>
       <OPTION value="USA">USA</OPTION>
       <OPTION value="France">France</OPTION>
       <OPTION value="Germany">Germany</OPTION>
</SELECTED>
```

The select tag has embedded within it a number of option tags. Each option tag holds one option. The value clause of the option statement is the value that is actually used by the form. The text immediately before the option tag is the text that is actually displayed on the page, although often the two will be the same.

If you want to show one of the options as preselected when the page loads, you include the selected attribute within the option tag.

You can also specify a size for the select tag, but this looks confusing to the user. But you can use the size tag when you add the multiple attribute to the select tag. This tells the select tag that you can select more than one option. The user does this by holding down the Ctrl key and then clicking more options with the mouse. You can also select a block of options by clicking the first option, moving down the select list until you get to the end of the block you want to select, and finally holding down the Shift key and clicking the last item. All the selections in the block then are selected and turn blue.

Now you can use the `size` attribute of the select tag. The `size` attribute determines how many options are visible.

Try the following to see an example of both types of select tags.

1. Open your editor.

2. Start a new file.

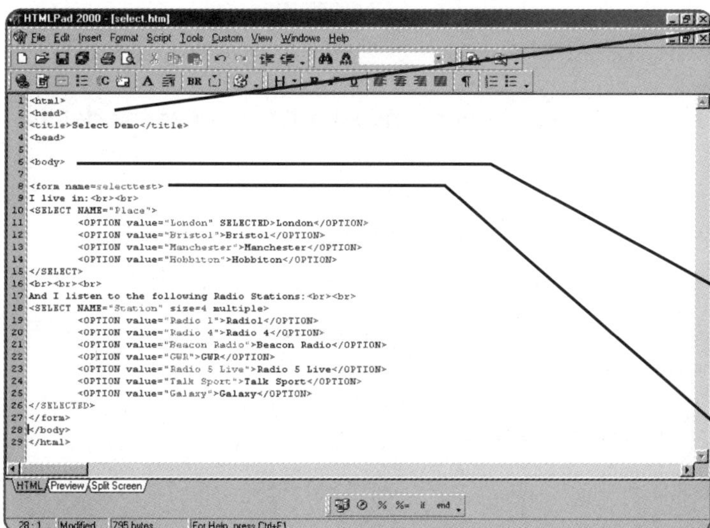

3. Start the HTML and add the header section like this:

```
<html>
<head>
<title>Select Demo</title>
<head>
```

4. Add the open body tag.

```
<body>
```

5. Code a form tag. Because you are not yet using a Perl program to process your form, you do not need to code an `action` or a `method` attribute.

```
<form name=selecttest>
```

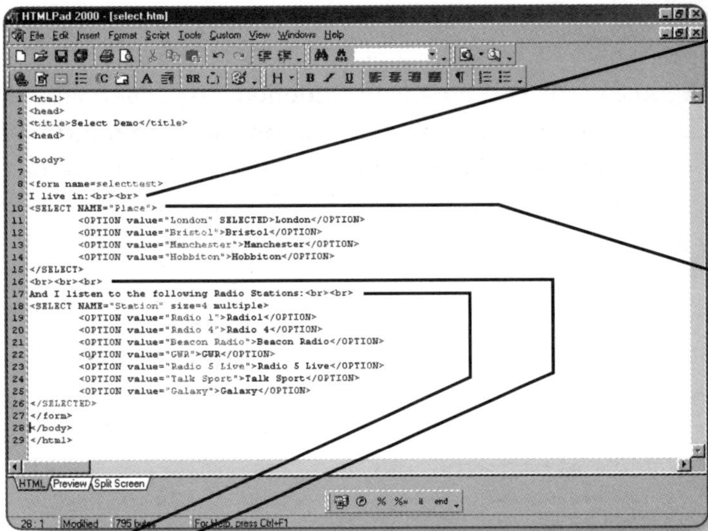

6. In this example, you are going to use two select tags. Add some text to label the first select.

```
I live in:<br><br>
```

7. Now code the first select.

```
<SELECT NAME="Place">
        <OPTION value="London"
            SELECTED>London
            </OPTION><OPTION
value="Bristol">Bristol
   </OPTION>
        <OPTION
value="Manchester">
   Manchester</OPTION>
        <OPTION
value="Hobbiton">Hobbiton
   </OPTION>
</SELECT>
```

In this case, `"London"` has the `selected` attribute and so will appear as the default choice.

8. Now add a few line breaks before adding the next bit.

```
<br><br><br>
```

9. And now some text for the second select.

```
And I listen to the following Radio Stations:<br><br>
```

10. Now add the second select.

```
<SELECT NAME="Station" size=4 multiple>
       <OPTION value="Radio 1">Radio1</OPTION>
       <OPTION value="Radio 4">Radio 4</OPTION>
       <OPTION value="Beacon Radio">Beacon Radio</OPTION>
       <OPTION value="GWR">GWR</OPTION>
       <OPTION value="Radio 5 Live">Radio 5 Live</OPTION>
       <OPTION value="Talk Sport">Talk Sport</OPTION>
       <OPTION value="Galaxy">Galaxy</OPTION>
</SELECTED>
```

> **NOTE**
>
> This time there is no selected option, but you do have the `multiple` attribute on the select tag, so more than one value can be selected.

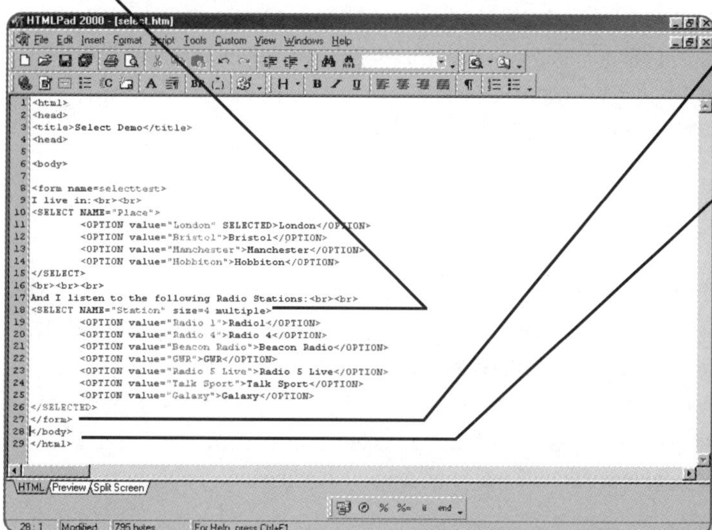

11. Now close the form.

```
</form>
```

12. Finally, close the body and html tags.

```
</body>
```

```
</html>
```

13. Save your new HTML page as select.htm.

14. Open your browser.

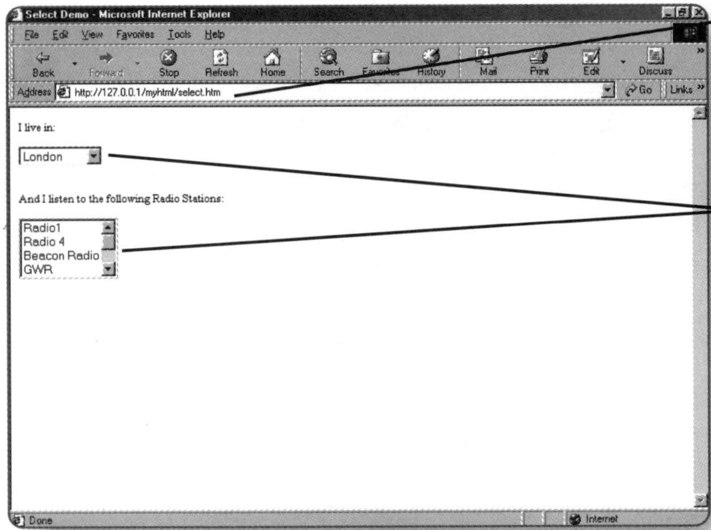

15. Enter the following URL into the address box: http://127.0.0.1/myhtml/select.htm.

You should see two select boxes, one of which is a single select and the other a multiple select.

You will find the `<select>` tags very useful for many reasons. Say you are going to save data from an HTML form in a database and you want to be able to manipulate that database later. Suppose you want to pick out the people who live in London. Some people will type **London**, some will type **london**, and some might even spell it wrong. If you use a select box for all such fields, you eliminate the possibility of input error for those fields.

Text Area Fields

The text area field is useful when users want to type in lots of text. You can provide a place for users to type with the <input type=text> tag, but with that method, the user can't see what he's typed once he's filled the box, because the text "tickertapes" out of the box to the left. With a text area field, you have a number of rows of text, so that as the user types the text scrolls up the box. You can also have a scrollbar so that the user can scroll up and down the text to review it.

```
<TEXTAREA NAME="comments" COLS="50" ROWS="50"></TEXTAREA>
```

There is not a value clause with the text area. If there is a default text, then you place it between the <textarea> and the </textarea> tags.

Here is an example of the text area box.

1. Open your editor.

2. Start a new file.

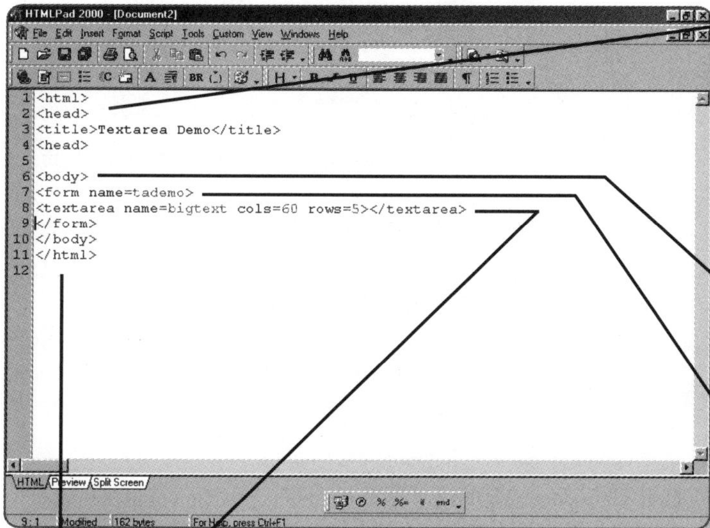

3. Start the HTML and add the header section like this:

```
<html>
<head>
<title>Textarea Demo</title>
<head>
```

4. Add the open body tag.

```
<body>
```

5. Code a form tag. Once again, as you are not yet using a Perl program to process your form, you do not need to code an `action` or a `method` attribute.

```
<form name=tademo>
```

6. Code the text area field. Make it 60 characters wide by 5 rows high.

```
<textarea name=bigtext cols=60
   rows=5></textarea>
```

7. Now close the form, body, and HTML tags.

```
</form>
</body>
</html>
```

8. Save your new HTML page as textarea.htm.

9. Open your browser.

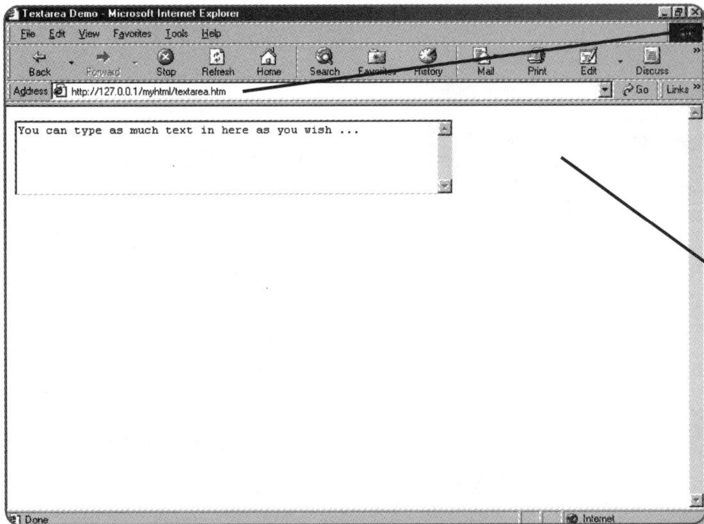

10. Enter the following URL into the address box, and try out the text area field.

http://127.0.0.1/myhtml/
textarea.htm

The page should look like this.

If you wanted default text in the text area, the HTML code would look something like this:

```
<textarea name=bigtext cols=60
   rows=5>Here is some default
   text</textarea>
```

That's enough about form input elements for now. Next, you can put together a complete form ready to send data back to your Web server and to your waiting Perl program. When you have written it, that is.

Submit and Reset Buttons

Before the form becomes really useful, you will need a submit button; that's pretty straightforward too.

Also, you might sometimes want a button to reset the form, so that if the user has made a hopeless mess of the form, he or she can click the reset button to clear all of the form entries and start again.

Try this.

1. Open your editor.

2. Open a previous program, such as select.htm.

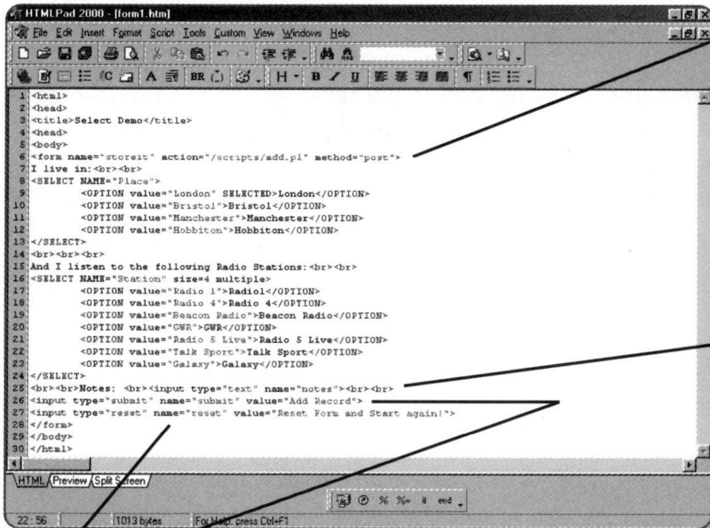

3. Make sure that the form tag has both a method and an action attribute specified, as shown here:

```
<form name="storeit"
   action="/scripts/add.pl"
   method="post">
```

4. Add a text field called Notes, after the second select tag, like this:

```
<br><br>Notes: <br><input
   type="text" name="notes">
   <br><br>
```

5. Now, insert a line immediately before the </form> tag that looks like this one:

```
<input type="submit" name="submit" value="Add Record">
```

6. Add a reset button.

```
<input type="reset" name="reset" value="Reset Form and Start again!">
```

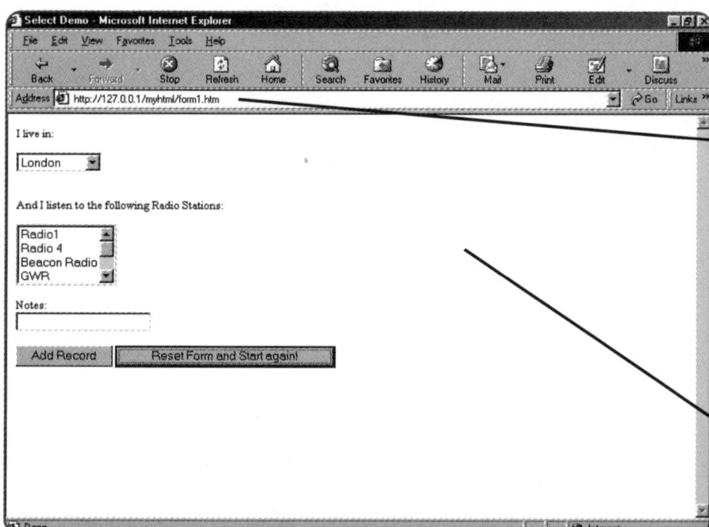

7. Now save your program in the myhtml folder as form1.htm.

8. Open your Web browser and type the following URL in the address box and then press the Enter key.

http://127.0.0.1/myhtml/form1.htm

You should see something like this.

Now the form will work, but if you click the submit button, you will get an error because you do not yet have a program to handle your form. You can test the Reset button by making your selections and typing something into the notes field, and then clicking the Reset button. Your selections should be reset and the text you typed into the Notes text box should disappear.

Now you know how to capture user input. Next you will learn how to handle that data at the server and how to send replies or "responses" back to the browser on the client machine.

11

CGI: Making the Connection

You now know the basics of Perl—you know how Perl variables work, you can build forms, and you even know what you can do with data after you get it onto the server. You can build an HTML page, and you have learned how to provide navigation through hyperlinks, how to add color, and how to build forms to capture data from users. You have even learned about environment variables and how useful they might be.

What you have not learned yet is how the information gets from your form into your Perl program on the Web server. Now you'll see how to make the connection from HTML form to Perl script.

In this chapter you will:

- Examine how data is received from forms
- Learn how to use HTML tables
- Learn how to get form data via the GET and POST methods

Receiving Data from Forms

As always, the best way to demonstrate the way you use forms is by way of a simple example. But first, you should learn about another feature of HTML: tables. This is a good time to discuss HTML tables, as they are very useful for creating neat form layouts!

HTML Tables

HTML tables are used to (amongst other things) format the contents of a Web page. In this section you'll learn how to use them to make a Web input HTML form look prettier. Tables are not essential for forms—but they do make them look better. You could just use spaces (` `) and breaks (<BR>) to position the form elements on the page, but it probably wouldn't look very good.

As you would expect, a table starts with the <TABLE> tag. The <TABLE> tag has a number of attributes; for example, you can use background = imagename.jpg to set the background image of a table, just like you did for the <BODY> tag. In the same way, you can set the background color using the bgcolor attribute.

You can set the width of the table using the `width=nnn` or `width=nn%` attributes of the table tag, rather like the `width` attribute of the <HR>, horizontal rule tag.

A typical table tag might look like this:

```
<table width=600 bgcolor=lightblue>
```

This code says to create a table 600 pixels in width with a light blue background color. Simple enough, isn't it?

A table achieves its aims by being what you would expect it to be: a table of rows and columns into which you can place the elements, pictures, or text you choose.

At the top of a table, you can have an optional "header" row, intended for things like titles. A header row looks like this:

```
<tr><th width=200>Column Title 1</th><th width=200>Column Title 2</th><th
width=200>Column Title 3</th><tr>
```

The <tr> tag signifies the start of a table row. The <th> tag defines a table header for a column, in this case the width of the header, and therefore the whole column has been fixed at 200 pixels (again, percentages could be used). The </th> tag closes this header. In this example, there are three identical headers containing three column titles for the table.

Note that although the width of the headers is set in this example to 200 pixels, if the title between the <th> and </th> tags exceeds 200-pixel width, the column will stretch (that is, any cells directly beneath the header tag will stretch) to accommodate the text, image, or whatever you choose to place within it.

At the end of the headers, the row is closed using the </tr> tag.

Following rows can contain what HTML calls *data*. The format of the data rows is very similar to the header row, except that the individual cells are defined by <td> tags instead of the <th> tag of the header row. A header row or a data row can also have its own width tags, background color tags, and so on.

A data row may look like this:

```
<tr><td>Column Title 1</td><td>Column Title 2</td><td>Column Title 3</td><tr>
```

An HTML table can contain many rows of data, which is, as you will see, very useful in Web-based applications.

Each <td> or <th> tag can have its own background color, `bgcolor`, `width`, and `height` attributes. They also can have tags for aligning the contents of the cell. Horizontally, alignment can be specified as left, center, or right. Vertically, alignment can be specified as top, middle, or bottom. So for example, a <td> tag can have its alignment attributes specified thus:

```
<td align="center" valign="top">
```

Note that the `valign` and `height` attributes can also be added to the <tr> tag.

The HTML table is closed, as you would expect, using the </table> tag.

The following form example shows how a table is used to position the form elements to produce a neat layout.

1. Open your editor.

2. Create a new HTML page.

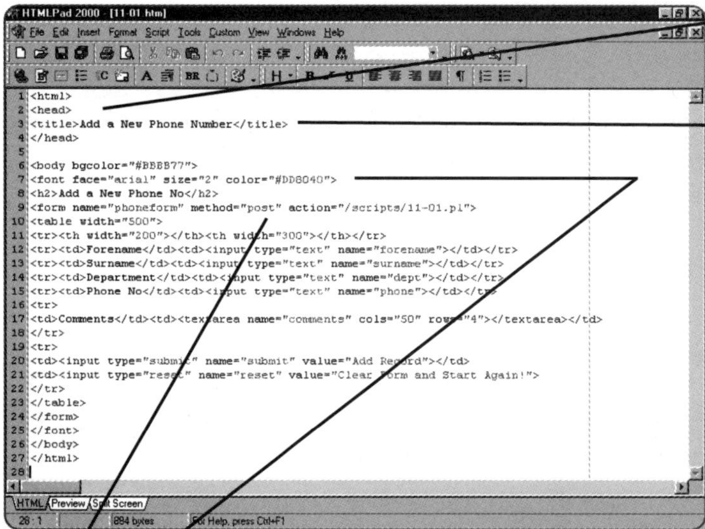

3. Start with the usual header tags and so on.

4. This time, the HTML is in lowercase (it doesn't matter whether you chose uppercase or lowercase but don't mix case on the same site; it might be confusing). Also note that all the attributes are enclosed in quotes. Often they don't have to be unless the attribute or an attribute value contains spaces.

5. Set up a default font and a title for your form page.

```
<font face="arial" size="2" color="#dd8040">
<H2>Add a New Phone No</H2>
```

6. After opening the body you will need a simple form HTML tag like this:

```
<form name="phoneform" method="post" action="/scripts/11-01.pl">
```

> **NOTE**
>
> You are using the POST method. You learned a bit about this method in Chapter 9. You will learn a little more about POST and GET in this chapter.

7. Open a table into which you are going to start positioning your form elements.

```
<TABLE width="500">
```

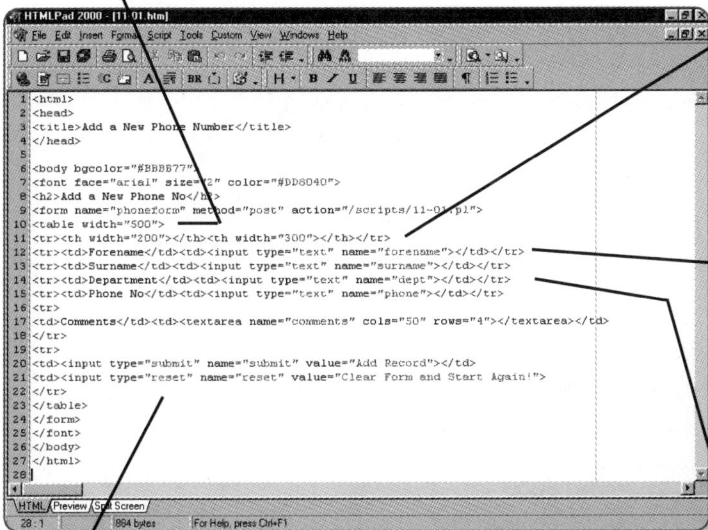

8. Use a table header row to fix the size and position of the form fields, text labels, and so on.

```
<tr><th width="200"></th><th
   width="300"></th></tr>
```

9. Now code a text box in a table data row to capture, say, forename (first name) from a user, like this:

```
<tr><td>Forename</td><td>
   <input type="text"
   name="forename"></td></tr>
```

10. Add more tags to capture typical work telephone data such as surname, department, phone number, and comments, again in table rows and columns, like this:

```
<tr><td>Surname</td><td><input type="text" name="surname"></td></tr>
<tr><td>Department</td><td><input type="text" name="dept"></td></tr>
<tr><td>Phone No</td><td><input type="text" name="phone"></td></tr>
<tr>
<TD>Comments</td><td><textarea name="comments" cols="50"
rows="4"></textarea></td>
</tr>
```

11. Now add a row with a submit button and a reset button to enable the user to send the data back to the server.

```
<tr>
<td><input type="submit" name="submit" value="add record"></td>
<td><input type="reset" name="reset" value="Clear Form and Start Again!">
</tr>
```

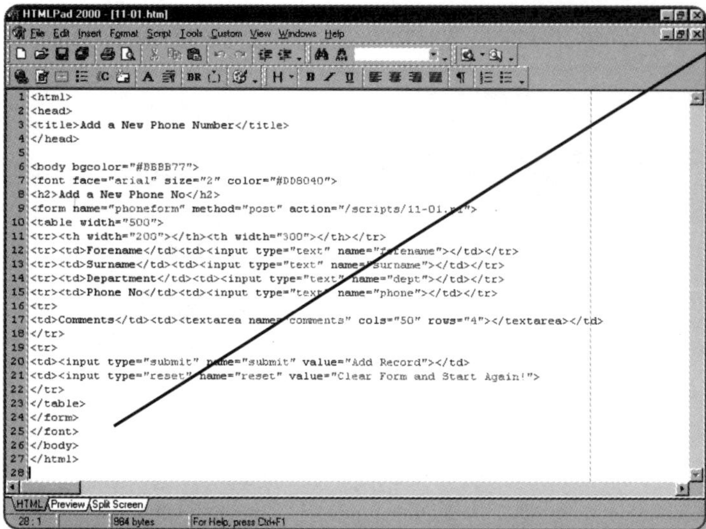

12. At this point close the table, form, font, body tag, and the HTML tags.

```
</table>
</form>
</font>
</body>
</html>
```

13. Save the form HTML as 11-01.htm in a suitable folder under the wwwroot folder in your Web server folders.

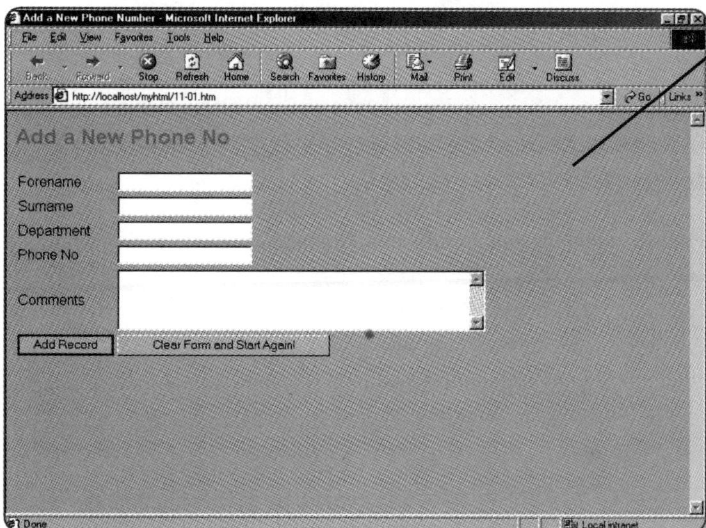

14. Open Internet Explorer, navigate to your new page, and make sure that your form looks okay.

At this point you cannot actually submit the form without receiving an error, as you have no Perl program yet to accept the data. That's what you are going to do next.

Getting Form Data via the POST Method

In your editor, start a new Perl program. Now you are going to add a Perl program to deal with the input from your HTML form. This small Perl program will require some explanation, as there will be some code you haven't seen before.

1. Start your program in the usual way, and add the HTTP header line.

```
#!c:/perl/bin

print "Content-type: text/html\n\n";
```

2. Add the following line to read the Form Input into your Perl program:

```
read(STDIN,$tempbuffer,$ENV{'CONTENT_LENGTH'});
```

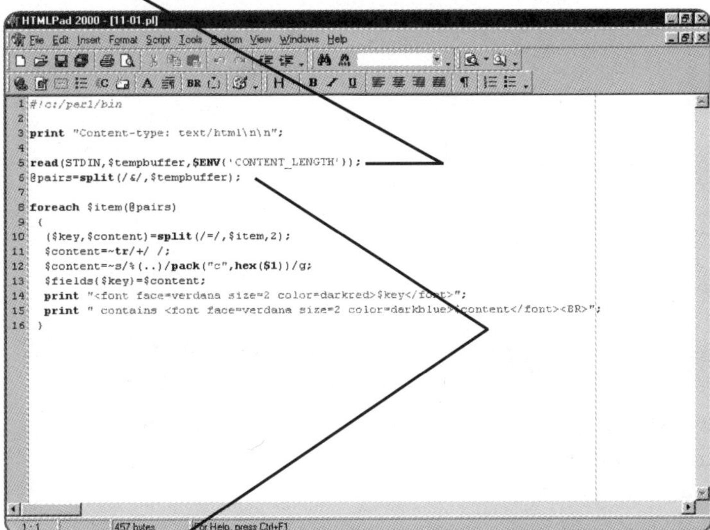

This line reads data from STDIN. STDIN is a reference to a built-in File Handle. In this case, the data from your form is being placed into a temporary buffer, called `$tempbuffer`, where you can then access the data. The amount of data taken from the form is arrived at by using an environment variable called CONTENT_LENGTH. So, this line knows how much data to expect and places it into `$tempbuffer`.

3. The data from the form is held as a single data item in `$tempbuffer`. To be of any use, you need to know what the original field was and what value it contained. The next line does this for you.

```
@pairs=split(/&/,$tempbuffer);
```

An array, called @pairs, is used to contain the key value pairs from the form. This line of code uses the split function to separate each key-value pair from all the other pairs so that you end up with an array of pairs each containing a field and its associated value. (Notice that each pair is separated from the next by an & character; the `split` function in this case uses this character to separate the data into discrete pairs.) You are almost at the stage where you have something useful.

4. Code a `foreach` line to perform a block of code (within the braces, {}) once for each item in the array, `@pairs`.

```
foreach $item(@pairs)
```

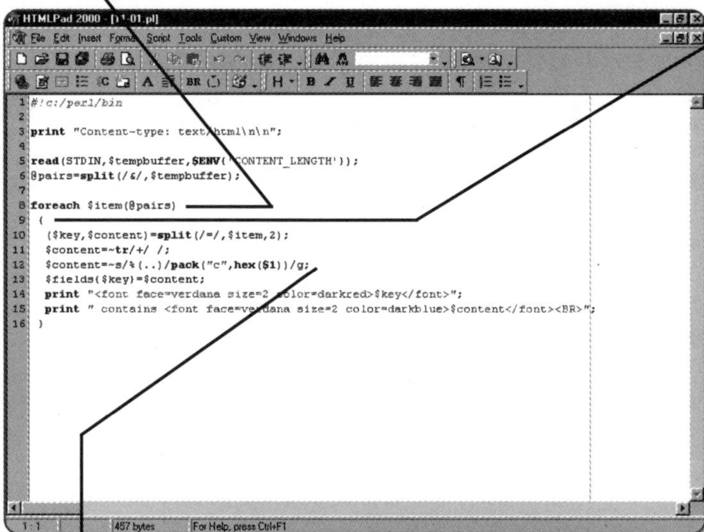

5. *Open the code block brace.*

```
{
```

6. Add the following line to separate the field names from the associated values.

```
($key,$content)=split
  (/=/,$item,2);
```

This line simply says: Split the value contained in each element, again using the `split` function, placing the results into `$key` and `$content`. The = is used to recognize where to make the split, and the 2 means there are only two elements, the key and the value—or in this application, the variable and its associated value.

7. The content received via the `HTTP POST` method contains a + where you would normally expect to find a space. Enter the following line to use the translate function to replace the + sign with spaces.

```
$content=~tr/+/ /;
```

Notice that you are using the binding operator, which means that the result of the pattern match on the right of the equal sign will be incorporated into the copy of the data loaded into the `$content` variable. The forward slash / is used as a delimiter in this case, so that the translate command, `tr`, knows what is intended to be in the translation.

8. Now enter this complicated-looking line:

```
$content=~s/%(..)/pack("c",hex($1))/g;
```

> **NOTE**
>
> Again you have a pattern-matching line using the binding operator. The command using the pattern is the substitute command, s. In this case, hexadecimal codes, which replace symbols during their transmission via HTTP, are substituted with their character equivalent. The /g at the end of the command simply means "global," that is, replace each occurrence found in the data.

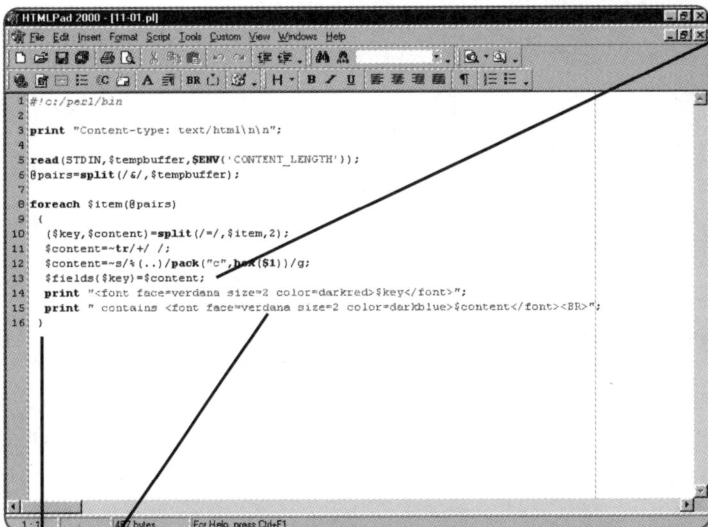

9. Now code this line to store the keys and associated values into the hash `%fields`. Note that as in each case you are storing a scalar variable into the hash, the element in the hash is also labeled as a scalar `$field`. At the end of the `foreach` loop, you will have a hash, `%field-s`, containing all of the fields with the associated values, which can then be "searched" by field name.

```
$fields{$key}=$content;
```

10. Now for the easy bit. Display each fieldname (key) and its associated value.

```
print "<font face=verdana size=2 color=darkred>$key</font>";
print " contains <font face=verdana size=2 color=darkblue>$content
   </font><BR>";
```

11. Finally, close the `foreach` code block.

```
}
```

That seemed like hard work didn't it? But read through each line and the notes attached to each step and I think you will agree it's a lot simpler than it might first appear.

12. Save your code as 11-01.pl.

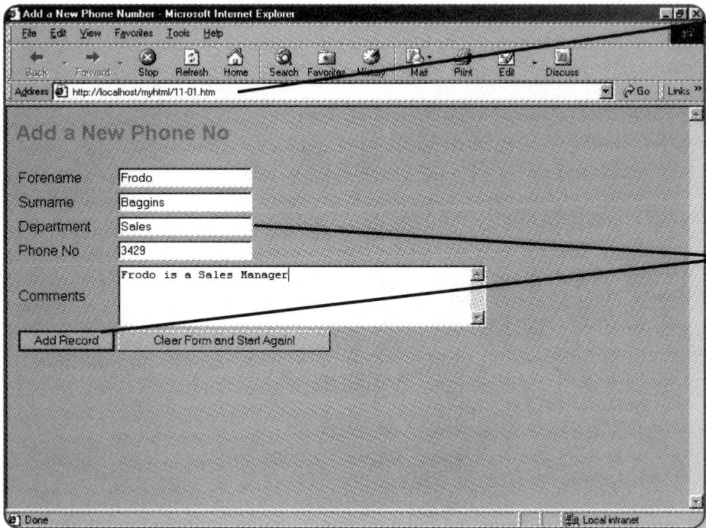

13. Type the following URL into your browser (or wherever you placed your html).

```
http://localhost/myhtml/
   11-01.htm
```

14. Enter some data into the form and click the Add Record button.

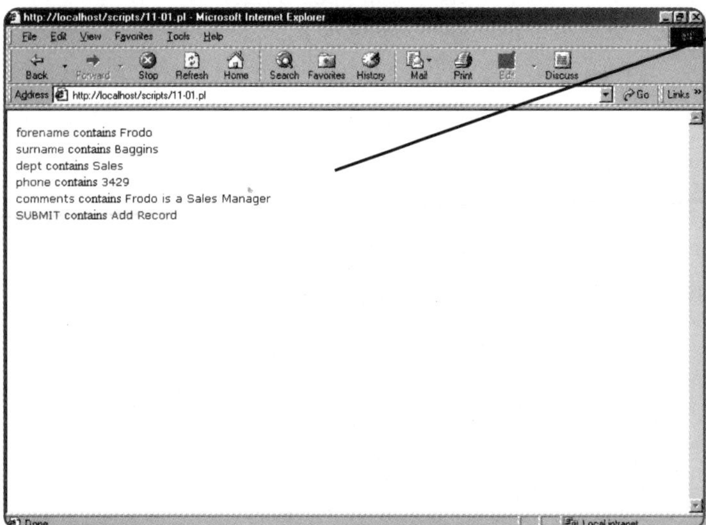

15. You should find that you get a list of all the variables from your form along with their values, like this.

Getting Form Data via the GET Method

Okay, now you know how to get at data sent from a form using the POST method. How about the GET method?

The good news is that most of the code is the same. In fact, in the form, all you need to do is to change the: `method= "post"` attribute to: `method= "get"`.

Try the following:

1. Re-open your 11-01.htm page into your editor.

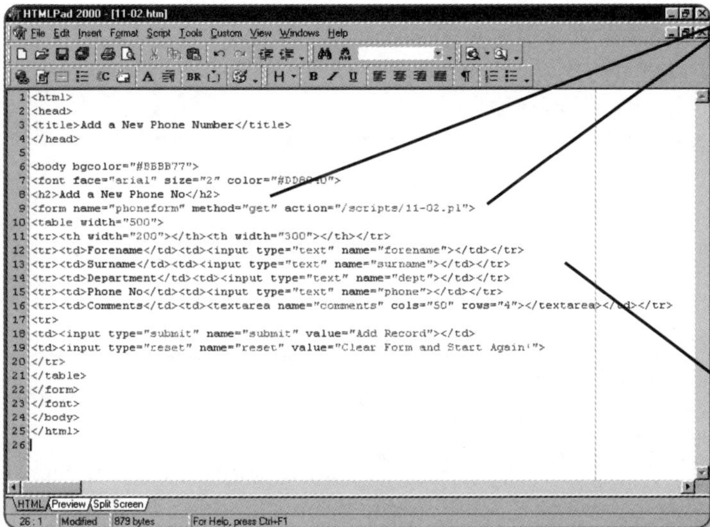

2. Replace the `method="post"` attribute of the form tag with the `method="get"`; then change the Perl program name from 11-01.pl to 11-02.pl, so that the form tag now looks like this:

```
<form name="phoneform"
   method="get
   action="/scripts/11-02.pl">
```

3. Your program should now look like this; save it as 11-02.htm.

4. Now re-open your 11-01.pl program.

5. Remove the following line:

```
read(STDIN,$tempbuffer,$ENV{'CONTENT_LENGTH'});
```

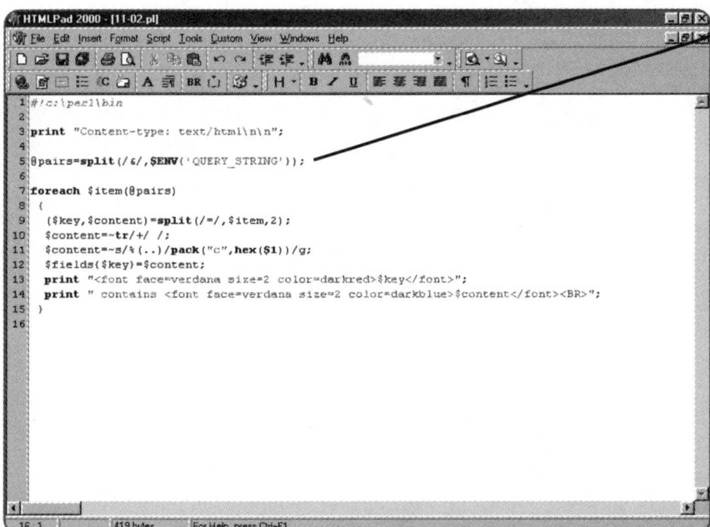

6. Replace the following line:

```
@pairs=split(/&/,$tempbuffer);
```

With this one:

```
@pairs=split(/&/,$ENV
   {'QUERY_STRING'});
```

NOTE

Now you are taking the data contained within the environment variable `QUERY_STRING` as your source for the form data.

Note that you do not have a "read" command anymore, as the data is, in the case of the `GET` method, simply a part of the URL, and therefore appears in `QUERY_STRING`.

7. The rest of the code is identical to the 11-01.pl; now save this code as 11-02.pl in your scripts folder.

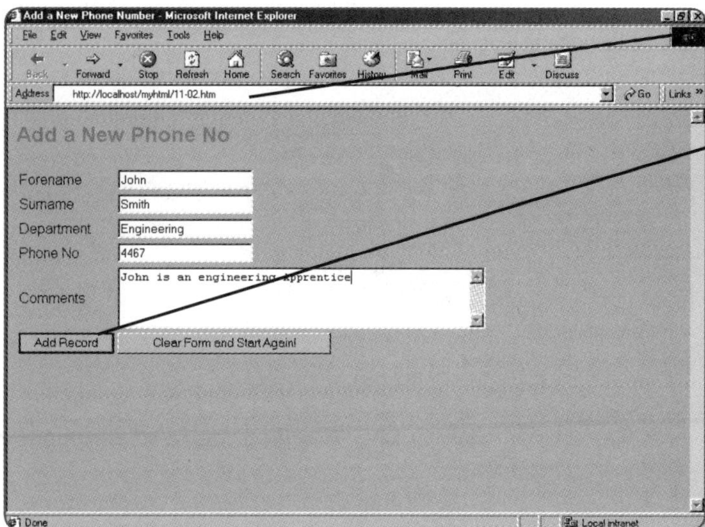

8. Open your browser and open your new page, 11-02.htm.

9. Enter some data and click the submit (in this case it's called Add Record) button.

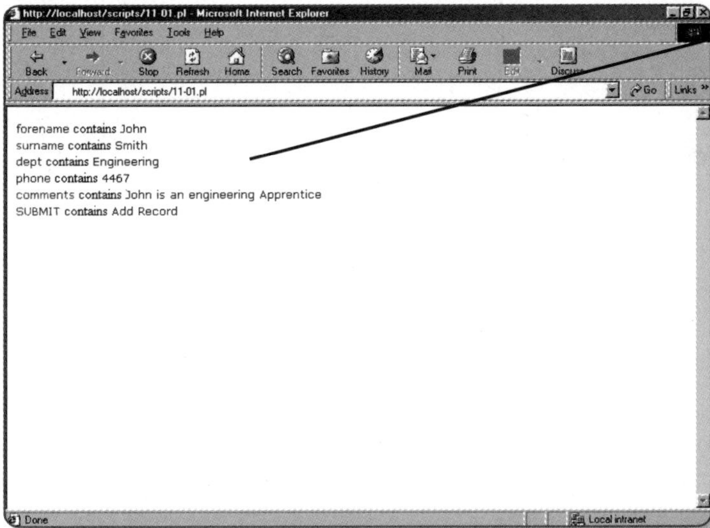

You should see something like this.

Once again the data fields used on the form are displayed along with their respective values.

In this chapter you learned how to obtain user input from an HTML form using both the `GET` and `POST` methods. This is a major milestone, as you have now made the link from user input at a form in the user's Web browser to actual data available for use on the server.

So, you can create the forms and you can grab the data in your Perl program. Now, what are you going to do? One thing you might like to do is to save the data into a file. So, in the next chapter you will learn about files.

12 Using Files in Perl

In this chapter, you'll learn how to use files in Perl—how to create them, write to them, read from them, and delete them. You will also learn how to create and remove directories in Perl.

In this chapter you will learn how to:

- Open a file in Perl
- Read data from a file
- Close a file
- Use directories
- Delete a file

Opening Files in Perl

Before you can do anything with a file, you need to open it. This is done using the Perl `open` function. The general syntax for the `open` function is

```
Open(MYFILE, "testfile.dat") || die "Error encountered when opening file ...";
```

This means that Perl will attempt to open a file whose file handle is MYFILE. A *file handle* is a reference variable that is used to store the *internal name* of the file, that is, the name by which the Perl program will recognize the file.

Following the file handle is the real name of the file; in this example, testfile.dat.

Notice in the line of code that the next thing on the line is a *double pipe*. This is the OR operator and is used here to execute whatever follows it if the file open code fails. In other words, if for any reason the file cannot be opened by Perl, the code following the || symbol will be executed.

The code after the double pipe OR operator simply says

```
die "Error encountered when opening file ..."
```

The `die` function then stops the program running after displaying the message "Error encountered when opening file…".

A general error message in itself isn't very helpful. However, Perl also has a special error variable that holds the error message for an event such as this. This is the `$!` variable. You can now add this variable to the `die` error message:

```
Open(MYFILE, "testfile.dat")
       || die "Error encountered when opening file ... $!";
```

As you would be unable to see anything when a file is successfully opened, trying an example would be a bit pointless right now. The next step will be to read a file so that you can see the `open` function in action and see how data is read from a file. If you want to, you can rename the input file so that the program cannot find it, and then try out the `die` function and error message.

Reading Data from a File

Data may be read from a file in Perl using the angle operator, < >. To get a line of data, you simply wrap the file handle in the angle operator like this:

```
$dataline = <MYDATA>;
```

This will take any data from MYDATA (testfile.dat) and store it into `$dataline`. The data will stop when a newline character is encountered.

The end of a file is recognized when the file handle returns "undefined." So to read and display the whole contents of a file you can do this:

```
while(defined($dataline=<MYFILE>))

  {
     print "$dataline <br>";
  }
```

This can be simplified still further if you do not have any other conditions in the `while` statement. The `while` statement will execute while the conditions in the following parentheses are True. The condition "undefined" of the file handle is effectively False.

Therefore, you can now say

```
while(<MYFILE>)
  {
     print;
  }
```

Note that now, unless you had <BR> tags at the end of your lines of data in the file, the data would all be joined together. Of course, you could put a separate print line after the empty one to provide the <br> tag.

```
while(<MYFILE>)
  {
     print;
     print "<br>";
  }
```

> **NOTE**
>
> You cannot add a <BR> tag to the first print statement, as it would then no longer be reading the data from $_, but would instead just directly print <br> and nothing else.

Now, providing you have a file to work with, you can try out both the `open` function and reading data from a file.

1. Open your editor and clear it of any default code that the editor might create so that you have a completely clear file.

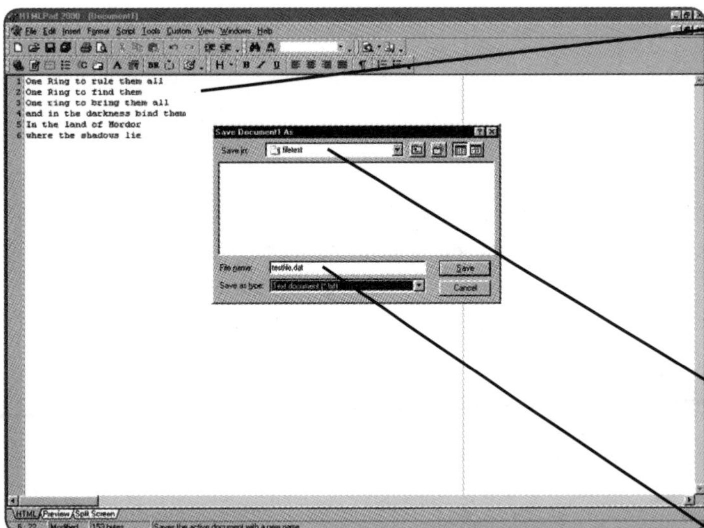

2. Use your editor to create some text (like this text, from J.R.R. Tolkien's *Lord of the Rings*):

```
One ring to rule them all
One ring to find them
One ring to bring them all
and in the darkness bind them
In the land of Mordor
where the shadows lie
```

3. Create a folder called filetest under the document root (wwwroot) on your Web server.

4. Save your text in your new filetest folder as, say, testfile.dat.

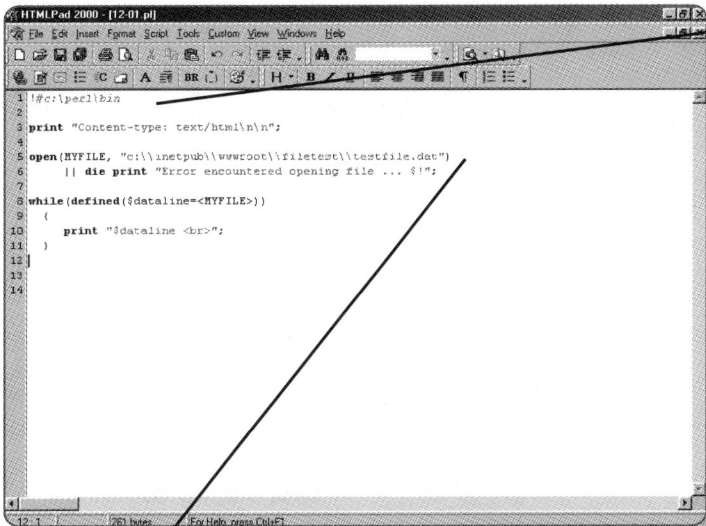

5. Open your editor and start a new Perl program with the shebang statement and the HTTP header:

```
!#c:\perl\bin
print "Content-type:
   text/html\n\n";
```

6. Open a file handle like this:

```
open(MYFILE, "c:\\inetpub\\wwwroot\\filetest\\testfile.dat")
      || die print "Error encountered opening file ... $!";
```

NOTE

Note the use of double backslashes. The string is double-quoted and so *interpolation* will occur. If this was not done, then, should any part of the path begin with an "n," it would be treated as a newline character. The double backslashes suspend the interpolation process for the characters following those double backslashes. An alternative to prevent character combinations being treated as special characters is to use forward slashes, as you will see in UNIX programs. This will work with Windows too, so you may prefer to use forward slashes rather than double backslashes like this:

```
open(MYFILE, "c:/inetpub/wwwroot/filetest/testfile.dat")
      || die print "Error encountered opening file ... $!";
```

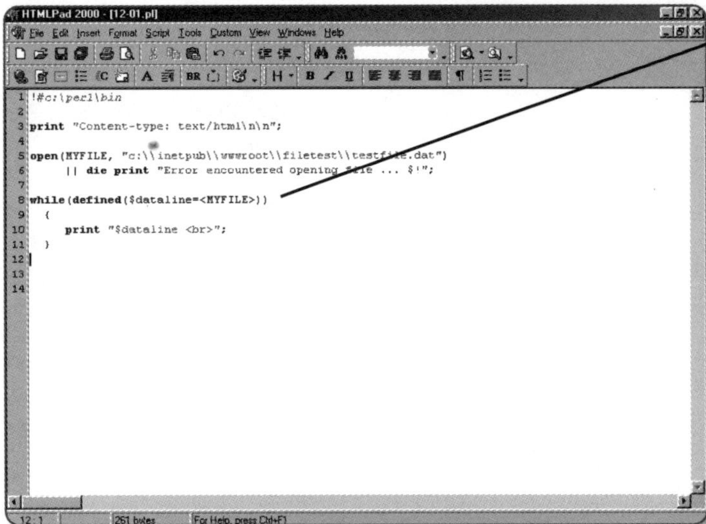

7. Now add the file record processing code as described earlier.

```
while(defined
   ($dataline=<MYFILE>))
  {
     print "$dataline <br>";
  }
```

NOTE

So you have a `while` loop, the terminating condition of which is when the input from the file is undefined; that is, you receive a null input from the file.

8. Save your file as 12-01.pl.

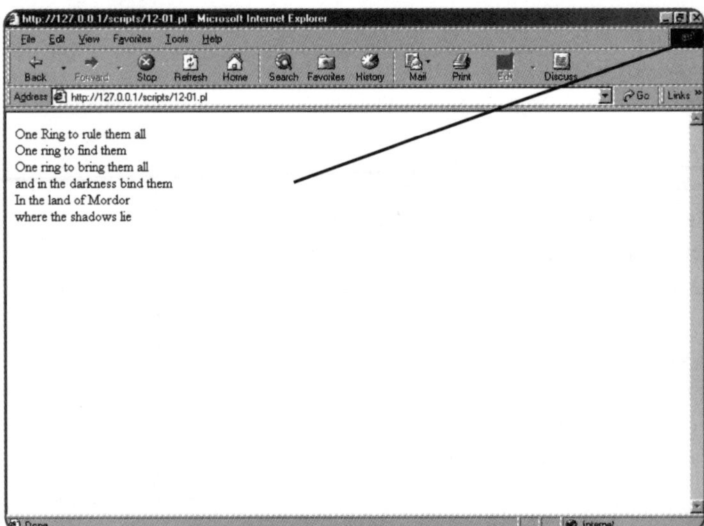

9. Now run your program by opening your browser and entering the URL for your script.

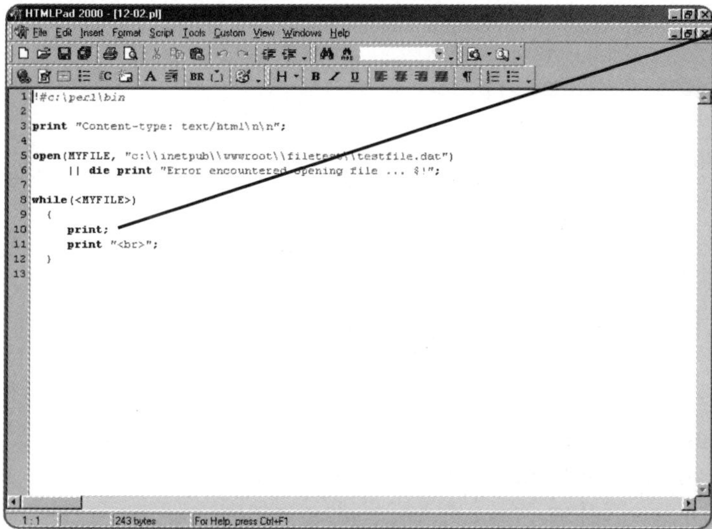

> **NOTE**
>
> You can even simplify your program further, as mentioned earlier. Remember that all the current data is held in a special variable called $_. Also, remember that a condition needs only to be tested as True or False. You can simplify your code further to look like this.

10. Save the program as 12-02.pl.

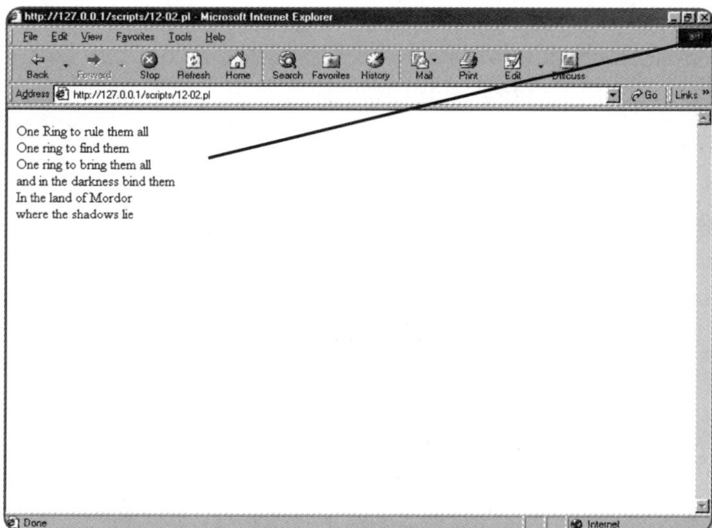

11. If you run the program again you should get the same results as with 12-01.pl.

Just to prove that the error condition is indeed trapped, try temporarily renaming your data file to anything you like and then re-running your code. You should get the error message.

Error Checking

The `die` function you have used so far is the simplest way of checking for errors. As an alternative you could use the code on the next page.

```
If (open(MYFILE, "testfile.dat"))
   {
        while(defined($dataline=<MYFILE>))
           {
                  print "$dataline <br>";
           }
    }
else
    {
       print "There was an error opening the file ...";
    }
```

This works because the `open` function returns a False value if it fails. (More correctly, if you displayed the value, you would find that it is returned as undefined). If it succeeds, it will return a non-zero value. Any non-zero value equates logically to True, so the rest of the code to read data from the file is executed.

The advantage of trapping errors in this way is that the program does not have to abort. The `die` function stops execution of the program, and therefore should be used where failure to open a file is considered a catastrophic error.

Closing a File

When you have finished with a file, you should always close it. Doing so is good programming practice and also ensures that resources no longer being used are returned to the operating system. If this is not done in large systems, the upper limit for the number of file handles that can be open at any one time may be reached and the system may then fail.

To close a file, simply use the `close` function. For the previous example, it would be coded like this:

```
close(MYFILE);
```

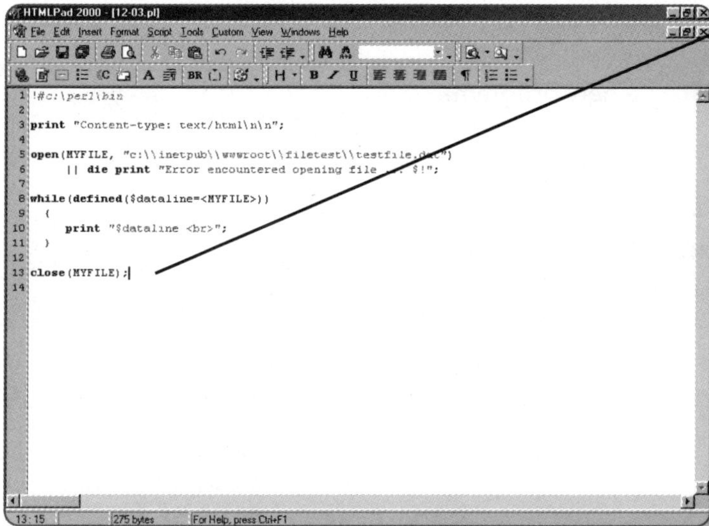

Now, the complete file read example would look like this.

Save your updated program as 12-03.pl and check that it works.

Writing to a File

You have learned one way to get data from a file. Now you are going to learn how to write data to a new file, and how to add data to an existing file.

Opening the File for Writing

Opening a file for writing is just as easy as opening a file for reading. You simply use the `open` function, like this.

```
open(MYFILE, ">c:\\inetpub\\wwwroot\\filetest\\outfile.dat")
```

Note that there is only a very subtle difference between this and opening the file for reading—the inclusion of the > symbol in front of the filename.

To create a file from a Perl program, do the following.

1. Open your editor and start a new program.

```
!#c:\perl\bin
print "Content-type: text/html\n\n";
```

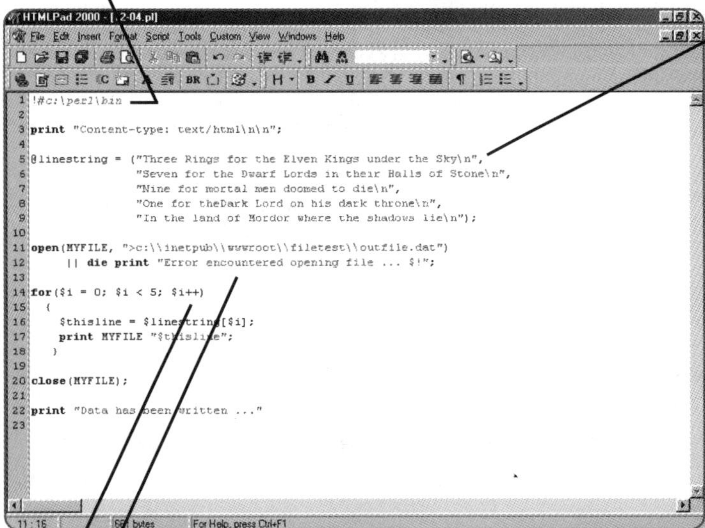

2. Create an array with some text like this (more Tolkien):

```
@linestring = ("Three Rings
   for the Elven Kings under
   the Sky\n",
       "Seven for the Dwarf
          Lords in their
          Halls of Stone\n",
       "Nine for mortal men
           doomed to die\n",
       "One for the Dark Lord
           on his dark
           throne\n",
       "In the land of Mordor
           where the shadows
           lie\n");
```

NOTE

Each entry in the array ends in \n and each entry is double quoted so that the newline \n characters are correctly interpreted.

3. Enter the code to open the file for writing:

```
open(MYFILE, ">c:\\inetpub\\wwwroot\\filetest\\outfile.dat")
     || die print "Error encountered opening file ... $!";
```

4. Now, as there are five lines of data in your array, start a loop to process the array:

```
for($i = 0; $i < 5; $i++)
  {
```

5. Copy the data into a scalar variable:

```
$thisline = $linestring[$i];
```

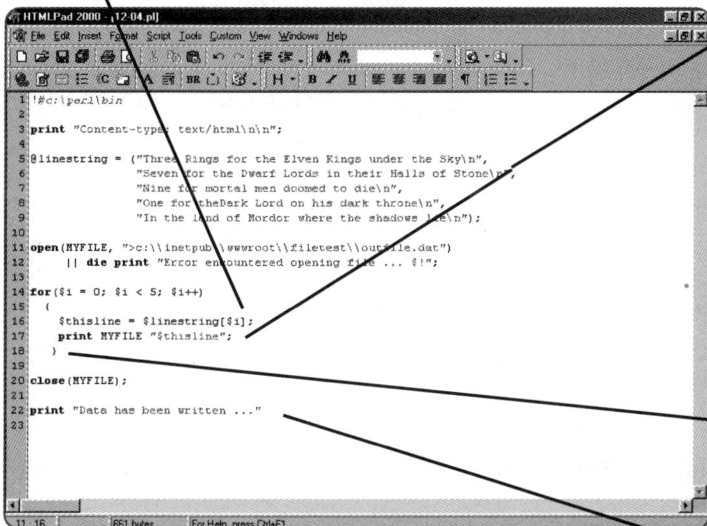

6. Print the data to your `MYFILE` handle so that it gets written to the file.

```
print MYFILE "$thisline";
```

Remember that the `MYFILE` handle directs output to the file you specified in the `open` function.

7. Now close the loop.

```
}
```

8. Finally, close the file and display a message saying that the data has been written.

```
close(MYFILE);
print "Data has been written ..."
```

> **CAUTION**
>
> In this example you used the > symbol at the front of the filename in the `open` function, causing a new file to be written. If you run the program again, it will still do the same. That is, any previous file will be overwritten. It is very important to remember this for the future to avoid losing important files.

9. Now save your file as 12-04.pl.

10. Run your program (http://127.0.0.1/scripts/12-04.pl).

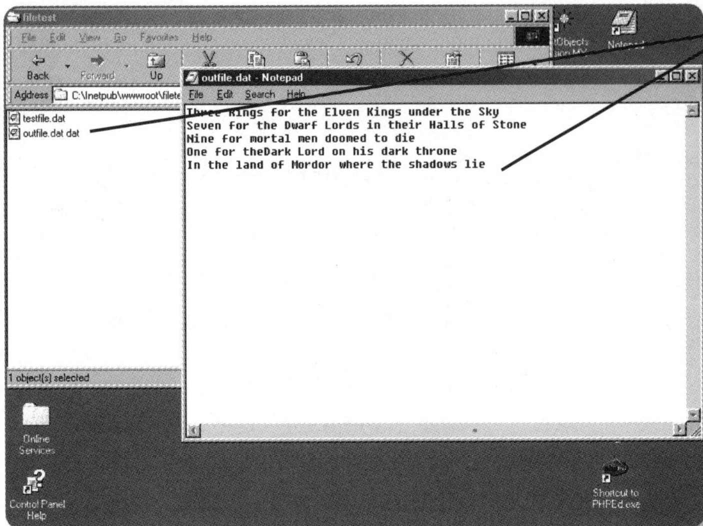

11. Go to your filetest folder, open the outfile.dat file, and check that your data has been written to the file.

Adding Data to an Existing File

You can also add data to an existing file. The change in the code to achieve this is very subtle. Remember that you added a > sign to the front of a filename in the `open` function so that you could write to the file. All you have to do to open a file to append data is to put two > signs at the front of the name.

Try it:

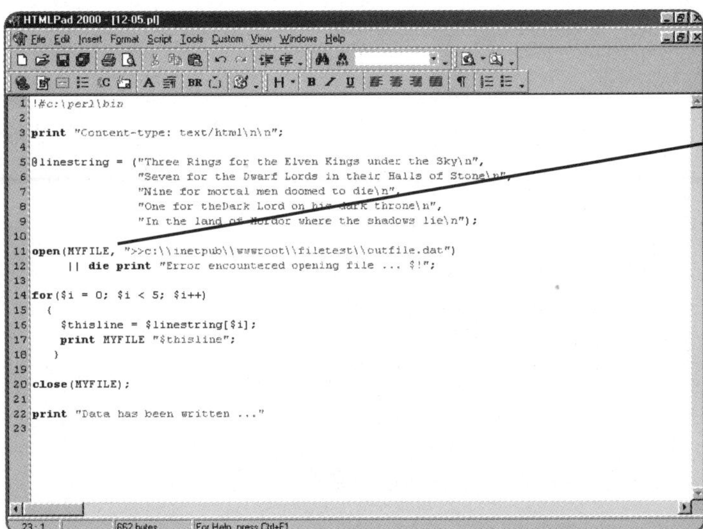

1. Re-open your write file program (12-04.pl).

2. Change the `open` statement to include two > signs, like this:

```
open(MYFILE, ">>c:\\inetpub\
   \wwwroot\\filetest\
   \outfile.dat")
      || die print "Error
         encountered opening
         file ... $!";
```

3. You now have >> at the front of the filename attribute of the file `open` statement.

4. Save your program as 12-05.pl.

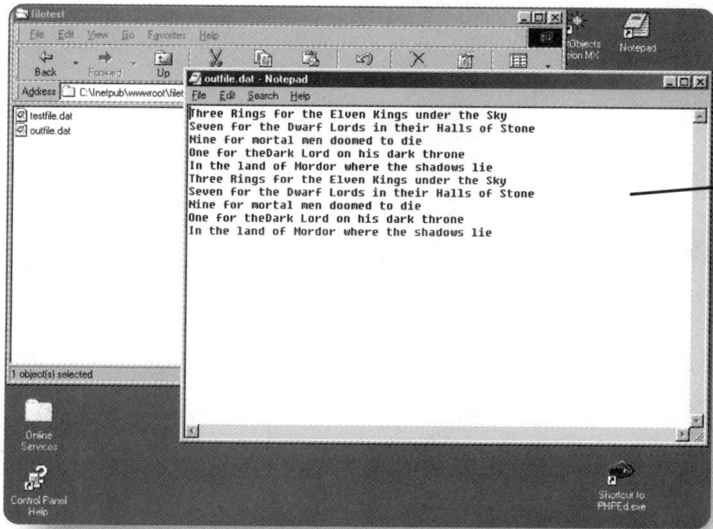

5. Run your program (http://127.0.0.1/scripts/12-04.pl).

6. The output on the page will be the same as for 12-04.pl. But now, open the file outfile.dat and you will see text from Tolkien's *Fellowhip of the Ring*.

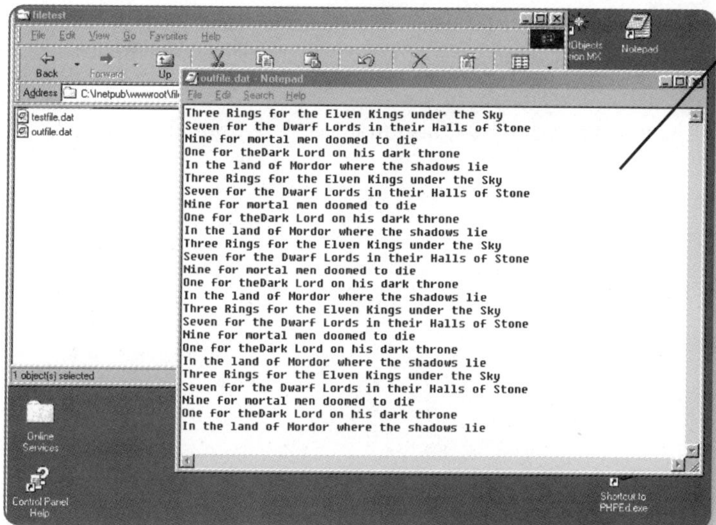

7. Run the program a few more times and view the file again.

As you can see, instead of overwriting the file outfile.dat as 12-03.pl would do, you are now adding each copy of the text in your program to the end of the file.

Deleting a File

Deleting a file is very straightforward. It is accomplished using the oddly-named `unlink` function.

To demonstrate the `unlink` function, delete the output file you just created.

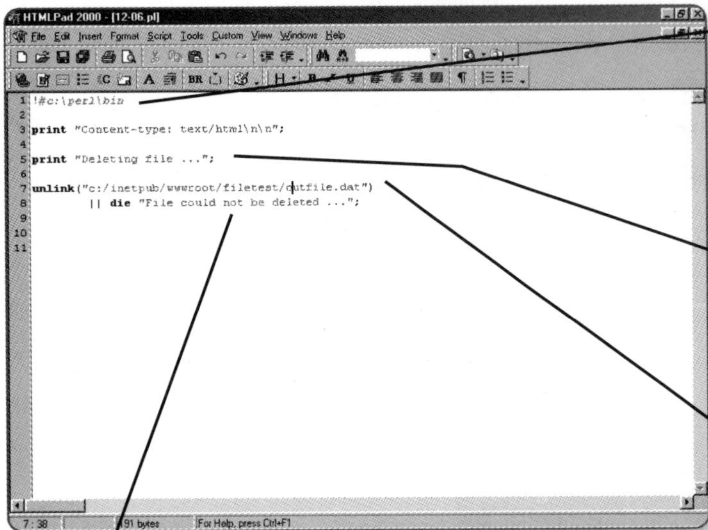

1. Again, start a new program in your editor.

```
!#c:\perl\bin
print "Content-type:
   text/html\n\n";
```

2. Display a message to show what you are doing.

```
print "Deleting file ...";
```

3. Now delete the file using the `unlink` function, not forgetting the `die` function to trap any errors.

```
unlink("c:/inetpub/wwwroot/filetest/outfile.dat")
        || die "File could not be deleted ...";
```

4. Note that you can use a scalar to store the filename so that your delete becomes

```
unlink($filename)
        || die "File could not be deleted ...";
```

NOTE

Multiple files can be specified by separating the filenames with commas.

```
Unlink("c:/inetpub/wwwroot/filetest/outfile.dat,
   c:/inetpub/wwwroot/filetest/anotherfile.dat ")
  || die "File(s) could not be deleted ...";
```

You can also store all the filenames to be deleted in an array so that your delete becomes

```
@files = {"c:/inetpub/wwwroot/filetest/outfile.dat",
   "c:/inetpub/wwwroot/filetest/anotherfile.dat"}
unlink(@files)
  || die "Files could not be deleted ...";
```

5. Save your program as 12-06.pl.

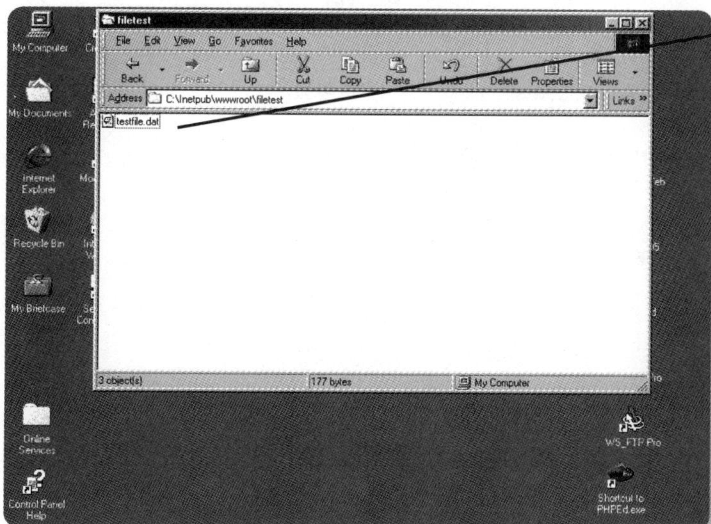

6. Run your program, then go to the filetest directory to check if your file has been deleted.

Using Directories with Perl

Perl is also able to create and remove directories or folders. This makes it very powerful, as it's able to create any environment or file and folder structure that your application needs.

Making a Directory

Making directories or folders with Perl is very easy, and the functions used are very similar to the equivalent DOS and UNIX commands. The function used to create a directory is `mkdir`.

Try this simple program.

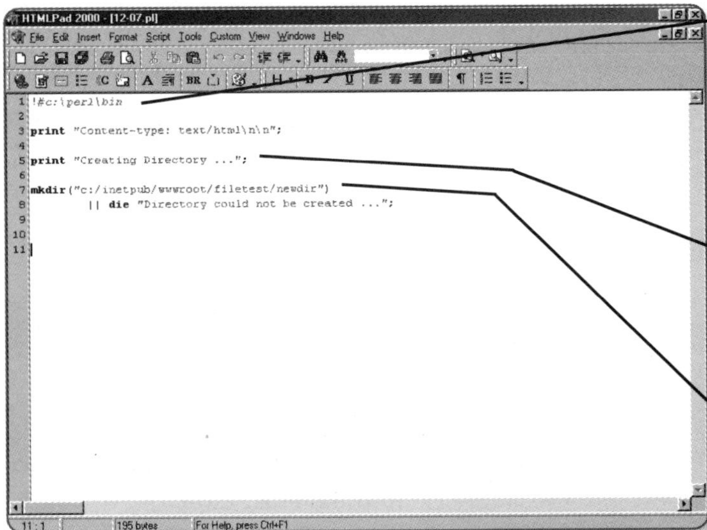

1. Open your editor and start a new program.

```
!#c:\perl\bin
print "Content-type:
   text/html\n\n";
```

2. Display a message to show what you are about to do.

```
print "Creating Directory ...";
```

3. Now enter the command to create your new folder or directory.

```
mkdir("c:/inetpub/wwwroot/filetest/newdir")
        || die "Directory could not be created ...";
```

4. Save your program as 12-07.pl.

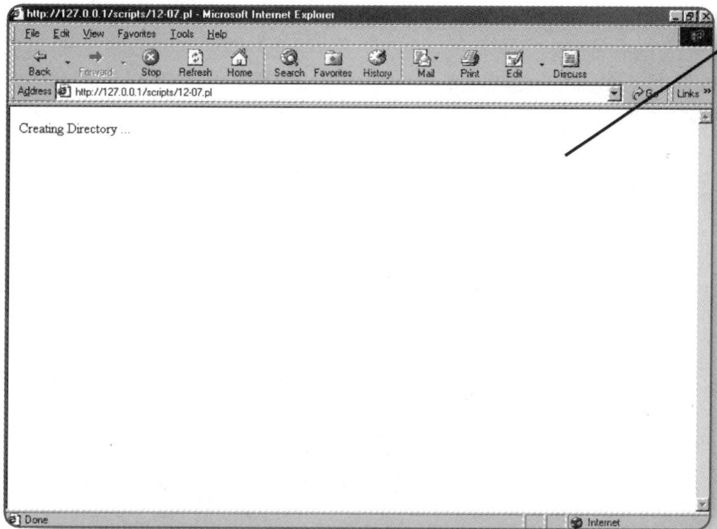

5. Run the program.

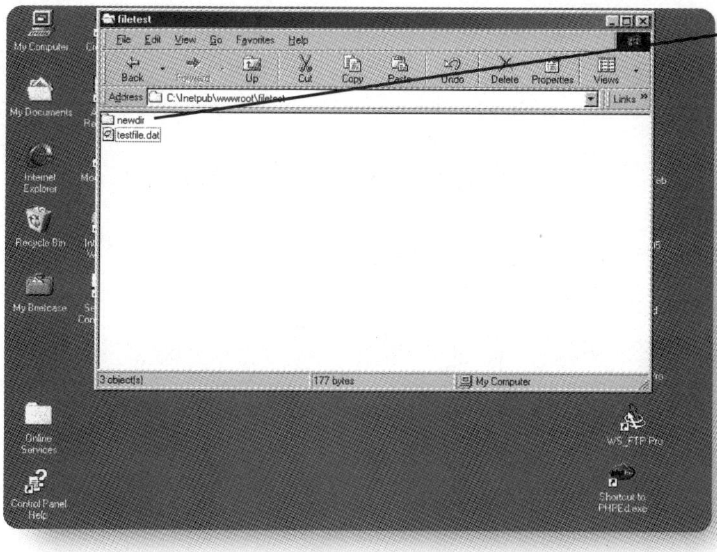

6. Go to the filetest folder; you should find you now have a new folder called newdir.

That was pretty simple, wasn't it?

Removing a Directory

Removing a directory is just as easy as creating one, and as you would expect, it uses a similar syntax to the DOS `rmdir` command.

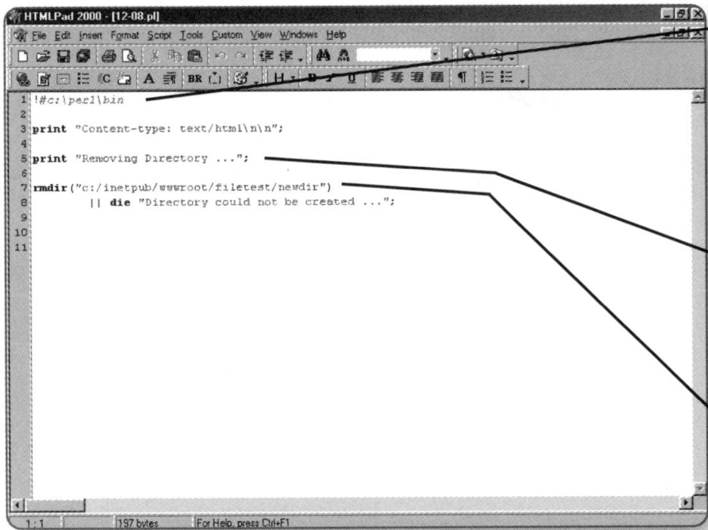

1. Open your editor and create a new program.

```
!#c:\perl\bin
print "Content-type:
   text/html\n\n";
```

2. Display the message stating what is happening.

```
print "Removing Directory ...";
```

3. Enter the code to remove the directory created by your program 12-07.pl.

```
rmdir("c:/inetpub/wwwroot/filetest/newdir")
        || die "Directory could not be created ...";
```

4. Save your program as 12-08.pl.

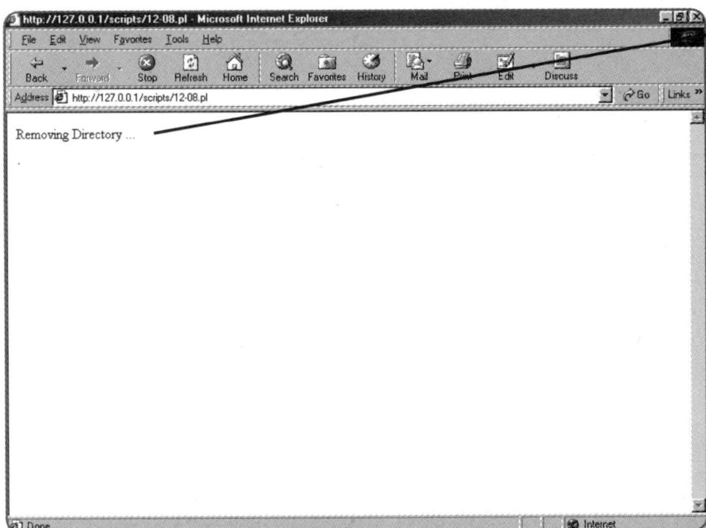

5. Run the program.

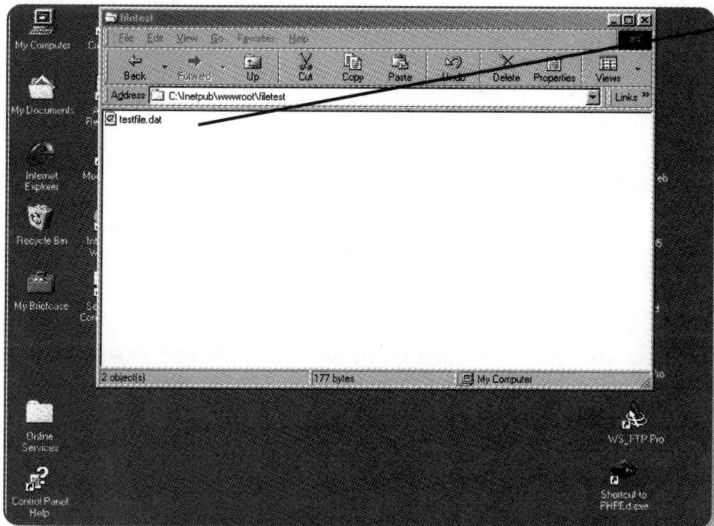

6. Go to the filetest folder. You should find that your newdir directory has been removed.

There are lots of other things you can do with folders, such as change permissions and so on, but that is beyond the scope of this book. In most cases, being able to change permissions on folders through a Web application could be pretty dangerous.

Data Files

You have already seen how to read data from and to write data to a file. But in that case, the data was simple strings of text. On most occasions your data will be more sophisticated than that. For example, a simple employee directory may store its data in separate fields for data items such as forename, surname, department, telephone number, and so on. How do you know which bit of data belongs where in a file?

You have to tell your program how to determine that. It's not as daunting as it sounds. All you have to do is to decide on a character to use as a *field separator*. Often, you will see the comma used for this purpose, but what if there are commas in the data? Just use a different character that is not likely to appear in the data. You can use any character you like; in the following examples you will see the *not* (¬) character used. It really doesn't matter what you use as long as you can use it to separate each data item from the next, and as long as that separator does not appear in the text.

> **NOTE**
>
> If you have a U.S. Keyboard (or any other besides British), you can get the ¬ character into your editor by holding down the ALT key and typing 170 on the numeric keypad on the right hand side of the keyboard. Release the ALT key and the character will appear in your editor code. But, as I said, you can use any character you like.

Right now, take a look at reading and writing data from and to files and see how you can retrieve the information as separate fields of data.

Writing Files

Try the following example, which is almost identical to a previous example except for the data, which is stored in a field called `$thisline`. The difference is that this is not *one* item of data but *four*, as you will see.

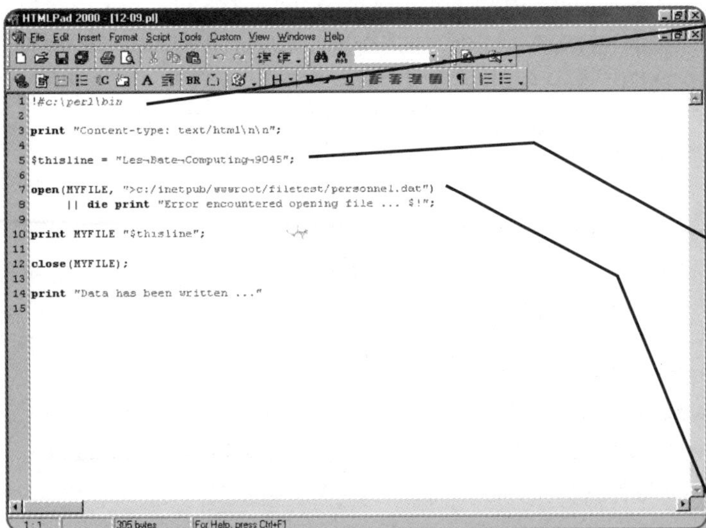

1. Open your editor and start a new Perl program.

```
!#c:\perl\bin
print "Content-type:
   text/html\n\n";
```

2. Create your four items of data, separated by ¬ symbols (or whatever you choose), and store them in a string scalar variable.

```
$thisline =
   "Les¬Bate¬Computing¬9045";
```

3. Enter the Perl code to open a file for writing (remember the >).

```
open(MYFILE, ">c:/inetpub/wwwroot/filetest/personnel.dat")
    || die print "Error encountered opening file ... $!";
```

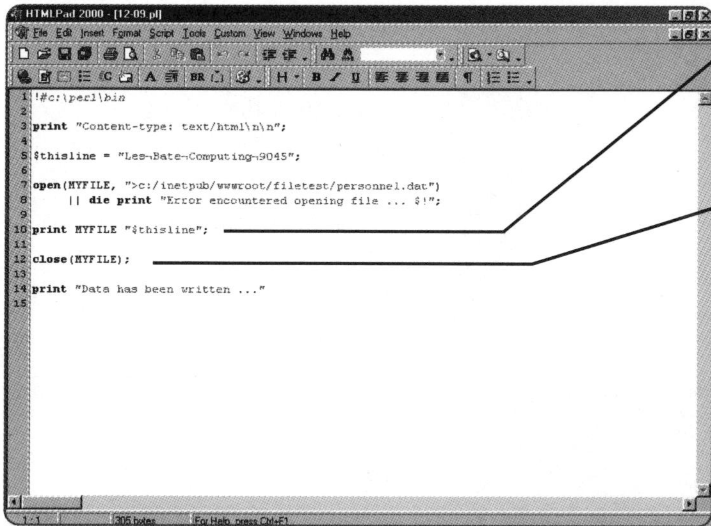

4. Now write the contents of the `$thisline` variable.

```
print MYFILE "$thisline";
```

5. Finally, close the file and write a message to the Web page telling the user what you have done.

```
close(MYFILE);
print "Data has been written
   ..."
```

6. Save your program as 12-09.pl.

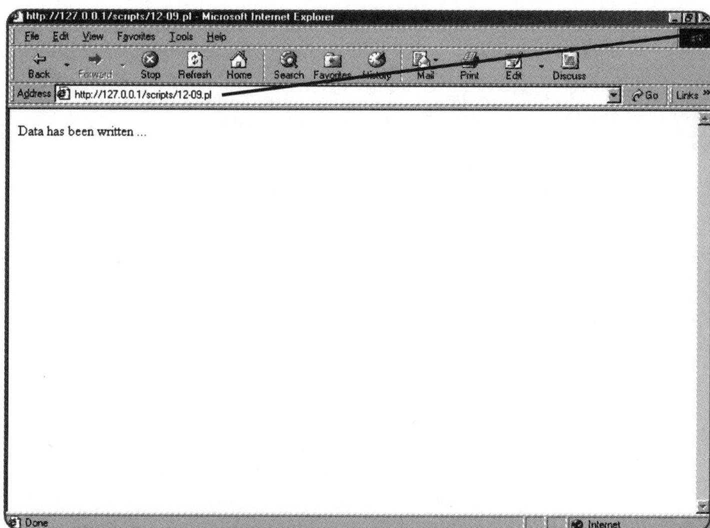

7. Open your browser and enter the URL (http://127.0.0.1/scripts/12-08.pl) to run your program.

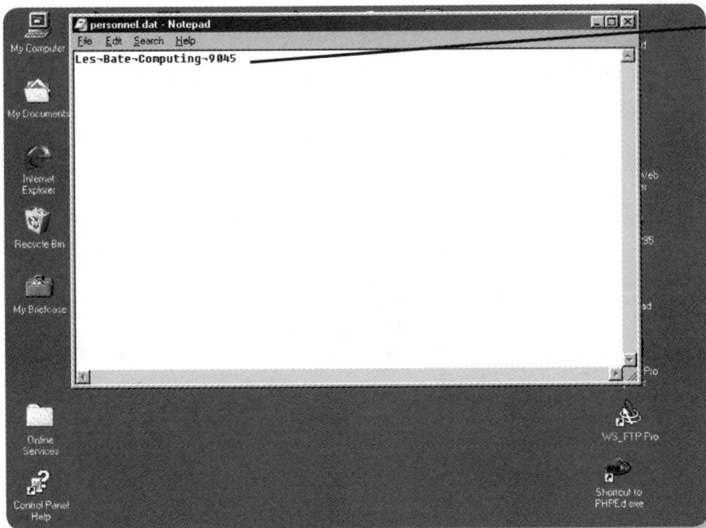

8. If you go to the filetest folder you should find that you have a new file called personnel.dat. Open it in an editor or Notepad or whatever you want to use, and there you will find the contents of your `$thisline` variable, proving that your Perl program has successfully written the data to a file.

The next step is to be able to get your data back from the file.

Reading Files

Now try retrieving the data you just wrote to the file called personnel.dat.

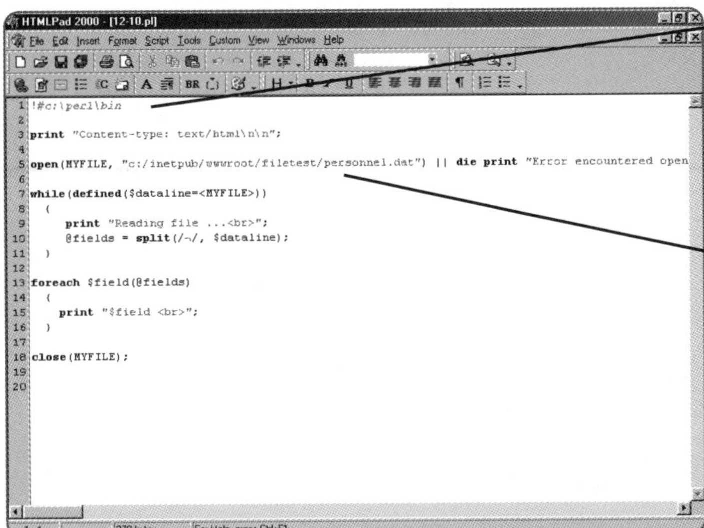

1. Open your editor and start a new program.

```
!#c:\perl\bin
print "Content-type:
   text/html\n\n";
```

2. Open the file in the usual way for reading files.

```
open(MYFILE,
"c:/inetpub/wwwroot
   /filetest/personnel.dat") ||
   die print "Error encountered
   opening file... $!";
```

3. Using a `while` loop, read the data from the file.

```
while(defined($dataline=<MYFILE>))
  {
     print "Reading file ...<br>";
```

4. The slight difference between this and earlier file reading programs you have tried is that you are going to store the data you read in from the file into an array, and data will be split up into separate pieces by looking for the ¬ symbols that were added to break up the data.

```
@fields = split(/¬/, $dataline);
```

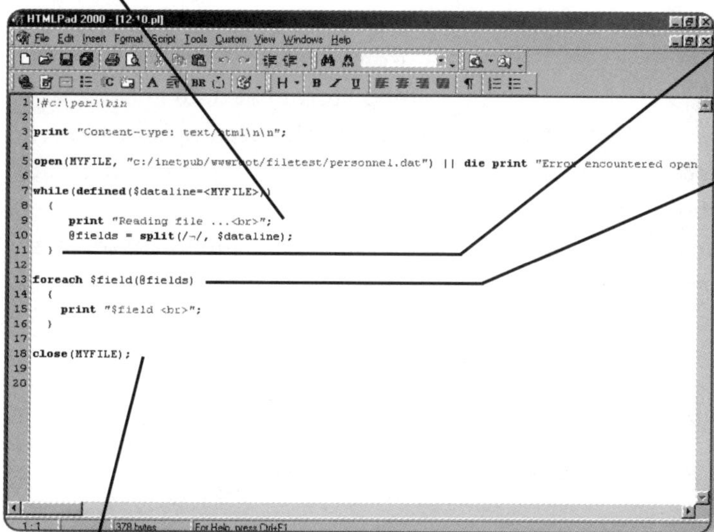

5. Close the `while` loop.

```
}
```

6. Now, to prove the point, display the value of each individual piece of data by "printing" the value of each element of the array you just created:

```
foreach $field(@fields)
  {
    print "$field <br>";
  }
```

7. And finally, of course, close the file.

```
close(MYFILE);
```

8. Save your program as 12-10.pl.

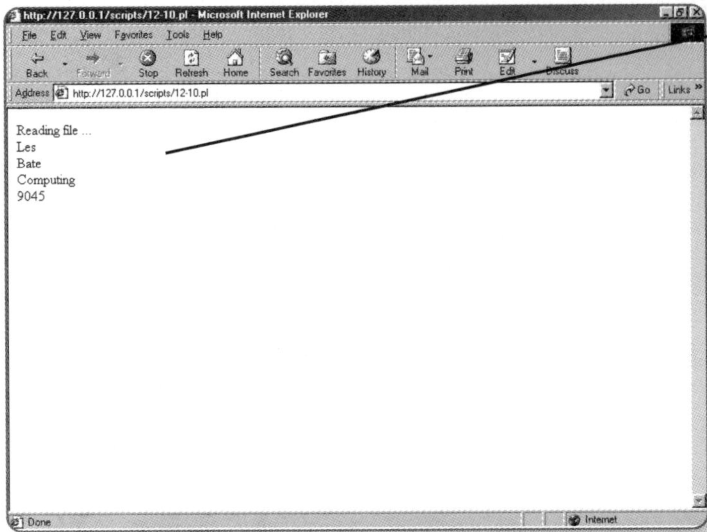

9. Open your browser and run your script. You should see a list of the data items like this.

As you can see, files are useful to have available when building applications, and indeed there is much you can do with them.

By now, you have learned the basics of the Perl language and now you can use some of the features of Perl to grab data from a user on your Web page and store that data in a file. You have learned how to retrieve that data and send it back to the user, or do whatever you want to do with it. You can now build applications that are fully interactive with the user. You may not be confident yet—so far this books has shown you brief, easy to understand examples, and the leap from those to a full application may seem a little daunting—but you are getting there.

Files have enabled you to complete the loop. They give permanence (often referred to as *persistence*) to your data, so that when your users come back another day, they can see their input staring back at them. And that is something that, as a budding Web developer, you will find immensely satisfying.

Even more powerful are databases, but before you learn about how to use them in Perl, you will learn about another subject that is very useful in Web applications: e-mail.

13

Sending E-mail in Perl

E-mail is a useful addition to the facilities in your Perl Web applications. And it is not difficult to send e-mail in Perl. Unfortunately, the methods used to do so differ, and it is largely a matter of asking your ISP for information. E-mail requires a program called a Mail Transfer Agent (MTA) to send the e-mail to an SMTP server. On the UNIX platform, the shell command `sendmail` does this. In Windows-type environments there is the SMTP server that comes with Microsoft's Internet Information Server (IIS), but there is no MTA in Windows. Instead, you can use a package called SMTP in Perl to help you send e-mail, or you can use a more recent module called sender.pm. A program called Blat.exe can also be used on Windows platforms to send e-mail via SMTP.

In this chapter you will learn:

- What FTP is and how to use it
- How to use SMTP in Perl to send e-mail
- How to send e-mail using Blat.exe
- How to send e-mail on a UNIX server using Sendmail

Because methods of using e-mail vary from ISP to ISP, I will describe each method generally, but with real code. Obviously, it is difficult to demonstrate with screenshots that e-mail has worked, but I'll describe and show the code as usual. Please check with your ISP if you have any problems, or ask your ISP before you start if there is anything you need to know about your particular environment. Most problems will be minor—you may have to change the path to the Blat.exe or the Sendmail program, for example.

Regardless of the platform that is being used, the method of sending e-mail is similar. Certain information is needed to send an e-mail, no matter what hardware or software you are using. For example, the following data items will always be required:

- Recipient
- Subject
- Message body
- Sender

Armed with this basic information, you can build a Perl program to send e-mail.

As I have said, the basic method of sending e-mail on all platforms is similar. The general method is to:

1. Define the path to the mail program.
2. Open the mail connection.
3. Supply the recipient and subject information.
4. Send the mail body data.
5. Close the e-mail connection.

Using FTP

Before you begin to learn about e-mail in Perl, you need to know how to get your files from your machine up to your ISP or hosting company Web space because, for this chapter, you need to step outside of your development cocoon (Microsoft Personal Web Server if you're using Windows 9x or Peer Web Services if you're using Windows NT). You will also need to use Web space that has an e-mail service attached to it. You need an SMTP server or some means of being able to send e-mail. To get your work onto your ISP Web space, you're going to have to learn how to get your files from your machine up to the ISP server using FTP (File Transfer Protocol)

What Is FTP?

FTP is the means by which you are able to transfer your files from your computer to another, usually a server at your ISP installation where you keep your Web sites and Web applications.

It isn't difficult to learn to use FTP, but it's a good idea idea to become familiar with it to remove some of the guesswork and to speed you along your way. So, before you start to learn about sending e-mail, read this short briefing on how to use FTP. I shall use one example of an FTP client; there are many, but they are basically very similar. There are a number of FTP clients on the market, and some of them are free for personal use.

> **NOTE**
>
> For the purposes of this discussion, I will concentrate on WS-FTP LE (the LE stands for Light Edition). This is an excellent, free FTP client that is easy to use and very effective.

How Do I Use FTP?

First of all, obtain a copy of WS-FTP from http://www.ipswitch.com. Download a copy of the installation file, follow the onsite instructions, and install a copy of WS-FTP LE. There are a number of FTP clients out there, so you may want to shop around to find a product that suits you once you are comfortable using FTP.

After you have installed the product, you have to configure it. To do so, follow this procedure.

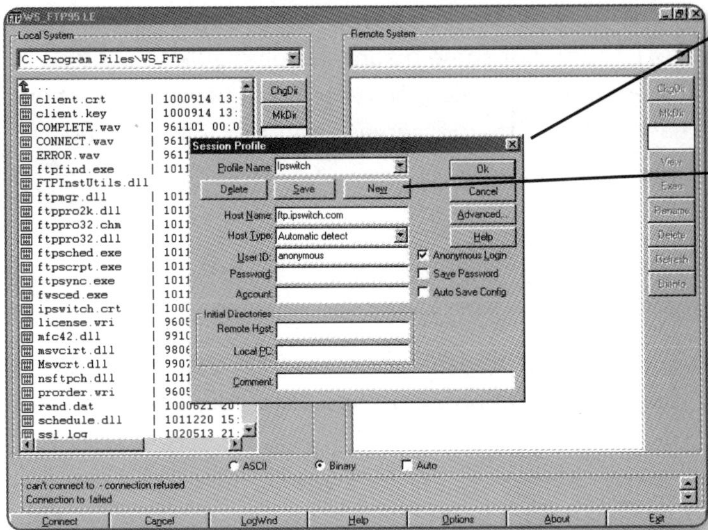

1. Start up the WS-FTP program and you will see something like this.

2. Click the New button.

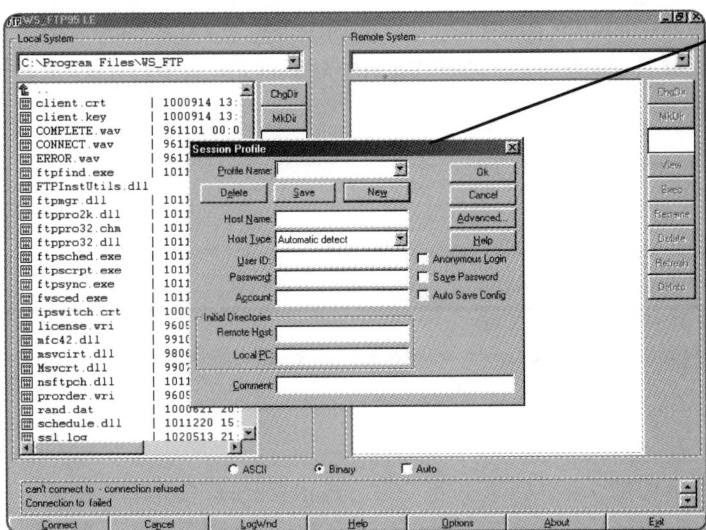

The display will now look like this.

3. In the Profile Name text box, enter a name for the profile that will remind you that this entry in your FTP client is for this particular ISP.

4. Now enter the host name of your ISP. Often this is something like www.myhostname.com or homepages.myisp.com (where *myisp* is the address of your ISP).

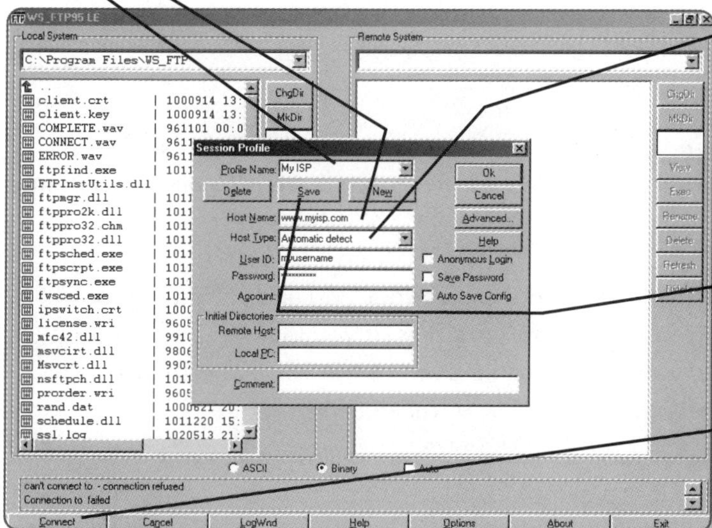

5. Leave the Host Type setting as Automatic detect.

6. Enter your user ID and password for your ISP into the appropriate boxes.

7. Click the Save button so that this profile is remembered when you next start WS-FTP LE.

8. When you click on Connect (or OK), provided you are connected to your ISP, you will be connected to your Web space.

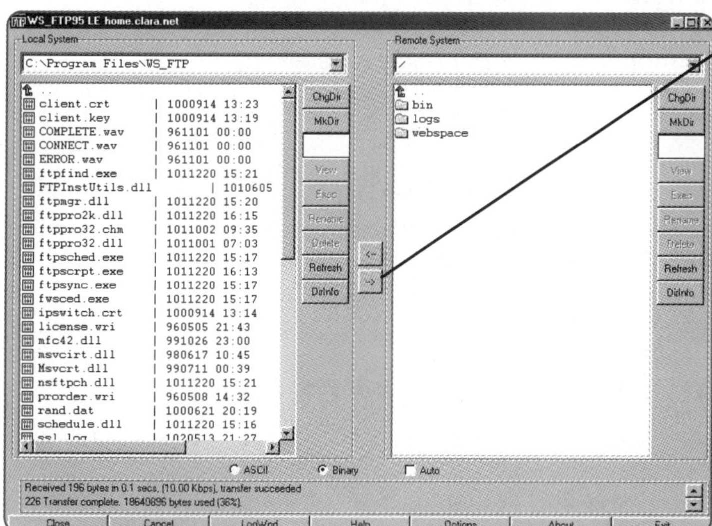

9. Now you can transfer files from the left window (your local machine) to the right window (the remote machine, your ISP's server). You do this by selecting the files in the left window, and then clicking the right arrow button.

> **NOTE**
>
> Of course, you can also transfer them the other way, by highlighting files in the right window and clicking the left arrow button.
>
> You can select more than one file by holding down the Shift key as you click with the mouse to select a list of files that are grouped together in the list, or by using the Ctrl key as you click the mouse to select files that are not together in the list.

Try transferring some files and you will soon see how easy WS-FTP is. Like most Windows-type tools, the easiest way to learn how to use them is to play with them and read the help screens.

One thing to note is that you will want to transfer your Perl and HTML files as ASCII. Your images will be transferred as binary files. If you look at the bottom of the WS-FTP transfer screen, you will see radio buttons for ASCII and Binary. Select the appropriate one for the type of file you are transferring.

> **TIP**
>
> The Auto button uses the file extension to determine whether to use binary transfer mode or ASCII. To set up the extensions in order to transfer files automatically, click the Options button, select the Extensions tab, then add all of the ASCII extensions you may want to use.

There are lots of settings for you to play with in WS-FTP LE, but I will leave you to discover them yourself; I suggest you read the help documentation before changing any setting.

Sending E-mail Using SMTP in Perl

Perl has a module called Net that contains its networking functions. One of the components of Net is the SMTP module that contains all of the functions needed to send e-mail via an SMTP server. Try the example on the next page.

1. Open a new program in your editor.

```
#!c:\perl\bin
```

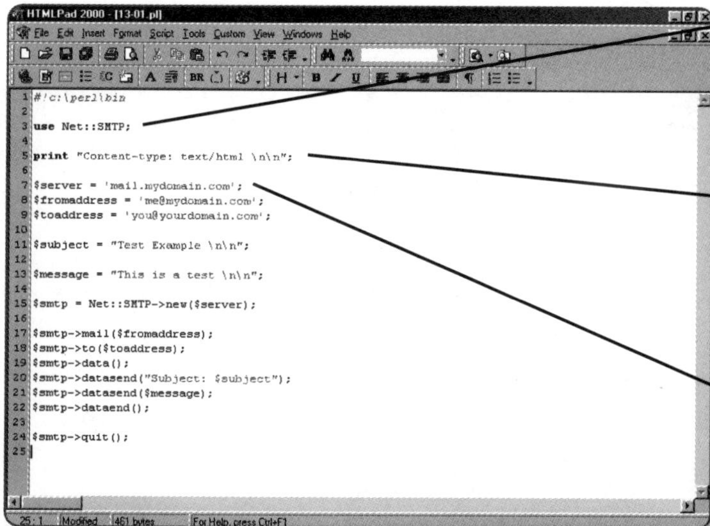

2. Include the SMTP component of the Net module.

```
use Net::SMTP;
```

3. Prepare to send data back to the Web browser.

```
print "Content-type: text/html
   \n\n";
```

4. Set up a variable containing the address of your mail server.

```
$server = 'mail.mydomain.com';
```

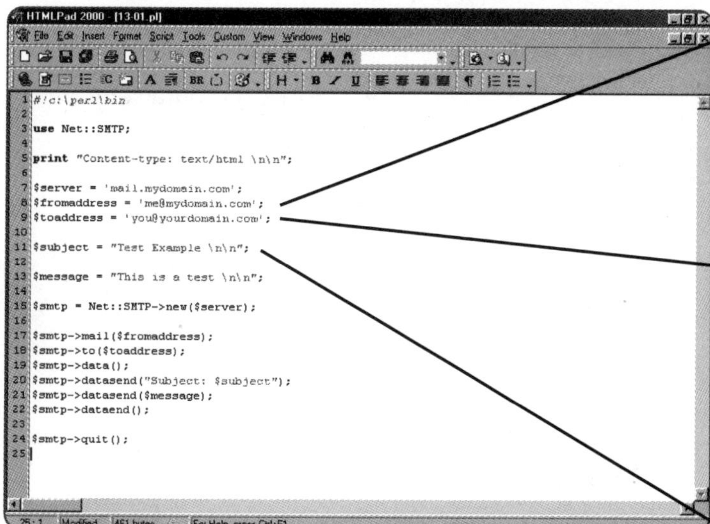

5. Now set up another variable to contain your own address.

```
$fromaddress =
'me@mydomain.com';
```

6. Add another variable to contain the address of the person to whom you are trying to send the e-mail.

```
$toaddress =
'you@yourdomain.com';
```

7. Set up a variable for the subject.

```
$subject = "Test Example
   \n\n";
```

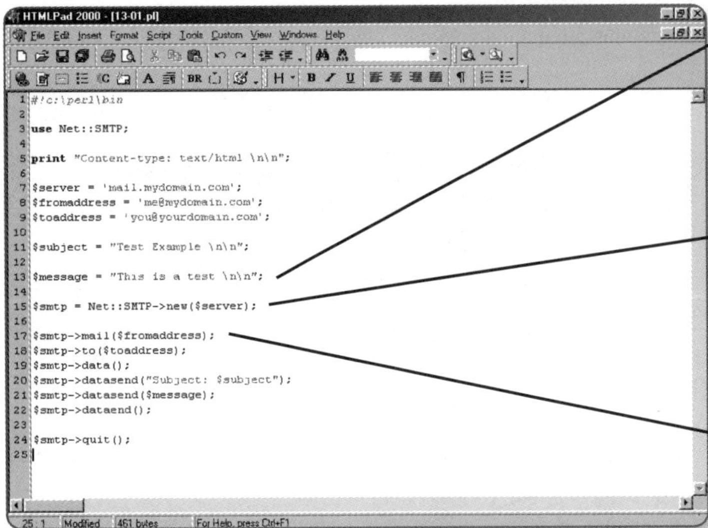

8. Set up a variable that contains your message body.

```
$message = "This is a test
   \n\n";
```

9. Now create a connection with the SMTP Server.

```
$smtp = Net::SMTP-
   >new($server);
```

10. Supply SMTP with the from address, using the variable you set up in Step 5.

```
$smtp->mail($fromaddress);
```

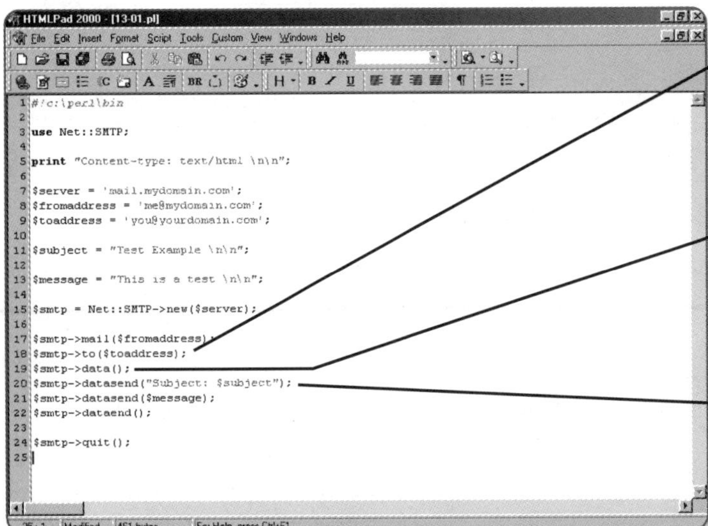

11. Supply the recipient address.

```
$smtp->to($toaddress);
```

12. Start the data send part of the program.

```
$smtp->data();
```

13. Send the subject.

```
$smtp->datasend("Subject:
$subject");
```

NOTE

The subject was terminated with two newline characters. This tells the SMTP server that this is the end of the header information, and that what follows is the body of the message. The message also ends with two newline characters, indicating that the end of the message has been reached, as you will see next.

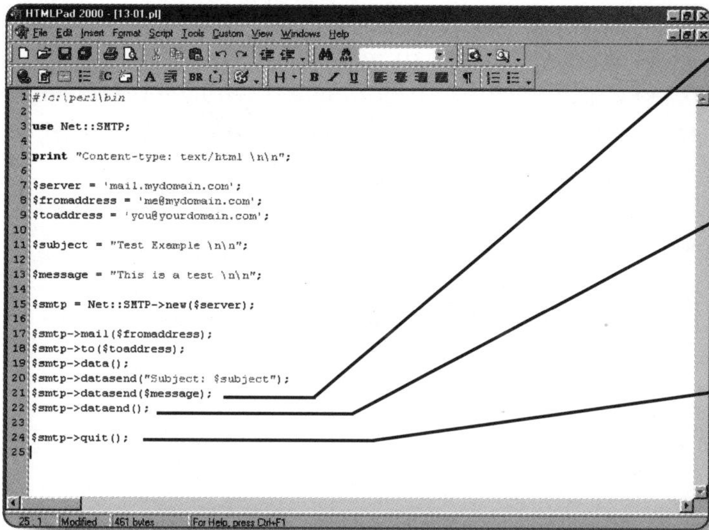

14. Now send the message itself.

```
$smtp->datasend($message);
```

15. Close the data send operation.

```
$smtp->dataend();
```

16. Close the SMTP connection.

```
$smtp->quit();
```

17. Save the program as 13-01.pl and upload it into your cgi-bin or scripts folder in your ISP or hosting company's Web space using a suitable FTP client.

18. Open your browser and enter the URL for your program (http://www.*yourdomain*.com/cgi-bin/13-01.pl). Notice that you will not see any output on the screen. If you want to see something to reassure yourself that the program completed, put in a print statement with a suitable message.

That's one way of sending an e-mail. There is another way that you may find useful if your site is hosted on a Windows server: using the Blat program.

Sending E-mail Using Blat.exe

Many Windows-based ISPs send e-mails by means of a freeware program called Blat.exe. This was actually originally developed as a command-line e-mail program, and it sends its e-mail text from a file. In fact, where this program is used on the Web, it still uses a file and it stills uses Blat.exe as a command-line program, sort of. You use the `system` Perl command that is designed to enable you to run any executable program from within a Perl program.

So, under normal circumstances, what you have to do is collect the address information and data (text) you are going to send from an HTML form. Then you save the text data to a file. Then call the Blat.exe program and send your data and message text file as parameters. *Parameters* are just individual items of data that a program needs to complete its job or to tell the program how to behave. In this case they are items of data such as recipient address, sender address, and name of the text file containing the message.

Try out the following program (if your ISP or hosting company offers the Blat.exe facility).

1. Start a new program in your editor.

```
#!c:\perl\bin
```

2. Create a variable to contain the recipient address.

```
$recipients = "admin\@domainname.com";
```

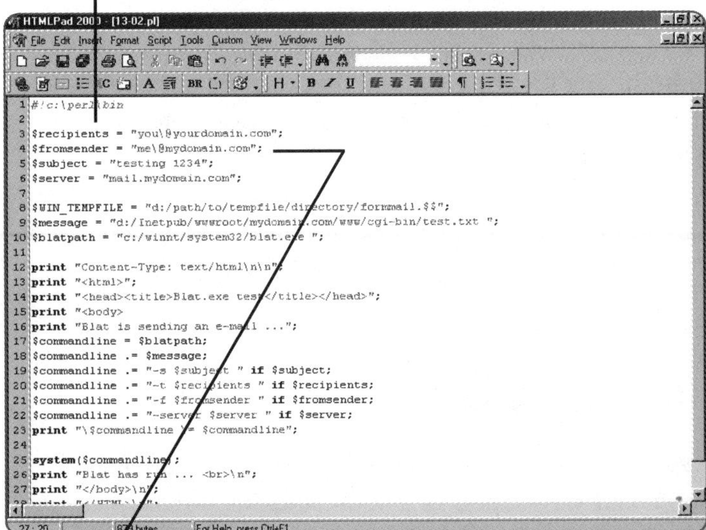

> **NOTE**
>
> Note the \ character; this enables you to escape special characters such as the @ character, which would otherwise be interpreted as an array indicator by Perl.
>
> For testing, you will probably want to put your own address in the `$recipient` variable.

3. Create another variable to contain the From address.

```
$fromsender = "admin\@domainname.com";
```

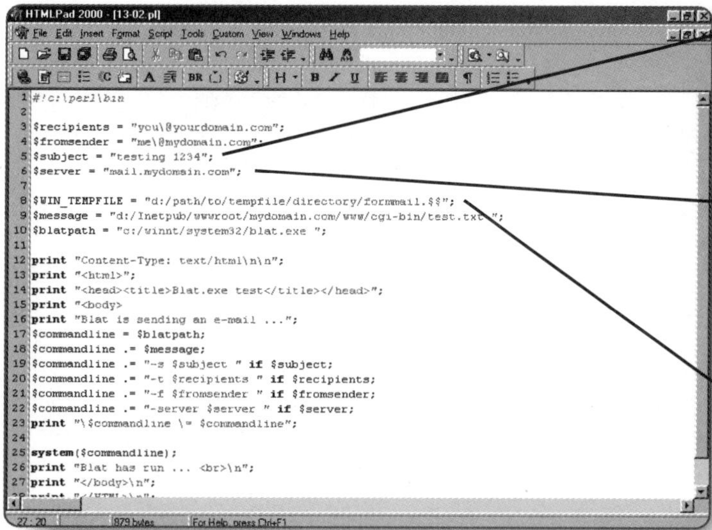

4. Create another variable to hold the subject heading.

```
$subject = "testing 1234;
```

5. Now create a variable to hold the mail server address.

```
$server =
"mail.domainname.com";
```

6. Blat also needs a temporary file location.

```
$WIN_TEMPFILE =
   "d:/path/to/tempfile/
   directory/formmail.$$";
```

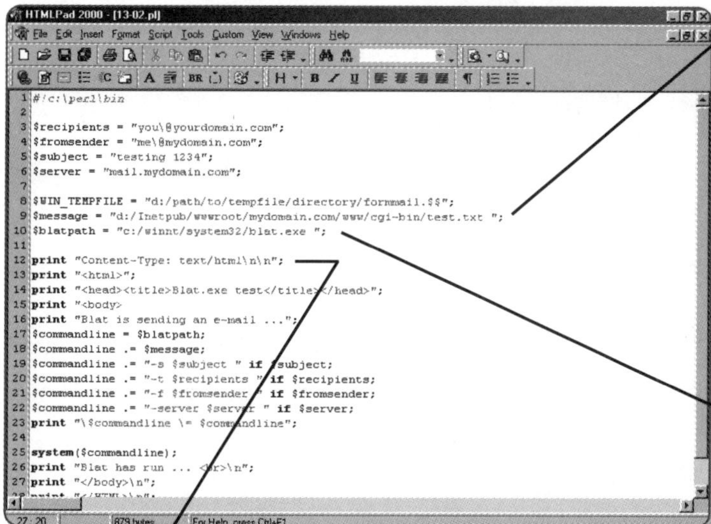

7. Blat does not take "instream" data in a program. It expects the body of the e-mail text to be found in a text file. So create a variable to contain the path to the file containing the file.

```
$message =
   "d:/Inetpub/wwwroot/
   mydomain.com/www/cgi-
   bin/test.txt ";
```

8. The system also needs to know where to find Blat.exe, so create a variable to contain the blat.exe location.

```
$blatpath = "c:/winnt/system32/blat.exe ";
```

9. Now prepare your program to send data back to the browser.

```
print "Content-Type: text/html\n\n";
```

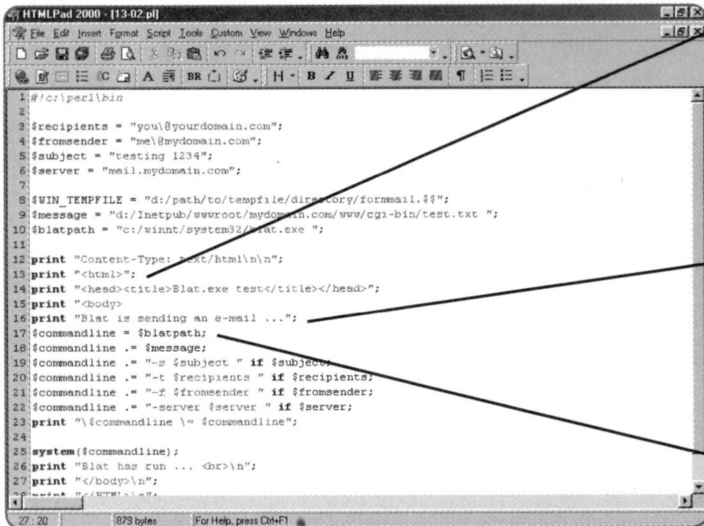

10. Start an HTML page.

```
print "<html>";
print "<head><title>Blat.exe
   test</title></head>";
print "<body>
```

11. Display a message showing that blat.exe is about to run.

```
print "Blat is sending an
   e-mail ...";
```

12. Now build a command line command using the concatenation operator to join the bits of the string together and store the command string in a suitable variable.

```
$commandline = $blatpath;
$commandline .= $message;
$commandline .= "-s $subject " if $subject;
$commandline .= "-t $recipients " if $recipients;
$commandline .= "-f $fromsender " if $fromsender;
$commandline .= "-server $server " if $server;
```

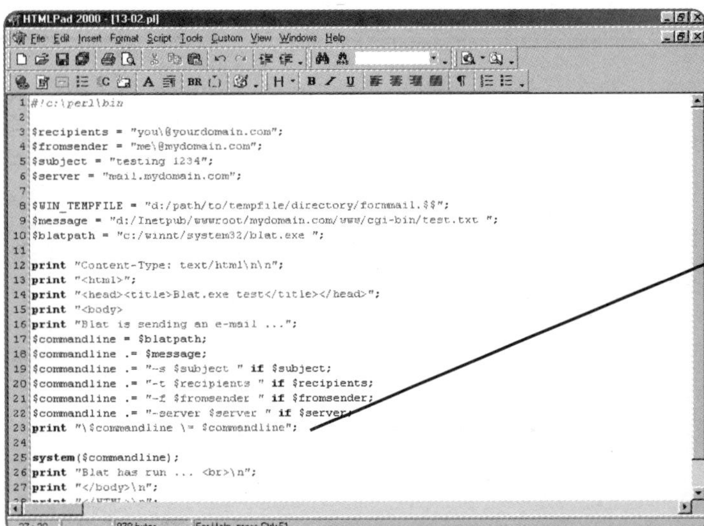

Note the different use of the `if` statement. It simply means do the first part of the statement if the variable being checked has something in it.

13. Display the command line you are about to run. You don't have to do this, but it is useful for debugging because you can see if the command line looks correct.

```
print "\$commandline \=
   $commandline";
```

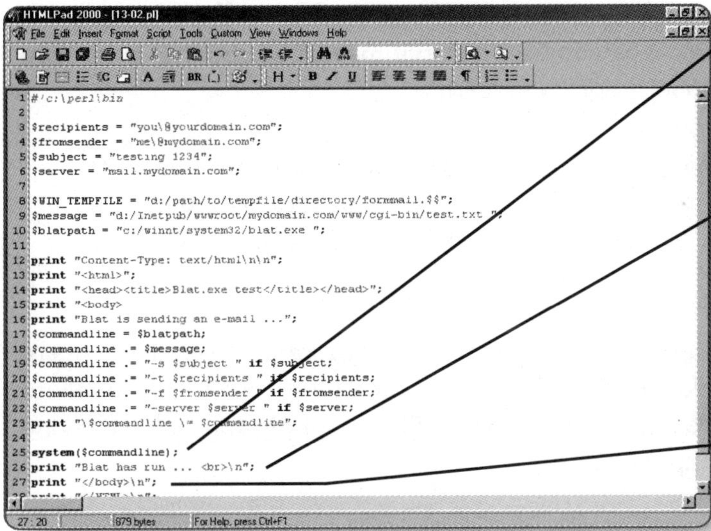

14. Now run the command line using the `system` command.

```
system($commandline);
```

15. Now display a reassuring message to let you know that Blat.exe has run.

```
print "Blat has run ...
   <br>\n";
```

16. Finally, close the HTML page.

```
print "</body>\n";
print "</HTML>\n";
```

17. Now save your program as 13-02.pl.

18. Upload the program to your Web space.

19. Create a text file containing a message and save it at the location you put in your `$message` variable.

20. Upload the message file to that location.

21. Open your Web browser and enter the URL (the location of your scripts folder will be determined by your ISP or hosting company) for your script to run it.

All being well, you will shortly receive an e-mail. If you do not, check your script again. If you can't see anything wrong with it, consult your ISP or hosting company and ask it for an example of how to use Blat.exe on its system (ISPs often have sample scripts that you can use, in which case you save yourself a lot of work).

The Blat program is not very sophisticated and the additional step of having to create a file is a nuisance. But it can be useful, and it may be all your ISP or hosting company offers, so it is a good program to learn.

You can also create a file using Perl from data that a user has given on a form. So you would get the data from the form (you already know how to do that now), write the text data to a file (you can do that too), and then let blat.exe run as shown previously.

The program given here is a typical example of a Perl program for sending e-mails, but there are lots of possible variations in terms of directories and so on, so talk to whomever you host with. You may find that your ISP will supply you with a working example to plug in to your applications.

Sending Mail on a UNIX Server Using Sendmail

The UNIX community has had for years a mail program called Sendmail. It is quite simple to use, but again, before you start, talk to your hosting company or ISP to learn about any local variations or hints for using sendmail from their servers.

Try this example, after you have spoken to your hosting company, making any modifications that your company indicates for its particular installation (again, the company may offer you a pre-written example that will save you time on debugging).

Following is a simple example of using Sendmail in Perl.

1. Open your editor and start a new program.

```
#!/usr/bin/perl
```

> **NOTE**
>
> Note the UNIX shebang statement—the path is different, which matters in the case of UNIX, as the shebang statement is not just a comment, but is used by the operating system to find Perl.

2. Set up variables to hold the from address, the recipient address (To), and the subject.

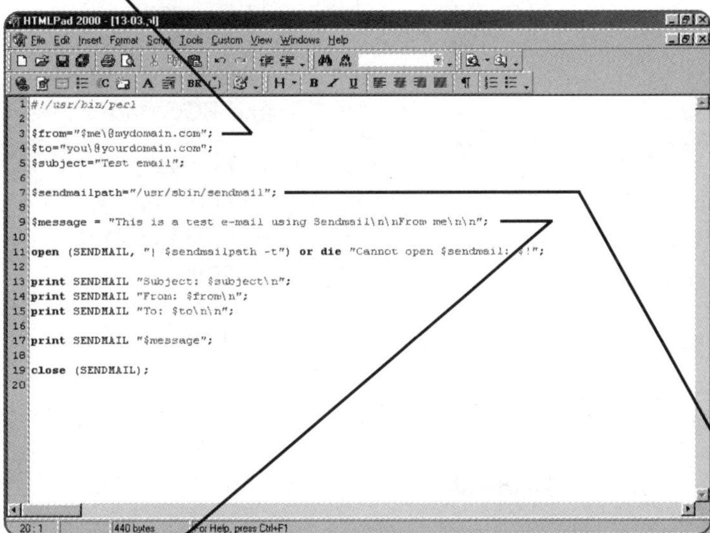


```
$from="$me\@mydomain.com";
$to="you\@yourdomain.com";
$subject="Test email";
```

> **NOTE**
>
> For testing, you will probably want to put your own address in the `$to` variable.

3. Create another variable to hold the path of the Sendmail program.

```
$sendmailpath="/usr/sbin/sendmail";
```

4. Create another variable to hold the message.

```
$message = "This is a test e-mail using Sendmail\n\nFrom me\n\n";
```

5. Now open the Sendmail program.

```
open (SENDMAIL, "| $sendmailpath -t") or die "Cannot open $sendmail: $!";
```

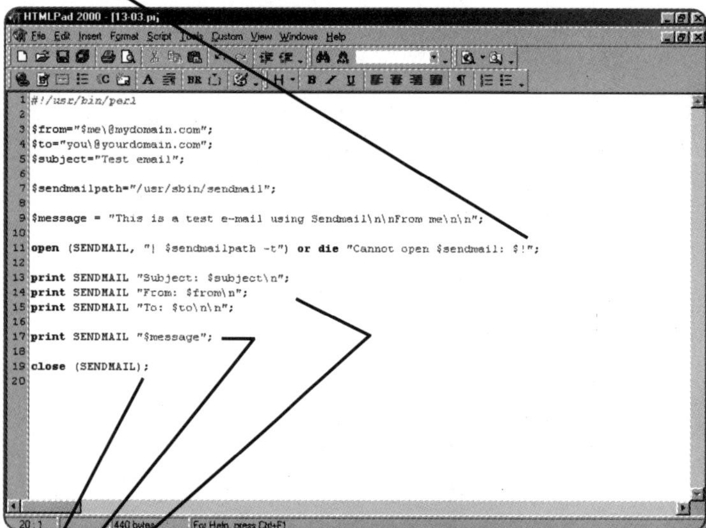

NOTE

Note the pipe symbol (|) before the `$sendmailpath` variable. This tells sendmail that its input can be taken from STDIN, which is the default input stream.

The option –t is added to the Sendmail `open` command. This simply tells Sendmail to scan for To, CC, and BCC data.

Also note the use of the `die` option and the use of the `$!` variable to report (hopefully) some meaningful information in the event of an error.

6. Now send the subject, from, and to information to Sendmail, like this.

```
print SENDMAIL "Subject: $subject\n";
print SENDMAIL "From: $from\n";
print SENDMAIL "To: $to\n\n";
```

7. Send the body of the message to Sendmail.

```
print SENDMAIL "$message";
```

8. Finally, close Sendmail.

```
close (SENDMAIL);
```

9. Save your program as 13-03.pl.

10. Now upload your program to your ISP host.

11. Open your browser and enter the URL for your Perl mail program and press the Enter key.

If all has gone well, you should receive an e-mail. If not, check the script and correct any errors. If you still have problems contact your ISP to check the details for Sendmail on its servers.

Sendmail is a very well-known, tried, and tested e-mail program, and you shouldn't find many problems with it. It is also the most commonly available program on UNIX type servers. It is also increasingly becoming available for Windows platforms.

Keep an eye on the Web and look out for new tools that suit you and your host environment. And remember, talk to your ISP and read the forums that many of them provide for new ideas and facilities. You'll be glad you did.

14

Using Perl with Databases

You have learned how, using Perl, you can collect data from users. You know how to store data in files and how to retrieve it. You know how to use Perl to respond to people who visit your Web site using e-mail. Now you are going to use Perl to store your data in a much more powerful way, by using relational databases.

Essentially, a *database* is almost any store of related data. For example, a filing cabinet is a database. But generally these days, what we really mean is an electronic database.

In this chapter you will learn how to:

- Add MS Access databases to your Web site
- Read, add, update, and delete records from a database using ADO
- Read, add, update, and delete records from a database using DBI

Access 97 and Relational Databases

Access 97 is a database package that includes sufficient code to enable the user to create complete standalone applications using forms, SQL, and so on. However, in this chapter you are only interested in using the database engine itself. There are many other database systems that are as good or better, such as MySQL, PostgreSQL, and SQL Server, but Microsoft Access is widely used and available to many users, so I'll use it for the examples in this chapter.

> **NOTE**
>
> You can also use Access 2000 for the exercises in this chapter.

Access 97 is a *relational* database system. A relational database allows the data structures to be defined or described. The data is organized into tables. A *table* is a collection of identically organized records and each record, or row, in a table contains the same *fields*, forming columns of that field. One or more fields may be designated as *keys*, allowing searches for specific values to be speeded up.

For the purposes of this chapter, you will learn how to write the scripts that would be the basis of building a simple address book. For simplicity, the HTML forms will be left out and values to enter into the database you are going to build will be hard-coded into the Perl code. Obviously this is not a practical arrangement, but you already know how to get data back from a form (if you have forgotten, refer to Chapter 11).

Right now, concentrate on learning the techniques and code necessary to manipulate a simple address book database.

The Database Design

This will be a simple database that will be easy to implement in Access 97. The data items you are going to use are given in Table 14.1, along with some typical test data that you might want to enter to test your code.

TABLE 14.1 Database Items and Test Data

ID	First name	Last name	Address
1	Joe	Bloggs	14 High Street
2	Fred	Smith	1 Sun Street
3	Jane	Doe	4 Love Lane
4	Angus	McCoatup	17 Lake Close

Note the ID column. This will not be used in this chapter, but you will have a use for it when you expand this simple example into the Contact Database case study in Chapter 17. Briefly, the ID field (or whatever you decide to call it) is a unique reference to each record (or row) in the database. This is needed, as certain operations on the database need to know precisely to which record you are referring. For example, if you had to delete a record from the database, a unique ID would ensure that the correct record and only the correct record is deleted. This is much better than a system where, for example, if you tried to delete a record for someone by the name of Smith, the database wouldn't know which one you meant and so would probably delete them all. Of course, there are times when you want to do something like that, but often you want to pluck out a certain record, and that is when the ID field, a unique key, is so useful.

Another consideration of databases is that of *data types*. Not all data is text data. There are date and time fields (notorious for creating problems), Boolean fields (which are used as flags and contain values that signify yes or no, on or off, 1 or 0, or True or False), and memo fields (which are able to hold large amounts of text).

Finally, there are *rules* and *default values*. An example of a rule might be "allow zero length strings." Default values are used to fill in a field with a value in the absence of a value coming back from a form.

Databases can be very complex. You can have a large number of tables, many of which link to each other through a system of foreign keys so that one table can do a lookup on another. This sort of database, and the complex SQL to go with it, are beyond the scope of this book, but as your experience and confidence in building simple applications grows, you will want to extend your knowledge in this area.

Creating a Database in Access 97

Let's build a database. In this section I'll run through the basics of creating a database table that you can use in your Web site application.

To build your first database table, do the following:

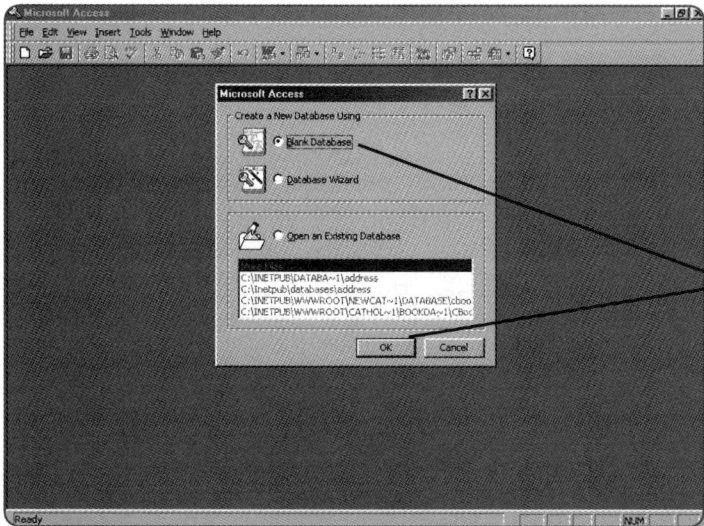

1. Start Microsoft Access 97. A dialog box will open, offering to let you open a blank database, use the Database Wizard, or to open an existing database.

2. Choose Blank Database and click OK. You will be presented with a dialog box asking you where you would like to put your database

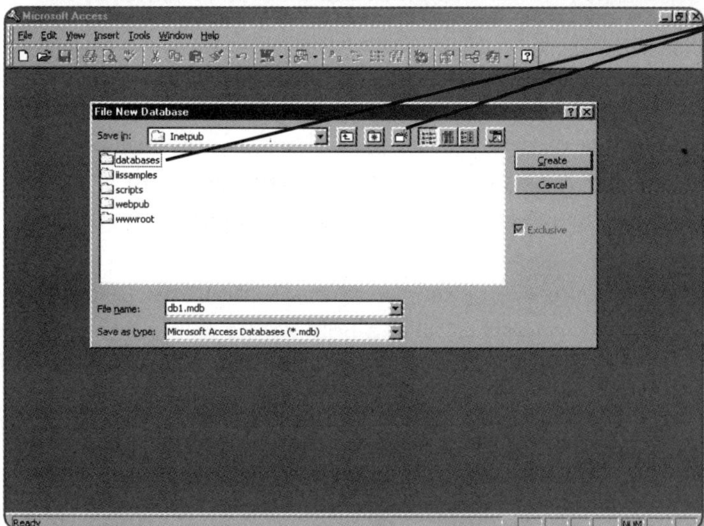

3. Navigate to your Inetpub folder, and create a new folder using the New Folder icon.

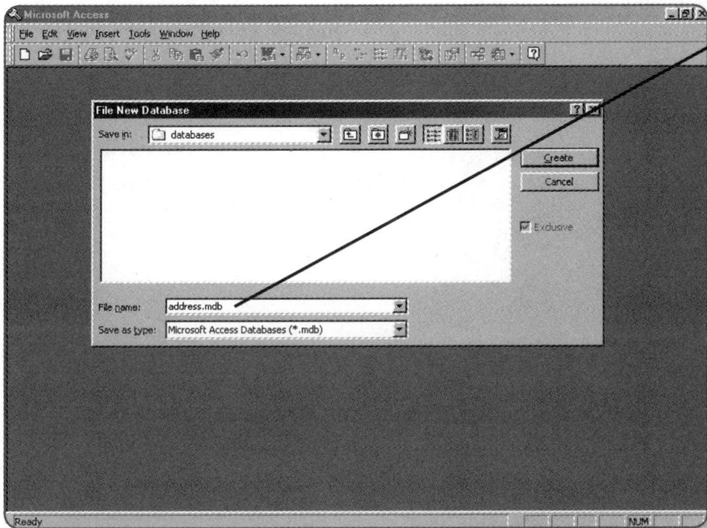

4. Double-click your new database folder and save your database as address.mdb. You will be presented with a new dialog box, from which you can administer and create many functions within Access. You are only interested in the Tables tab for Web applications now.

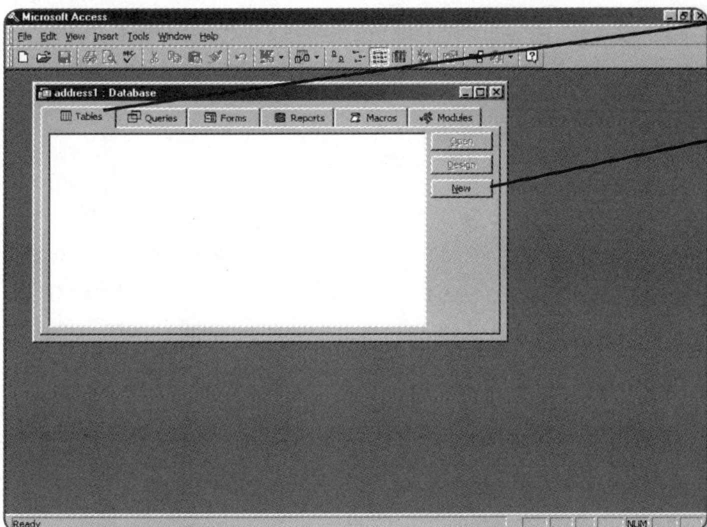

5. If it is not already selected, select the Tables tab.

6. Click the New button. The New Table dialog box will open.

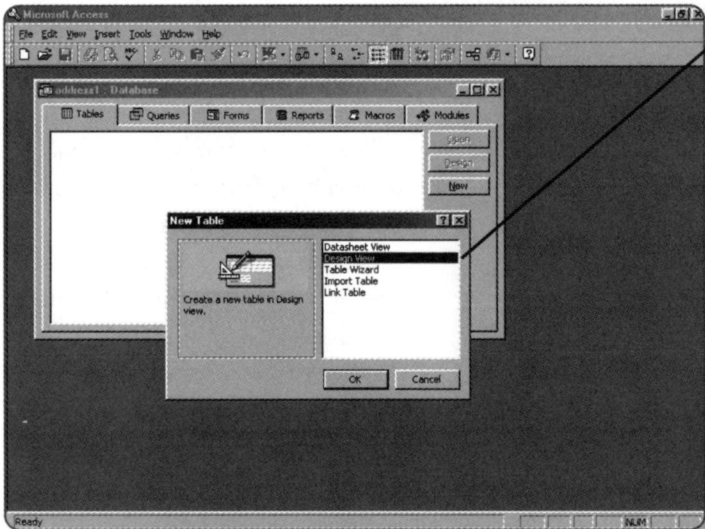

7. Select the Design View option in the window and click OK. You will see a grid into which you can enter all the details of your database table

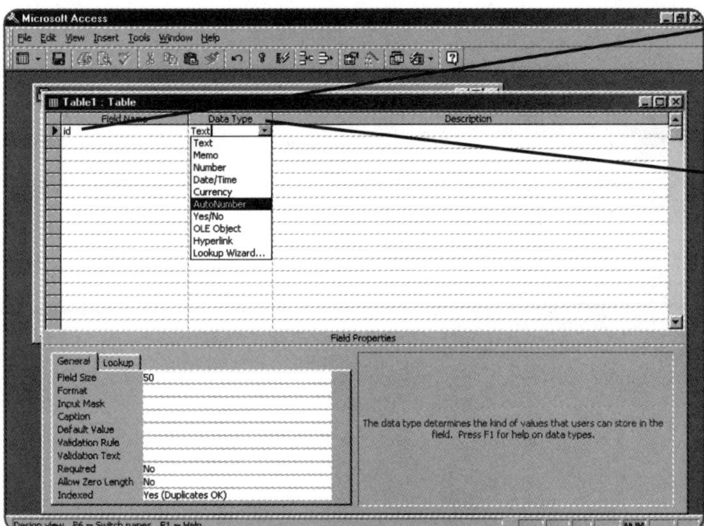

8. Click your mouse cursor into the first Field Name box and type **id**.

9. Click on the Data Type field and a small gray button will appear with a black downward arrow. Click on this button and select AutoNumber from the drop-down list that appears.

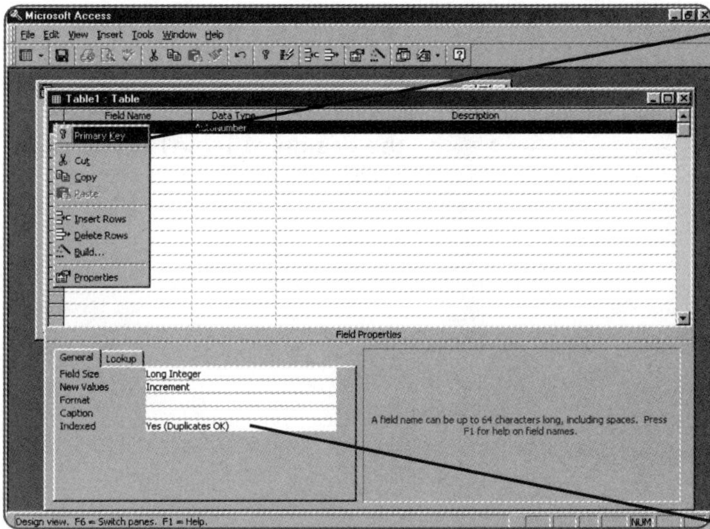

10. To the left of the id Field Name you will see a small right-pointing (back) arrow. Right-click on that arrow and a gray box with a list of options will appear. Select the first item on the list, Primary Key. You have now set the key for this database table.

> **NOTE**
>
> Notice that the Indexed option at the bottom of the dialog box has changed to Yes (No Duplicates), which is what you would expect, as the primary key must be unique.

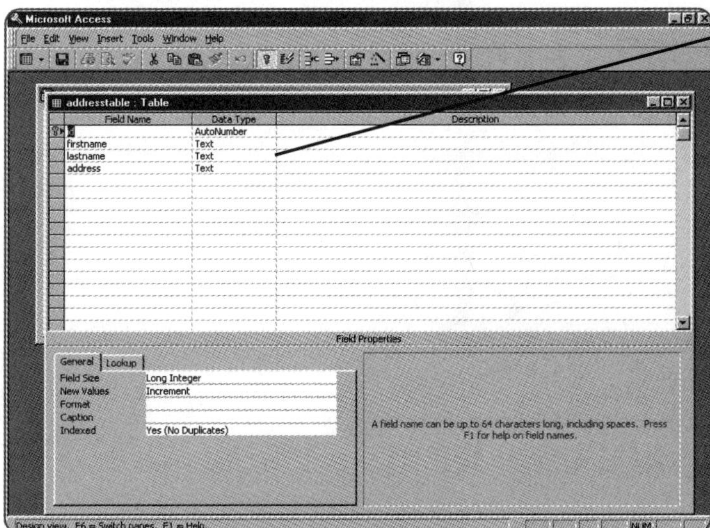

11. Now add the remaining fields to the database table, accepting the default type of Text for the data types, until your table looks like the one shown here.

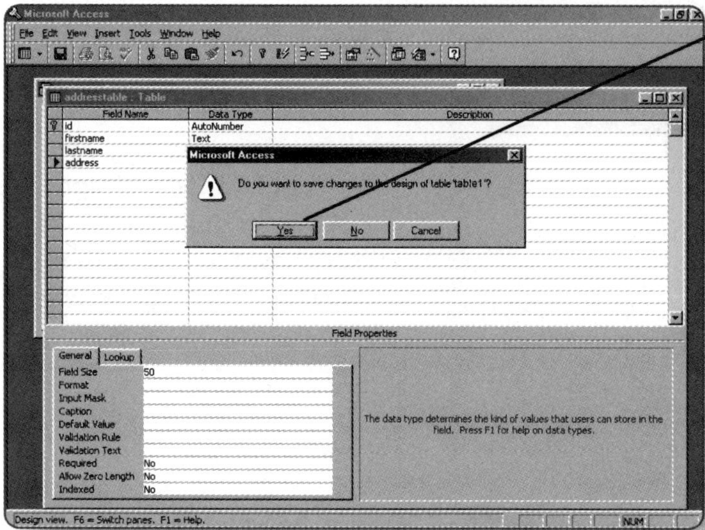

12. Close the Table Design dialog box. A prompt asking if you want to save the changes to the design of Table1 will appear. Click Yes.

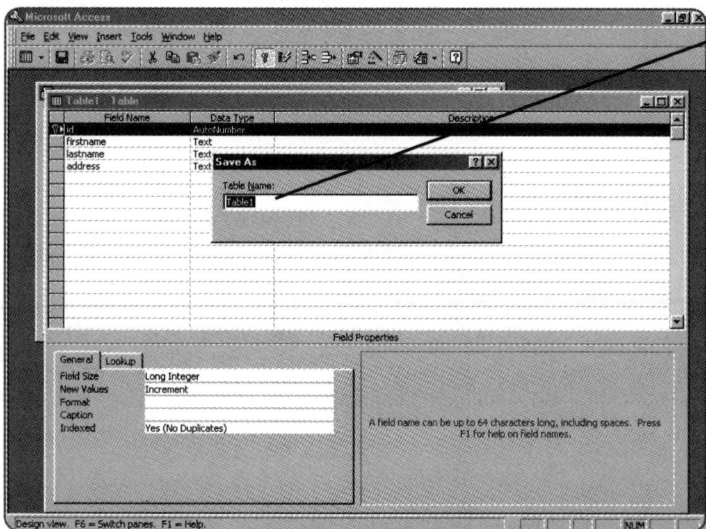

13. This is not the name you want, so click in the highlighted text box and enter **addresstable**, then click OK. You will return to the Table dialog box and your new table will be visible in the window.

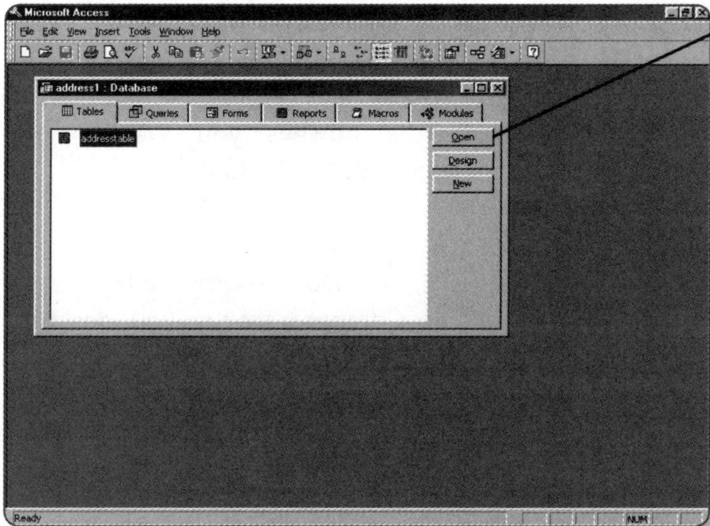

14. Now click the Open button. You will see a new grid into which you can enter data into each field.

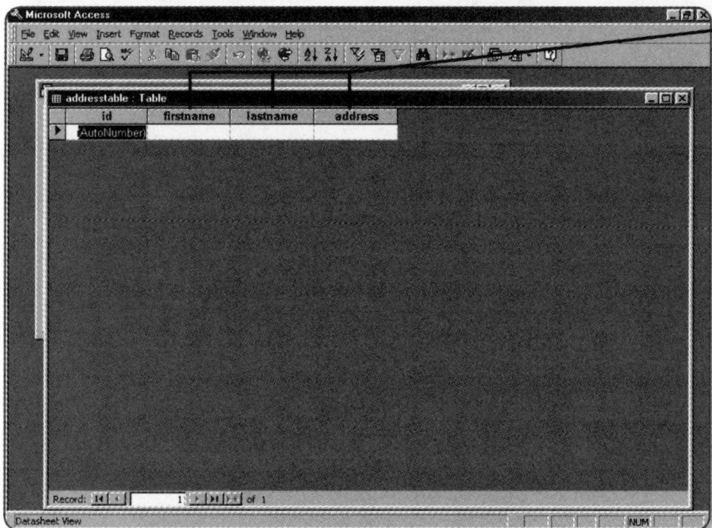

15. Click into the firstname field and type some data. Then click into the lastname field and enter a surname. Finally, click into the address field and type an address.

16. Click into the next firstname field and enter another name. Complete the other two fields as you did for the first one, but with different names and addresses.

17. Close the database Table dialog box and then close Access 97.

Creating a Data Source Name (DSN)

Now you have a database with some data in it; soon you will write a Perl program to read the records from the data. Before you do that, however, you have one more thing to do. You need to create a Data Source Name (DSN). To do that, follow these simple steps:

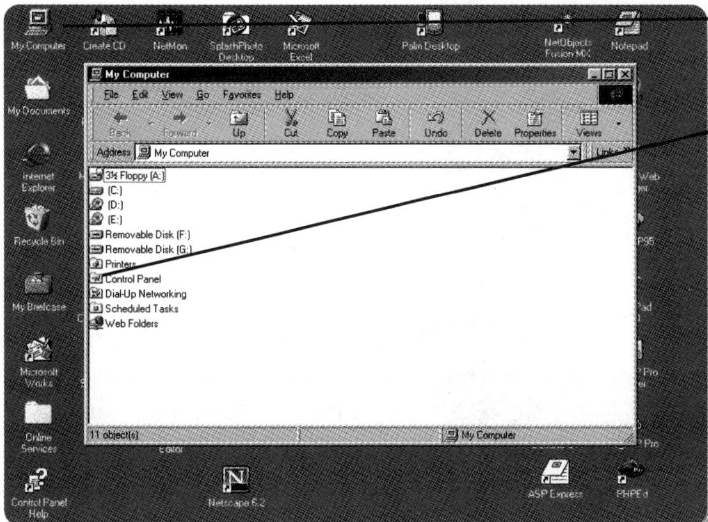

1. Double-click the My Computer icon on your desktop.

2. Double-click the Control Panel icon. The Control Panel window will open.

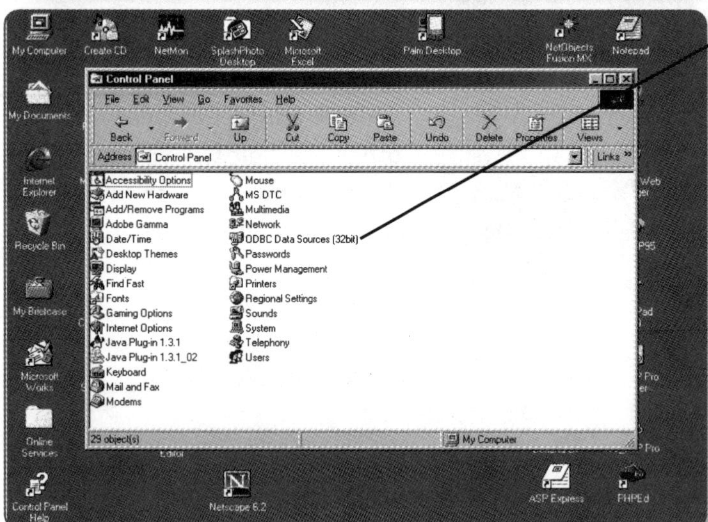

3. Double-click the ODBC Data Sources icon. The ODBC Data Source Administrator dialog box will open.

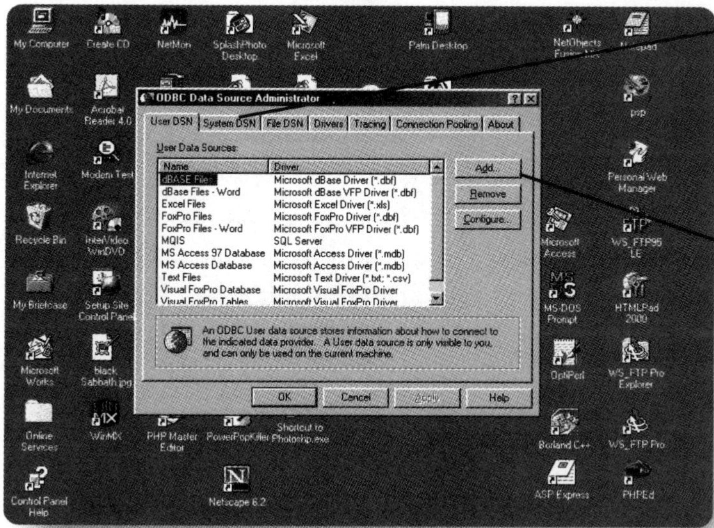

4. Select the System DSN tab. In the user Data Sources window, you will see a list of data sources that already exist (if any).

5. Click the Add button.

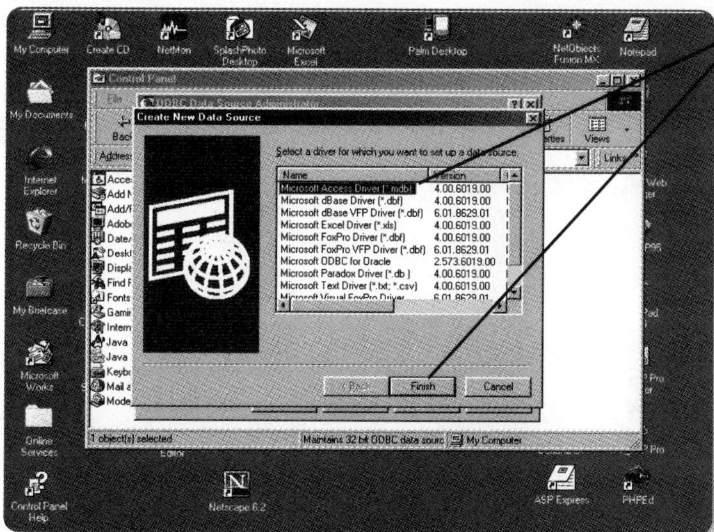

6. Make sure the Microsoft Access Driver (*.mdb) entry is highlighted, then click Finish.

The ODBC Microsoft Access Setup dialog box will open.

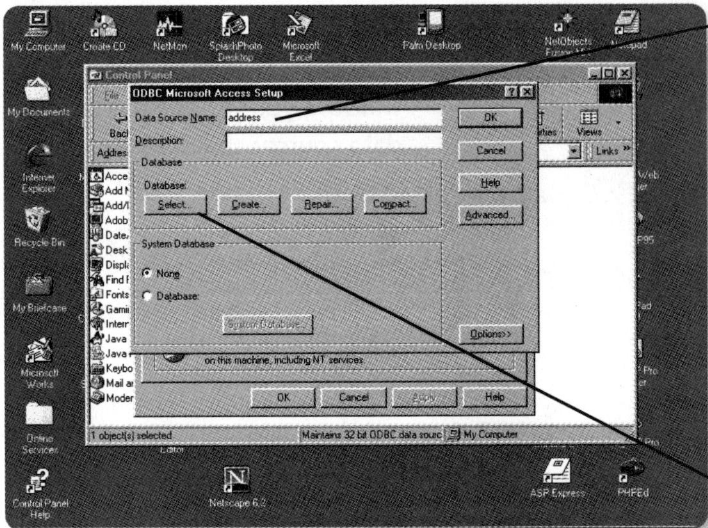

7. In the Data Source Name field, enter **address** as the name.

> **NOTE**
>
> The Description field is just for documentation; leave it blank or enter some text to remind you what this database is for.

8. Click the Select button. The Select Database dialog box will open.

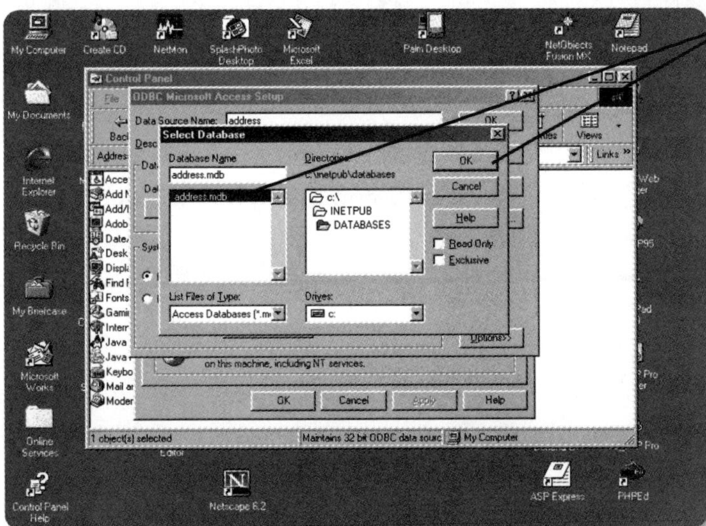

9. Navigate to your database and click OK.

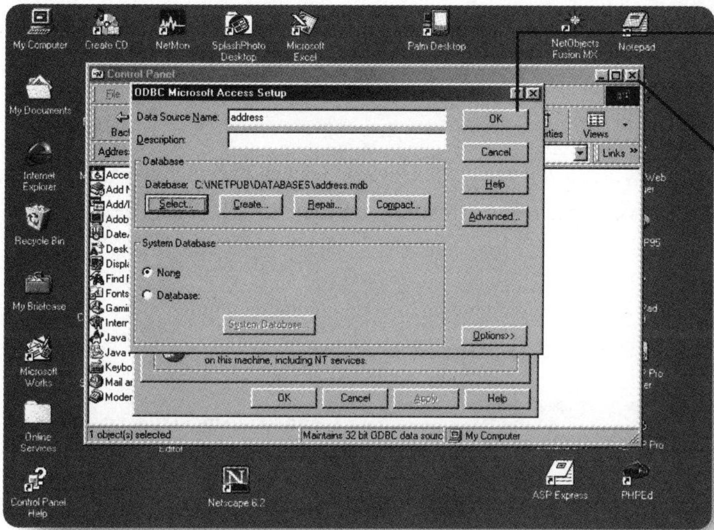

10. Click OK on the Microsoft Access Setup dialog box.

11. Click OK on the ODBC Data Source Administrator dialog box.

12. Close the Control Panel and My Computer.

Reading Records from a Database Using ADO

In this chapter you are going to learn two methods of using databases with Perl—using OLE (Object Linking and Embedding) database access, and the Perl DBI method. The first method is often referred to as ActiveX Data Objects, or ADO. In this section you will learn how to select records from a relational database using ADO and SQL (Structured Query Language, the language used to select records from the database, write records to it, and so on). An in-depth discussion on SQL is beyond the scope of this book, but you will learn sufficient SQL here to be able to perform the most common database functions—read, write, delete, and so on.

1. Open your editor and start a new program.

```
#!c:/perl/bin
```

2. Bring a couple of required modules into your Perl program. These contain the code required to enable you to manipulate databases using the Win32 OLE method.

```
use Win32::OLE;
use Win32::OLE::Const 'Microsoft ActiveX Data Objects';
```

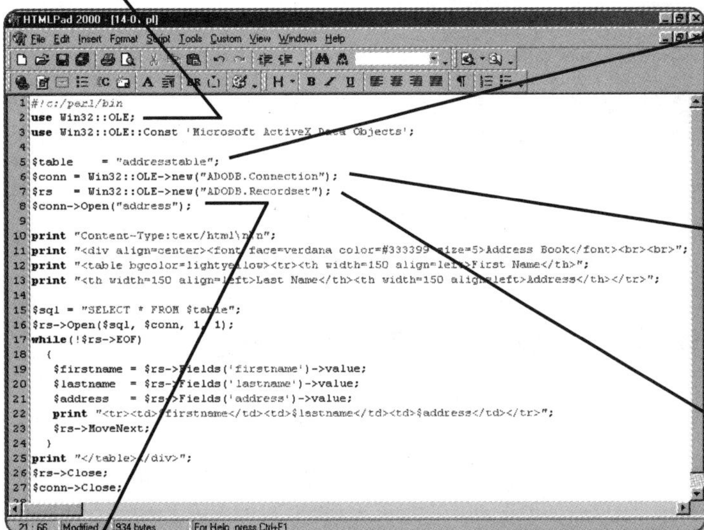

3. Create a variable to hold the name of your database table.

```
$table    = "addresstable";
```

4. Now create an ADO database connection.

```
$conn = Win32::OLE-
   >new("ADODB.Connection");
```

5. Create an ADO recordset to hold the records returned from the database.

```
$rs    = Win32::OLE->new("ADODB.Recordset");
```

> **NOTE**
>
> A *recordset* is a temporary table containing the records that are returned from your database SQL query.

6. Using the connection you created, open the address database.

```
$conn->Open("address");
```

7. Prepare your Perl program to be able to write back to the Web browser.

```
print "Content-Type:text/html\n\n"";
```

8. Now create an HTML table with a table header with titles for the fields. Note the table is centered on the page by means of the <div align=center> tag.

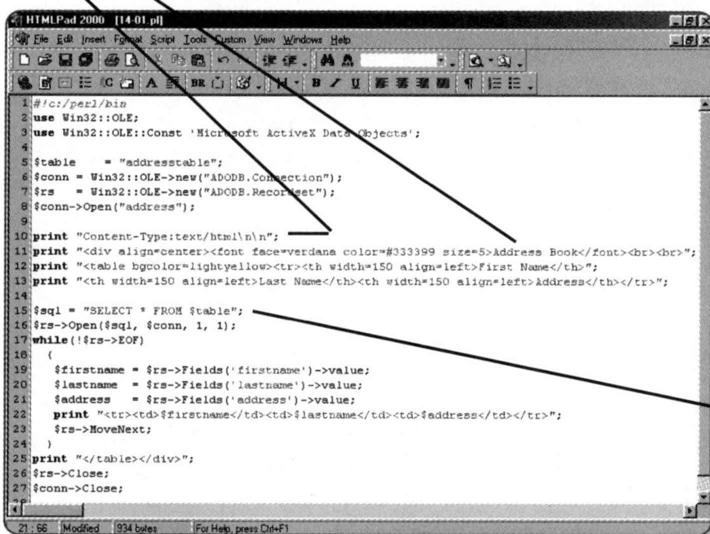


```
print "<div align=center><font
   face=verdana color=#333399
   size=5>Address
   Book</font><br><br>";
print "<table
   bgcolor=lightyellow><tr><th
   width=150 align=left>First
   Name</th>";
print "<th width=150
   align=left>Last
   Name</th><th width=150

align=left>Address</th></tr>";
```

9. Create a variable to hold the SQL query.

```
$sql = "SELECT * FROM $table";
```

NOTE

This statement means: Select all the columns from a table whose name is held in the variable `$table`. That is, `*` means "all columns." You could instead simply name all the fields you want returned from the query, like this:

```
$sql = "SELECT firstname, lastname, address FROM $table";
```

You can also add a `WHERE` clause, which filters the records, like this:

```
$sql = "SELECT * FROM $table WHERE lastname='Bate'";
```

Finally, you can change the order of the records by using the `ORDER BY` clause, like this:

```
$sql = "SELECT * FROM $table ORDER BY lastname";
```

10. Now, open the recordset using the SQL statement you just created and the connection you created called `$conn`.

```
$rs->Open($sql, $conn, 1, 1);
```

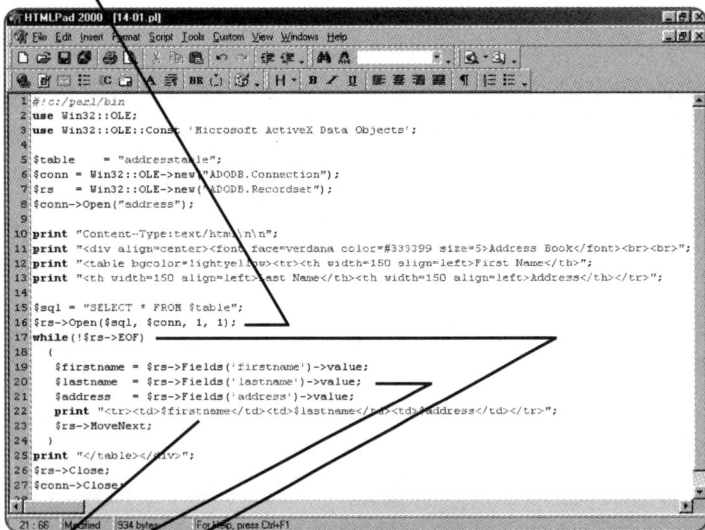

> **NOTE**
>
> The 1,1 is an advanced feature that controls the way in which the records are read using cursors (you can have different cursors for reading and writing to database tables) and LockTypes (as they are called in ADO parlance), which determine what kind of locking should be used for different purposes. These are advanced features that we will not delve into here; for now, just code them as they are.

11. Now loop through the records until EOF (end of file) is reached on the recordset.

```
while(!$rs->EOF)
  {
```

12. In the loop, store the value held in each column of the recordset into an appropriate variable.

```
$firstname = $rs->Fields('firstname')->value;
$lastname  = $rs->Fields('lastname')->value;
$address   = $rs->Fields('address')->value;
```

13. Now display the values in an HTML table row.

```
print "<tr><td>$firstname</td><td>$lastname</td><td>$address</td></tr>";
```

14. Get the next record (or row) in the recordset.

```
$rs->MoveNext;
```

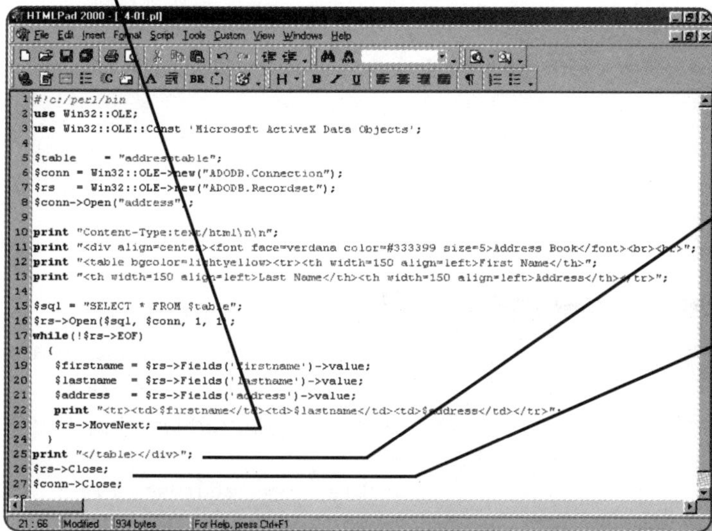

15. Close the loop code block.

```
}
```

16. Close the HTML table.

```
print "</table></div>";
```

17. Close the recordset and connection objects.

```
$rs->Close;
$conn->Close;
```

18. Save your program as 14-01.pl in your scripts folder.

19. Open your browser and enter the URL for your new program; you should see something like the results shown here.

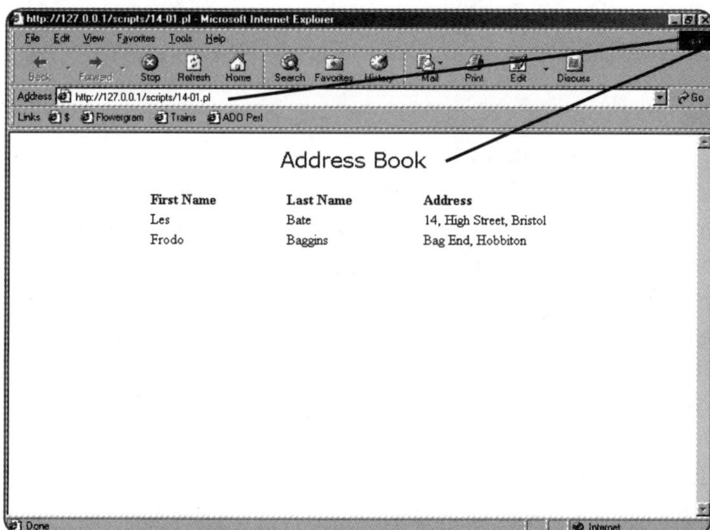

If you don't get results like this, check the code and try again.

Adding Records to a Database with ADO

The code for adding a record to the database is even simpler than that in the last example.

1. Open a new program in your editor, and again bring in the WIN32::OLE modules.

```
#!c:/perl/bin
use Win32::OLE;
use Win32::OLE::Const 'Microsoft ActiveX Data Objects';
```

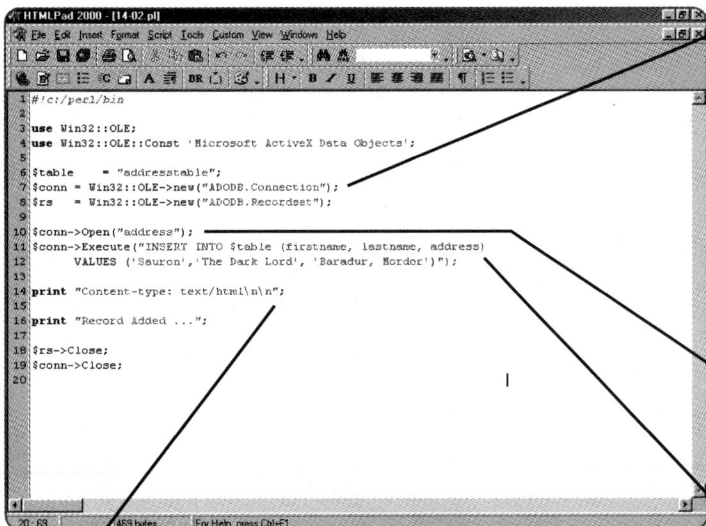

2. Set up a variable to hold the name of the table, and create the connection and recordset objects as you did last time.

```
$table    = "addresstable";
$conn = Win32::OLE-
   >new("ADODB.Connection");
$rs   = Win32::OLE-
   >new("ADODB.Recordset");
```

3. Open the connection.

```
$conn->Open("address");
```

4. Now execute the SQL to add a record to the database table. As it says, this just means insert a new record into the table and set the fields firstname, lastname, and address to the values `Sauron`, `The Dark Lord`, and `Baradur, Mordor`, respectively.

```
$conn->Execute("INSERT INTO $table (firstname, lastname, address)
      VALUES ('Sauron','The Dark Lord', 'Baradur, Mordor')");
```

5. Prepare to send data back to the user's browser.

```
print "Content-type: text/html\n\n";
```

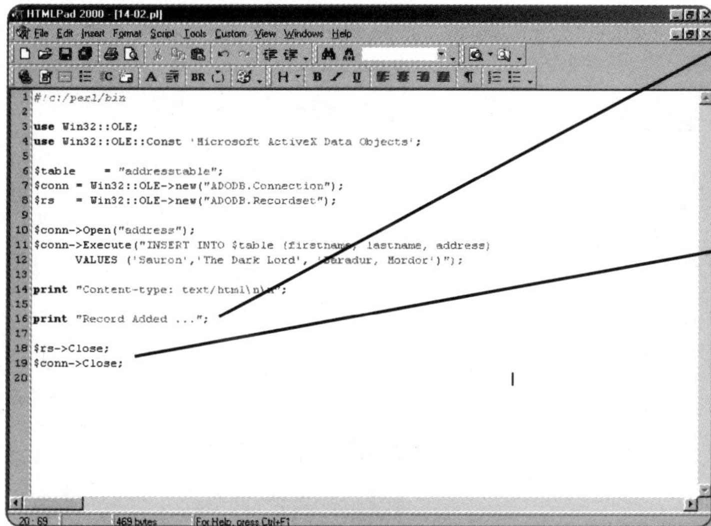

6. Print a comforting message to say that the program completed correctly.

```
print "Record Added ...";
```

7. Finally, close the recordset and the connection.

```
$rs->Close;
$conn->Close;
```

8. Save your program as 14-02.pl.

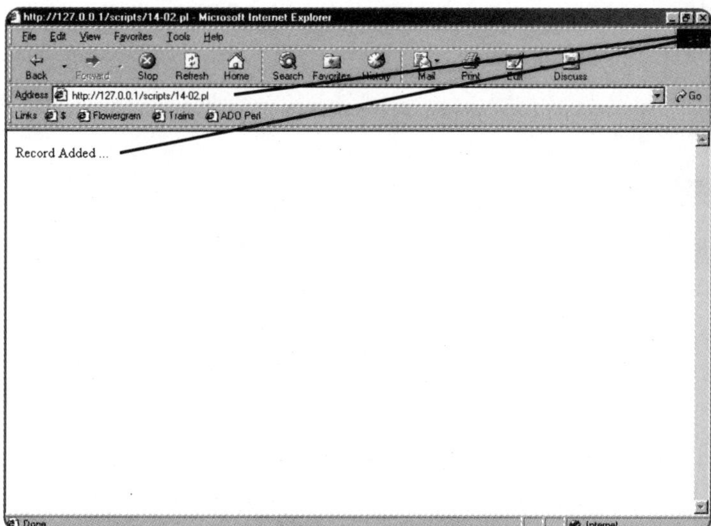

9. Now open your browser and enter the URL for your new program. You should see your simple message saying you have added a record to the database table.

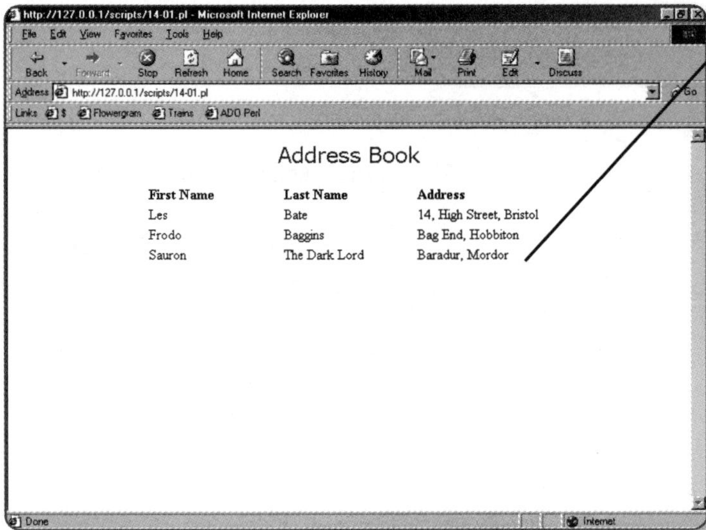

10. Now go back to your 14-01.pl. You should see the new record in the list.

Next, you are now going to learn how to update a record in a table.

Updating a Record in a Database Table Using ADO

This is almost identical to the previous example, except that the SQL is slightly different, as you would expect.

1. Re-open your 14-02.pl program.

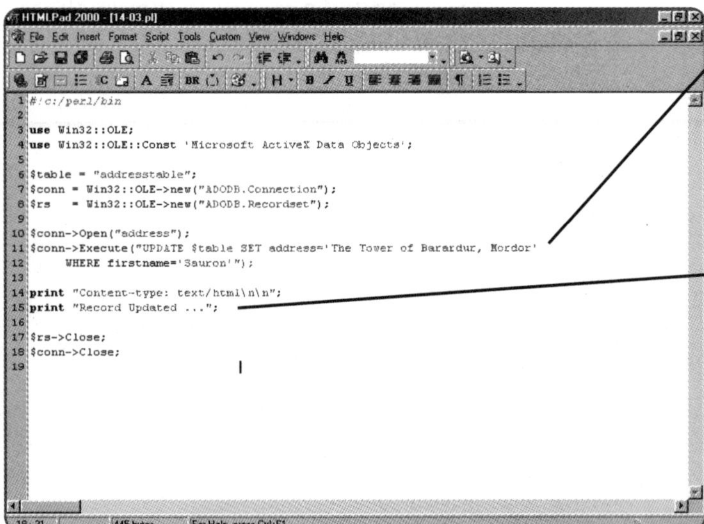

2. Replace the old SQL line with the one here.

```
$conn->Execute("UPDATE $table
   SET Address='The Tower of
   Barardur, Mordor'WHERE
   firstname=Sauron");
```

3. Replace the confirmation message with this one.

```
print "Record Updated ...";
```

4. Save your program as 14-03.pl.

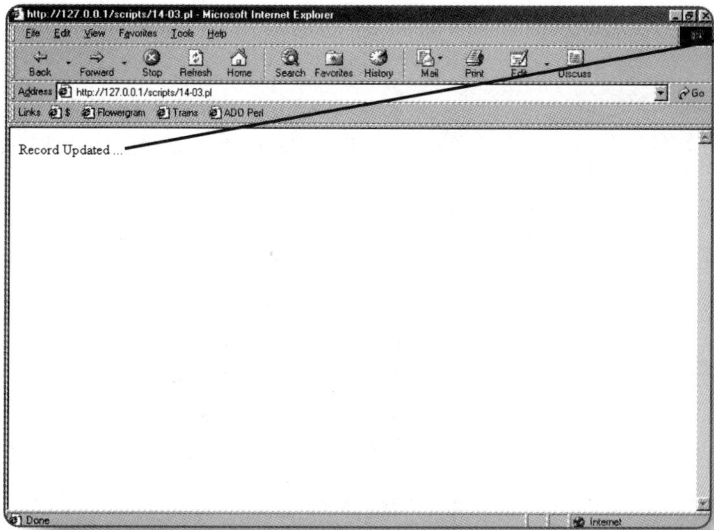

5. Open your 14-03.pl program in your Web browser and you should again get the message that the record has been updated.

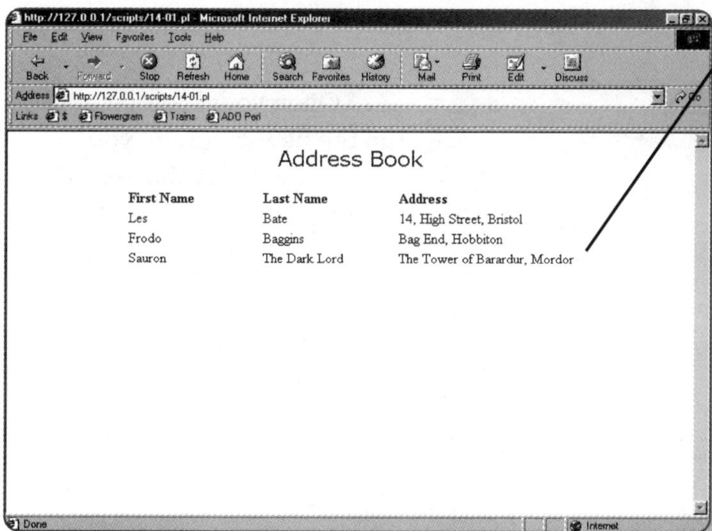

6. Once again, go back to your 14-01.pl program in the browser (if you use the Back button you will need to click the browser's Refresh button) to confirm that the update took place.

All you need to know now is how to delete a record from the database table.

Deleting a Record from a Database Table with ADO

Once again, this is just a simple change to the programs SQL.

1. Re-open your previous program.

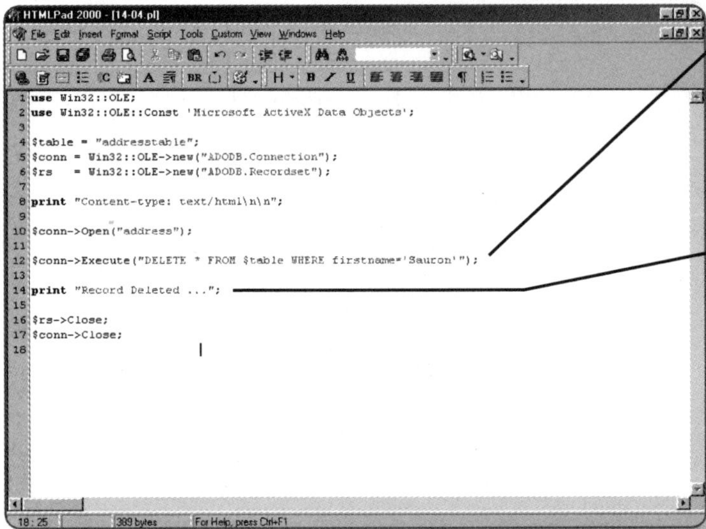

2. Change the line containing the SQL so that it looks like this:

```
$conn->Execute("DELETE * FROM
   $table WHERE
   surname='Sauron'");
```

3. Change the confirmation message to look like this:

```
print "Record Deleted ...";
```

4. Save your program as 14-04.pl in your scripts folder.

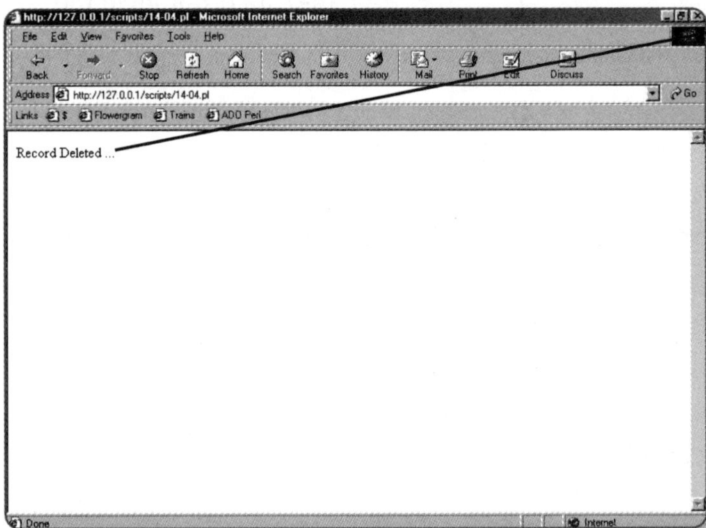

5. Open your browser and run the new program; you should see the confirmation message.

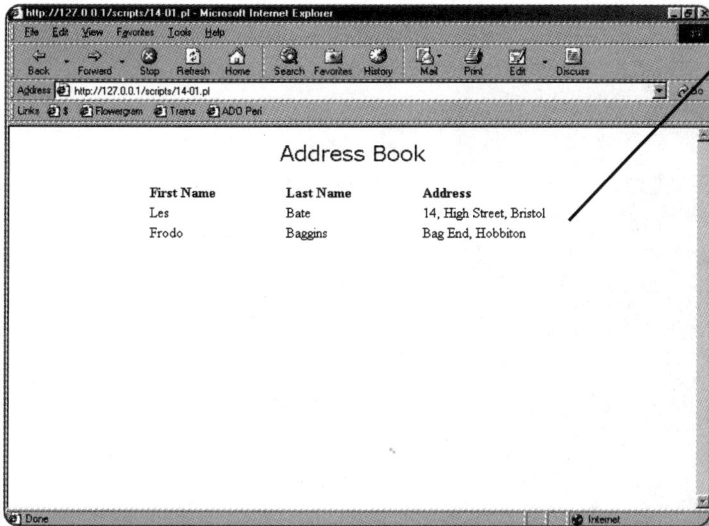

6. Again, go to the 14-01.pl program in your browser to confirm that the Sauron record has been removed from the database table.

So there you have it. You are now able to carry out all of the CRUD (Create, Read, Update, and Delete) operations on a database table.

Perl DBI

DBI, Perl's database interface, has been around for some time. It is used extensively on UNIX-type platforms but also works on Windows platforms, so it is worth covering that briefly here.

Installing DBI

Before you can use DBI, you must install the DBI module in Perl. To do this on Windows, follow these simple instructions. Of course, your ISP may already have DBI installed for you.

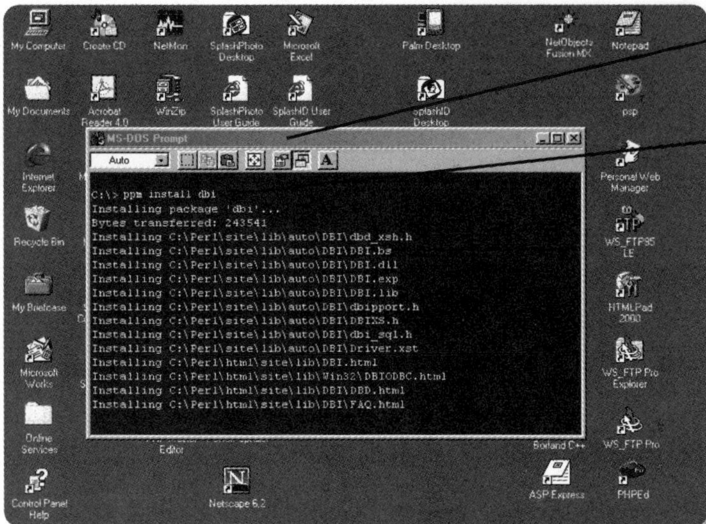

1. Open an MS-DOS command window.

2. Type the following command and press the Enter key:

```
ppm install dbi
```

The process may take several minutes, and when it completes, you will see a list of all the modules currently installed.

Any time you want to confirm what modules you have installed, simply enter the command **ppm query** at an MS-DOS command line (or at the command prompt on a UNIX machine).

Reading Database Tables Using DBI

Okay, now let's look at how you can use DBI. You will run through the same set of exercises as you did with ADO, but using DBI instead.

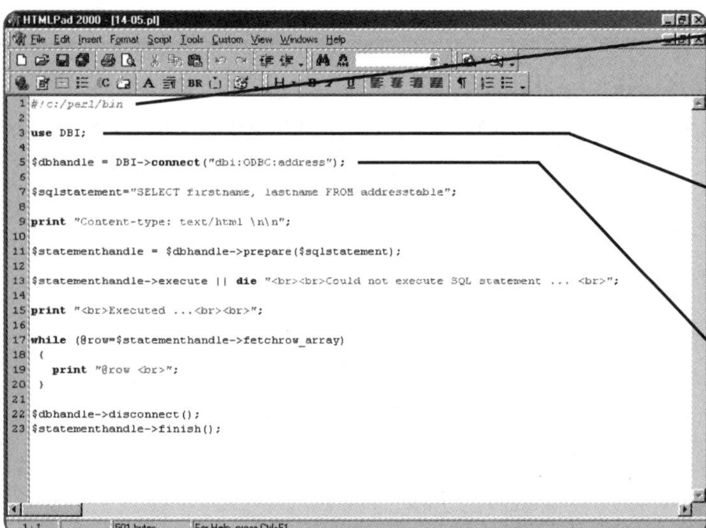

1. Open a new program in your editor.

```
#!c:/perl/bin
```

2. Bring the DBI module into your program.

```
use DBI;
```

3. Connect to the database via DBI.

```
$dbhandle = DBI->connect
   ("dbi:ODBC:address");
```

This operation returns a handle that is used to reference the database in future operations in your program. The connect string specifies the database is being accessed via DBI, that it is an ODBC database (you can substitute this for any database type supported by DBI), and finally, that the name of the database is address.

4. Set up a variable to hold your SQL statement, as you did with the ADO version.

```
$sqlstatement="SELECT firstname, lastname FROM addresstable";
```

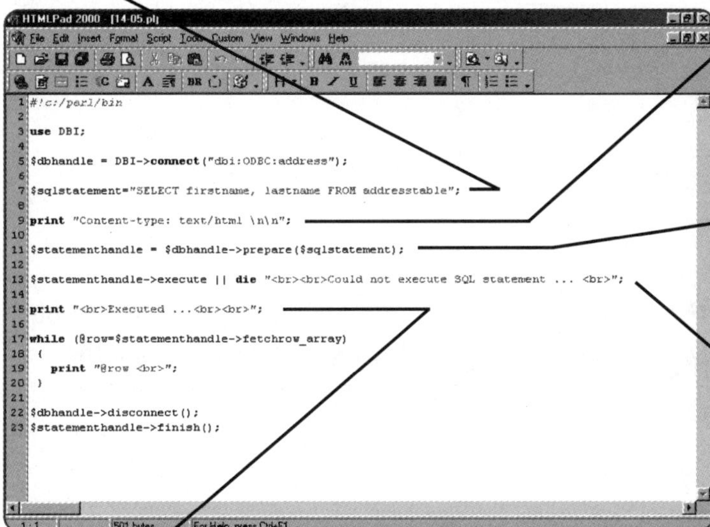

5. Prepare to send data back to the browser.

```
print "Content-type: text/html
   \n\n";
```

6. Prepare to run the SQL.

```
$statementhandle = $dbhandle-
   >prepare($sqlstatement);
```

7. Now enter the DBI code to run the SQL query. This time you are checking for errors.

```
$statementhandle->execute || die "<br><br>Could not execute SQL statement ...
   <br>";
```

8. Display a confirmation message.

```
print "<br>Executed ...<br><br>";
```

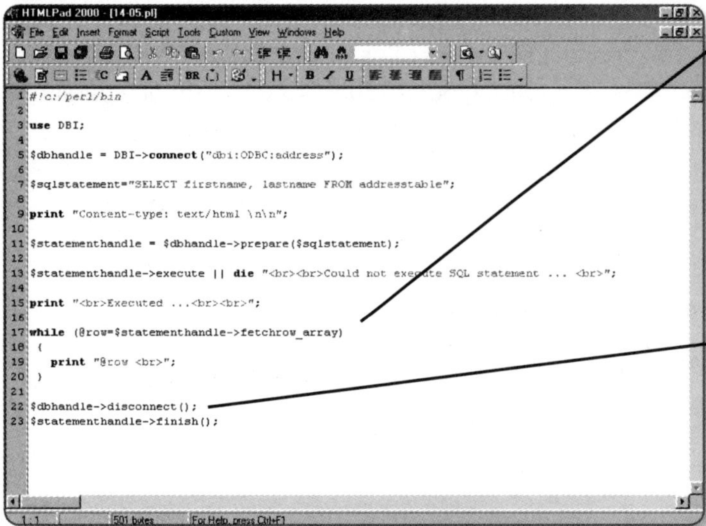

9. Display the rows that are returned.

```
while (@row=$statementhandle-
>fetchrow_array)
 {
   print "@row <br>";
 }
```

10. Finally, tidy up by closing the connection and statement handles.

```
$dbhandle->disconnect();
$statementhandle->finish();
```

11. Save your program as 14-05.pl.

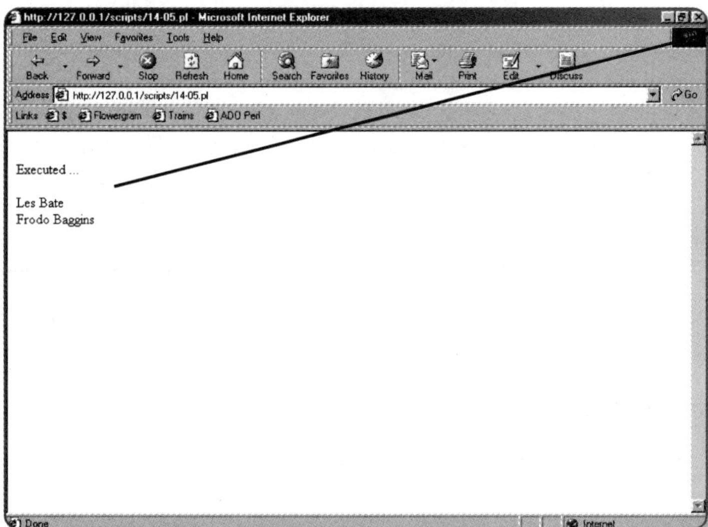

12. Run the program in your browser. You should see the database records displayed.

Writing to Database Tables Using DBI

The method of writing to a database with DBI is very similar to the previous example.

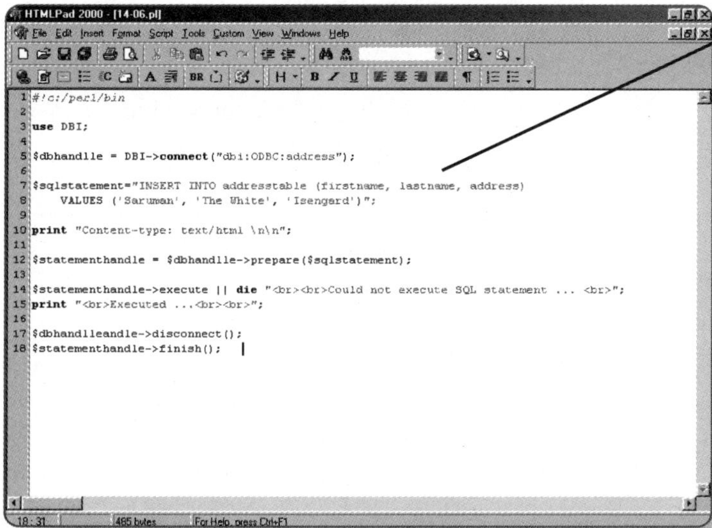

1. Open the previous example and replace the SQL statement line(s) with the following:

```
$sqlstatement="INSERT INTO
  addresstable (firstname,
  lastname, address)
      VALUES ('Saruman', 'The
         White', 'Isengard')";
```

2. Now remove the loop and read through the records in the previous example.

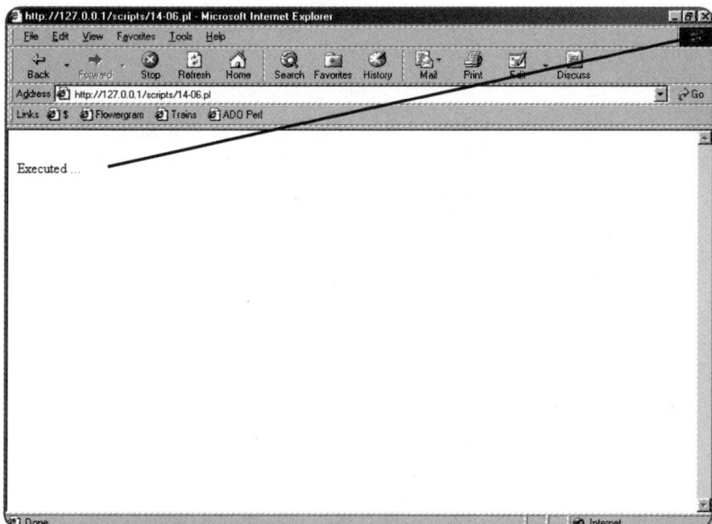

3. Open your browser and run the new program. You should see a confirmation message.

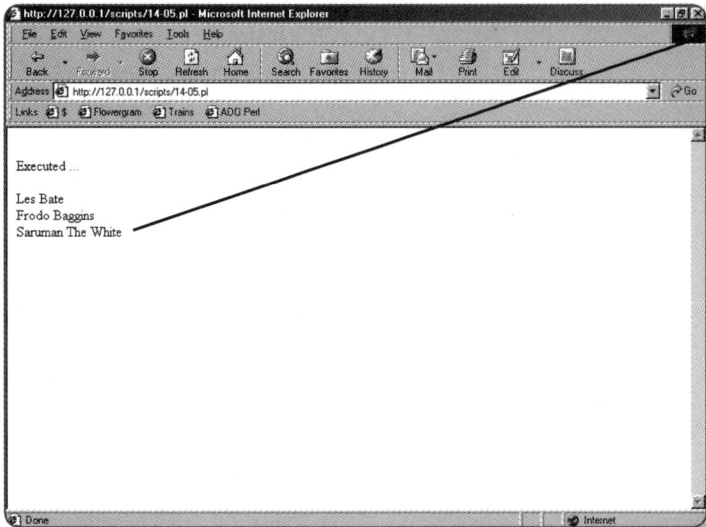

4. Now return to the first DBI program, 14-05.pl, to confirm that the new record has been added.

> **TIP**
>
> If you do not always see what you expect in the Web browser, try clicking the Refresh button.

Updating Database Tables Using DBI

The following example of updating database tables using DBI is identical to the previous example, except for the SQL statement.

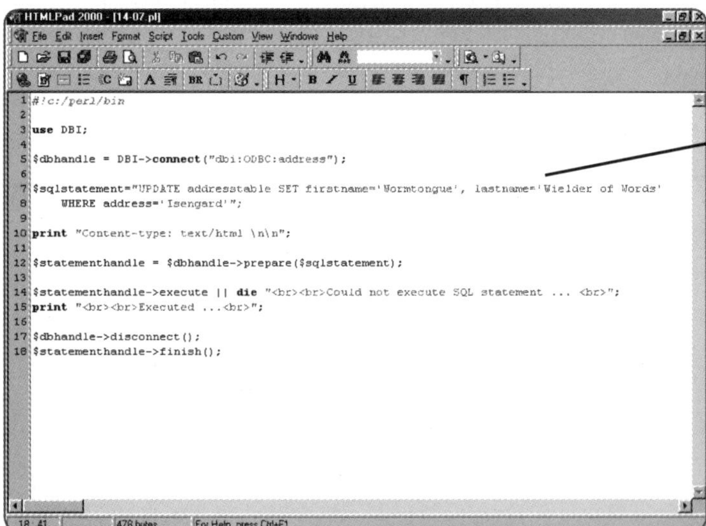

1. Open your previous program (14-06.pl).

2. Replace the SQL statement with the following:

```
$sqlstatement="UPDATE
   addresstable SET
   firstname='Wormtongue',
   lastname='Wielder of Words'
      WHERE address='Isengard'";
```

3. Save your program as 14-07.pl.

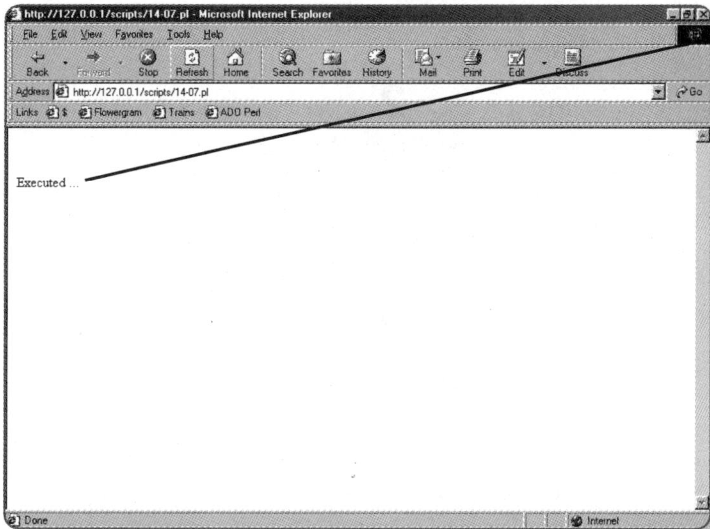

4. Run the program in your browser; again you should see the confirmation message.

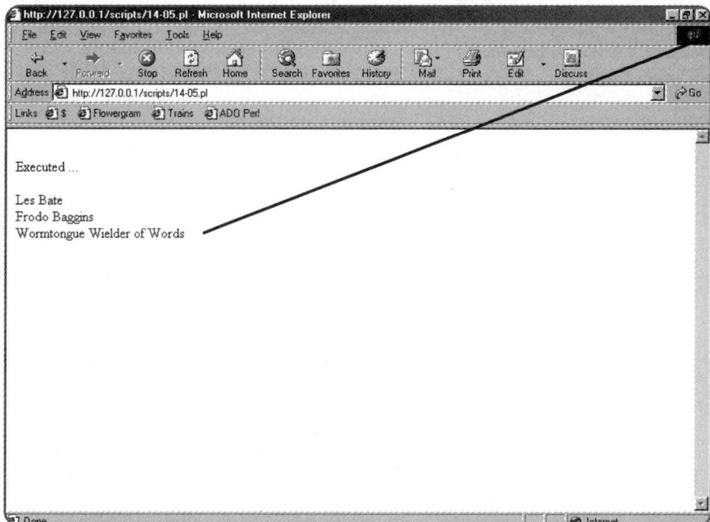

5. Return to program 14-05 in your browser to confirm that the updates have been made.

Now, if you're still with me, let's take a look at deleting records with DBI.

Deleting Records from Database Tables Using DBI

Once again, the code to remove a record from the database is identical to that used in the previous example.

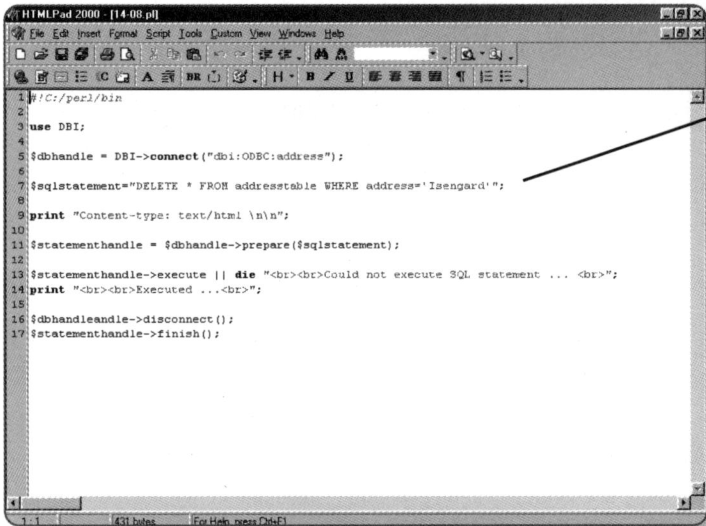

1. Re-open 14-07.pl.

2. Replace the SQL statement with the following:

```
$sqlstatement="DELETE * FROM
   addresstable WHERE
   address='Isengard'";
```

3. Save your program as 14-08.pl.

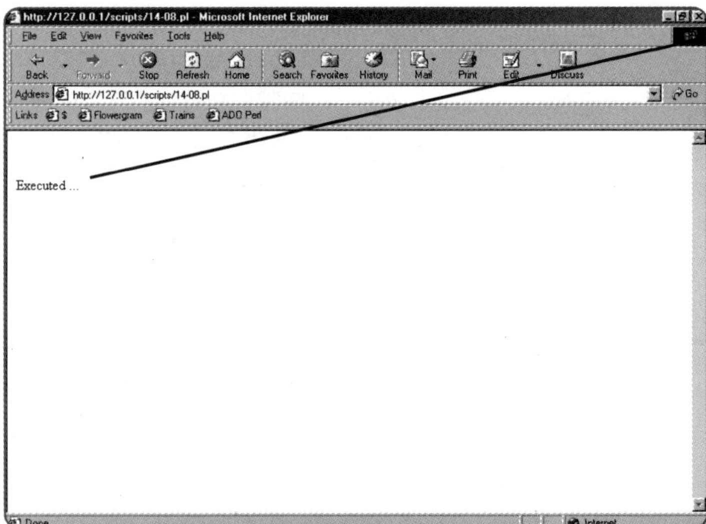

4. Open your program in your browser and you should see the usual confirmation message.

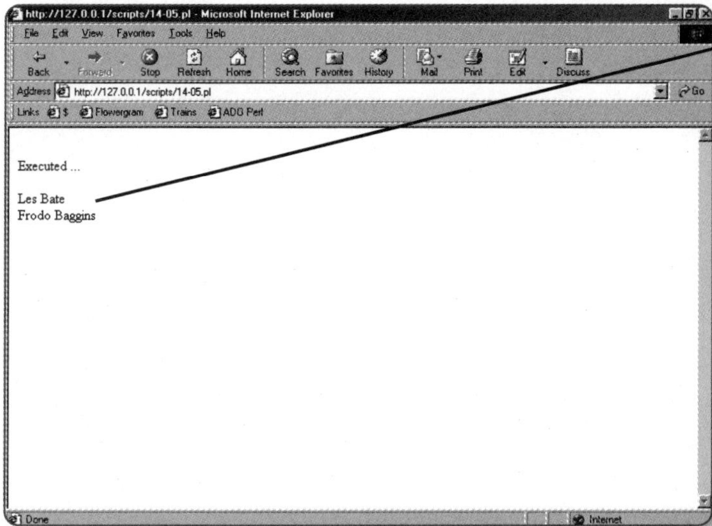

5. Finally, check that the record has disappeared from the database by re-running 14-05.pl in your browser.

And that's it. You now know the basics of manipulating databases through two possible methods, ADO and DBI.

You will see more examples of practical code in the case study in Chapter 17.

15

Another Diversion: JavaScript

You know how to create a form and how to get the data sent by the form into your Perl program. But what if the data entered by the user is invalid? You can get your Perl program to return the form with an indication of what the problem is, but this is an inefficient way of checking the form data because each error discovered means that the page is re-sent over and over until the user has corrected all of his mistakes. Wouldn't it be nice if you knew (as far as possible) that the data being received into your Perl program was okay?

This is where JavaScript comes in. JavaScript can check your form data at the client (that is, within your Web page) and can prevent your form being submitted until all the errors in the entered data have been corrected. This means that you get instant notification of any errors and there is (hopefully) only one trip across the Internet for your form.

In this chapter you will learn about:

- Object orientation
- JavaScript syntax
- JavaScript variables
- Using JavaScript to validate form data

A Few Notes about JavaScript

JavaScript is an interpreted, object-oriented programming language developed for use in HTML Web pages (that is, client-side programming). Although it can also be used as a server-side programming language, we are not going to discuss that aspect of JavaScript here.

JavaScript is similar in its syntax to Java and C++, and behaves in much the same way. However, JavaScript is not the same as Java. Java enables you to build full-blown, stand-alone applications; JavaScript does not. It simply reacts with *objects* within a Web page.

Object Orientation

Object orientation attempts to bring the real world into programming. Real world objects (I'll give an example of such an object soon) are represented as software objects. In theory, object-oriented programs are simpler, more reliable, and more closely model their real-world subjects.

Object orientation should also be more efficient in terms of software creation, as you do not, in theory, have to keep re-writing things. Objects are described using what is known as a *class*. This class contains all the definitions of the data that are relevant to that object and all of the functions that operate upon that data. Classes can be reused and modified to suit a particular purpose without having to re-write things from scratch. This gives rise to a property known as *inheritance*.

An example of a real-world object is a bank account. You could have a class describing such an account. The data for a bank account would include

- Account number
- Account name
- Sort node
- Balance

These items describe the data contained within the description of the class.

Having decided upon the data that might be contained within a class, you now need to be able to manipulate these data items to read, write, update, and delete them. That is, to use the account you need to be able to

- Open the account
- Add funds
- Debit funds
- Close the account

In a class definition you would write methods (know as functions in normal programming terms) to deal with each of these actions.

With the definition of the object (in the form of a class) you can now create the bank account object itself; in fact you can create lots of them. Where ordinary languages might have arrays of integers and so on, in object-oriented languages you can have arrays of objects too. This is very powerful indeed. Imagine trying to keep track of loads of accounts in a normal procedural language.

One of the main points of object orientation is that the data within an object can be set up to be accessed only via that object's methods. This helps to ensure the integrity of the data and reduces bugs. This feature is known as *data hiding*.

Creating an object from the class definition is referred to as *instantiation*.

A form of notation has been developed to help you to describe the act of accessing the methods within an object. This is sometimes referred to as *dot notation*. For example, if you want to access the `add_funds()` method of an object you can write it as

```
account.add_funds()
```

Note the dot between `account` and `add_funds( )`.

If you are with me so far, here is another twist.

Having created your account class, you can now slightly change the purpose of the account. For example, you can have current accounts and savings accounts. The basic information that defines an account (account number, balance, and so on) can be held in a super class. Then other classes can inherit from this class and provide the more specific information that describes a particular type of account. This is an illustration of the potential flexibility of object orientation. This use of inheritance is an example of the much-discussed code re-use advantage of object-oriented languages.

Let's go for a silly example, and create a class called Animal.

What data can you hold about an animal?

```
Carnivore (true/false)
Number of legs (integer)
```

What methods (functions) could you have? Most animals make a sound of some sort, so you could have a method called

```
talk( );
```

This gives a basic animal class. You can inherit from this class and specialize into more specific subclasses. Your subclasses can inherit the basic methods from the superclass, or higher level class. So you can create a class for a cat and one for a dog, both based on the animal superclass but with their own specializations that describe the differences from the basic animal class.

Now calling the `talk()`method for each object you create, such as `dog.talk()`, `cat.talk()`, causes an appropriate response from each object—the dog will bark and the cat will meow.

This ability to produce an equivalent but appropriate response is known as *polymorphism*. Perhaps you can begin to see the possible uses of such behavior.

An in-depth discussion about all the aspects of object orientation is beyond the scope of this book, but I hope that you can begin to see there are possible advantages of object orientation over conventional procedural programming. Now let's turn back to discussing JavaScript.

Elements of JavaScript

JavaScript uses objects. The HTML page that you might be on at any particular time is referred to as the *document object*. There are many other objects as well, such as the window object, the form object, the form element object (containing the <INPUT TYPE=...> elements), and the button object.

Many of these objects produce *events*, that is, a result of the user's action or a change in the state of some element on a page or in a window. For example, clicking a button on a form triggers the `onClick` event. When you roll your mouse over an image you trigger the `onMouseOver` event. You can attach JavaScript code to these events to cause things to happen.

As in other object-oriented languages, you use methods to cause something to happen to an object. Here is a simple example. If you want to move the cursor into a text field called Surname on a form called MyForm1 you would write

```
document.MyForm1.Surname.focus();
```

Note the dot notation again. This means that the document object contains a form object called `MyForm1`, and object `MyForm1` contains an object called `Surname`. The object called `Surname` has a method within it called `Focus()`, which is what is being called, or executed, in the example. So you have objects contained within objects, a bit like a Russian nesting doll.

Also notice the parentheses at the end of the method name. These show that this is a method, but they are also used to pass parameters to methods that accept them. In our earlier bank account example, you might want to add funds. When you use the method to do this, you can write

```
account1.addfunds(500.00)
```

This means (in this example) you are adding $500.00 to `account1`.

Much of the time, the parentheses following a method name are empty. Sometimes, as in the previous example, the parentheses are used to pass information to the method.

So now you have an idea of how objects are used; you will start to build upon this with some examples. But before you do that, you must learn how to incorporate JavaScript into your Web pages.

Where Do You Put Your JavaScript?

Now you have some idea of what JavaScript is all about, it is time to look at where to put it. To tell the Web browser that you are using any kind of script, you have to use the <SCRIPT> tag. This is a general HTML tag and not anything to do with JavaScript itself. It is used to point out that some kind of script follows. The default script language (for IE5 at least) is VBScript. So, if you want to use JavaScript, you should use

```
<SCRIPT LANGUAGE="JavaScript">
```

If you don't specify the language, the browser is usually clever enough to recognize which language you are using, but don't assume anything.

</SCRIPT> is used to end all script sections, whether they are VBScript, JavaScript, or another language.

Note also that there are several versions of JavaScript, so you might see:

```
<SCRIPT LANGUAGE="JavaScript1.0">
```

or

```
<SCRIPT LANGUAGE="JavaScript1.1">
```

or

```
<SCRIPT LANGUAGE="JavaScript1.2">
```

These versions offer more updated functionality, and you will need to become more aware of the differences as you become more proficient at using JavaScript and want to extend the complexity of your scripts.

Another thing to remember is that you can place script either in the <BODY> of an HTML document or in the <HEAD>.

Generally, you use JavaScript in the body of a document if you want it to execute as the page loads. JavaScript placed in the head of a document is generally used as it is required, or *called*, as the action of executing it is called. The script in the head usually takes the form of *functions* (discrete sections of code), each function having a specific purpose.

More JavaScript Syntax

JavaScript uses code blocks all over the place. These are lines of code enclosed in braces, very much like Perl.

For example:

```
{
  Document.write ("Hello There!");
  Alert("This is a pop-up box!");
}
```

It is unusual to see a block of code like this on its own. Often it is the body of a function, as in this example:

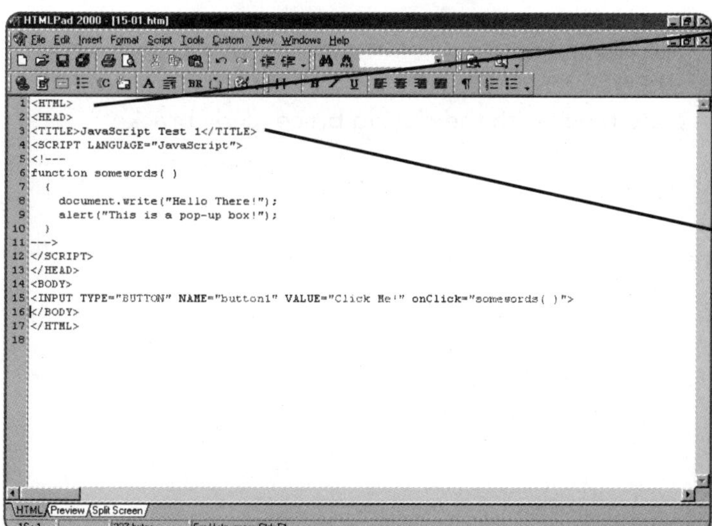

1. Open your editor and start an HTML page.

```
<HTML>
<HEAD>
```

2. Give your HTML page a title (for the title bar at the top of the browser).

```
<TITLE>JavaScript Test
   1</TITLE>
```

3. Start a <Script> tag, describing JavaScript as the script language.

```
<SCRIPT LANGUAGE="JavaScript">
```

4. Start a function as shown below. Notice the comment start tag placed there so as not to confuse older browsers.

```
<!--
function somewords()
```

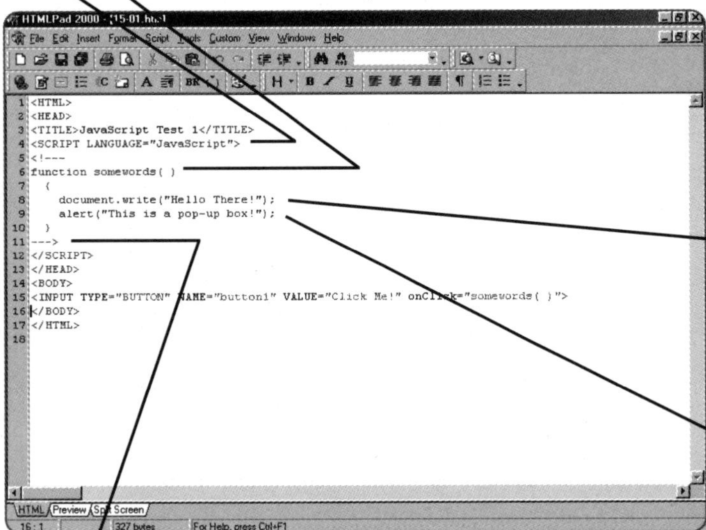

5. Open a block of code using the curly braces we talked about a little while ago.

```
{
```

6. Type the following JavaScript command to write some text to the Web page:

```
document.write("Hello There!");
```

7. Type this JavaScript statement to cause an Alert box to pop up on the screen:

```
alert("This is a pop-up box!");
```

8. Now close the function code block with the closing brace (curly bracket).

```
}
```

9. Close the HTML comment.

```
-->
```

10. Close the <Script> tag and the HTML <HEAD> tag.

```
</SCRIPT>
</HEAD>
```

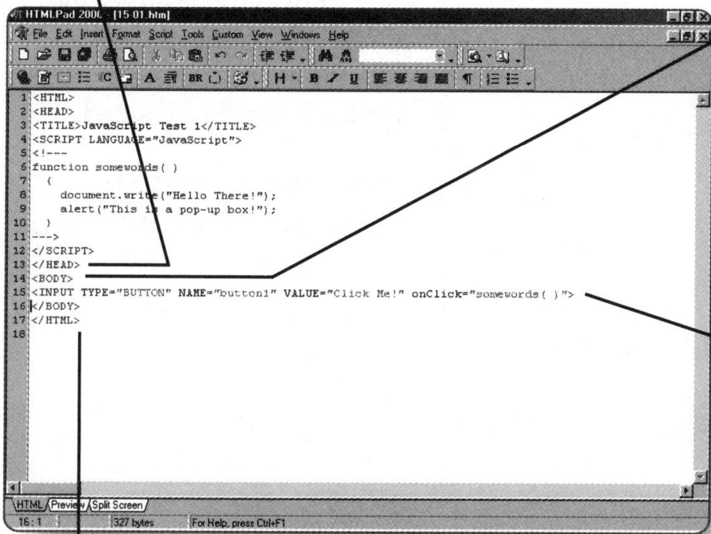

11. Now open a <BODY> tag. This, as you have learned, is where you normally put the main part of your Web page, containing your images, text, and so on.

```
<BODY>
```

12. Create a button. These are normally used to interact with HTML forms, as you have seen. But you can use them on their own.

```
<INPUT TYPE="BUTTON"
   NAME="button1" VALUE="Click
   Me!" onClick="somewords()">
```

13. Finally, close the <BODY> tag and the <HTML> tag.

```
</BODY>
</HTML>
```

NOTE

Normally, you would save this either in a folder under your wwwroot folder, or you would upload it to your hosting company to use on the Internet and you would then access it using the appropriate URL as you do when you are connecting to a normal Web site.

If you saved this page into a folder called *test* at the top level of your ISP Web space, you would enter something like

http://www.mydomainname.com/test/15-01.htm

14. Save it as 15-01.htm.

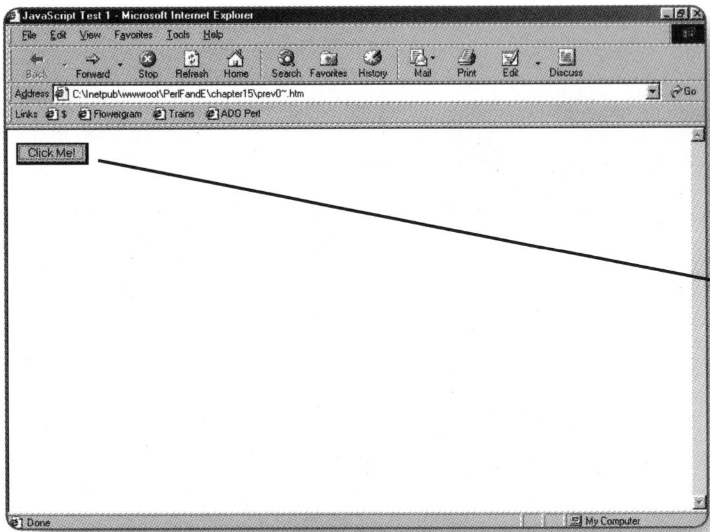

15. Use the preview option in your editor to test your JavaScript, or double-click the 15-01.htm file and it will open in your browser. Either way, you will see the button you created.

16. Click the Click Me! button and observe the effect.

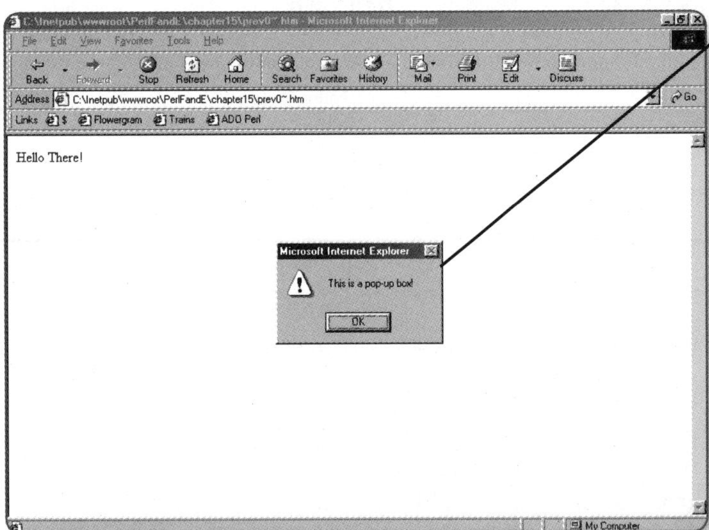

You should get a message box like this.

This is a full example of a very simple JavaScript function, showing the use of braces, {}, around the code. It also shows where functions are placed and one method of calling a function (`onClick=`).

Just to remind you, the <!--- and ---> tags are normally used to embrace HTML comments (text that is designed to be informative to humans but is ignored by the browser) and therefore anything inside them is ignored. Modern browsers recognize that there is script inside them and therefore execute it. Older browsers (that do not understand JavaScript) ignore the JavaScript code; this prevents unnecessary error messages. Of course, the JavaScript code won't work on an older browser, either. The opening HTML comment needs a less than symbol (<) followed by at least two dashes like this:

```
<!--
```

It should end with at least two dashes followed by a greater than symbol (>), like this:

```
-->
```

Note that case is very important when specifying keywords in JavaScript—function is a keyword, *Function* isn't.

JavaScript Variables

As do all other languages, JavaScript uses variables to store information. Variables can be created on-the-fly as and when you need them, but it is a good idea to create them at the beginning of your script so that it is easier to follow, and so you know where to look for them. To create a variable you use the `var` keyword.

```
var age;
var name;
```

And so on.

To assign a value to a variable you use the assignment operator, =.

```
age = 17;
name = "fred";
```

Most JavaScript statements end with a semicolon. JavaScript, like most modern languages, is *free format*, that is, it can be split over many lines if desired, usually to aid readability. It uses the semicolon to indicate the end of a statement, a form of notation borrowed from C++ and Java (and of course, Perl) languages.

Other things you will want to do with JavaScript include

- Add numbers together
- Subtract
- Multiply
- Divide

You might add the values of a couple of variables like this:

```
firstNumber = 13;
secondNumber = 23;
ressultOne = firstNumber + secondNumber;
```

Note that the standard convention is to capitalize the second word in a variable. This makes the code easier to read and reduces mistakes. It is up to you whether to follow this convention, but doing so will make it easier for other people following along behind you to update your code.

Subtraction, multiplication, and division are performed in a similar manner to the previous example, using the -, *, and / operators, respectively.

There are many other things that you might want to do; for example, you might want to get the length of a character string.

```
stringVar = "fred";
sLength = stringVar.length;
```

There are no parentheses after length because this is not a method, but an attribute of the string object, `stringVar`.

To test a value you use the equals operator, = = (remember that you already used the = operator to assign a value to a variable).

So you would say

```
if(numVar = = 5)
 {
```

Other operators are

- > (greater than)
- < (less than)
- <= (less than or equal to)

You can do many hundreds of other things too with JavaScript, including opening new windows, jumping to different Web pages, opening dialog boxes, and so on. JavaScript is a large, complex, and immensely powerful language.

You will learn more features of the language with experience, but now we have to be ruthless and stick to things that will help you with your Web applications.

Your First Form Validation JavaScript Function

One of the most interesting and useful things you can do with JavaScript is client-side validation. But before we go any further, let us briefly re-visit the object discussion. All things in JavaScript are regarded as objects. An HTML page is called a *document object*. As you learned a short time ago, a form is another object that lives inside a document and has a name by which you can refer to it. Therefore, you refer to a form that has a `NAME="addrecord"` attribute like this.

```
document.addrecord
```

Note the dot!

This is not a complete statement yet, but it means "go to the form `addrecord` contained within the document."

Any fields in the form are referred to in a similar way. So, if you have a field called `surname`, like this:

```
<INPUT TYPE=TEXT NAME="surname">
```

Then you would refer to it like this:

```
document.addrecord.surname
```

This gets you to the field object inside the form object, which is inside the document object. Now you have reached the field object. But this object has many attributes, such as length, value, and so on. So, to access the value of your field, you refer to the value of the field like this:

```
document.addrecord.surname.value
```

Now, you can have a look at what is in the field. To do this, use the JavaScript `if` statement. If you want to check that the field is empty, you can do this:

```
if (document.addrecord.surname.value == "")
 {
  Do something ...
  Do something else ...
 }
back to the rest of the code that doesn't care if the field is empty or not …
```

As you can see, the braces are used here again, and now you can see why. They limit the scope of the `if` statement. In other words, only the code inside the braces is dependent upon the condition in the `if` statement.

Also, note that you use two equal signs (= =) to check for equality. A single = in JavaScript is used to assign a value to a variable. Other tests are:

- != not equal to
- > greater than
- < less than
- <= less than or equal to
- >= greater than or equal to

You can have multiple conditions in your `if` statement. These conditions can be ANDed or ORed together (or a combination of the two) by using the JavaScript AND operator, which is the double ampersand, &&, and the JavaScript OR operator, which is the double pipe, || .

So, a JavaScript `if` statement might look like this:

```
if ((document.formname.department.value = = "HR" ||
  document.formname.expenses.value != 0) &&
   (document.formname.jobtitle.value = = "Manager"))
 {
```

The parentheses force conditions to be grouped together in the way you intend rather than the way JavaScript decides if you leave the inner parentheses out. There are rules about operator precedence that define in what order conditions will be tested. If you do not want to learn them, or you are at all unsure as to how your conditions will be interpreted, use parentheses to group them together.

Submitting Forms Using JavaScript

You can submit your form to a server-side script or program (such as your Perl programs) from within a JavaScript function. This can be done by using the `submit()` method of the form object, like this:

```
document.addrecord.submit();
```

Conditional Form Submission

Now you can check the value contained within fields in your form and you can submit your form. But there is much more to learn yet.

How do you check for the possibility that a field is blank? You have met the `if` statement briefly; the full syntax for the `if` statement is

```
If (condition)
 {
   do something[...]
   do something else[...]
 }
else
  {
   do some other stuff[...]
   do some more other stuff![...]
  }
```

So, putting it all together, try the following example and see what you get.

1. First, open a new HTML page in your editor.

```
<HTML>
<HEAD>
<TITLE>JavaScript Example</TITLE>
```

2. Open a <Script> tag to hold your JavaScript function.

```
<SCRIPT LANGUAGE="JavaScript">
```

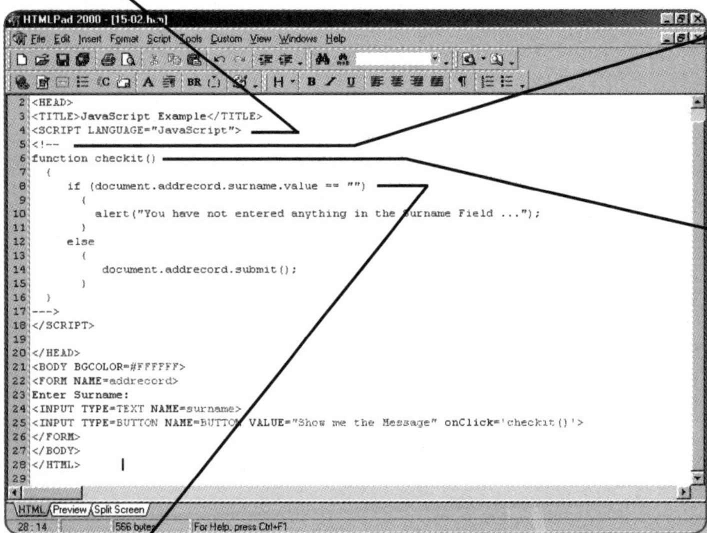

3. Open your HTML comments to hide your script from old browsers.

```
<!–
```

4. Start your function using the keyword `function` and the name of your function with parentheses at the end, and add an opening brace to mark the start of the function code block.

```
function checkit()
  {
```

5. Now code an `if` statement to check whether the `surname` field on a form called `addrecord` is empty.

```
    if (document.addrecord.surname.value == "")
```

6. The `if` statement has its own code block, so you will need to open a new brace.

```
      {
```

7. Inside this code block, enter the code you need to give the response you want to the empty surname field, in this case a JavaScript pop-up alert box displaying the nature of the problem.

```
alert("You have not entered anything in the Surname Field ...");
```

8. You have finished with the `if` part now, so close the brace of that code block.

```
}
```

9. But now you are going to tell JavaScript what it must do if there is something in the surname field, so now code the `else` statement.

```
else
```

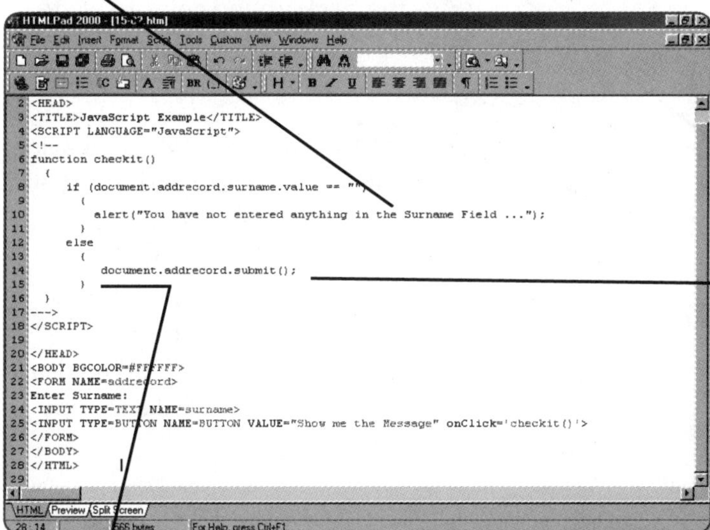

10. Again, the `else` statement needs its own code block, so an opening brace will be needed.

```
{
```

11. If there is something in the surname field on this simple form, you can assume that everything is okay and submit the addrecord HTML form, like this:

```
document.addrecord.submit();
```

12. Close the brace belonging to the `else` statement and then close the function code block using another closing brace.

```
    }
}
```

13. To finish off the script, close the script tag.

```
-->
</SCRIPT>
```

14. Now close the HTML header.

```
</HEAD>
```

The rest of the HTML now contains the body of the HTML document, including the form to be submitted by your JavaScript function.

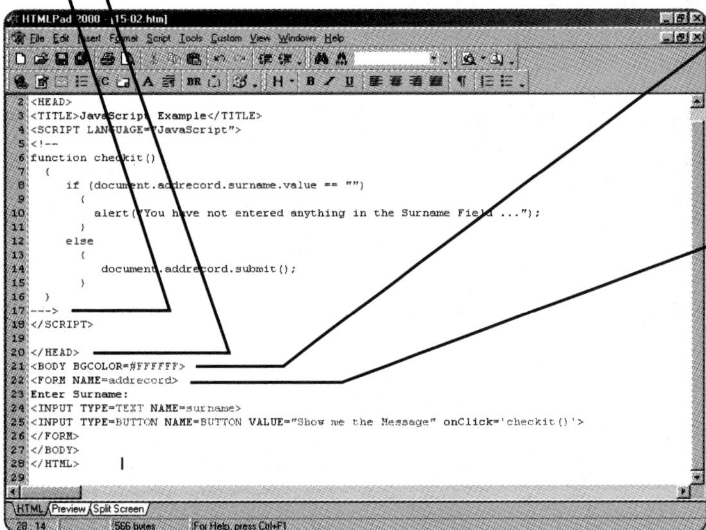

15. Open your <BODY> statement, in this case setting the background color to white.

```
<BODY BGCOLOR=#FFFFFF>
```

16. Add a FORM tag, leaving out the METHOD and ACTION attributes. You are merely going to verify that your JavaScript works. If your form works, the form will be submitted but nothing will happen; otherwise you should get the JavaScript alert box.

```
<FORM NAME=addrecord>
```

17. Enter some text to label the surname field.

```
Enter Surname:
```

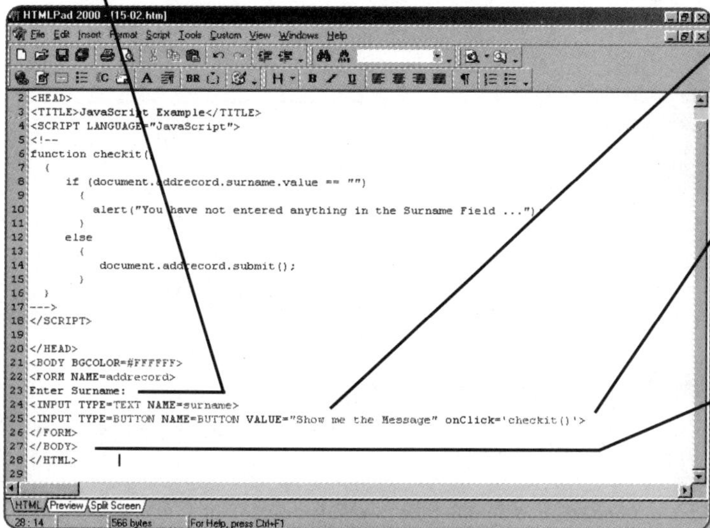

18. Now code the surname HTML text field itself.

```
<INPUT TYPE=TEXT NAME=surname>
```

19. Add your form button.

```
<INPUT TYPE=BUTTON NAME=BUTTON
VALUE="Show me the Message"
   onClick='checkit()'>
```

20. Finally, close your form, body, and HTML tags.

```
</FORM>
</BODY>
</HTML>
```

> **NOTE**
>
> TYPE=BUTTON is used rather than TYPE=SUBMIT, preventing the form contents being immediately sent to the server. Instead, you can invoke your JavaScript function which can check that you have completed any required fields, displaying any error messages where appropriate, or, if there are no errors, can submit your form.

21. Save your page as 15-02.htm and check it to make sure it works.

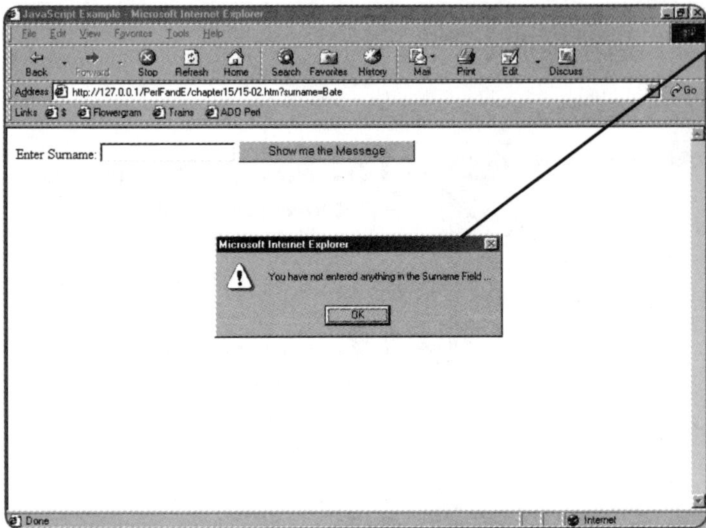

If you leave the surname field blank and click the button you should get a message telling you that you have not entered anything in the field.

NOTE

If you add a name in the surname field, then as has been said, you will see nothing happen except perhaps the page refresh and the surname field will empty.

There is one other method that makes the form more useful and friendly, especially on a form with lots of fields. You can direct the user back to a field in error by using the `focus()` JavaScript method.

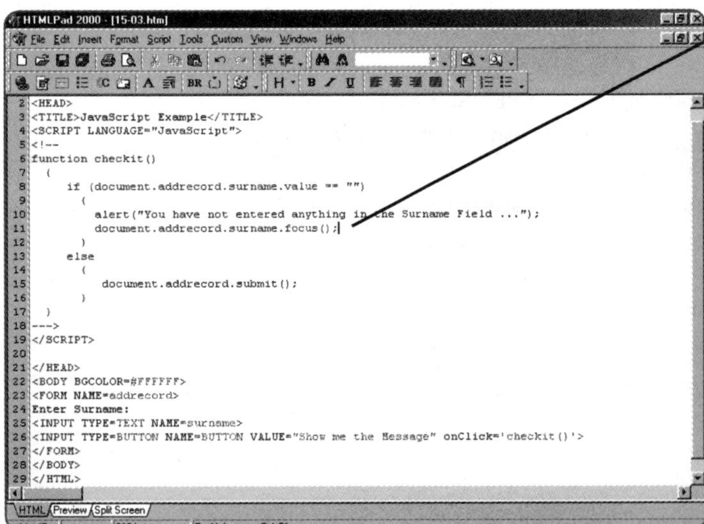

1. Modify your last HTML page by adding the `focus()` function to your JavaScript function, like this:

```
document.addrecord.
   surname.focus();
```

2. Save your page as 15-03.htm and make sure it works.

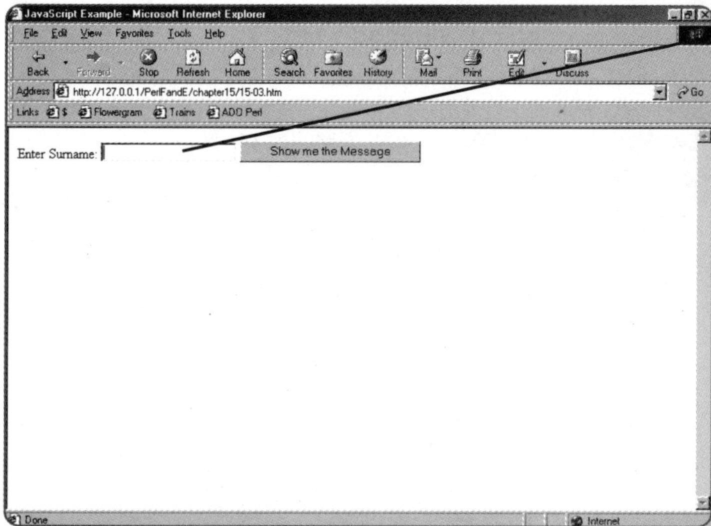

3. Notice the subtle difference: this time when you click the OK button on the message box, you will see the cursor jump back into the text box. In the previous example, the Show me the message button was highlighted instead.

More JavaScript Functions

What if you wanted to check that what the user typed was a number? JavaScript has a function called `isNaN( )` which means "is not a number." This function returns a Boolean result (True or False), True being returned if the number sent to it is not a number.

You use `isNaN` like this:

```
if(isNaN(variable)
  {
```

1. Load your program again into your editor and modify it to include the following lines of code:

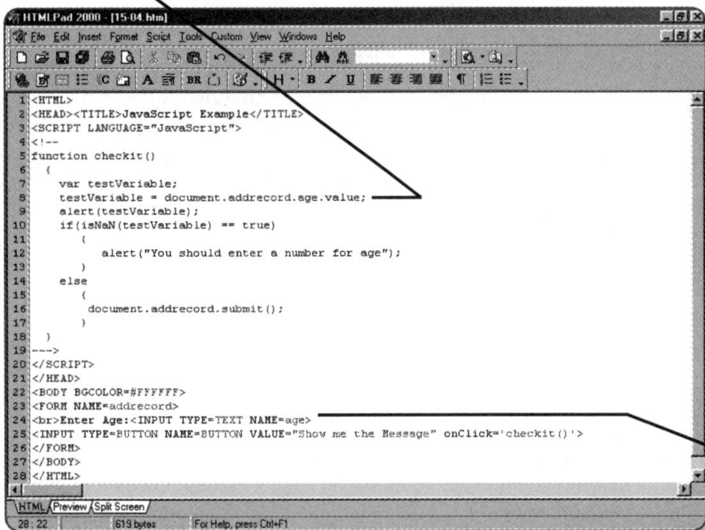


```
var testVariable;
testVariable =
   document.addrecord.age.value;
if(isNAN(testVariable)
   {
       alert("You should enter
         a number for age");
   {
 else
    {

document.addrecord.submit();
    }
```

2. Replace the surname text field to your form with another field to hold age data like this.

```
<BR>Enter Age:
<INPUT TYPE=TEXT NAME="age">
```

3. Save the page as 15-04.htm.

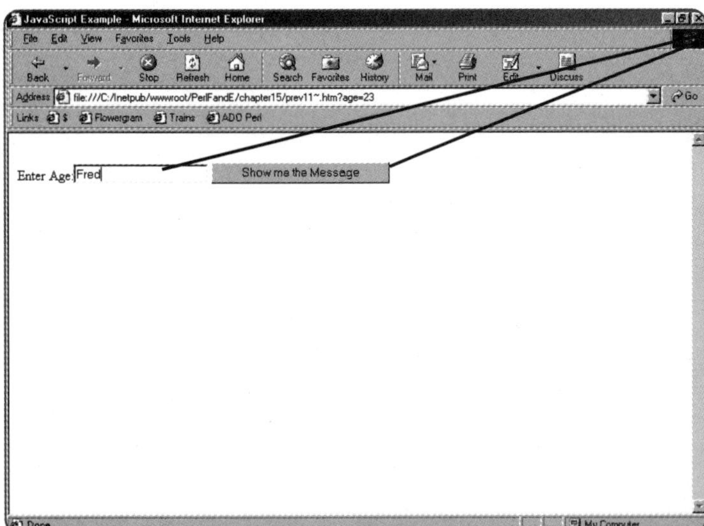

4. Load the page into your browser and enter some letters into the Age field, and click the Show me the Message button.

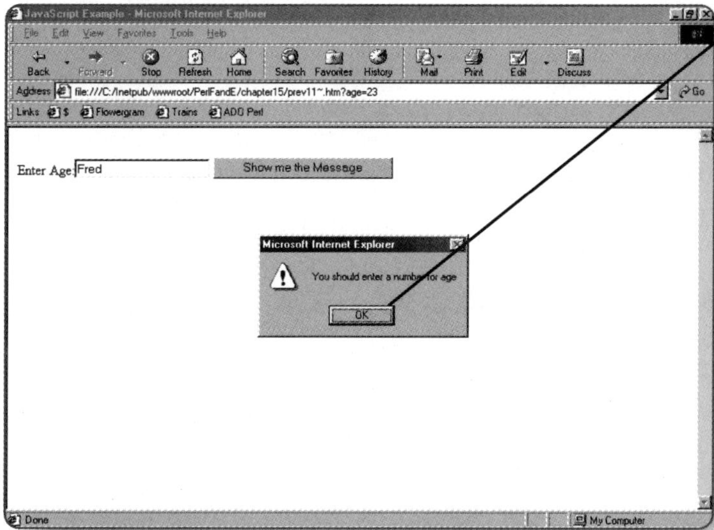

You should get an error message.

What if you want to check two fields, such as age and surname? You can put both of the checks in one function, which will work fine. But what if the form contains 15 or 20 fields? And what if there are a lot of errors?

Well, the user will get lots of error messages, but will probably only remember the last two or three; he or she will then have to click the button again to get the rest of the errors. A better way is to check each field in turn and when you find a problem, skip the rest of the checks and display the first error message. The user then corrects that error and then when he or she clicks the button again, the next error message appears until the form is free from errors, at which point the form is submitted.

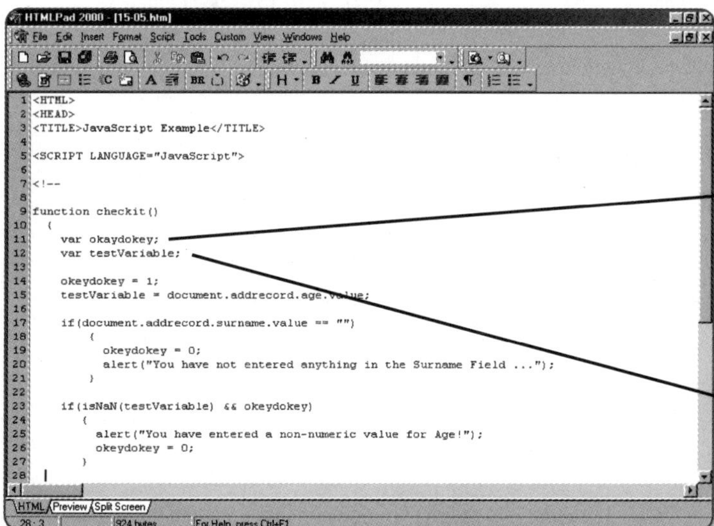

This is easy to do.

1. Open your HTML page again.

2. At the beginning of your function add the following variable.

```
var okeydokey;
```

3. Also add the variable to hold the value of surname from the form.

```
var testVariable;
```

4. Set the `okeydokey` variable to 1.

```
okeydokey = 1;
```

5. Now code an `if` statement to check if the surname field is empty.

```
if (document.addrecord.surname.value == "")
```

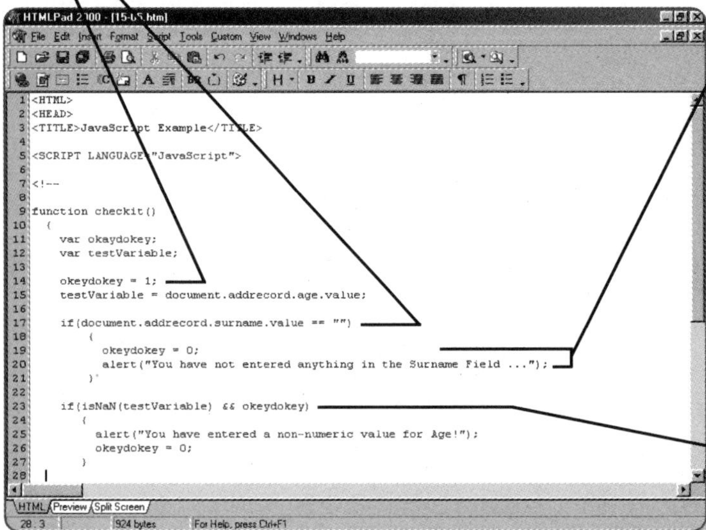

6. If it is, set `okeydokey` to 0 and display the error message. Note that there is no `else` statement this time.

```
{
      okeydokey = 0;
      alert("You have not
         entered anything
         in the Surname
         Field ...");
}
```

7. Now code the `isNaN` check for the Age field, but at the same time check to see if `okeydokey` is set to 1 (or is True).

```
If (isNaN(testVariable) && okeydokey)
  {
    alert("You have entered a non-numeric value for Age!");
    okeydokey = 0;
  }
```

> **NOTE**
>
> Notice that the `if` statement says
>
> `If (isNAN(testVariable) && okeydokey)`
>
> Remember I said that any non-zero value was True? This means that the above okeydokey gets substituted by the value True.
>
> Follow the logic and see if you can understand how this works!

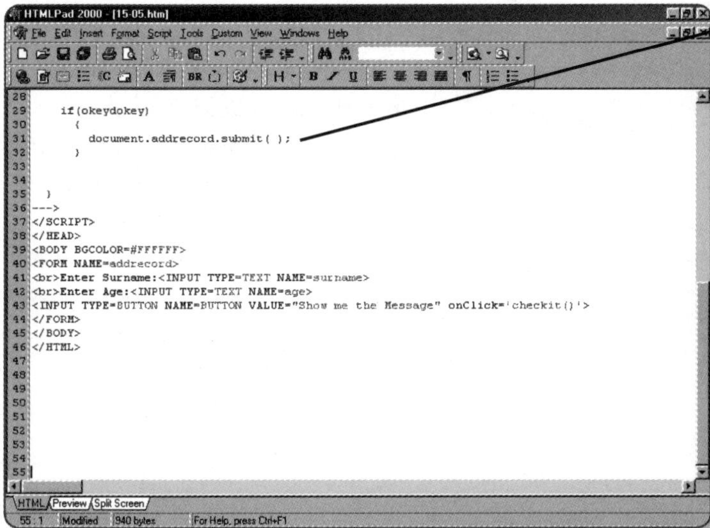

8. Now you need one more `if` statement to decide whether you are going to submit the form.

```
if(okeydokey)
  {
   document.addrecord.submit(
);
  }
```

9. Save the page as 15-05.htm.

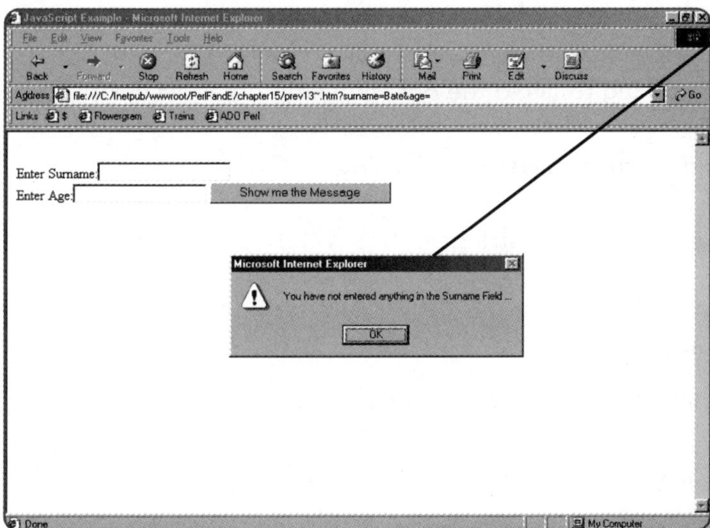

10. Test the page and ensure that it works by entering nothing in the Surname field and then clicking the button. You should get the You have not entered anything in the Surname Field message.

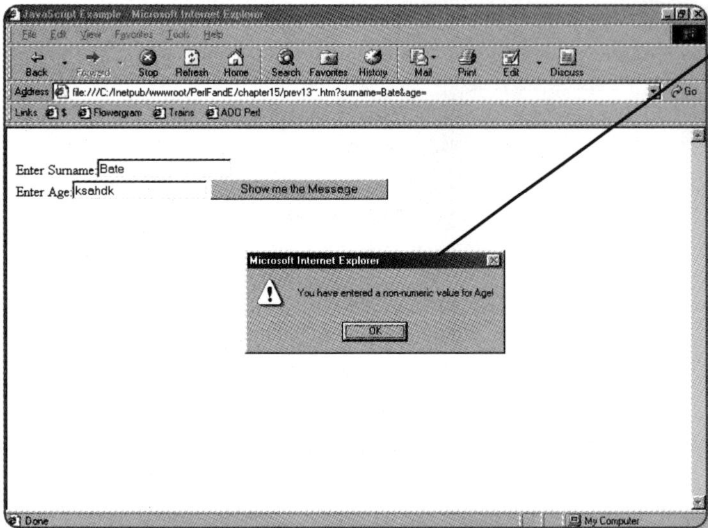

11. Now enter a name in the Surname field and enter words into the Age field. You should get the You have entered a non-numeric value for Age! message.

Now you know how to check for empty fields in a form and how to guide the user back to the fields that were completed incorrectly.

E-mail Address Validation

E-mail address validation is one more useful function that you might want to achieve with JavaScript. But how do you check an e-mail address? There are a few basic checks that are worth making to avoid the occasional typographic error.

A valid e-mail address would normally have the following:

- An @ symbol within the e-mail address string.
- Some characters before the @ symbol.
- Some text after the @ symbol.
- A period amongst the characters after the @ symbol.

If these checks do not reveal a problem, the address is probably okay.

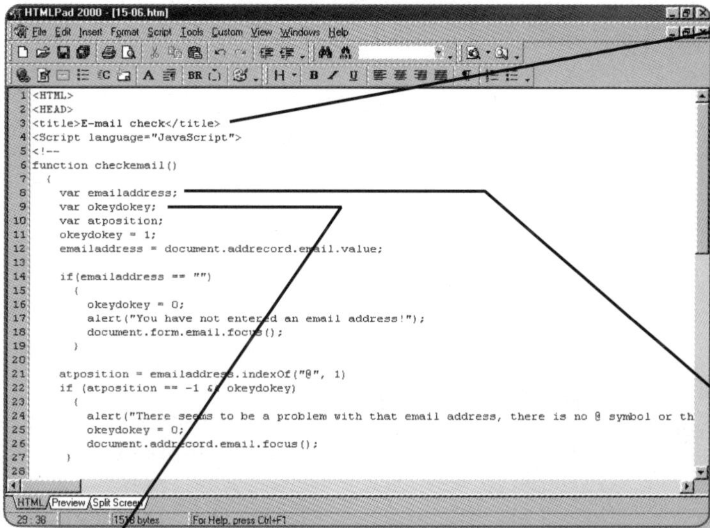

1. Start a new HTML file in your editor.

```
<HTML>
<HEAD>
<title>E-mail check</title>
<Script language="JavaScript">
<!—
function checkemail()
  {
```

2. Create a variable to hold the e-mail address.

```
var emailaddress;
```

3. Create another variable to check the progress and prevent further checks when a failed test is encountered, as you did in the previous example.

```
var okeydokey;
```

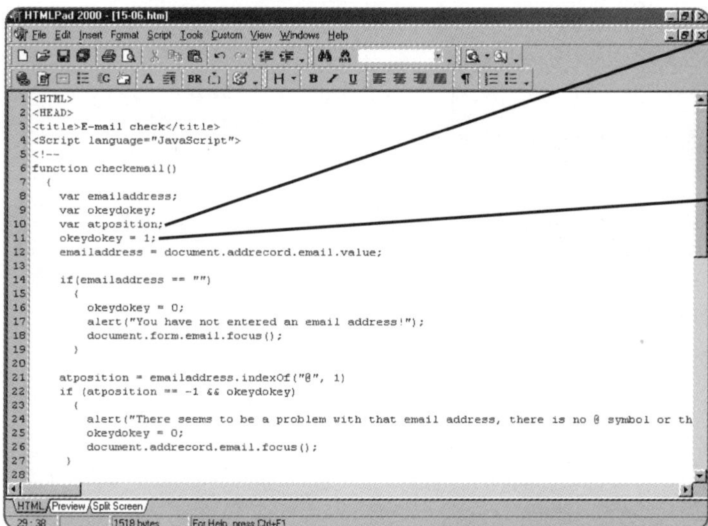

4. Create a variable to hold the position of the @ symbol.

```
var atposition;
```

5. Set the check variable to 1.

```
okeydokey = 1;
```

6. Check that the e-mail address has been provided.

```
emailaddress = document.addrecord.email.value;

if(emailaddress == "")
   {
        okeydokey = 0;
       alert("You have not entered an email address!");
       document.form.email.focus();
   }
```

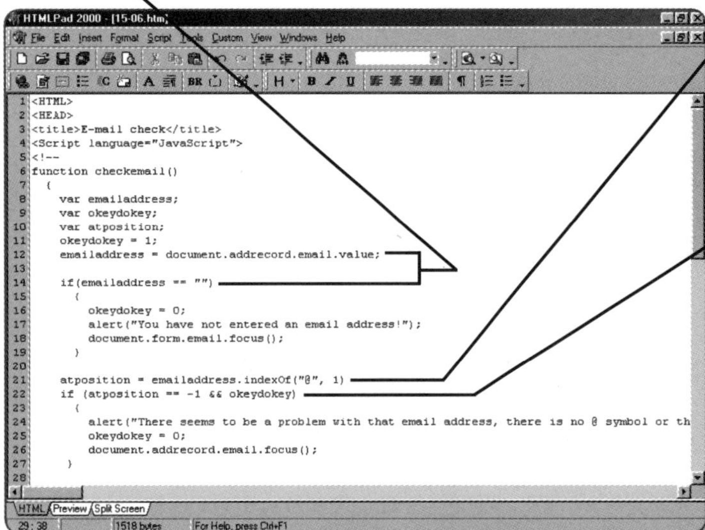

7. Find out where the @ symbol is in the e-mail string.

```
atposition = emailaddress.
   indexOf("@", 1)
```

8. Now do some checks on that position. If the @ symbol is not found from the second character position onwards then this is an error.

```
if (atposition == -1 &&
      okeydokey)
   {
alert("There seems to be a problem with that email address, there is no @
   symbol or there is nothing in front of it");
      okeydokey = 0;
      document.addrecord.email.focus();
   }
```

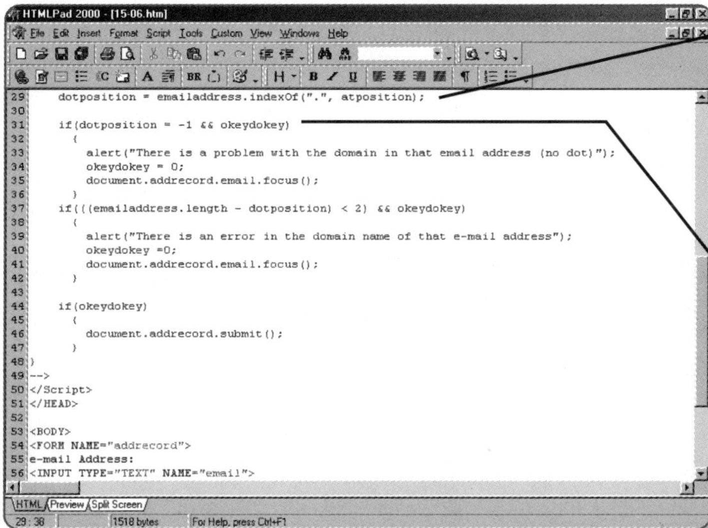

9. Assuming that the last check was okay, now look for the period after the @ symbol.

```
dotposition =
   emailaddress.indexOf(".",
   atposition);
```

This looks for the index position (`indexOf`) of the dot (.) after the position at which the @ symbol is located.

```
if(dotposition == -1 &&
   okeydokey)
   {
      alert("There is a
         problem with the
         domain in that email
         address (no dot)");
      okeydokey = 0;
      document.addrecord.
      email.focus();
   }
```

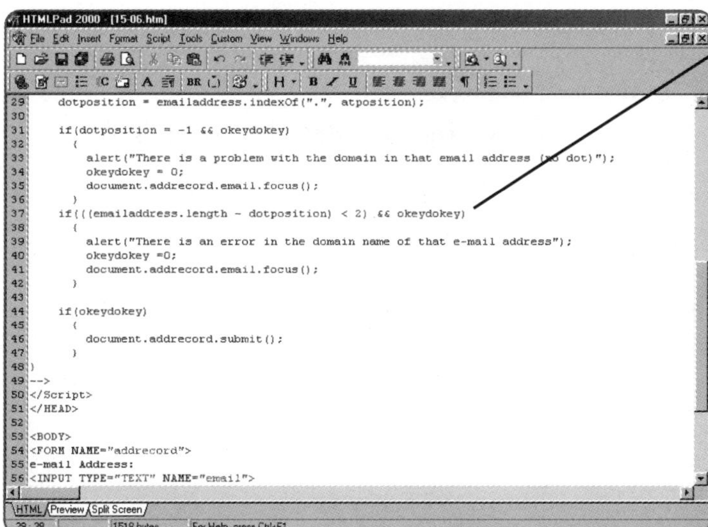

10. The last part of a domain name (after the dot) should be at least two characters long.

```
if(((emailaddress.length -
   dotposition) < 2) &&
   okeydokey)
     {
       alert("There is an
          error in the domain
          name of that e-mail
          address");
       okeydokey =0;
       document.addrecord.
          email.focus();
     }
```

11. If your e-mail address has passed all your tests, you can submit your form.

```
If(okeydokey)
   {
      document.addrecord.submit();
   }
```

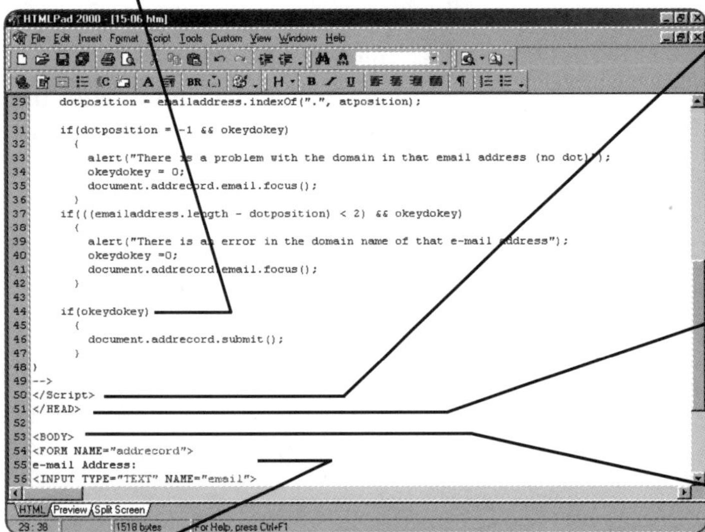

12. That will do for now, so close the function and the script tag.

```
}
- ->
</Script>
```

13. And close the HTML header.

```
</HEAD>
```

14. Now open the HTML body.

```
<BODY>
```

15. Create a form similar to the ones you have been using so far, but this time just having a field for the e-mail address, and giving the e-mail address field the name "e-mail", like this.

```
<FORM NAME="addrecord">
e-mail Address:
<INPUT TYPE="TEXT" NAME="email"><BR>
<INPUT TYPE="BUTTON" NAME="BUTTON" Value="Go!" onClick='checkemail()'>
</FORM>
```

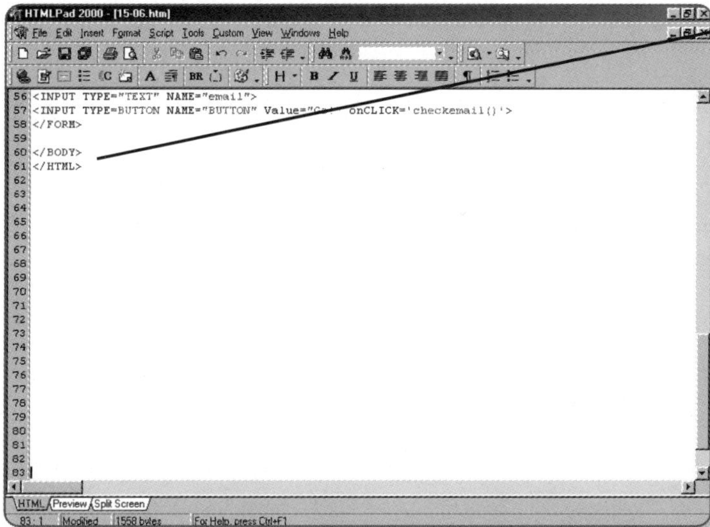

16. Now close the page.

```
</BODY>
</HTML>
```

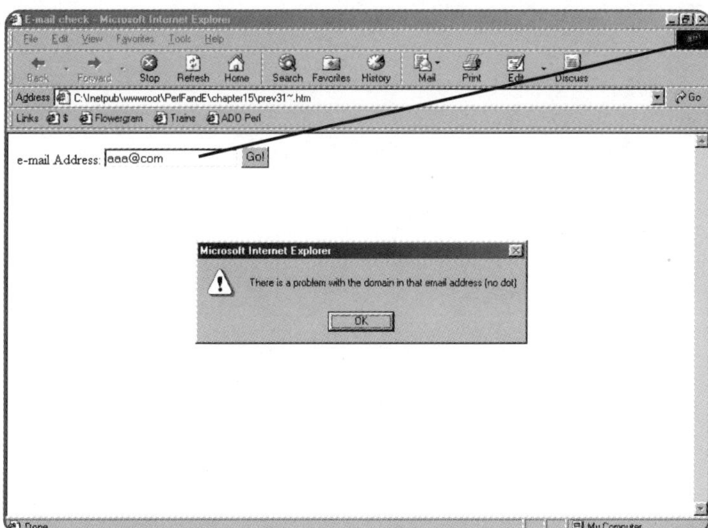

17. Save the file as 15-06.htm and test it out using lots of different e-mail error combinations. Check that the error tests all work and if they don't then check your code and try again.

There are many books, Web sites, and courses set up to teach JavaScript. I urge you to look deeper into JavaScript, as it is a really useful tool that can save you lots of server-side work and time.

16

The CGI.pm Module

In this book, you have so far learned (amongst other things) about Perl, HTML, and how to create HTML from Perl. This has been useful, as learning about how to create HTML on-the-fly from Perl has reinforced the HTML that you have learned. In this chapter you'll learn a little about a module called CGI.pm, which simplifies the creation of HTML from Perl.

Specifically, you'll learn:

- What CGI.pm does
- How to start and end an HTML page with CGI.pm
- How to use forms with CGIpm
- How to use GGI.pm in object-oriented mode

What's the Idea Behind the CGI.pm Module?

The CGI.pm module attempts to simplify and formalize the functions used in CGI applications. Some of the actions that need to be taken in the execution of CGI programs are not intuitive, and the reason for the necessity of some of them is lost in the mists of time—way back in the 1990s!

Perl is a powerful language and yet it still has to perform some pretty obscure gymnastics to do some things that should be fairly easy. The truth is that the existing technologies have moved on and some new technologies have arrived, but in many cases, we still have fairly primitive mechanisms available to us to access these technologies.

You have seen how tedious it is to have to send headers (`print "Content-type: text/html \n\n";`) and how cumbersome it can be to get data back from forms. The CGI.pm module is intended to simplify all of this and provide an interface into the CGI functions and to enable you to create HTML forms and back-end CGI scripts much more quickly and easily. There are many functions available in the CGI.pm module, and in this chapter you are going to learn some of the most commonly used.

To use the CGI.pm functions, you must import the CGI.pm module methods. You do this by using the following statement; this statement makes the functions contained within the CGI.pm module available within your program:

```
use CGI qw(:standard);
```

The `qw` is simply a way of wrapping `:standard` in quotes.

You can also use

```
use CGI ':standard';
```

The `':standard'` refers to the standard set of functions, so that you can use a less long-winded way of referring to functions.

The best way to learn some of theses CGI.pm functions quickly is by example, so let's get right on with it.

Starting and Ending an HTML Page with CGI.pm

Starting and ending a page using conventional HTML is not difficult. You can use the Perl `print` statement to create the HTML line by line (a bit tedious) or you can use the document as described in Appendix A, "More Perl Functions," or as demonstrated in Chapter 17, "Case Study: A Contact Database."

But try this:

1. Open your editor and start a new Perl program.

```
#!c:/perl/bin
```

2. Include the CGI.pm module using the `use` statement.

```
use CGI ':standard'
```

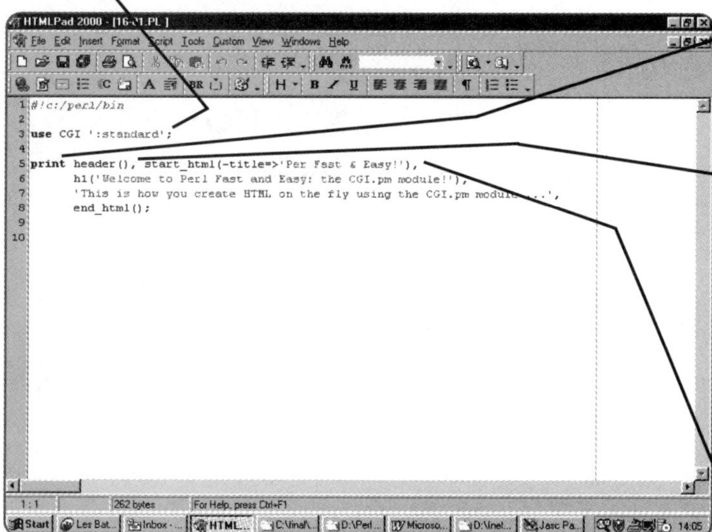

3. Add a `print` statement passing the functions as parameters.

4. First add the `header()` function.

```
print header(),
```

This creates the <HTML><HEAD>. Note the comma—you haven't finished yet.

5. Insert a title into the header. This is the title that appears on the title bar at the top of the browser.

```
start_html(-title=>'Perl Fast & Easy!'),
```

6. Now add a header in the HTML.

```
h1('Welcome to Perl Fast and Easy: the CGI.pm module!'),
```

> **NOTE**
>
> This is the same as using
>
> `<H1>Welcome to Perl Fast and Easy: the CGI.pm module!</H1>`

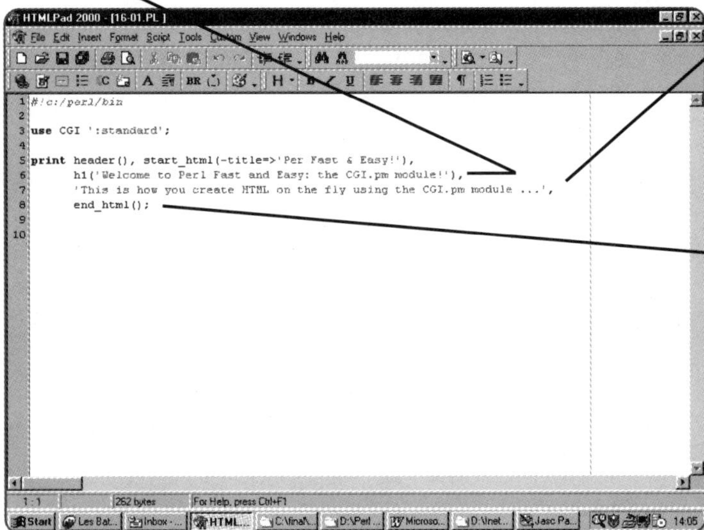

7. Now add some text to the page.

```
'This is how you create HTML
   on the fly using the CGI.pm
   module ...',
```

8. Close off the HTML.

```
end_html();
```

> **NOTE**
>
> This is like using
>
> `</BODY>`
>
> `</HTML>`

9. Save your program as 16-01.pl in your scripts folder.

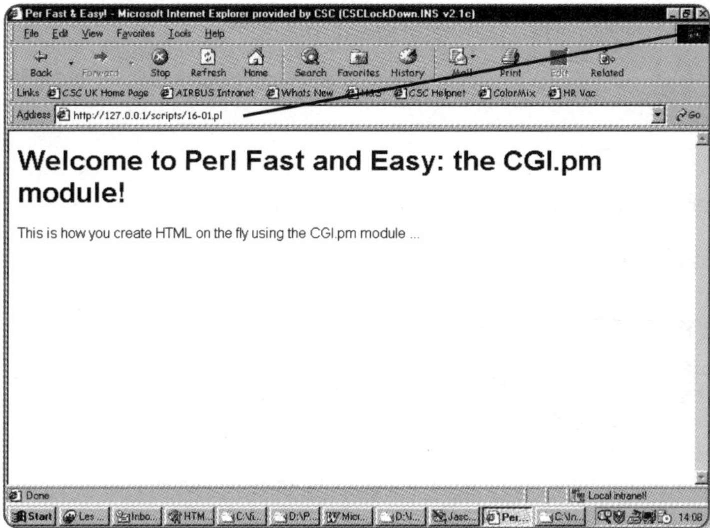

10. Now try out your program in your browser by entering the following URL:

```
http://localhost/scripts/
   16-01.pl
```

That's a bit neater than standard HTML, isn't it?

Some things don't appear to be any easier using the CGI.pm functions than using the `print` function and the usual HTML. Here is an example. To print a horizontal rule using CGI.pm, you would do this:

```
print hr();
```

Not difficult, but not exactly shorter. Of course, in these days of modern programming there is much to be said for consistency, and if you are using the CGI.pm module, perhaps you might want to use it throughout your program to avoid confusing others who come along after you. But to be honest, mixing and matching of standard Perl with CGI.pm stuff allows you to mix useful features of the CGI.pm module with other standard features of Perl that you are already familiar with.

Other similar "unpaired tags" such as the <BR> and the <P> tags are treated in a similar way. Try the short program on the next page to demonstrate the use of some other tags via CGI.pm.

1. Start a new program and bring in the CGI ':standard' module.

```
#!c:/perl/bin
use CGI ':standard';
```

2. Create an HTTP header using the CGI.pm header function.

```
print header();
```

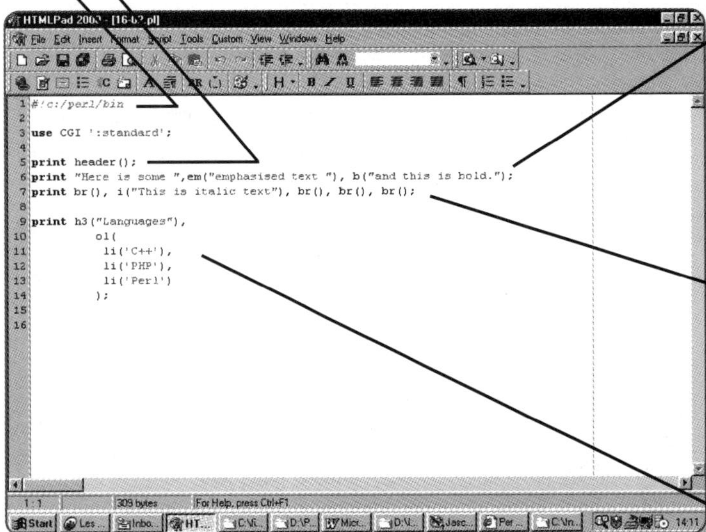

3. Display some emphasized text and some bold text like this:

```
print "Here is some ",
   em("emphasized text "),
   b("and this is bold.");
```

4. Now move onto a new line and display some italic text, followed by a few <br> tags.

```
print br(), i("This is italic
text"), br(), br(), br();
```

5. Add this code to create an ordered list.

```
print h3("Languages"),
         ol(
          li('C++'),
          li('PHP'),
          li('Perl')
         );
```

> **NOTE**
>
> The ordered list is preceded by the CGI.pm equivalent of the `<h3>Languages</h3>` header in HTML.

6. Save this program as 16-02.pl in your script folder.

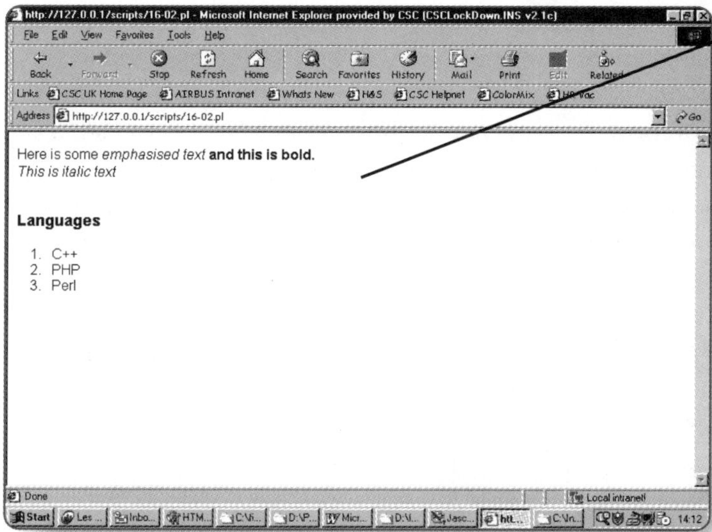

7. Run it in your browser.

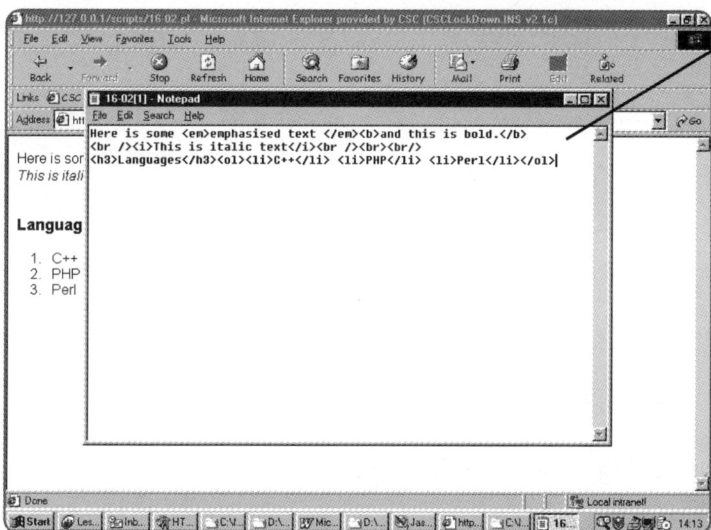

8. Take a look at the source code (choose View, Source) and you will see some pretty conventional (if perhaps a little unformatted) HTML.

Let's take a look at a few more things that CGI.pm can do.

Forms and CGI.pm

CGI.pm can also build forms. You can generate the HTML on-the-fly to create forms, including all the usual elements, such as select boxes, text areas, and a submit button. Try the following program, which has many of the usual elements you might expect to find in a form. I'll leave you to judge how easy it is to use.

The page you are going to create here is going to call itself. This form will also remember the state or values of all the fields on each execution of the form. You will see what I mean in a moment.

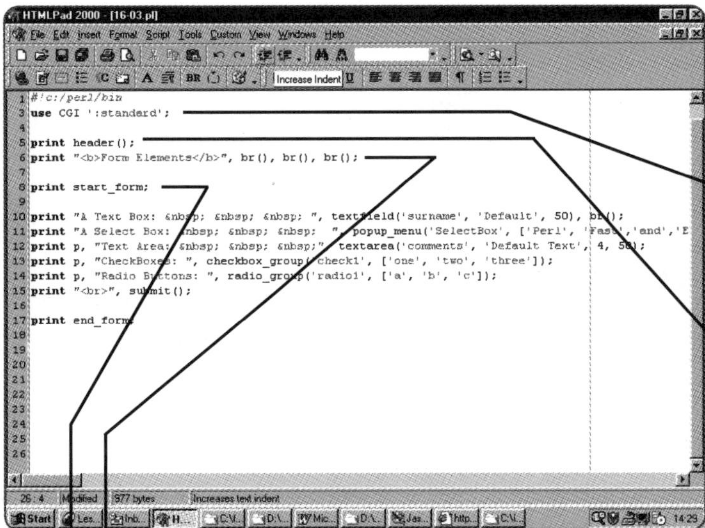

1. Open a new program in your editor.

```
#!c:/perl/bin
```

2. Bring in the CGI.pm module.

```
use CGI ':standard';
```

3. Create an HTTP header using the CGI.pm header function.

```
print header();
```

4. Add a title and a few new lines

```
print p, "<b>Form Elements</b>", br(), br(), br();
```

5. Tell CGI.pm that you are going to start a new form.

```
print start_form;
```

6. Now add a text box.

```
print p, "A Text Box:       ", textfield('surname', 'Default',
   50), br();
```

> **NOTE**
>
> Note the parameters: `Default` is any text you want the field to have when the form is displayed, the 50 is the length of the field.
>
> This is the same as `<INPUT TYPE="TEXT"., NAME="surname" VALUE="Default" SIZE="50">`

7. Add a pop-up box.

```
print p, "A Select Box:        ", popup_menu('SelectBox',
   ['Perl', 'Fast','and','Easy','Web', 'Development'], 'Fast');
```

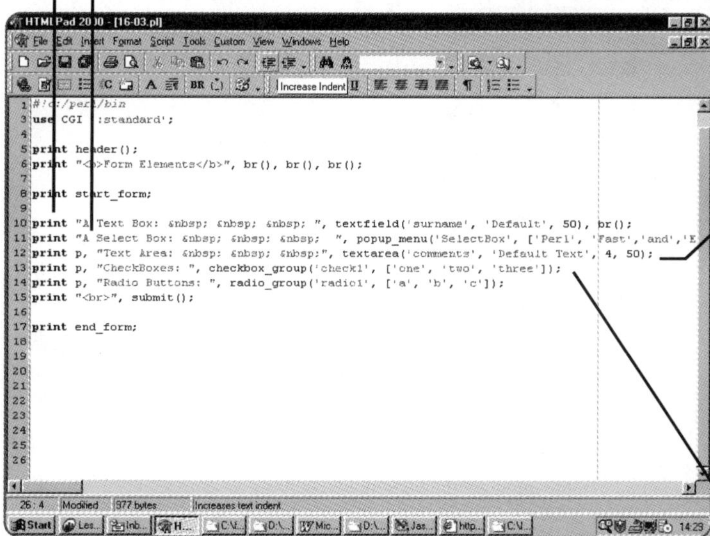

The pop-up box also has parameters. Above, it has name, a list of values, and then a default value if required.

8. Enter this code to create a <TEXTAREA>. Once again there are parameters for default text, row size, and column size.

```
print p, "Text Area:  
      ", textarea
   ('comments', 'Default
   Text', 5, 50);
```

9. Now create a check box.

```
print p, "CheckBoxes: ", checkbox_group('check1', ['one', 'two', 'three']);
```

Note the parameters for the name of the check box group, and the value for each check box.

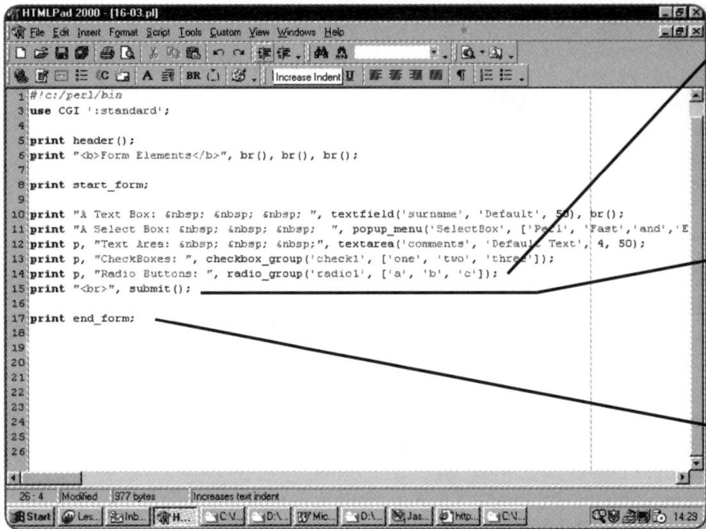

10. Radio buttons are created in a similar way.

```
print p, "Radio Buttons: ",
   radio_group('radio1', ['a',
   'b', 'c']);
```

11. Add the submit button.

```
print p"", submit();
```

12. Now close the form.

```
print end_form;
```

13. Save the script as 16-03.pl.

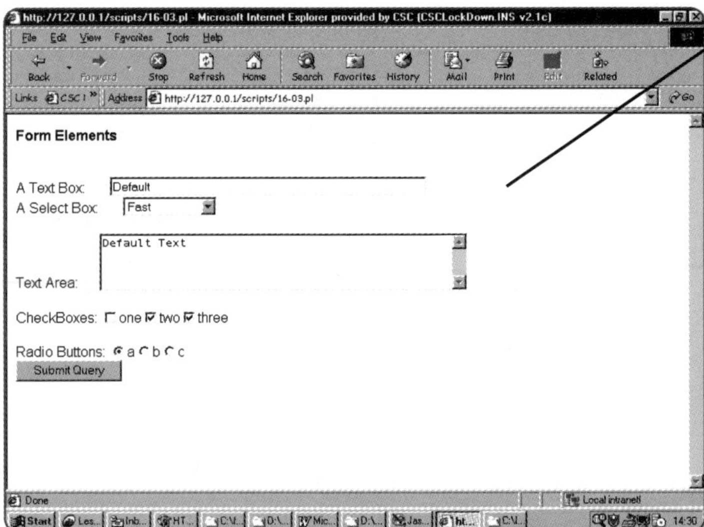

14. Run it in your browser. You should see a pretty conventional (if a little untidy) form.

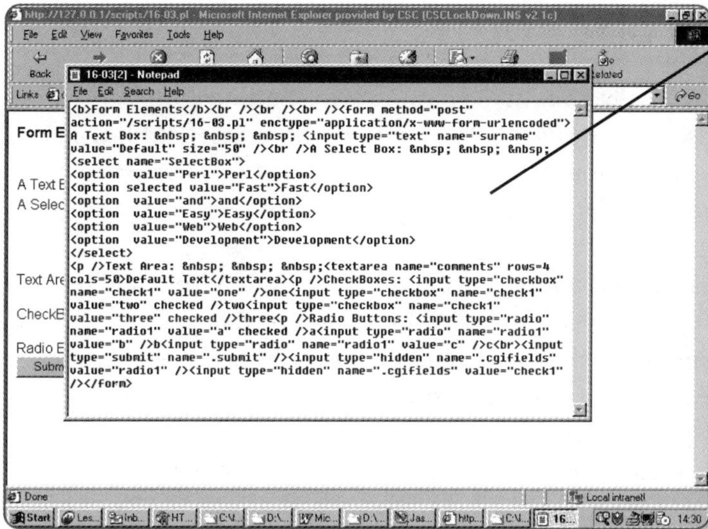

15. Once again, view the source code to see the HTML that has been created.

Before you go any further, a word of warning: There are a few cases that may cause confusion, the most common being that if you use the `tr()` function to try to create a table row (yes CGI.pm handles tables, too) you will end up invoking the Perl `translate` function. A similar conflict occurs with `select` (as in select lists). To be honest, you are better off creating tables using the conventional HTML; then you won't encounter the conflicts.

Incidentally, if I've left you wondering, you can generate a table like this:

```
print table(Tr( td('Some Data'), td('Some More Data'), td('Even More Data')));
```

which will generate the normal HTML, like this:

```
<table><tr><td>Some Data</td> <td>Some More Data</td> <td>Even More
   Data</td></tr></table>
```

Next you'll learn something really useful, something that the CGI.pm does that really takes the hard work out of grabbing data from HTML forms.

Getting Data from Forms

Here is an area where CGI.pm really does come into its own. Getting data from forms using CGI.pm is so much easier and more intuitive for the programmer. With CGI.pm, you don't have to think about how you're going to separate the key value pairs, or how you are going to separate the form field name from its accompanying value.

Remember all that stuff you learned about getting the data from a form and having to convert characters, splitting on = and so on? Well, thanks to CGI.pm you can now dodge all that. If you are using the POST method, you can simply get at form data by using CGI.pm's `param('fieldname')` function.

The `param()` function simply returns the value of the field named in the `param()` function parentheses. So

```
myfield = param('surname');
```

returns the value that had been typed into a field called Surname on the sending form. Now that's useful!

Try this:

1. Re-open your last program in your editor.

2. Add the following `if` statement (the p's are simple paragraph tags):

```
if (param())
  {
    print "The surname you entered was: ",em(param('surname')),
       p, "The Selections are: ",em(join(", ",param('SelectBox'))),
       p, "The comments box contains: ",em(param('comments')),
       p, "you selected checkbox: ",em(param('check1')),
       p, "you selected radio: ",em(param('radio1'));
}
```

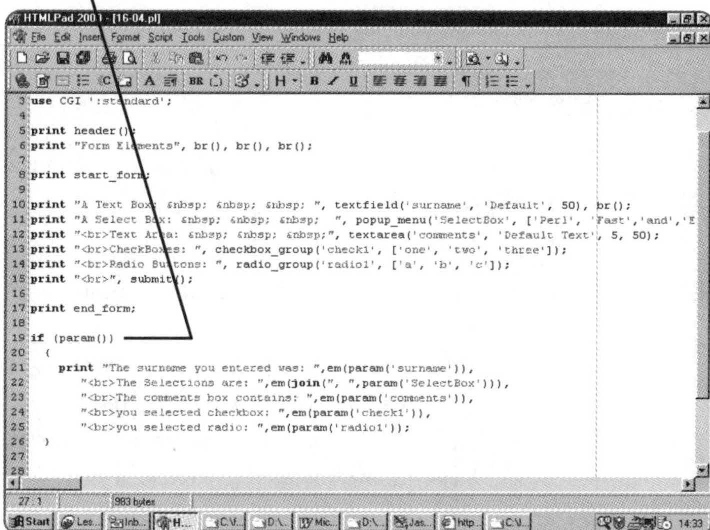

3. The `if` statement checks to see if there are any values in the fields and displays them if there are. Which is what I mean by saying the page *calls itself* and remembers its state between executions.

4. Save the program as 16-04.pl.

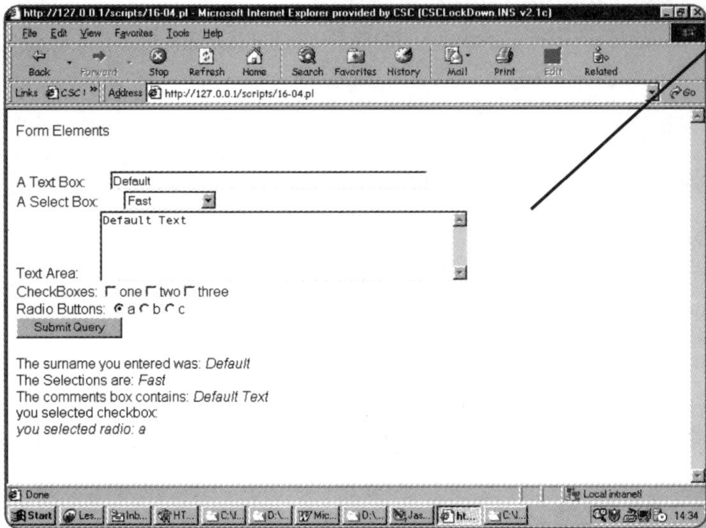

5. Now run your program, enter some data, and observe the result.

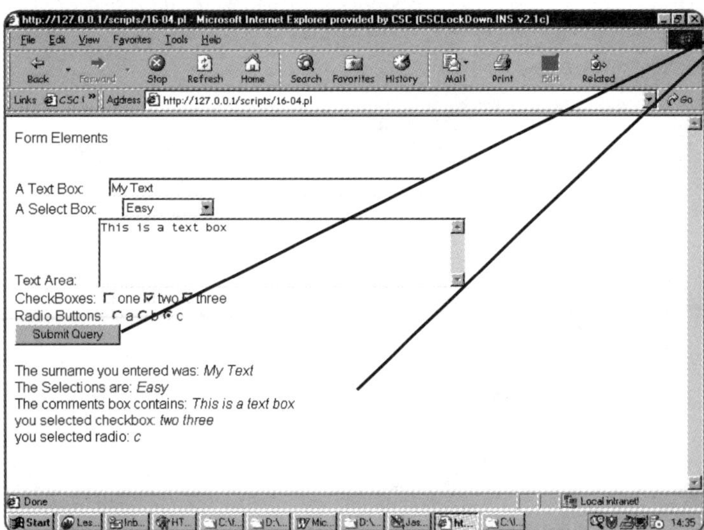

6. Try changing the values in the fields and clicking the Submit Query button again.

Form manipulation is a very useful area in which to use CGI.pm. In my opinion, the most useful of all! However, there is one other aspect that will interest you—the object-oriented mode of CGI.pm.

CGI.pm in Object-Oriented Mode

Before we leave the subject of CGI.pm, there is a little more you should know about it. You have so far used CGI.pm in what is known as *function-oriented* mode. CGI.pm can also be used in an *object-oriented* way.

This has a few advantages:

- If you treat CGI as a class, you can have more than one CGI object.
- You can inherit from a CGI class and modify the resulting object's behavior to suit your requirements.
- Using CGI.pm in object-oriented mode uses less memory.
- You can use parameters of tags generated by name, so you don't have to learn the positional location of a parameter; you just name it and assign a value in any order you like.
- You can save a CGI object to disk and reload it.

However, the object-oriented mode is also more verbose, so it means more typing.

Just for fun, let's do a program similar to the last program (16-04.pl) in object-oriented mode and you'll see what I mean.

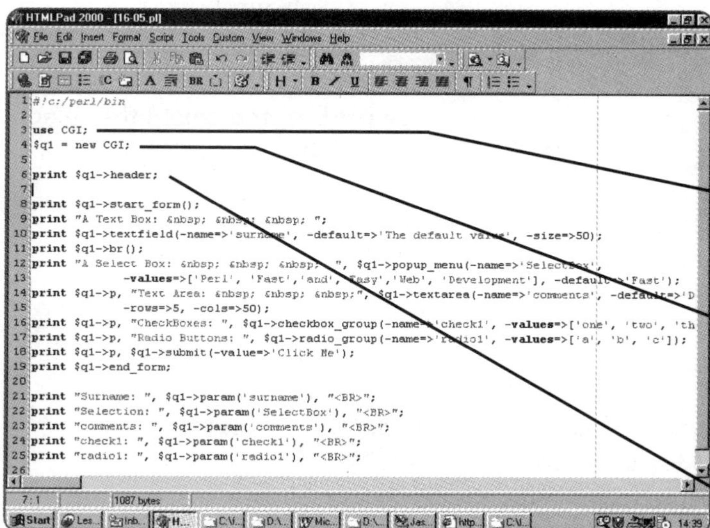

1. Start a new program in your editor.

```
#!c:/perl/bin
```

2. Import the CGI module.

```
use CGI;
```

3. This time, create a new CGI object; call the object q1.

```
$q1 = new CGI;
```

4. Call the header method of your new CGI object, q1.

```
print $q1->header;
```

5. Start an HTML form.

```
print $q1->start_form();
```

6. Print some text for a text box label.

```
print "A Text Box:       ";
```

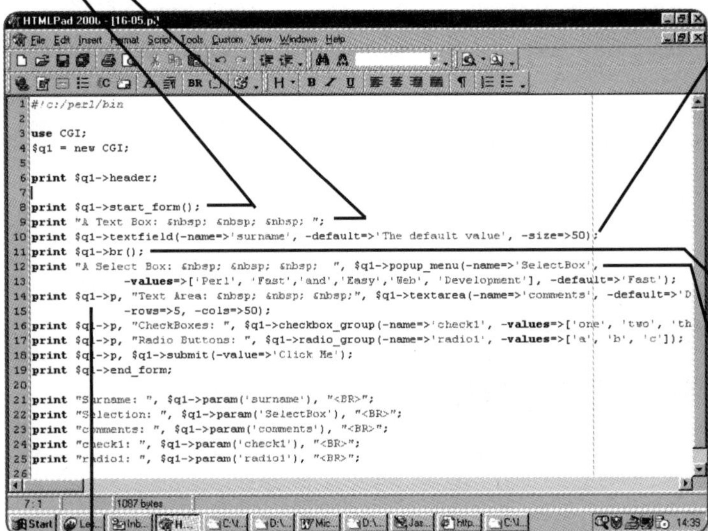

7. Now create a text box in the form of your q1 object.

```
print $q1->textfield(-
name=>'surname', -
default=>'The default value',
-
   size=>50);
```

8. Add a <BR> tag.

```
print $q1->br();
```

9. Add some text for your select box and create the select box itself.

```
print "A Select Box:        ", $q1->popup_menu(
     -name=>'SelectBox',  -values=>['Perl', 'Fast','and','Easy','Web',
     'Development'], -default=>'Fast');
```

10. Now add a text area.

```
print $q1->p, "Text Area:      ", $q1->textarea(
      -name=>'comments', -default=>'Default Text',
      -rows=>10, -cols=>50);
```

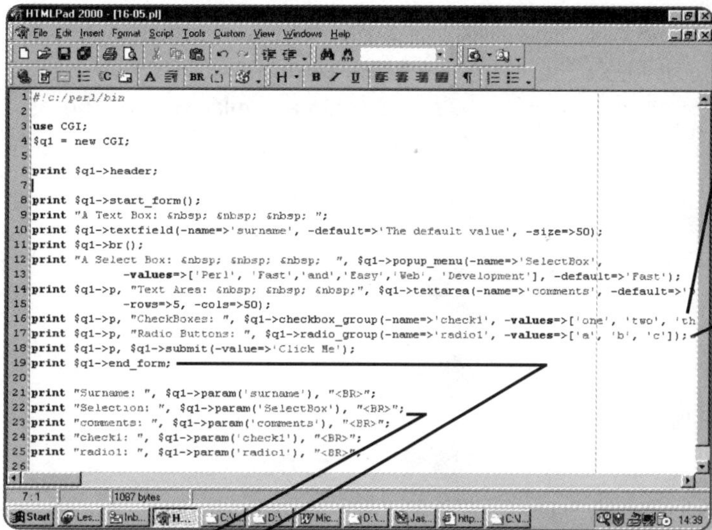

11. Add a group of check boxes.

```
print $q1->p, "CheckBoxes: ",
   $q1->checkbox_group(-
   name=>'check1',
      -values=>['one', 'two',
          'three']);
```

12. Add a group of radio buttons.

```
print $q1->p, "Radio Buttons:
   ", $q1->radio_group(-
   name=>'radio1',
        -values=>['a', 'b',
            'c']);
```

13. And of course, you'll need a submit button.

```
print $q1->p, $q1->submit(-value=>'Click Me');
```

14. Now close your form.

```
print $q1->end_form;
```

15. Now you can display the values of the fields in your form using these lines of code:

```
print "Surname: ", $q1->param('surname'), "<BR>";
print "Selection: ", $q1->param('SelectBox'), "<BR>";
print "comments: ", $q1->param('comments'), "<BR>";
print "check1: ", $q1->param('check1'), "<BR>";
print "radio1: ", $q1->param('radio1'), "<BR>";
```

16. Save your program as 16-05.pl.

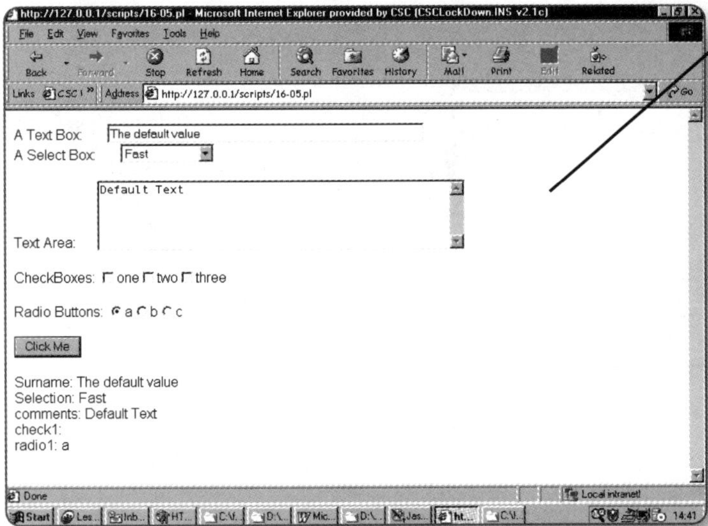

17. Run your program in your browser and confirm that it works in a similar way to the previous program (16-04.pl).

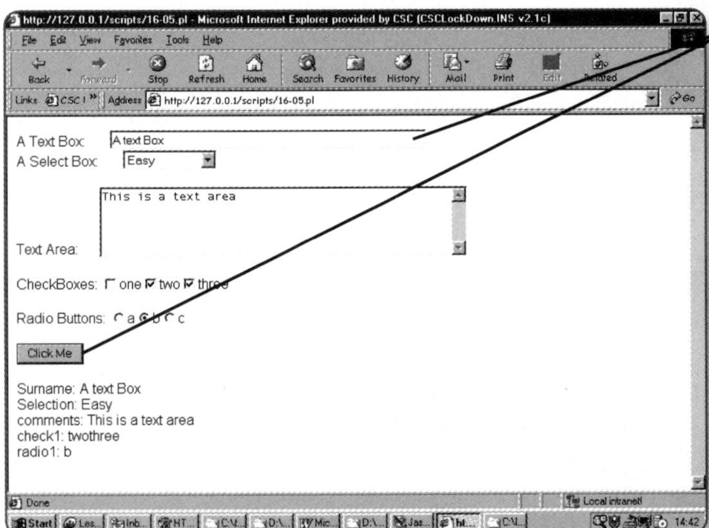

18. Confirm that your program works by changing the data in the fields and pressing the Click Me button.

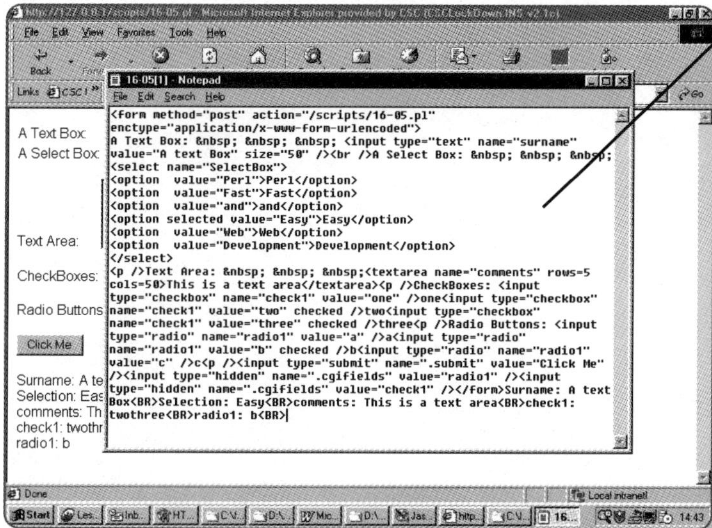

19. View the source code of the generated page to see what has been generated.

The significant thing about the object-oriented way of using CGI.pm is that you can have lots of independent CGI objects and handle them all separately (`q2`, `q3`, and so on). In fact, Perl itself now has an object-oriented mode, which is unfortunately beyond the scope of this book. But should you wish to learn more about it, there is lots of information at the Web sites listed in Appendix B in the back of this book.

17

Case Study: A Contact Database

In this chapter you are going to see how all of the things you have learned so far can be brought together to demonstrate a complete Perl database-driven application. This application is a simple contacts database. You can, of course, modify it to do any number of different jobs including the ubiquitous Guest book. I think you will find many useful things to do with the techniques used in this application.

In this chapter you will:

- Create a home page
- Use the listcontacts.pl program to read and list the contents of a database table
- Use the editcontact.pl program to insert data in the database
- Use the editcontact.pl program to load data into fields

The Requirements

What are the requirements for a contacts database application?

Very simply, you need to be able to:

- Add a new contact
- Update an existing contact
- Delete a contact
- List contacts

Yes, there are variations and refinements that can be applied, but basically this is the core requirement of any database application. Everything else is a tweak (although some of the tweaks are very useful). I will mention some tweaks that you might like to try at the end of this chapter.

You know what you want to do with the database, so what data items might you be interested in? Here is a set to begin with.

- First name
- Middle initial
- Last name
- Address (number, street, and so on)
- Town/City
- Post code/ZIP code
- Telephone number
- E-mail address

This forms the basis of a useful set of information. There are other bits of information you might want to store, and you can go back and add any extra bits you would like. Or, of course, you can change all the data and use the application for something else entirely.

Now you know what we are going to do and what we are going to do it with. It's time to visualize what the application should look like, and how it should behave. When I say "look like," I don't mean aesthetically—that isn't important, and it is something you can tinker with when you're happy with your application. What I mean is how it is going to work.

A good place to start is to imagine you are the user of the new application. What would you expect to see when the application started? How do you see new records being added and how should this work? How would you navigate around the system? In short, how can you best make your application friendlier and less cumbersome?

A good starting point is draw out your ideas on paper and plan out what your application is to consist of and how it should hang together, paying attention to navigation and to a logical sequence of events.

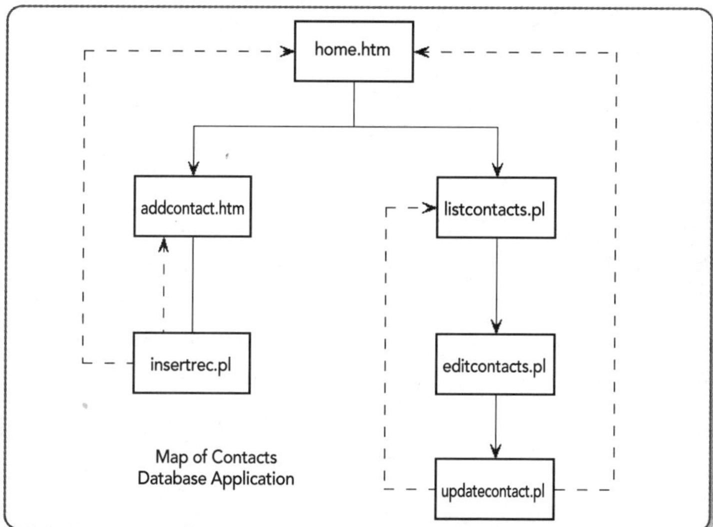

Here is the approach I took for this simple application. I think this simple design is fairly self-explanatory. I have named the files to give you an idea of what they should be doing. The solid lines are links to the different parts of the application. The dotted lines are possible links that you might want to have to ease navigation.

Now you can start putting together your application.

The Home Page

A good place to start is with the home.htm page, which is a simple HTML page to act as the home page and the menu for your application.

The top-level page (home.htm) is nothing exciting. It is as simple an HTML page as you can get with a couple of links to the List Contacts program and the Add a New Contact Page.

1. Open your editor and start a new HTML page.

```
<html>
<head>
```

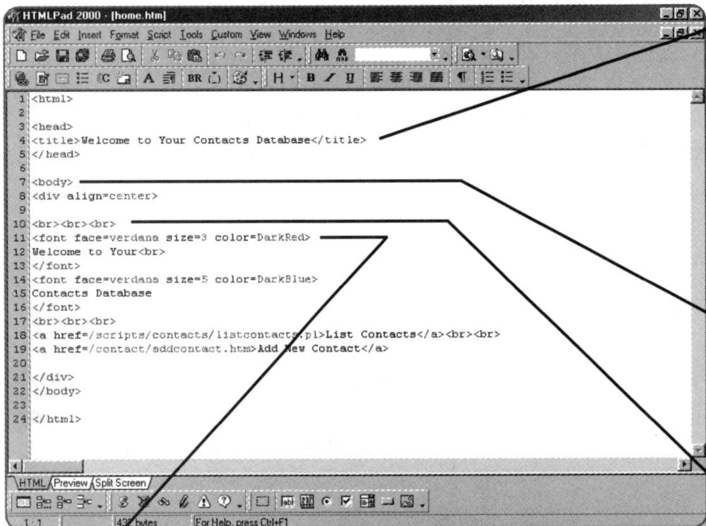

2. Give your page a title to appear on the title bar of your browser and close the HTML header.

```
<title>Welcome to Your
   Contacts Database</title>
</head>
```

3. Open the <BODY> of your page

```
<body>
```

4. For the purposes of this menu type page, center the contents of the page using the <DIV> tag, and insert a few line break <BR> tags so that the main content of the page is well below the top of the page.

```
<div align=center>
<br><br><br>
```

5. Set a suitable font and create a simple title for your page so that your users know what it is about.

```
<font face=verdana size=3 color=DarkRed>
Welcome to Your<br>
</font>
<font face=verdana size=5 color=DarkBlue>
Contacts Database
</font>
```

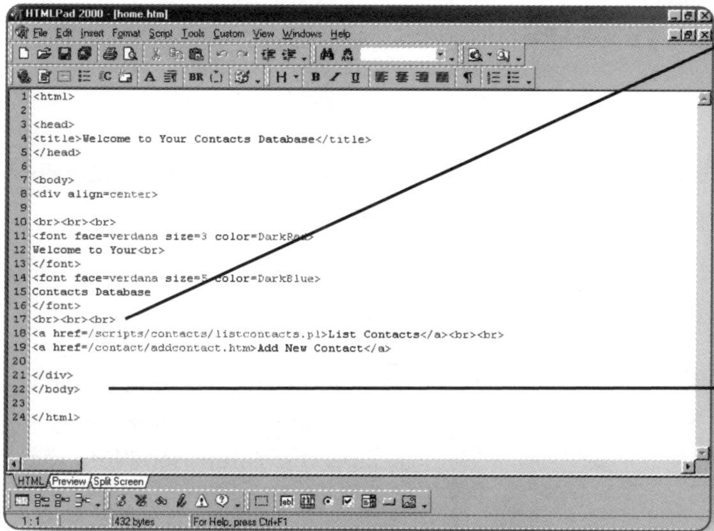

6. Now after a few more line breaks, add your menu links.

```
<br><br><br>
```

```
<a href=/scripts/contacts/
   listcontacts.pl>List
   Contacts</a><br><br>
<a href=/contact/addcontact.
   htm>Add New Contact</a>
```

7. Finally, close the <DIV>, <BODY>, and <HTML> tags.

```
</div>
</body>
</html>
```

8. Save your page as home.htm in a suitable folder called, say, Contacts.

9. If you wish, open your browser and view your home.htm page.

Okay, so you have made a start on your contacts database application. You will also want a Perl script to display the contacts from your database as a list. Let's do that next.

The listcontacts.pl Program

The listcontacts.pl program simply reads the contents of the database table and lists the first name, last name, and town fields for each record. (A view of the database design is at the end of this chapter). In this program, ADO is being used to connect with the Access database. There should be no surprises here, but if something doesn't make sense to you, refer to Chapter 14, "Databases."

1. Open your editor and start a new Perl program.

```
#!c:/perl/bin
```

2. You are going to be using ADO to access the database, so you'll need to bring into your program the appropriate Perl modules, like this:

```
use Win32::OLE;
use Win32::OLE::Const 'Microsoft ActiveX Data Objects';
```

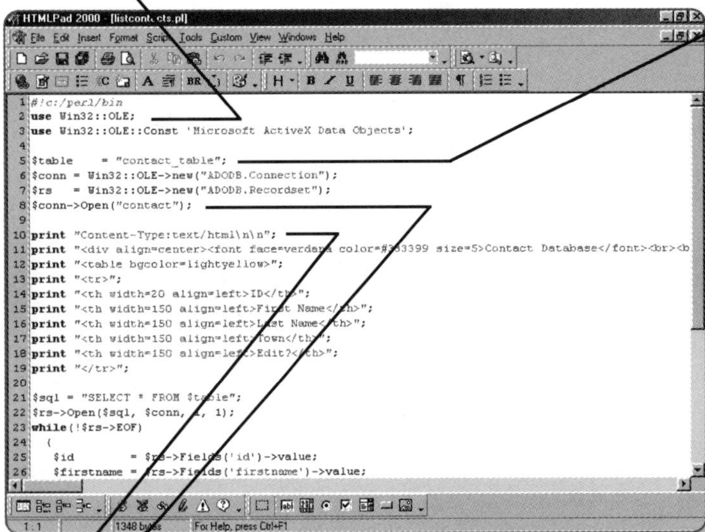

3. Now create some variables to enable your program to access the database. Note that the table has been named `"contact_table"`. When you come to create your table in Microsoft Access, you will need to call it by this name so that you can reference it in your database.

```
$table    = "contact_table";
$conn = Win32::OLE-
   >new("ADODB.Connection");
$rs   = Win32::OLE-
   >new("ADODB.Recordset");
```

4. You will also need a connection to the database. Do you remember ODBC? Your database will be recognized by the name that you give it in ODBC. The following command allows you to establish a connection with the database.

```
$conn->Open("contact");
```

5. Create a table to contain a neat list of the results that you receive from the database. Use a Table Header row to set the width of the table columns and to supply headings for each column.

```
print "Content-Type:text/html\n\n";
print "<div align=center><font face=verdana color=#333399 size=5>Contact
   Database</font><br><br>";
```

```
print "<table bgcolor=lightyellow>";
print "<tr>";
print "<th width=20 align=left>ID</th>";
print "<th width=150 align=left>First Name</th>";
print "<th width=150 align=left>Last Name</th>";
print "<th width=150 align=left>Town</th>";
print "<th width=150 align=left>Edit?</th>";
print "</tr>";
```

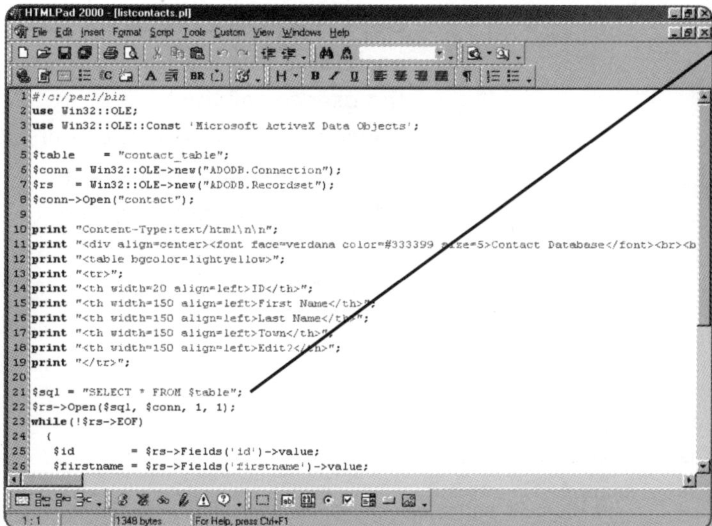

6. Now create a variable to contain your SQL statement for requesting the records from your contacts database, and then open a recordset containing the results of your SQL statement.

```
$sql = "SELECT * FROM $table";
$rs->Open($sql, $conn, 1, 1);
```

NOTE

Note that you are using the `SELECT * FROM $table` type of SQL statement, meaning get all of the columns. This is fine for a small program like this, but you are actually bringing back columns that you do not need and therefore the database and the network are doing unnecessary work. It keeps things simple for this example, but a better SQL statement would be:

```
$sql = "SELECT id, firstname, lastname, town  FROM $table";
```

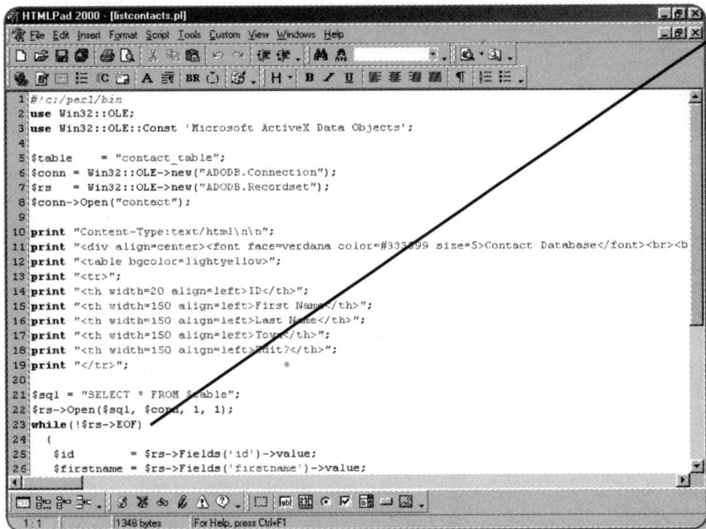

7. Now you can extract all of the field values from the table for every record that exists on the database table. Here you are using a `while` loop to process each record in the recordset. For each record, you are writing a table row to the page. Note that at the end of each table row is a form to allow the user to call the editcontact.pl program, sending the record `id` as a key so that editcontact.pl can call up the required details from the database.

```
while(!$rs->EOF)
  {
   $id        = $rs->Fields('id')->value;
   $firstname = $rs->Fields('firstname')->value;
   $lastname  = $rs->Fields('lastname')->value;
   $town      = $rs->Fields('town')->value;
   print
"<tr><td>$id</td><td>$firstname</td><td>$lastname</td><td>$town</td>";
   print "<form name=editrec" . $id . " method=post action=editcontact.pl>";
   print "<input type=hidden name=id value=$id>";
   print "<td><input type=Submit name=submit value=Edit></td>";
   print "</form>";
   print "</tr>";
   $rs->MoveNext;
  }
```

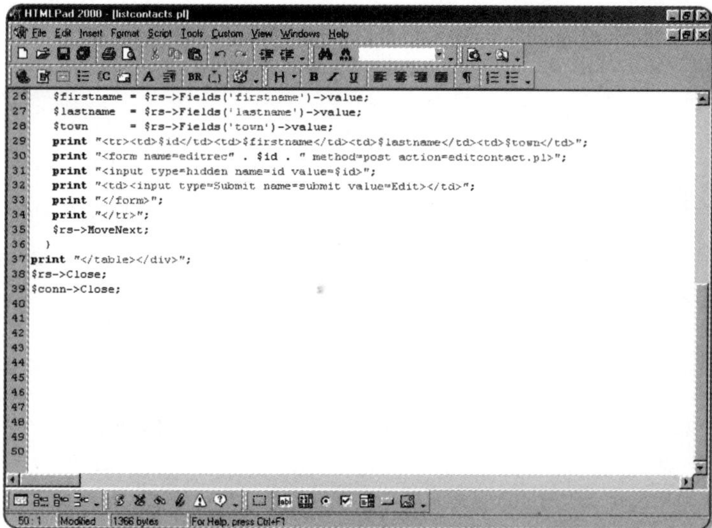

8. Just to tidy things up, close the <body> and <html> tags.

```
</body>
</html>
```

9. Save your program as listcontacts.pl in your scripts folder.

That completes the listcontacts.pl program. Of course, you cannot run it yet, as you do not have a database to run it against! Next you are going to create the HTML form to add data to your database and a Perl script to actually insert the data into the database table.

addcontact.htm

This is a simple HTML form that sends data to the insertrec.pl program. You are also going to check, using JavaScript, if the user has entered the data he or she should have and then give them an appropriate message if they did not.

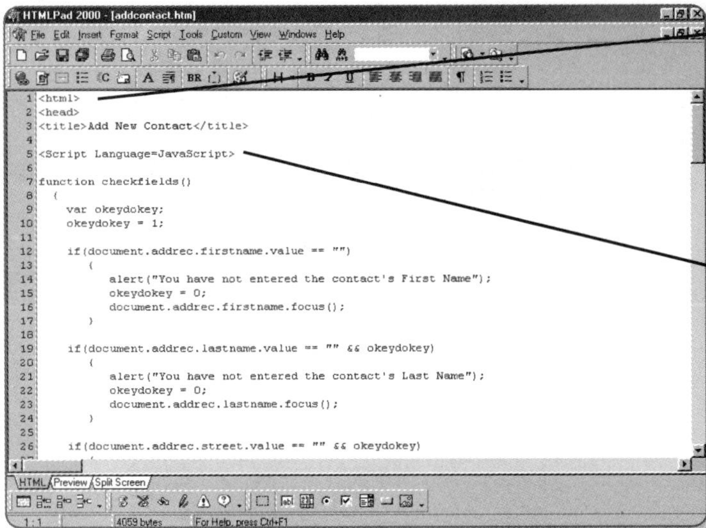

1. Start a new HTML page in your editor.

```
<html>
<head>
<title>Add New Contact</title>
```

2. In the <HEAD> of the page, create a JavaScript function in which you are going to check that a value has been entered into all the fields of your form.

```
<Script Language=JavaScript>

function checkfields()
  {
    var okeydokey;
    okeydokey = 1;

    if(document.addrec.firstname.value == "")
       {
          alert("You have not entered the contact's First Name");
          okeydokey = 0;
          document.addrec.firstname.focus();
       }

    if(document.addrec.lastname.value == "" && okeydokey)
       {
          alert("You have not entered the contact's Last Name");
          okeydokey = 0;
          document.addrec.lastname.focus();
       }

    if(document.addrec.street.value == "" && okeydokey)
       {
          alert("You have not entered the contact's Street Address");
```

```
            okeydokey = 0;
            document.addrec.street.focus();
         }

      if(document.addrec.town.value == "" && okeydokey)
         {
            alert("You have not entered the contact's Town");
            okeydokey = 0;
            document.addrec.town.focus();
         }

      if(document.addrec.postcode.value == "" && okeydokey)
         {
            alert("You have not entered the contact's Zip / Post Code");
            okeydokey = 0;
            document.addrec.postcode.focus();
         }

      if(document.addrec.phone.value == "" && okeydokey)
         {
            alert("You have not entered the contact's Phone No.");
            okeydokey = 0;
            document.addrec.phone.focus();
         }

      if(document.addrec.email.value == "" && okeydokey)
         {
            alert("You have not entered the contact's e-mail address");
            okeydokey = 0;
            document.addrec.email.focus();
         }

      if(okeydokey)
         {
           document.addrec.submit();
         }

   }
</script>
```

> **NOTE**
>
> Note the last part of the function. It uses the `if(true)` check on the `okeydokey` variable to decide whether or not to submit the form. If there are errors and `okeydokey` is False, the `submit` method will not be executed and the form will sit there waiting for the user to correct the errors. Each time the errors are corrected, the `checkfields()` function will be executed again. If all is well, the form will be submitted and your data will be sent to the Perl program that will insert the data into the database table.

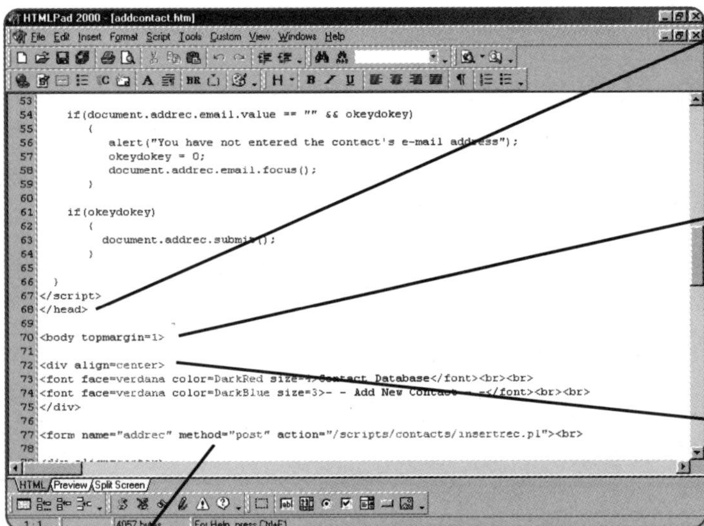

3. Now you can close the HTML <HEAD> tag.

```
</head>
```

4. As with all HTML pages, the next step is to open the <BODY> part of the page.

```
<body topmargin=1>
```

5. Add a header to your HTML page, explaining what you are about to do on this page.

```
<div align=center>
<font face=verdana color=DarkRed size=4>Contact Database</font><br><br>
<font face=verdana color=DarkBlue size=3>- - Add New Contact - -
</font><br><br>
</div>
```

6. Now create the form tag to call your insertrec.pl Perl program (which you will create shortly).

```
<form name="addrec" method="post" action="/scripts/contacts/insertrec.pl"><br>
```

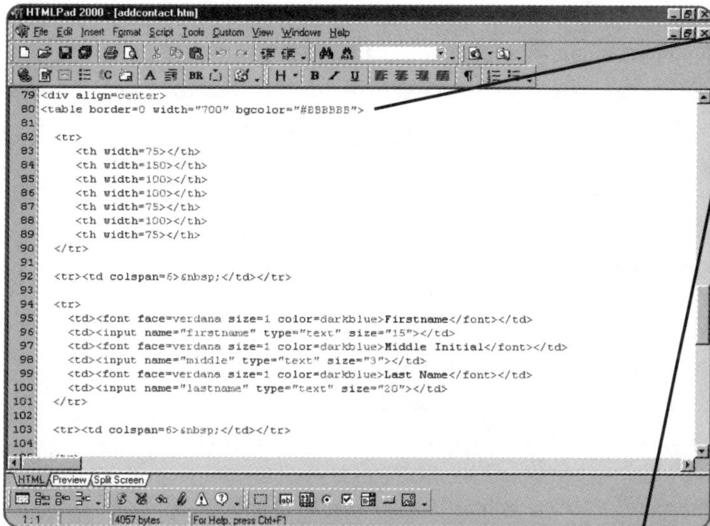

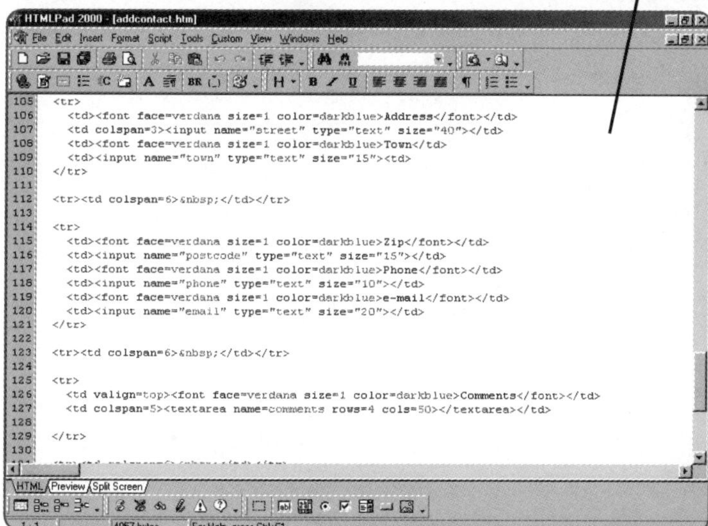

7. Using a table to keep things neat, create all the form field tags for each field that you need in order to pass data to the database:

```
<div align=center>
<table border=0 width="700"
bgcolor="#BBBBBB">


  <tr>
     <th width=75></th>
     <th width=150></th>
     <th width=100></th>
     <th width=100></th>
     <th width=75></th>
     <th width=100></th>
     <th width=75></th>
  </tr>


  <tr><td
    colspan=6> </td></tr>


  <tr>
    <td><font face=verdana
      size=1
color=darkblue>Firstname
   </font></td>
      <td><input
name="firstname" type="text"
size="15"></td>
    <td><font face=verdana
       size=1 color=darkblue>
       Middle Initial</font>
       </td>
    <td><input name="middle" type="text" size="3"></td>
    <td><font face=verdana size=1 color=darkblue>Last Name</font></td>
    <td><input name="lastname" type="text" size="20"></td>
  </tr>



  <tr><td colspan=6> </td></tr>
```

```
<tr>
  <td><font face=verdana size=1 color=darkblue>Address</font></td>
  <td colspan=3><input name="street" type="text" size="40"></td>
  <td><font face=verdana size=1 color=darkblue>Town</td>
  <td><input name="town" type="text" size="15"><td>
</tr>

<tr><td colspan=6> </td></tr>

<tr>
  <td><font face=verdana size=1 color=darkblue>Zip</font></td>
  <td><input name="postcode" type="text" size="15"></td>
  <td><font face=verdana size=1 color=darkblue>Phone</font></td>
  <td><input name="phone" type="text" size="10"></td>
  <td><font face=verdana size=1 color=darkblue>e-mail</font></td>
  <td><input name="email" type="text" size="20"></td>
</tr>

<tr><td colspan=6> </td></tr>

<tr>
  <td valign=top><font face=verdana size=1
color=darkblue>Comments</font></td>
  <td colspan=5><textarea name=comments rows=4 cols=50></textarea></td>

</tr>

<tr><td colspan=6> </td></tr>
```

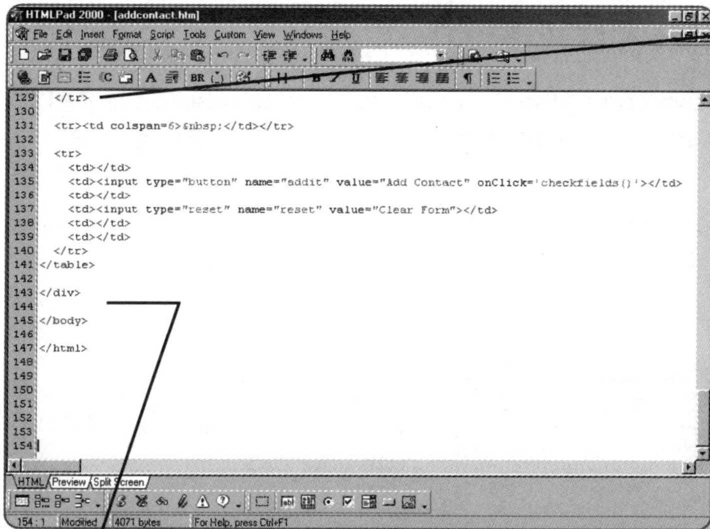

8. Supply a submit and a reset button to enable the user to submit the form or clear it and start again.

```
  <tr>
    <td></td>
    <td><input type="button"
        name="addit" value="Add
        Contact"
onClick='checkfields()'></td>
    <td></td>
    <td><input type="reset"
name="reset" value="Clear
   Form"></td>
     <td></td>
     <td></td>
   </tr>
</table>
```

Note in this case that your submit button is a `"button"` tag. Also note that there is an `onClick` function attached to it. This means that your button will not directly submit your form; instead, it will call your `checkfields()` function you created at the top of the page, which, as I explained, will decide whether or not your form should actually be submitted!

9. Now, as usual, close your HTML <BODY> and <HTML> tags, not forgetting to first close the <DIV ALIGN=CENTER> tag that you used at the beginning to center everything on the page.

```
</div>
</body>
</html>
```

10. Save your HTML page as addcontact.htm in, say, a Contacts folder beneath wwwroot.

The insertrec.pl Program

You now have your HTML form and all the data that you need to pass to the Perl program that's going to insert the data into the database; here it is going to be called insertrec.pl.

1. Open a new Perl program in your editor:

```
#!c:/perl/bin
```

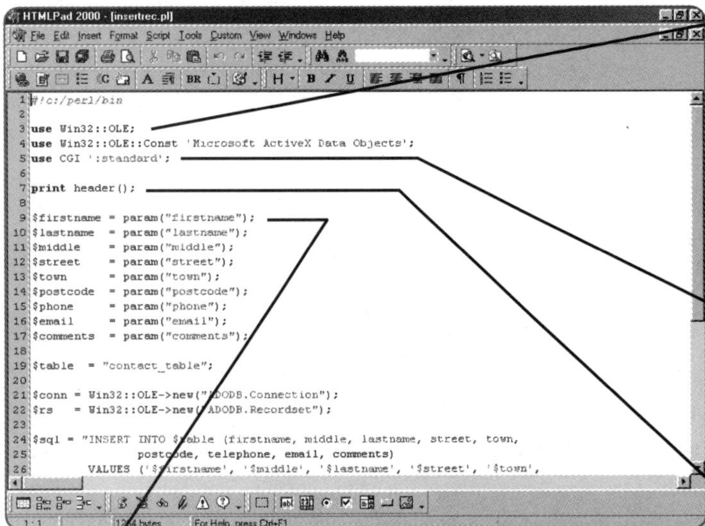

2. Bring the Perl modules that you need in order to use ADO into your program.

```
use Win32::OLE;
use Win32::OLE::Const
   'Microsoft ActiveX Data
   Objects';
```

3. Next, import the CGI.pm module.

```
use CGI ':standard';
```

4. Now send the HTTP header.

```
print header();
```

Remember? This is the equivalent of:

```
print "Content-type: text/html
   \n\n";
```

5. Get all of the values from the fields in your form and store them into appropriately named variables.

```
$firstname = param("firstname");
$lastname  = param("lastname");
$middle    = param("middle");
```

```
$street    = param("street");
$town      = param("town");
$postcode  = param("postcode");
$phone     = param("phone");
$email     = param("email");
$comments  = param("comments");
```

6. Add the following variable to store the name of the table:

```
$table  = "contact_table";
```

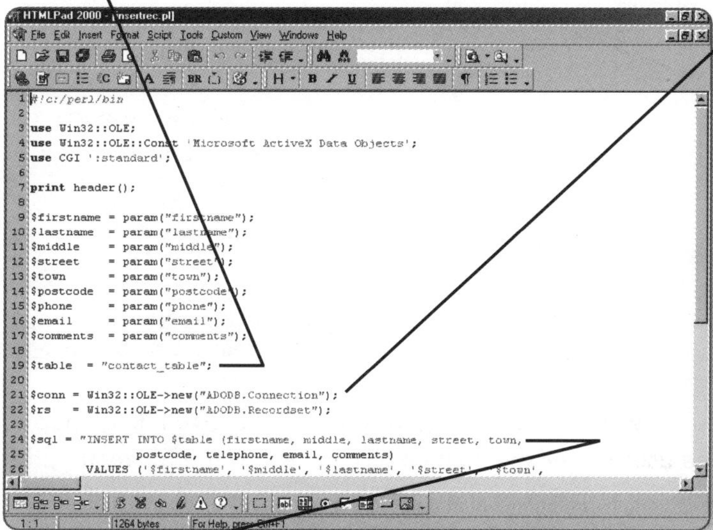

7. Now create two new objects, one for the connection and one for the recordset that is going to hold the new record details for insertion into the database.

```
$conn = Win32::OLE-
   >new("ADODB.Connection");
$rs   = Win32::OLE-
   >new("ADODB.Recordset");
```

8. Create a variable to hold the SQL statement that you need in order to add the values you just got from the form, and add the values to the appropriate column of the recordset.

```
$sql = "INSERT INTO $table (firstname, middle, lastname, street, town,
               postcode, telephone, email, comments)
        VALUES ('$firstname', '$middle', '$lastname', '$street', '$town',
              '$postcode', '$phone', '$email', '$comments')";
```

9. Open the connection object.

```
$conn->Open("contact");
```

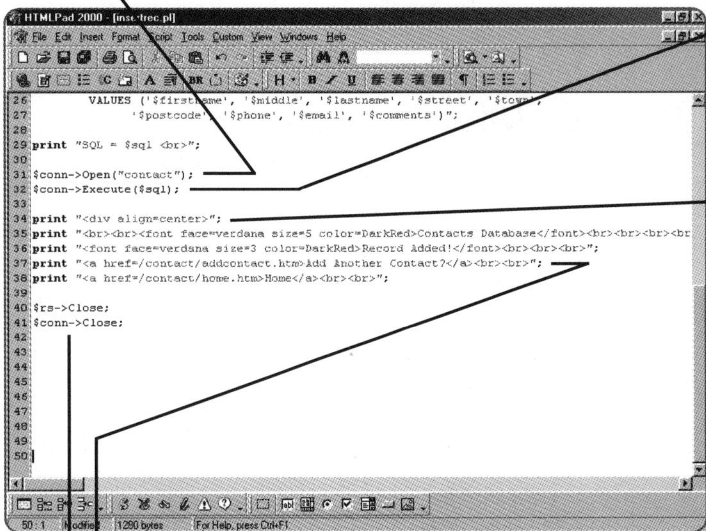

10. Execute the SQL statement you just created.

```
$conn->Execute($sql);
```

11. Display a confirmation message so that the user knows that the program has finished.

```
print "<div align=center>";
print "<br><br><font
   face=verdana size=5
   color=DarkRed>Contacts
Database</font><br><br>
   <br><br><br><br>";
print "<font face=verdana
   size=3 color=DarkRed>Record
   Added!</font><br><br><br>";
```

12. At this point the user does not know where to go next, so give him a couple of options. You can offer the user either the chance to go back to the form and add a new record or return to the home page of the application. Code the links like this:

```
print "<a href=/contact/addcontact.htm>Add Another Contact?</a><br><br>";
print "<a href=/contact/home.htm>Home</a><br><br>";
```

13. Finally, just to tidy things up, close the record set and connection objects.

```
$rs->Close;
$conn->Close;
```

14. Save your program as insertrec.pl

The editcontact.pl Program

Remember that the listcontacts.pl program had a form sending the record number of any selected record? Now you are going to look at how your new program, editcontact.pl, will load all of the data for a record into the fields ready to be modified by the user. Then you will examine how to pass any changes (in fact you will pass all of the fields, changed or not) to the database update program, updaterec.pl.

1. Open a new Perl program in your editor.

```
#!c:/perl/bin
```

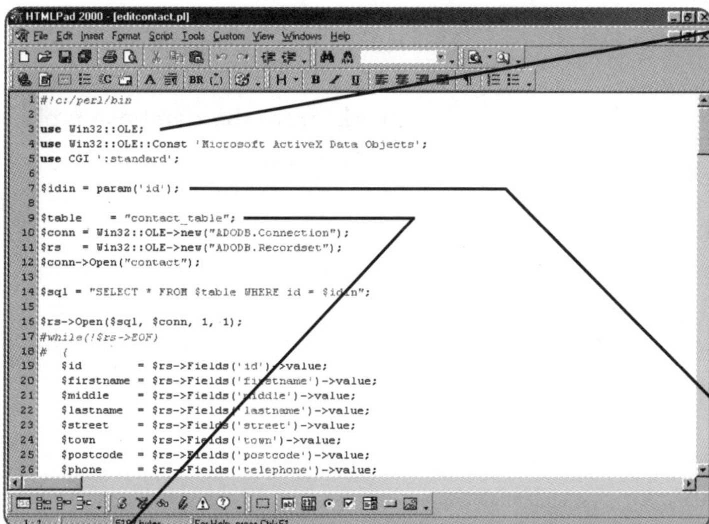

2. As you did in the last program, import the modules that you need to allow you to use ADO, then import the CGI.pm module.

```
use Win32::OLE;
use Win32::OLE::Const
   'Microsoft ActiveX Data
   Objects';
use CGI ':standard';
```

3. Now get the `id` fields value from the listrecords.pl program (remember the little form at the end of each row?). Store the `id` of the record that is to be edited into a variable:

```
$idin = param('id');
```

4. Create a variable to hold the name of the table in the database:

```
$table    = "contact_table";
```

5. Create object variables for the database connection and for the recordset.

```
$conn = Win32::OLE->new("ADODB.Connection");
$rs   = Win32::OLE->new("ADODB.Recordset");
```

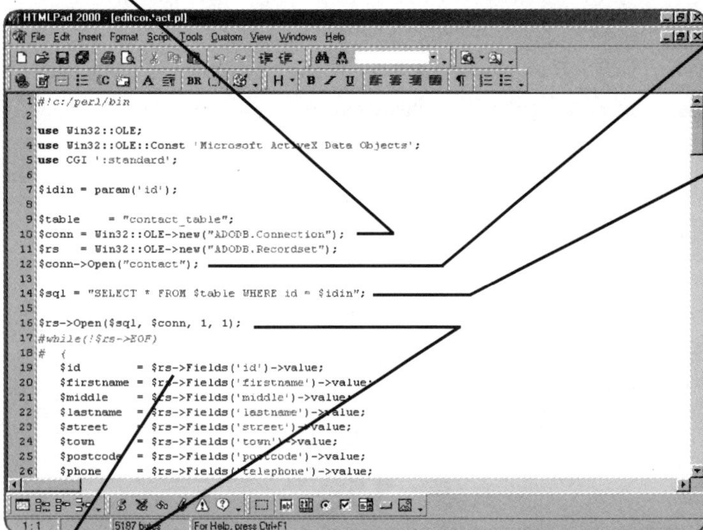

6. Now open the connection.

```
$conn->Open("contact");
```

7. Create a variable to hold your SQL statement, like this:

```
$sql = "SELECT * FROM $table
   WHERE id = $idin";
```

Here the SQL statement is saying: "Get all of the columns (fields) from the database table called contact_table where the id of the record is that stored in `$idin`, which came from the form in listcontacts.pl." (Remember, `$table` will be substituted by the name of the table assigned to the `$table` variable). If you only wanted, say, a couple of fields from the table then instead of using the asterisk, which means "get them all," you would just code the name of each column or field separated by commas.

8. Open the recordset, like this:

```
$rs->Open($sql, $conn, 1, 1);
```

9. Now get the value stored in each column of the recordset and assign each to its own appropriately-named variable.

```
$id        = $rs->Fields('id')->value;
$firstname = $rs->Fields('firstname')->value;
$middle    = $rs->Fields('middle')->value;
$lastname  = $rs->Fields('lastname')->value;
$street    = $rs->Fields('street')->value;
$town      = $rs->Fields('town')->value;
$postcode  = $rs->Fields('postcode')->value;
```

```
$phone      = $rs->Fields('telephone')->value;
$email      = $rs->Fields('email')->value;
$comments  = $rs->Fields('comments')->value;
```

> **NOTE**
>
> Note that this is very similar to the listcontacts.pl processing, except there you were processing a list and so there was a `while loop` wrapped around the above statements. Here you only want one record, and you know that it exists because your listcontacts.pl program found it.

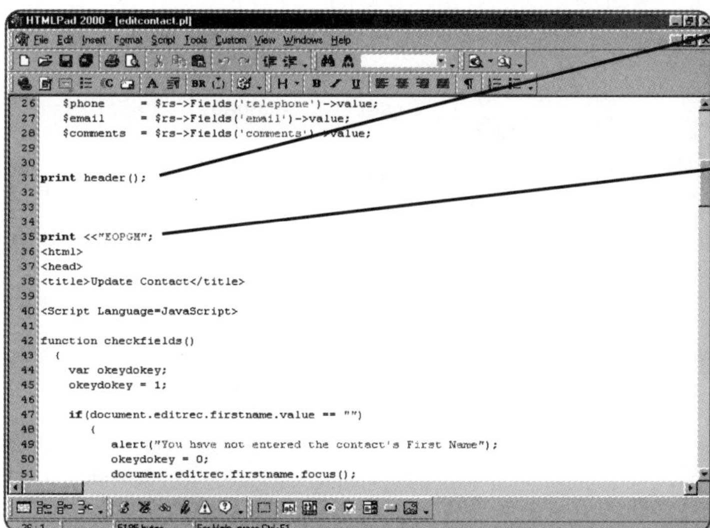

10. Create the HTTP header.

```
print header();
```

11. Now start a Here document. Basically, the Here document will pass everything through as it was HTML, with the exception that, because the label (in this case EOPGM, which I chose arbitrarily as meaning End Of ProGraM) is double quoted, you can include variables and they will be interpolated. Code your Here document like this:

```
print <<"EOPGM";
```

From now on, everything is almost identical to the addcontact.htm program, so you can copy and paste the form from your addcontact.htm page. Following are a few of things that you will have to change.

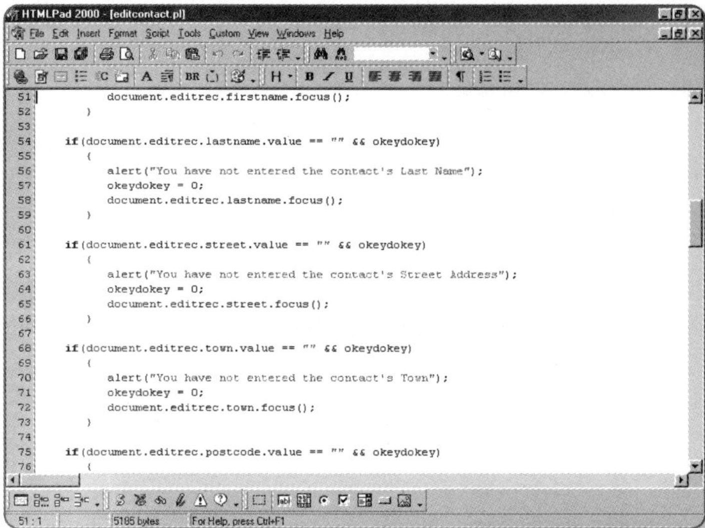

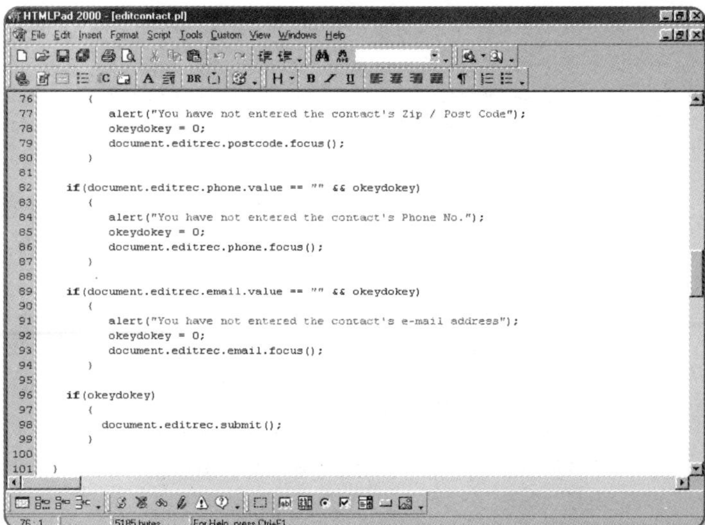

12. Change the name of the form referred to in the JavaScript `checkfields()` function to "editrec" Doing so doesn't alter the way it works, but it looks appropriate to anyone reading your code! As long as the form name reference in the JavaScript matches the name of the form, everything will work.

```
<html>
<head>
<title>Update Contact</title>

<Script Language=JavaScript>

function checkfields()
  {
    var okeydokey;
    okeydokey = 1;

    if(document.editrec.
   firstname.value == "")
       {
          alert("You have not
             entered the
             contact's First
             Name");
          okeydokey = 0;
          document.editrec.
            firstname.focus();
       }

    if(document.editrec.lastname.value == "" && okeydokey)
       {
          alert("You have not entered the contact's Last Name");
          okeydokey = 0;
          document.editrec.lastname.focus();
       }
```

```
      if(document.editrec.street.value == "" && okeydokey)
       {
          alert("You have not entered the contact's Street Address");
          okeydokey = 0;
          document.editrec.street.focus();
       }

    if(document.editrec.town.value == "" && okeydokey)
       {
          alert("You have not entered the contact's Town");
          okeydokey = 0;
          document.editrec.town.focus();
       }

    if(document.editrec.postcode.value == "" && okeydokey)
       {
          alert("You have not entered the contact's Zip / Post Code");
          okeydokey = 0;
          document.editrec.postcode.focus();
       }

    if(document.editrec.phone.value == "" && okeydokey)
       {
          alert("You have not entered the contact's Phone No.");
          okeydokey = 0;
          document.editrec.phone.focus();
       }

    if(document.editrec.email.value == "" && okeydokey)
       {
          alert("You have not entered the contact's e-mail address");
          okeydokey = 0;
          document.editrec.email.focus();
       }

    if(okeydokey)
       {
         document.editrec.submit();
       }

  }
```

```
</script>
</head>
```

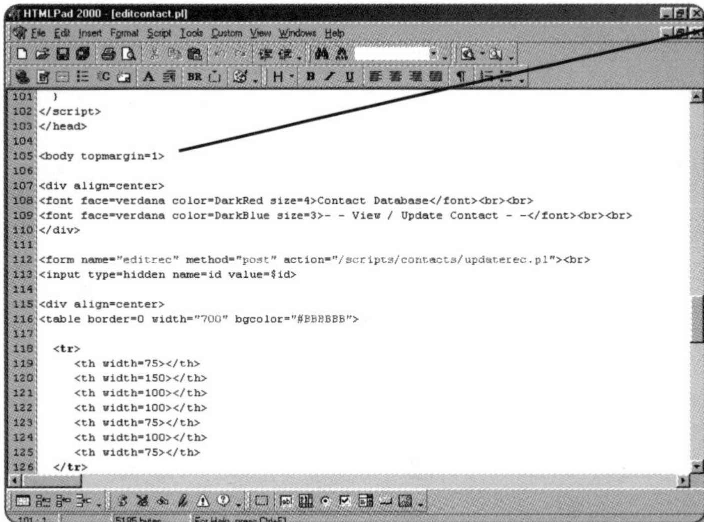

13. Change the name of the form to "editrec" and the program name in the HTML form to "updaterec.pl".

```
<body topmargin=1>

<div align=center>
<font face=verdana
   color=DarkRed size=4>
   Contact Database</font>
   <br><br>
<font face=verdana
   color=DarkBlue size=3>- -
   View / Update Contact - -
   </font><br><br>
</div>

<form name="editrec"
   method="post"
   action="/scripts/contacts/
   updaterec.pl"><br>
```

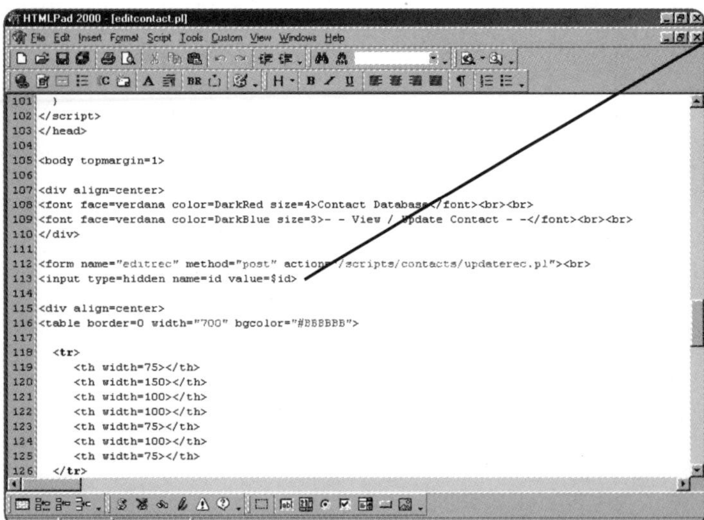

14. Add the names of the variables that store the values for each field from the database table to the "value" attributes of the form fields. (The figure shows only the first part of this rather long code.)

```
<input type=hidden name=id
   value=$id>

<div align=center>
<table border=0 width="700"
   bgcolor="#BBBBBB">

  <tr>
     <th width=75></th>
```

```
    <th width=150></th>
    <th width=100></th>
    <th width=100></th>
    <th width=75></th>
    <th width=100></th>
    <th width=75></th>
  </tr>

  <tr><td colspan=6> </td></tr>

  <tr>
    <td><font face=verdana size=1 color=darkblue>Firstname</font></td>
    <td><input name="firstname" type="text" size="15" value='$firstname'></td>
    <td><font face=verdana size=1 color=darkblue>Middle Initial</font></td>
    <td><input name="middle" type="text" size="3" value='$middle'></td>
    <td><font face=verdana size=1 color=darkblue>Last Name</font></td>
    <td><input name="lastname" type="text" size="20" value='$lastname'></td>
  </tr>

  <tr><td colspan=6> </td></tr>

  <tr>
    <td><font face=verdana size=1 color=darkblue>Address</font></td>
    <td colspan=3><input name="street" type="text" size="40"
value='$street'></td>
    <td><font face=verdana size=1 color=darkblue>Town</td>
    <td><input name="town" type="text" size="15" value='$town'><td>
  </tr>

  <tr><td colspan=6> </td></tr>

  <tr>
    <td><font face=verdana size=1 color=darkblue>Zip</font></td>
    <td><input name="postcode" type="text" size="15" value='$postcode'></td>
    <td><font face=verdana size=1 color=darkblue>Phone</font></td>
    <td><input name="phone" type="text" size="10" value='$phone'></td>
    <td><font face=verdana size=1 color=darkblue>e-mail</font></td>
    <td><input name="email" type="text" size="20" value='$email'></td>
  </tr>

  <tr><td colspan=6> </td></tr>
```

```
    <tr>
     <td valign=top><font face=verdana size=1
color=darkblue>Comments</font></td>
     <td colspan=5><textarea name=comments rows=4
cols=50>$comments</textarea></td>

  </tr>

  <tr><td colspan=6> </td></tr>

  <tr>
     <td></td>
     <td><input type="button" name="addit" value="Update Contact"
onClick='checkfields()'></td>
     <td></td>
     <td><input type="reset" name="reset" value="Clear Form"></td>
     <td></td>
     <td></td>
  </tr>
</table>

</div>

</body>


</html>
```

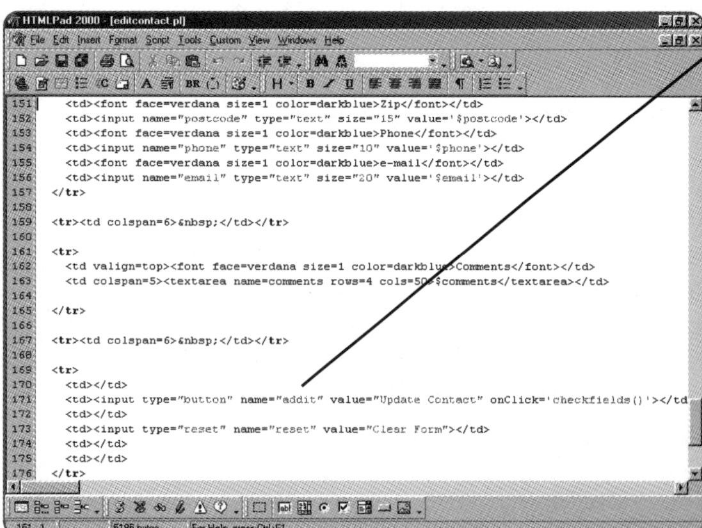

15. Change the name of the button to make it more appropriate, as shown here.

```
<td><input type="button"
   name="addit" value="Update
   Contact" onclick=
   checkfields()'></td
```

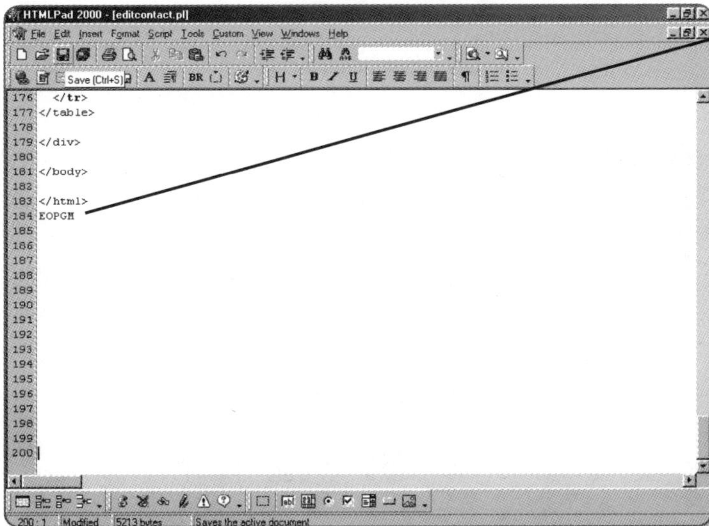

16. Finally, enter the label name for the Here document, then press enter a couple of times. The Here document expects an empty line after the closing label if this is the end of the program.

```
EOPGM
```

17. Save the program as editcontact.pl.

And that is the editcontact.pl program completed. This program will "call" the program updaterec.pl, which is what you are going to code next.

The updaterec.pl Program

The form in the editcontact.pl program points at the updaterec.pl program. Again, a hidden field is used to pass the `id` to the updaterec.pl program, as the user does not need to see it displayed. This is another simple program using SQL and ADO to update the data as supplied by the form in editcontact.pl.

1. Open a new Perl program in your editor.

```
#!c:/perl/bin
```

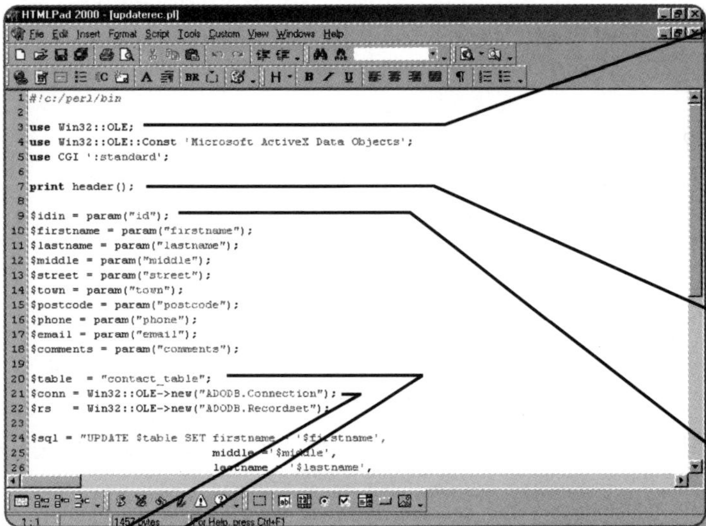

2. Import the ADO and CGI.pm modules.

```
use Win32::OLE;
use Win32::OLE::Const
   'Microsoft ActiveX Data
   Objects';
use CGI ':standard';
```

3. Create the HTTP header.

```
print header();
```

4. Get the field values from the form in editcontact.pl using the CGI.pm `param()` function.

```
$idin = param("id");
$firstname = param("firstname");
$lastname = param("lastname");
$middle = param("middle");
$street = param("street");
$town = param("town");
$postcode = param("postcode");
$phone = param("phone");
$email = param("email");
$comments = param("comments");
```

5. Create a variable to contain the table name.

```
$table  = "contact_table";
```

6. Create the now-familiar connection and recordset objects.

```
$conn = Win32::OLE->new("ADODB.Connection");
$rs   = Win32::OLE->new("ADODB.Recordset");
```

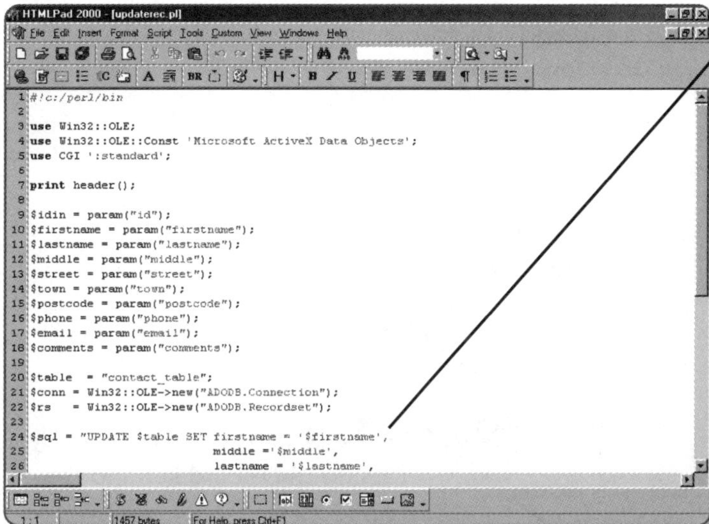

7. Now create a variable to contain the UPDATE SQL string, like this:

```
$sql = "UPDATE $table SET
  firstname = '$firstname',
middle ='$middle',
lastname = '$lastname',
street = '$street',
town = '$town',
postcode = '$postcode',
telephone = '$phone',
email = '$email',
comments ='$comments'
WHERE id = $idin";
```

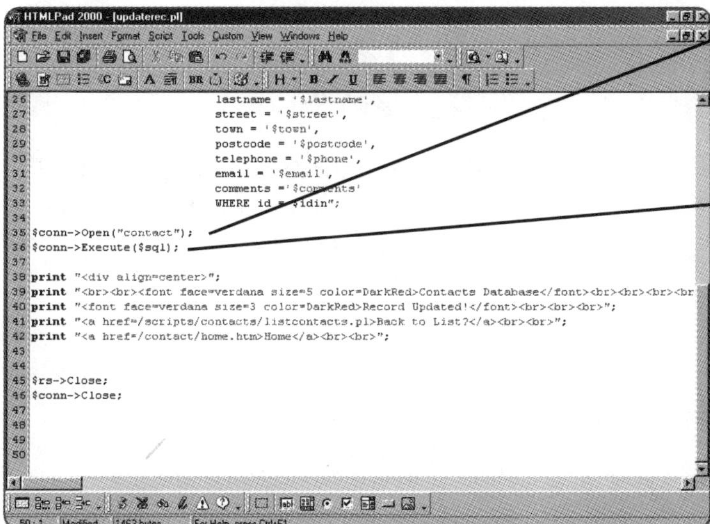

8. Open the connection to your database.

```
$conn->Open("contact");
```

9. And add the code to execute your UPDATE SQL.

```
$conn->Execute($sql);
```

10. As in the insertrec.pl program, add a confirmation message and links to give the user the opportunity to return to the list of records or to go the contacts home page.

```
print "<div align=center>";
print "<br><br><font face=verdana size=5 color=DarkRed>Contacts
   Database</font><br><br><br><br><br><br>";
print "<font face=verdana size=3 color=DarkRed>Record
   Updated!</font><br><br><br>";
print "<a href=/scripts/contacts/listcontacts.pl>Back to List?</a><br><br>";
print "<a href=/contact/home.htm>Home</a><br><br>";
```

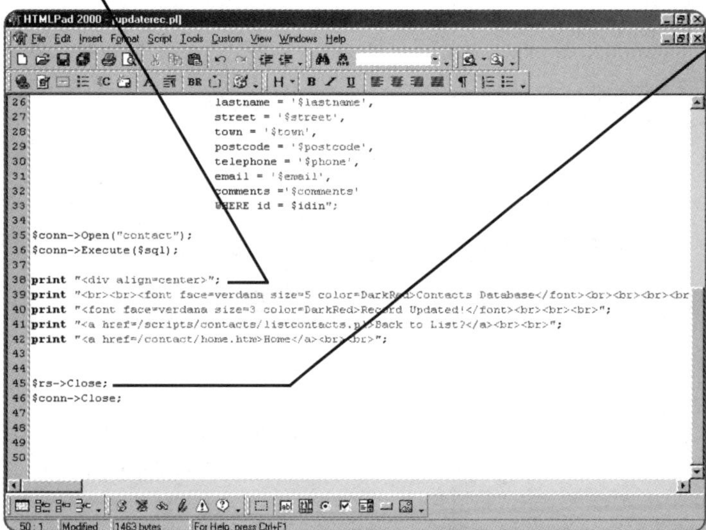

11. And as usual, tidy up by closing the record set and the connection.

```
$rs->Close;
$conn->Close;
```

12. Save your program as updaterec.pl

And that's it! All you have to do now is to create the database itself and then you're in business.

The Database

This is the last step in creating your application. You are going to create the database that your application "talks" to. Create the database (contact.mdb) in exactly the same way as you did in Chapter 14. Don't forget that for added security, the database should be stored above the Web root (wwwroot).

Make sure that the option "Allow Zero Length" for each field is set to "Yes." This prevents errors if you decide that completion of a field is not mandatory and you therefore remove the JavaScript code pertaining to that field.

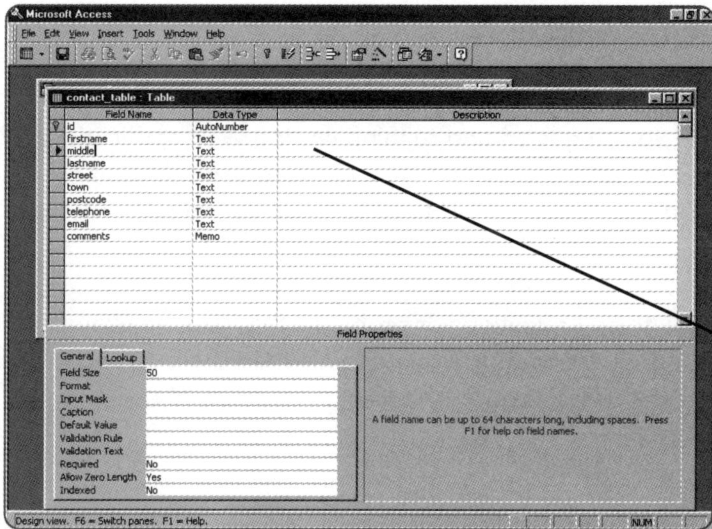

Don't forget to set up the data source name using the ODBC feature of the control panel. If you can't remember how, refer to Chapter 14.

Save your database as contact.mdb.

And here it is. Go to the home page of your application (home.htm) and test it. If you find any errors, go back and check your code for typos.

You now have a full, working application. I did leave out one function: the `delete` option. See if you can work out how to do it. Here's a clue: the deleterec.pl would be almost identical to the updaterec.pl program. Do you remember how the listcontacts.pl program links to the editcontact.pl program using the hidden `id` field? The `delete` function will work in exactly the same way! You will need another separate form like that used for the edit buttons in the listcontacts.pl program. But this time you can go directly to the deleterec.pl program because you're not editing anything.

There are a number of improvements you can make to this program. You can improve the look and feel, you can add a search facility (remember the `"LIKE %data%` option in SQL?), and you could add a separate view option that doesn't have edit options, so that you can just look at the data. You could even allow an e-mail to be sent directly from your program.

A Final Word

That brings us to the end of this book. I have not tried to make you an expert in Perl, but I hope I have helped you to get up and running writing Web applications with the minimum of fuss and complexities. There is much more you will want to learn that is beyond the scope of this book; I will have to leave you to research this on your own.

Please feel free to e-mail me with any questions or problems that you may have. I cannot promise to answer every question, but I will certainly read them all and create a FAQ page to answer the most frequently asked.

E-mail me at perl@sparksoft.net.

Good Luck and happy Perl Fast & Easy programming!

Appendixes

A

More Perl Functions

This appendix is a ragbag of functions and other features in Perl that you might find useful in your future applications.

The length() Function

The `length()` function returns the length of a scalar variable. The syntax for the length function is

```
$size = length($variable);
```

For example, the following code:

```
$variable = "fred";
$size = length($variable);
print "The length of  \$size = $size";
```

would display

```
The length of  $size = 4
```

The reverse() Function

The `reverse()` function takes an array as its argument, and returns an array in which the order of the elements has been reversed. The syntax is

```
@reversedarray = reverse( @startarray );
```

So, if you do this

```
@startarray = (A .. K);
@reversedarray = reverse( @startarray );
print "Array = @reversedarray \n";
```

Then you will see

```
K J I H G F E D C B A
```

The index() Function

The `index()` function finds the postion of the first occurrence of another string. By default, it starts at the leftmost character of the string being searched. If you add a third optional parameter, the function will start at the location in this parameter.

The syntax is as follows:

```
$position = index($teststring, $substring);
```

Or

```
$position = index($teststring, $substring, $startposition);
```

So, for example

```
$teststring = "Perl Fast & Easy Web Development";
$position = index($teststring, "Web");
print "The position of \"Web\" in \$teststring is: $position \n";
```

will display

```
The position of "Web" in $teststring is: 17;
```

> **NOTE**
>
> The first location in the string is 0. If the substring being searched for is not found, the function will return the value –1.

The rindex() Function

The `rindex()` function finds the rightmost position of the first occurrence of another string. That is, it searches the string backwards. In all other respects, this function is the same as the `index()` function.

The syntax is as follows:

```
$position = rindex($teststring, $substring);
```

Or

```
$position = rindex($teststring, $substring, $startposition);
```

So, for example

```
$teststring = "Perl Fast & Easy Web Development";
$position = rindex($teststring, "Web");
print "The position of \"Web\" in \$teststring is: $position \n";
```

will also display

```
The position of "Web" in $teststring is: 17;
```

The substr() Function

The `substring()` function enables you to extract a partial string from another string. The syntax is as follows:

```
Substr( $wholestring, offset, length, $replacementstring);
```

This means inspect `$wholestring` (which can be a variable or a literal), starting at offset position, for a length of length, and replace the substring if found with the contents of `$replacementstring` (which can also be a literal).

So the following:

```
$wholestring = "Cats are cute";
$substring = substr( $wholestring, 0, 4, "Dogs");
print $substring;
```

will you give you

```
Cats are cute
```

If you leave out the `$replacementstring` parameter, then just the substring is returned so that the same code as above but without the `$replacementstring` parameter, would give

```
Cats
```

`substr()` is quite a powerful function.

The tr/// Operator

The tr/// operator is not, strictly speaking, a function, but it can be argued that it provides one. The syntax of the tr/// operator is

```
tr/ searchstring / replacestring /
```

The forward slashes are simply delimiters.

The tr/// operator is very powerful. Consider the following:

```
$newstring =~ tr/a-z/A - Z/
```

This will replace every character in a string, of the range a to z, and replace it with the uppercase equivalent A to Z.

Note the =~ symbol. This is called the *binding operator* and if it is not used, the operation is carried out on whatever is in `$_`. In this case you will not use a variable on the lefthand side, like this:

```
tr/a-k/A-K
```

You can also add modifiers onto the end of the translation operator. So

```
tr/a-k/h-k/c
```

(where /c is the modifier) replaces any character that is not in the search string.

```
tr/a-k/h-k/d
```

deletes any characters that are found that match the searchstring characters, but where no replacement is present in replacestring.

The chr() Function

The `chr()` function returns the character corresponding to the ASCII code supplied in the parentheses.

```
Chr(67)
```

returns the letter C.

This function can be useful for issuing special codes such as linefeed characters, tab characters, and so on.

The ord() Function

Essentially, the `ord()` function does the opposite of the `chr()` function. So if you provide C as an argument or parameter, 67 will be returned.

If you send more than one character to the function, only the first character is used.

So

```
$asciinumber = ord("Cat");
```

returns 67 in the variable `$asciinumber`.

The join() Function

The `join()` function is an interesting function. It joins together lists or strings into one string, but separates them by a supplied separator. The syntax is like this:

```
$wholestring = join (separator_character, list);
```

Often the separator will be a comma or some other character considered useful as a field separator. This has obvious uses in creating comma-separated value (csv) files.

For example:

```
@array1 = ( "Lord", "of", "the", "rings");
$string1 = join( ', ' @array1);
print $string1;
```

will display

```
Lord, of, the, rings
```

The separator can be any string you like.

The sort() Function

The `sort()` function sorts lists of values.

The syntax is

```
sort (@listofvalues);
```

For example, if you do this:

```
print  sort("animal", "vegetable", "mineral");
```

then

```
animalmineralvegetable
```

would be displayed. You can separate the words again using the join() function.

The rand() Function

The `rand()` function generates a random floating-point number that is less than 1 but greater then zero. If you want a larger number you have to supply the maximum value you want. If you want an integer you must use the `int()` function to return a whole number, like this:

```
print int(rand(10);
```

This prints an integer between 0 and 9.

The Here Document

This is a peculiar but very useful feature. The Here document enables you to pass everything that follows an opening identifier to pass straight through so that everything is quoted as though it were text until Perl sees a closing identifier.

If you put an unquoted identifier at the beginning of the Here document, Perl will interpolate any variables it finds in the text. This is very useful if you are sending a form back to use with variables assigned to form elements. It saves a lot of coding.

This is the basic syntax:

```
<<an_identifer_string;
a line of text
and another line of text
and yet another line of text
an_identifer_string
```

If the closing identifier is the last line of your Perl program, there must be another carriage return.

A quoted opening identifier such as

```
<<'an_identifer_string';
```

prevents interpolation.

There is an example of this in use in Chapter 17, "Case Study: Contact Database."

I hope you find these additional functions and features useful. This book does not describe or constitute a full list of the features and functions available in Perl, nor has every possible use of every parameter of every function been described. But I hope there has been enough to whet your appetite without scaring you away.

B

Web Site Resources

Official Sites for Obtaining Perl and More

Here are a list of some of the best Perl Web sites, where you can find just about any information you need regarding Perl. As you will find, the available resources for this powerful and ubiquitous language are huge, and the list grows daily. My small list will help to get you started. Happy Surfing!

- http://www.perl.com/
- http://www.activestate.com/
- http://www.perl.org/
- http://www.cpan.org/

Learning More about Perl

If you want to study Perl in more depth, these sites will give you a good start. There is a lot of good quality content on the sites, and even if you can't find exactly what you are looking for, you will probably find something that will nudge you into generating a solution of your own.

Following are some sites where you can get all the official downloads of Perl, Perl news, version information and lots more:

- http://www.perlmonks.org/index.pl?node=Tutorials
- http://www.webreference.com/perl/
- http://cgi.resourceindex.com/Documentation/Programming_Languages/Programming_in_Perl/
- http://www.devshed.com/Server_Side/Perl
- http://www.perlmasters.com/tutorial/

Free Perl Scripts

Here are some sites offering free Perl scripts that do lots of jobs. These scripts make great learning tools. If you want to find something fast or you're having an idle day, try one of these sites!

- http://www.scriptarchive.com/ (This site is probably one of the best for code examples and ideas..)
- http://www.bignosebird.com/cgi.shtml
- http://cgi.resourceindex.com/
- http://www.freeperlcode.com/

Learning More about HTML and JavaScript

Did you find the sections on HTML and JavaScript interesting? Would you like to learn more? These sites will teach you lots more:

- http://www.w3schools.com/
- http://www.htmlgoodies.com/
- http://www.w3schools.com/html/
- http://www.pageresource.com/jscript/
- http://www.w3schools.com/js/default.asp
- http://javascriptkit.com/
- http://developer.netscape.com/tech/javascript/resources.html

I hope these have given you a good taste of what is on the Web for the Perl developer. As I have said, there are vast resources waiting to be tapped.

Index

Symbols

E

K

L

M

P

W

X-Z